SOBRAL PINTO, "THE CONSCIENCE OF BRAZIL"

JOHN W. F. DULLES

Sobral Pinto

"The Conscience of Brazil"

LEADING THE ATTACK
AGAINST VARGAS
(1930–1945)

UNIVERSITY OF TEXAS PRESS, AUSTIN

COPYRIGHT © 2002 BY THE UNIVERSITY OF TEXAS PRESS

All rights reserved

Printed in the United States of America

First edition, 2002

Requests for permission to reproduce material from this work should be sent to Permissions, University of Texas Press, P.O. Box 7819, Austin, TX 78713-7819.

⊚ The paper used in this book meets the minimum requirements of ANSI/NISO Z39.48-1992 (R1997) (Permanence of Paper).

LIBRARY OF CONGRESS CATALOGING-IN-PUBLICATION DATA
Dulles, John W. F.
Sobral Pinto, "the conscience of Brazil" : leading the attack against Vargas (1930–1945) / John W. F. Dulles.—1st ed.
     p.   cm.
Includes bibliographical references and index.
ISBN 0-292-71616-8 (hardcover : alk. paper)
1. Pinto, Heráclito Sobral, 1893–   2. Brazil—Politics and government—1930–1945.   3. Vargas, Getúlio, 1883–1954.
I. Title.
F2538.P4784 D85   2002
981.06′1′092—dc21
2001008557

In Memory of
Edith Foster Dulles
and
Eleanor Foster Lansing

CONTENTS

Soon after I finished writing this story about Sobral Pinto, two oc-
currences added to earlier recognition of his influence. At an impressive ceremony in Brasília, attended by leading magistrates and
jurists of the country, his name was given to the *sala dos advogados*
(the chamber used by lawyers) at the Supreme Court of Brazil. And
steps were taken by Brazilian Catholic figures for his canonization,
which, if successful, will place him at the side of Saint Ivo of Brit-
tany, the patron of lawyers, as well as Saints Thomas Becket and
Thomas More, also lawyers.

For three reasons, it seemed to me, attention should be given to
Sobral Pinto's activities and writings during what Catholic leader
Alceu Amoroso Lima said in 1945 was "the illegality of the last fifteen years":[1] (1) his correspondence, (2) his role as the most constantly forceful oppositionist, and (3) his unusual character.

(1) Because the press was so much of the time under government
control and because *memórias* and police records, while useful, have
occasional drawbacks, historians can be grateful for the additional
information and observations in the vast correspondence of Sobral
Pinto, known as "the Marquise de Sévigné of the regime."[2] They can
also be grateful that Sobral was continually in close touch with the
great figures of the period and with so many victims of the violence
and that he was an inveterate faultfinder who made it a point to
analyze political developments. It was his duty, he felt, to scold his
friends, among them Justice Minister Francisco Campos and Catholic Church leaders, and to exchange letters with his jailed clients
and their families (such as the distressed relatives, living abroad, of
Communist prisoners Luiz Carlos Prestes and "Harry Berger"). His
polemics with prominent journalists and his scathing denunciations
of authorities, who included the top officers of the National Secu-

rity Tribunal, the police, and the censorship bureau, sometimes developed into sensational conflicts. The correspondence, filled with judgments and accounts of the conflicts, throws light on the institutions, events, and personalities, but is so massive that only the tip of the iceberg appears in the pages that follow.

Alceu Amoroso Lima, in the United States in 1951, had some advice for a young professor at Princeton University who was trying to write about Brazil: "Put your work aside and wait until you can go to Rio. There you must look up Dr. Sobral Pinto and try to become familiar with his files of letters, at least with the parts that are not confidential. It is, at present, impossible to write the history of Brazil's last thirty years without making use of the files of Dr. Sobral Pinto, who has been preserving copies of the letters he has written." They represented, Alceu said, "the most extraordinary political apostleship" and revealed, in the best manner ever carried out in Brazil, secrets about morals to be found in the relations between persons.[3]

(2) Sobral Pinto has been called "the epistolary chief of the resistance." But, as fellow lawyer Evandro Lins e Silva has made clear, his "famous letters" were only one of the tools of "this intrepid Don Quixote," who "fought against an avalanche of stupidity, incomprehension, and prejudices . . . and, with a solitary voice, . . . against accommodations, halfheartedness, and cowardice."[4] Other tools were his arguments in government offices (leading in one case to a physical scuffle), his weekly newspaper articles (until silenced by the censorship), and the legal briefs that he turned into condemnations of the regime. Veteran jurist Clemente Hungria writes that he has known no other lawyer who could equal Sobral in demonstrating courage and vehemence when facing judges, tribunals, and men in power, and that Sobral did this with so much virility that his accusations were viewed by many as "acts of insanity" (along with his "vow of poverty").[5] The Ordem dos Advogados do Brasil, official organ of Brazil's lawyers, adopted a resolution, worded in 1944 by Dario de Almeida Magalhães, to point out that "the causes Sobral Pinto represents are not simply those that are submitted to him as a lawyer. Most of his time and extraordinary effort are expended on behalf of his fellow-citizens, the law, morality, justice, and the noblest of ideals. His voice is not intimidated by the powerful or by threats of the use of force."[6] Unlike some of the other Brazilians who attacked the Vargas regime from the outset, Sobral did not have his effectiveness reduced by a forced exile.

Sobral, although a critic of the administration that fell in October 1930, denounced Brazil's new leaders as early as November of that year. In 1931 he railed against "the military mentality" that pushed civilians out of the governments of the states, and, starting in June 1932, he began his series of attacks on the influence of positivism on President Getúlio Vargas. As he wrote Archbishop Jayme Câmara in April 1944, he did recognize that some "important steps" had been taken "by our government to improve the future of our workers"; but he detested dictatorship and terrorism by the police.[7]

(3) With the collapse of censorship in 1945, the Rio press, over-whelmingly anti-Vargas, was filled with articles praising Sobral and his long struggle. *Diário Carioca* columnist Joaquim de Sales de-clared that Sobral, "one of those rare heroic figures out of Plutarch," was Brazil's most fearless fighter for Christian truth. Columnist Raphael Corrêa de Oliveira wrote in the *Diário de Notícias* that no fulfillment of legal duty, even in the glorious age of defense lawyers during and after the French Revolution, exceeded that "achieved in Latin America a century later by Sobral Pinto."[8]

Writers recalled that, without concern about legal fees, he had defended many far leftists during the repression. They could have added that the waiting room of the modest office of this dedicated Christian democrat became filled with desperate families of other unfortunates whose appeals he heeded, certain that justice and char-ity should be his first considerations, regardless of his excessive workload and the slim prospects of reducing his financial indebted-ness. His clients included members of the fascist-like Integralista movement, soldiers and officers expelled from the military, Ger-mans persecuted during the war, and many victims of the improper use of "popular economy" legislation. Among the latter was a lowly greengrocer whose imprisonment was ordered by the National Secu-rity Tribunal when he tried to collect payments for the fruit and vegetables he had been delivering to the home of the Tribunal's president.

Sobral came to the defense of priests and foreign missionaries who suffered at the hands of the dictatorship, and he preached the Gospel in his articles and speeches, frequently using his favorite adjectives, virile and arduous. He appealed to Church leaders and others for steps that would rid Brazil of its social structure, which he repeatedly described as un-Christian and unfair to the downtrod-den majority. Denouncing the Catholic hierarchy for cooperating with the dictatorship, he was called "a naughty boy" by Rio's archbishop. This lack of understanding of what he saw as his "gigantic struggle"—a struggle that he attributed to the drama that raged in his religious conscience—was the cause of one of his many moments of acute agony.

Throughout his life he attended Mass daily and adhered strictly to the principles that he demanded of others. He sought nothing for himself. In declining government positions, such as a National Security Tribunal judgeship, he adhered to his statements that government positions should not be accepted by those who, like himself, were officers of Ação Católica Brasileira; and in declining appeals that he run for Congress in 1945 he remained true to his word about keeping apart from political posts (while offering plenty of comments about candidates). He became, rather, a sort of oracle, the conscience of Brazil—a "severe, indomitable and virile conscience" according to the Ordem dos Advogados do Brasil. Jurist Victor Nunes Leal called Sobral "the vigilant critic of public life" and "the conscience of every one of us in those cases when our own consciences fail us on account of passion, fear, anger, insecurity, pride, ambition, and vanity, and even in those cases of minor errors such as are sometimes made by the very best of men."[9]

During debates, Sobral frequently mentioned his hard work, sacrifices, and poverty, leading adversaries to accuse him of the sin of ostentation. In reply, he pointed out that Saint Paul had revealed his good works not for reasons of ostentation but in order to strengthen his fellow Christians. Sobral, who remarked that "no lesson equals that of an example," would even speak, if he believed it useful, of his own youthful sin (adultery) and the great pain it had brought him. He discussed the unfortunate affair when he tried to persuade Francisco Campos to lead a more honorable private life and when he comforted Alceu Amoroso Lima with the explanation that Alceu's suffering was the result of Alceu's virtue and bore no resemblance to his own suffering, caused by his single act of infidelity.

Following Sobral's death in 1991 at the age of ninety-eight, the press was filled with tributes expressed by men who were familiar with his battles against the military regime that began in 1964. Evandro Lins e Silva, familiar also with episodes narrated in these pages, wrote that Sobral had left mankind a legend of altruism, abnegation, and honorability, and had died "in the most Franciscan poverty." "Yes," Evandro wrote, "Sobral Pinto was different from others; he was an anomaly; he was a marvel; he was enormous."[10]

In 1945 Alceu Amoroso Lima called Sobral "the chief of the Moral Resistance." He explained: "If I see in Sobral Pinto the leading figure of our generation and the best one to guide us . . . , it is precisely because his moral fortitude and juridical and democratic convictions are based on the immovable rock of Faith, Hope, and Charity, the supreme virtues that take us to God."[11]

J.W.F.D.

ACKNOWLEDGMENTS

This book owes its existence to Roberto Sobral Pinto Ribeiro, grandson of Heráclito Fontoura Sobral Pinto, and, as Roberto points out, to Cecília Silva ("Cecy"), the devoted secretary of Heráclito. Cecy, held in affection by the family, spent her life assisting Heráclito and is responsible for the preservation in an orderly form of his vast collection of papers.

Although Roberto's grandfather, before he died, expressed reservations about a book such as I had in mind, Roberto gave me the green light to proceed. Subsequently, while he organized and studied the mountain of papers (two tons, I am told), he graciously provided me with copies of thousands of letters, making possible the selection that forms the heart of our story. He assisted me in every way possible, and so I have had the advantage of his recollections and, thanks to him, the recollections of others. Together we visited places of interest in Rio, such as the big house of his grandfather on Pereira da Silva Street and the palace of the cardinal, where collections include copies of *A Ordem*.

Flávia Araripe and John Cuttino, graduate students at the University of Texas at Austin, have helped with their research, as have Francisco G. Gazzaneo, in São Paulo, and Maria Cecília Ribas Carneiro, in Rio. A very special delight has been the receipt of precious papers and books sent in abundance from Rio by Clemente Hungria. I am deeply grateful to Clemente also for his encouragement and enthusiastic cooperation, for his clarifications about legal matters and lawyers' organizations in Brazil, and for making it possible for me to have the benefit of assistance from some of his many friends, such as Evandro Lins e Silva and Tito Lívio Cavalcanti de Medeiros.

Helpful comments about the manuscript submitted by César Parreiras Horta and Daphne F. Rodger are much appreciated, along with the work of producing it carried out by Jan E. Rinaldi, Dr. Cacilda Rêgo, Roslyn E. Rosales, and Shameela Keshavjee.

The Sobral Pinto family in Porto Novo do Cunha, Minas Gerais, in 1903. From left to right: Rubens, Idalina, Príamo, Natalina, and Heráclito. (Kindness of Sobral Pinto family)

The railroad station at Porto Novo do Cunha, where Príamo was station master. (Kindness of Sobral Pinto family)

The Anchieta School in Nova Friburgo, Rio de Janeiro state, where Heráclito was a boarding student, 1906–1912. (Kindness of Sobral Pinto family)

Heráclito on his graduation from law school, Rio de Janeiro, 1917. (Kindness of Sobral Pinto family)

Maria José Azambuja, whom Heráclito married in 1922, is standing. Seated (from left): her father Alberto and mother Luiza (at center), 1914. (Kindness of Sobral Pinto family)

Heráclito convalescing in Queluz de Minas, 1920. (Kindness of Sobral Pinto family)

Jackson de Figueiredo, 1921, lay Catholic leader who drowned while fishing in Rio de Janeiro in 1928. (Kindness of Centro Dom Vital)

"Protógenes Conspiracy" trial, May 1927. Judge Sá Albuquerque (center) hearing Procurador Criminal Sobral Pinto. At right: Protógenes Guimarães. (Drawing in O Jornal, May 5, 1927)

Sobral Pinto, procurador geral of the Federal District, 1928. (Drawing by Gerson in O Paiz, September 8, 1928)

José Barreto Filho, lawyer who
served as congressman from the
state of Sergipe, 1935–1937.
(Kindness of Luiz Paulo Horta)

Evandro Lins e Silva at his law
school graduation in Rio de Janeiro,
1932. (Kindness of Clemente
Hungria and Evandro Lins e Silva)

President Getúlio Vargas and Cardinal Sebastião Leme, leader of the Brazilian
Church from 1928 until his death in 1943. (Kindness of *Correio da Manhã*)

The house on Pereira da Silva Street, Rio de Janeiro, that was the home of
Sobral Pinto from 1935 until his death in 1991. (Kindness of Sobral Pinto family)

Francisco Campos, minister
of justice, 1937–1941. *(Jornal
do Brasil)*

Frederico de Barros Barreto, the judge
who headed the Tribunal de Segurança
Nacional, 1936–1945. *(O Globo)*

Vitório Caneppa, warden of the
Casa de Correção (prison), 1937–
1945. (Correio da Manhã/Arquivo
Nacional. From R. S. Rose, One of
the Forgotten Things)

Euzébio de Queiroz Filho, head of
the Special Police at the time of the
arrest of Luiz Carlos Prestes (1936).
(O Globo)

Antônio Emílio Romano, assistant of Sobral Pinto in the procuradoria in the
1920s and later political section chief of the Delegacia Especial de Segurança
Política e Social until his dismissal in 1938. (Arquivo Público do Estado do
Rio de Janeiro. From R. S. Rose, One of the Forgotten Things)

Filinto Müller, chief of the Federal
District police, 1933–1942. (*Correio
da Manhã*/Arquivo Nacional.
From R. S. Rose, *One of the
Forgotten Things*)

Police Chief Müller (tall, in center) observing his birthday in his office.
Euzébio de Queiroz Filho is third from the left. (Arquivo Público do Estado
do Rio de Janeiro)

Arthur Ernst Ewert ("Harry Berger"), German Communist arrested in Rio in 1935 and tortured until he went insane. (Arquivo Público do Estado do Rio de Janeiro)

Auguste Elise Ewert, wife of Arthur, whose expulsion to Germany in 1936 was followed by her death in a Nazi concentration camp. (Arquivo Público do Estado do Rio de Janeiro)

Luiz Carlos Prestes being brought to testify before a military council about the charge of desertion from the army, February 1937. (Arquivo Público do Estado do Rio de Janeiro)

Prestes testifying about the charge of desertion from the army.
(Arquivo Público do Estado do Rio de Janeiro)

1	63	62	4	5	59	58	8
16	50	51	13	12	54	55	9
17	47	46	20	21	43	42	24
32	34	35	29	28	38	39	25
33	31	30	36	37	27	26	40
48	18	19	45	44	22	23	41
49	15	14	52	53	11	10	56
64	2	3	61	60	6	7	57

One of the arrangements of numbers (adding up the same vertically and
horizontally) made by Prestes and given by the prisoner to Sobral Pinto as a
souvenir, May 1937. (Kindness of Sobral Pinto family)

Leocádia Prestes, mother of Luiz Carlos Prestes, whose letters to Sobral Pinto and her son flowed from France and then Mexico. *(O Globo)*

Olga Benário, companion of Prestes, who was deported to Germany in 1936. In a German prison she gave birth to a daughter of Prestes. Later she perished in a Nazi concentration camp. Painting by Di Cavalcanti. (Arquivo Público do Estado do Rio de Janeiro)

Posters demanding the freedom of Luiz Carlos Prestes, Paris, 1936–1937. (Hélio Silva collection)

OLGA ☐ BENARIO ☐ PRESTES
La Femme de l'héroïque défenseur du peuple brésilien extradée du Brésil en Allemagne hitlérienne, détenue à Berlin avec son enfant nouveau-né dans la prison de la gestapo. 0f.50

French postcard demanding the freedom of Olga and her baby from a German prison. *(O Globo)*

Prestes with diplomat Orlando Leite Ribeiro, friend of Vargas and Prestes, who made visits to the prisoner. *(O Globo)*

Sobral Pinto with his client Luiz Carlos Prestes at the Tribunal de Segurança Nacional, November 7, 1940. (Kindness of Sobral Pinto family)

Alceu Amoroso Lima, lay Catholic leader and Jackson de Figueiredo's successor as president of the Centro Dom Vital. *(O Globo)*

Sobral Pinto with fingers bandaged on account of eczema. *(O Globo)*

Pedro de Oliveira Ribeiro Sobrinho, the last Rio police chief of the regime that fell in 1930 and, in 1945, before the fall of Vargas, São Paulo state secretary of security. (Kindness of Sobral Pinto family)

Lawyer Dario de Almeida Magalhães. (Kindness of Almeida Magalhães family)

Lawyer Mário Bulhões Pedreira. (Kindness of his son, José Luís Bulhões Pedreira)

Lawyer Jorge Emílio Dyott Fontenelle. (Kindness of his son, Celso Augusto Fontenelle)

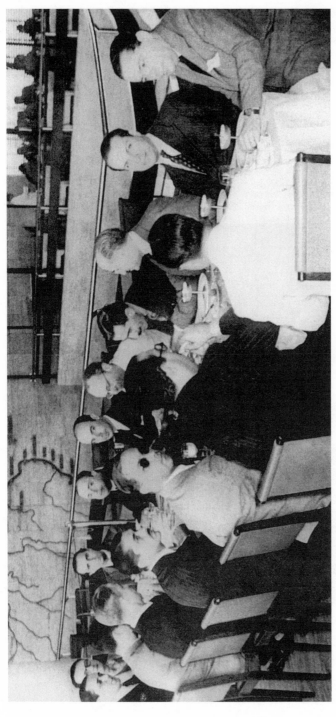

One of the annual lunches on the birthday of Alceu Amoroso Lima. Around the table, starting from the right, facing camera: Mário Bulhões Pedreira and then Dario de Almeida Magalhães. The fourth is Sobral Pinto (in dark suit, bending downward) followed by Alceu Amoroso Lima, Hamilton Nogueira, and Edmundo Luz Pinto. Adaucto Lucio Cardoso, on the table's near side (wearing dark glasses and light suit), is flanked by Evandro Lins e Silva (with mustache) and Augusto Frederico Schmidt (with glasses on his mostly hidden face). At head of the table (far left) is Rubens Maximiano de Figueiredo and close to him (extreme left) Aloísio Salles. (Kindness of Sobral Pinto family)

Sobral Pinto, at home, dictating to Cecília Silva (Cecy). (Kindness of Sobral Pinto family)

SOBRAL PINTO, "THE CONSCIENCE OF BRAZIL"

Advocate of Order during the Old Republic (pre-1930)

1. Catholic Upbringing (1893–1912)

For his early devotion to the Catholic faith, Heráclito Fontoura Sobral Pinto could thank principally his father, Príamo Cavalcanti Sobral Pinto. Príamo's devoutness, Heráclito wrote later, "was something rare in Brazil in those days."[1]

When Heráclito was born on November 5, 1893, Príamo was a station master, working for the Central do Brasil Railroad in Barbacena, in the interior state of Minas Gerais. The station master found his paychecks barely adequate to support his wife Idalina and himself and their three children, of whom Heráclito was the youngest; but his importance locally, Heráclito explained later, was exceeded only by that of the judges and the vicar.[2] A railroad station master was recognized as a key figure in the life and commerce of the community.

Within a couple of years of Heráclito's birth the family moved to southern Minas because Príamo was named station master at Porto Novo do Cunha, a suburb of the busy city of São José de Além Paraíba. Porto Novo is on the Paraíba River, which separates Minas from the more southerly state of Rio de Janeiro, and was an important railroad transshipment point for goods moving across a bridge between the broad-gauge Central do Brasil, in Minas, and the narrow-gauge Leopoldina Railroad, south of the river.

Príamo supervised the movements of the two railroads and the work at six warehouses. He employed hundreds of men who loaded and unloaded freight, or who drove horse-drawn wagons. An unruly border-town atmosphere prevailed, and Príamo's men needed to be vigilant to prevent robberies by thugs, such as the men who served a political boss across the river.[3]

The family spent twelve years in the pleasant climate of Porto Novo, living in a one-story house amidst mango trees. Like Príamo, Idalina was eager to provide a strong Catholic upbringing to the children: Natalina (born in 1886), Rubens (born in 1891), and Heráclito. Church services were faithfully attended, and thus Heráclito came under the religious influence of Padre Carloto Távora, his father's best friend.[4]

The boy, unlike his less studious older brother, achieved excellent grades in school. A legal career was seen as an appropriate possibility in view of Heráclito's expressed determination to do something, when he grew up, to prevent the atrocities he witnessed, such as a thrashing in Porto Novo of a railroad station wagon driver by criminals known across the river as policemen. Besides, the boy could argue well. He impressed Príamo's friends when he discussed the Russian-Japanese war of 1904–1905 and disputed the prevailing support for the Japanese, whom he described as "cowards and traitors."[5] Heráclito, an obedient boy, was brought up in a household that was austere and severely devoted to good morals. Recalling later those "idyllic years" of his youth, he wrote: "I was brought up and educated in Brazil's interior, in touch with the exuberance of our tropical nature . . . , far from everything artificial and insincere."[6]

Horse-drawn buses took the family on visits to relatives in the area and occasionally to see friends who owned *fazendas* (large estates) north of the Paraíba River. Prized above all other visits were those made to Ouro-Fino, the 1,500-hectare *fazenda* of Eduardo de Almeida Magalhães, who had married Príamo's sister Cândida after his first wife had died, bequeathing him the *fazenda*. There two hundred workers tended cattle and raised crops, chiefly the coffee for which Ouro-Fino was famous. Eduardo and Cândida, known to Heráclito as "Aunt Candóca," presided over a large family, because Cândida had added ten children to the four born of Eduardo's first wife. Heráclito, who spent vacations at Ouro-Fino between the ages of eight and thirteen, became close to numerous cousins.[7]

The main Ouro-Fino house, an extensive and formidable two-story structure of stone, was poorly lit except for the dining room, which boasted a large gas lamp from Belgium. And so it was in the dining room that Eduardo played solitaire or read, while the women occupied themselves with weaving when they were not receiving music instruction from a German piano player, an occasional visitor. Before 9:00 P.M. everyone retired to bedrooms, carrying candles.

Heráclito, after being awakened at 5:00 A.M., would join one of the boys at the *fazenda* for a breakfast of milk in a cowshed and then for a horseback ride to the fields of coffee plants and sugarcane, where they observed the workers, many of them former slaves.

Lunch, announced at 9:30 A.M. by a bell struck by a butler, would be followed by a look at the mail and the *Jornal do Commercio*, the leading newspaper of the city of Rio de Janeiro, capital of Brazil. Later Heráclito and other youngsters might visit the mills or the rice paddy, drive an oxcart, and swim in the pool. Occasionally they attended dances, held sometimes to observe birthdays, with music provided by an accordion.[8]

Visits to Ouro-Fino ended for Heráclito in 1907, when his father was transferred to Conselheiro Lafaiete, Minas Gerais, less accessible to Ouro-Fino. By then Heráclito had spent a year with his brother Rubens as a boarding school student at the Colégio Anchieta in Nova Friburgo, in the state of Rio de Janeiro. Príamo was determined to spare nothing to assure for his two sons the solid Jesuit education of Anchieta, known as Brazil's best Catholic school;[9] but soon it became clear that he could not pay for it. When he wrote the school about his predicament, the *reitor* (school director) replied with a fervent appeal against the withdrawal of Heráclito, whose "application, discipline, and piety" he found outstanding. Arrangements were made for Príamo's younger son to stay in the school at only half the annual fee of 800 milreis (equivalent to $250 at the time)—a payment that became less onerous after Rubens dropped out of the school.[10]

Heráclito, a well-built youth, was assigned the task of pulling the rope that rang the bell in a tower of the school's imposing main building, and he became well known also for his prowess on the soccer field. He made lifelong friends, among them his roommate Leonel Franca, who would go on to have a distinguished career as a Jesuit Father.[11]

Like other students in 1910, Heráclito was fascinated by the polished arguments presented strikingly in speeches by oppositionist Ruy Barbosa, campaigning for the Brazilian presidency.[12] But, as Heráclito and his friends knew very well, political practices in Brazil made it impossible for any oppositionist to dislodge the group that had always controlled the presidential elections.

During his seven years at the Colégio Anchieta, Heráclito learned history, French, and Latin. Above all, he came to feel that the Jesuits there completed the training in the Catholic faith begun by his parents. In a message he wrote in 1986, for the observance of the *colégio's* hundredth anniversary, he said that he had received instruction "in the Truths of Dogmatic Theology and of Moral Theology" that were "indispensable to the life of a Catholic as a family man, a professional man, and a man in public life."[13]

2.   Law School and Later (1912–1924)

After graduating from the Colégio Anchieta late in 1912, Heráclito joined his parents, who had moved to Rio de Janeiro following Príamo's retirement. The young man set out to study law at Rio's Faculdade de Ciências Jurídicas e Sociais with the help of money he earned as a clerk at a government telegraph office near the school.[1]

Heráclito participated in the activities of the Marian Church and joined the União Católica de Moços (Catholic Union of Young People), which held weekly meetings, published a journal, and sought to put into practice the Catholic social doctrine advocated by the Vatican. Entries in his diary in 1915 stressed his belief that only the Catholic Church, unfortunately of no interest to men in government, could overcome the "moral and intellectual anarchy" of society that was encouraged by the all-powerful "modern press." The entries revealed also his resolve in the future to write volumes, with God's help, that would combat principles of the French Revolution, which, he wrote, had "enshrined individualism and killed religion."[2]

Eager to spread the faith where he most desired to see it accepted, he gave, in 1915, a copy of *A Vida Devota de São Francisco de Sales* to his godmother, Luiza Rocha de Azambuja. In his long inscription, encouraging his parents' dear friend to embrace Christianity, the twenty-one-year-old law student expressed the hope of one day persuading Luiza's youngest daughter, then eighteen, to become his wife.[3]

Fellow law students, Heráclito has written, never missed reading a single speech of Ruy Barbosa, who again campaigned unsuccessfully for the presidency in 1914 following his defeat by army marshal Hermes da Fonseca in 1910. According to Heráclito, the speeches of Ruy Barbosa, champion of *civilismo* (civilian domination of politics), awakened public interest in the selection of presidents.[4]

With his wealthier classmate Benjamin Antunes de Oliveira

Filho, Heráclito discussed French literature that persuaded them to resolve to work, after graduation, for a better Brazil.[5] Another classmate with whom Heráclito developed close and lasting ties was Mário Bulhões Pedreira, whose graduation at the top of the class was followed by a legal career far more successful than that of Benjamin. Criminal law, which became Heráclito's specialty, was taught by Professor João Martins de Carvalho Mourão, later a Supreme Court justice before whom Heráclito argued cases.[6]

Heráclito's brother Rubens found jobs in bookkeeping without completing much education. Idalina, had she not died in 1916, would have been proud to witness the receipt of a law degree in December 1917 by her exemplary younger son.

The first legal work of Heráclito was to assist a Rio lawyer whose malady, cancer of the throat, gave the new graduate early experience in the oral presentation of cases.[7] By 1919 his income from his profession allowed him to leave the responsible telegraph office position to which he had been promoted. He formed a law partnership and, after recovering from a lung problem in Conselheiro Lafaiete, married the devoted Maria José Azambuja in February 1922. They rented a home in Rio's Tijuca district, where, in August 1923, they became the parents of the first of their seven children. They named the girl Idalina.

By then Maria José knew that Heráclito was an avid soccer fan, liked occasional music, and had little interest in the cinema; and she knew that it would be well to keep the kitchen supplied with fruit, especially bananas. Her husband smoked small Havana cigars and drank on social occasions, especially enjoying *cachaça* (a raw sugarcane rum).[8] Social occasions for him included the discussions at bars and cafés by groups of friends, such as Francisco Karam, a talkative poet. Heráclito prized these "Bohemian" interludes[9] in a busy life— so busy that he could not fulfill his wish to practice with the soccer team of the América Football Club. Starting in 1922, however, he became a member of the club's directorship, and, as such, helped set up Rio's soccer championship matches. He wrote Brazil's first Code of Sports, a document chiefly about soccer.[10]

In 1923 Heráclito participated in a legal case concerning the right of Rio's new Copacabana Palace Hotel to run a gambling casino. Evidence showed that the entitlement had been formalized in a contract signed by the government when it had persuaded investors to build the hotel for distinguished visitors attending the 1922 centen-

nial of Brazil's independence. Indignant at the government's failure to keep its word, Heráclito argued in favor of the casino, and
it opened its doors in 1924. For this work he received a large fee,
5 contos de reis (or 5,000 milreis, a sum then worth $1,000). But he
came to regret his role in the case. "I never imagined," he wrote
later, "how great a cancer gambling was."[11]

Heráclito envisioned the ideal society as one combining both liberty and the authority to maintain order. Because revolutionaries
defied order, he was critical of the brief and unsuccessful uprising
in Rio in July 1922 by young army officers who opposed Brazil's
unsavory electoral practices and the forthcoming inauguration of
President-elect Arthur Bernardes, of Minas Gerais.[12]

Survivors of the July 1922 uprising, known as revolutionary tenentes (lieutenants), continued plotting. With the aid of adherents,
they took control of the city of São Paulo in July 1924. Although
troops loyal to President Bernardes forced them out of the city, the
revolutionaries remained determined to defy the regime. About
1,200 of them, belonging to contingents from São Paulo and the
southern state of Rio Grande do Sul, set out in April 1925 on a march
that made its way throughout much of the Brazilian interior and
ended up in Bolivia early in 1927. During their struggles against federal and state troops, and against outlaws armed by the government,
hundreds of lives were lost. But the revolutionary movement and
especially this "Long March of the Prestes Column," a name reflecting the leadership of former army officer Luiz Carlos Prestes, won
the admiration and sympathy of much of the public and the press.
With the help of an unpopular "state of siege," or martial law, the
Bernardes government used strong measures against supporters of
the revolution.

The troubles of those times were the cause of Heráclito's emergence in 1924 from the obscurity of a model but unspectacular
youth.

3.   Procurador Criminal Interino (1924–1926)

The legal case against the tenentes who rebelled in Rio in July 1922
was being drawn up by Carlos da Silva Costa, the procurador criminal da república (top criminal prosecutor). However, following the
more serious tenente uprising of July 1924 in São Paulo, President

Bernardes sent him there because the law required that cases be tried where the crimes had been committed.

Heráclito Sobral Pinto had been making a name for himself in criminal law, and, as a substitute federal judge in March 1924, had written a thirty-five-page document condemning men he had found guilty of what the press had called the "scandal of the counterfeit stamps."[1] Carlos Costa, about to leave for São Paulo, recommended that Sobral handle the work of the *procuradoria* in Rio, with the title of Brazil's *procurador criminal interino* (interim), allowing Costa to retain the top title. In August 1924 Bernardes acted on the recommendation, and Sobral assumed the post, which paid a monthly salary of 3.6 contos de reis, to which was added a percentage of the fines collected.[2]

"I had the sole responsibility," Sobral wrote later, "of directing the legal repression of political, civilian, and military criminals who attacked constitutional order." This was true of the Federal District, whose prisons in the 1920s held most of the country's political prisoners.[3] Sobral became a familiar figure in the police department's Fourth Delegacia Auxiliar, which, after its creation in 1922, had been given a "social order section" to repress antigovernment activities by agitators and labor organizations, and a "public security section" to prevent antigovernment activities of a political nature.[4]

President Bernardes relied heavily on the Fourth Delegacia to uncover plots and was in constant touch with Sobral and Rio Police Chief Manuel Lopes Carneiro da Fontoura. Fontoura, an army marshal known as "General Stupidity" by his belittlers, made use of a bevy of investigators and secret police. Sobral worked with them, directing some investigations and collecting evidence.[5]

Police spies late in 1924 reported on subversive meetings attended by navy officers and others, and this led to the major case of the *procurador interino:* "the Protógenes Conspiracy." Sobral, who felt that almost a hundred men were plotting, drew up a long list that included navy Commander Protógenes Pereira Guimarães, navy Lieutenant Ary Parreiras, army Captains Carlos da Costa Leite and Gustavo Cordeiro de Farias, army Lieutenant Odílio Denys, and Congressman João Baptista de Azevedo Lima. Commander Protógenes and men who had met with him were arrested, an exception being Azevedo Lima, whose fellow congressmen refused even to consider Sobral's demand that his congressional immunities be set aside.[6]

Conspirators who were still at large managed to overpower six hundred legalists on the battleship *São Paulo*. Although the Rio coastal artillery sank two hydroplanes that the conspirators planned to use, shots from the Rio forts were unable to prevent the *São Paulo* from going to sea under the command of conspirator Herculino Cascardo, a navy lieutenant. The seafaring revolutionaries were thwarted in their attempt to land in Rio Grande do Sul and went on to Montevideo, where they left the ship in the hands of the government of Uruguay. Then Cascardo and a few companions joined a group that fought against Rio Grande's autocratic Governor Antônio Borges de Medeiros. After the group was defeated in battle, Borges' men cut the throats of eleven captured revolutionaries,[7] and Cascardo turned his attention to commercial activities in a town in Uruguay.

Sobral, appearing at Rio's First Vara (Circuit Court), denounced Cascardo and thirty-one other navy men, such as Augusto do Amaral Peixoto, a lieutenant who had made prisoners of legalists on the *São Paulo* and then became another exile in Uruguay. Navy Lieutenant-Captain Edmundo Jordão Amorim do Valle was arrested in Rio for his failure to combat the *São Paulo* uprising at its outset.[8]

In a decision handed down in March 1926, First Circuit Judge Olímpio de Sá e Albuquerque ruled that Sobral's denouncements should be thrown out because of his weak case against the Protógenes conspirators and because the *São Paulo* battleship defendants should be tried by the military justice system. He ordered the release from prison of Protógenes Guimarães and the others; but the Bernardes government, calling the men dangerous, kept them locked up "not for judicial reasons but to ensure public order during the state of siege."[9]

Sobral, appealing to the Supreme Court, maintained that the conspirators, who included civilians, were guilty of political crimes similar to those of the revolutionaries of July 1922 and July 1924. Asserting that Sá e Albuquerque's "ridiculous decision" had been made after a "superficial study," he said it should be overturned.[10]

Sá e Albuquerque's reaction, a message to the Supreme Court which he made known to the press, denied the superficiality of his study and declared that "no moral value" could be found in the testimonies of witnesses presented by the government. He criticized the "rude language" of the young *procurador interino*, who, he said, had obviously failed to consult his superiors.[11]

Sobral furnished the press copies of a long letter he wrote the judge to strike back at his "brutal words." He said he did not need to consult his superiors in a clear-cut case like the Protógenes Conspiracy, and he showed, from correspondence, that his friend Carlos Costa had praised his handling of it. He revealed also that Targino Ribeiro, although a lawyer for the defense, considered his work "brilliant," and he quoted from the speech of a senator who supported the *procurador interino* against the attacks of oppositionist lawmakers. Asserting that he was no coward, Sobral rejected the judge's "perfidious insinuations" against his personal and professional behavior.[12]

In May 1926, a majority of the Supreme Court ministers agreed with their *relator* (recommender of a decision), who said that the case of the *São Paulo*'s venture to sea belonged to the military justice system and that the Protógenes conspirators had not been shown to have carried out specific revolutionary acts.[13] Sobral, a tenacious fighter, remained determined to prove their guilt.

Besides denouncing conspiring *tenentes*, Sobral took on Communists in Brazil, many of whom, he maintained later, were foreigners who "began to come to Brazil in 1924–1926."[14] By 1924, however, the Communists in Brazil were principally Brazilians, as is clear from the pages of *Bastilhas Modernas* by Communist Everardo Dias. In one of his passages, Dias describes an "infernal scene," during which Sobral relaxed "impassively" at the navy arsenal while Dias and seven companions, boxed in an armored car, screamed about the heat and their fear of asphyxiation. Two hours later they were shipped to a prison camp on Ilha Rasa, a nearby rocky island, where they found over forty soldiers guarding fifty political prisoners, among them anarchist writer José Oiticica, oppositionist politician Maurício de Lacerda, and Paulo Bittencourt, of the Rio newspaper *Correio da Manhã*. Some weeks later, Everardo Dias writes, Sobral visited the island prison camp to confer with guards about the escape of José Eduardo de Macedo Soares, an anti-Bernardes politician from Rio state. After Sobral's visit, the island prison guards instituted a regime considered "iniquitous and debasing" by the prisoners.[15]

Writing later to his Catholic friend Alceu Amoroso Lima, Sobral said: "With the sole collaboration of the civilian police of Rio, I was the initiator of the efficient campaign against the communism that infiltrated Brazil."[16]

Sobral was not involved in the decision to send, in 1924 and 1925, over nine hundred prisoners (thieves, laborers, anarchists, and military conspirators) to the Centro Agrícola Clevelândia in the north, on the river separating Brazil from French Guiana. He understood that the climate was good at the Clevelândia prison camp. In a reference to the more than four hundred who died of diseases there, he stated that an epidemic of malaria had broken out on a ship carrying some of the prisoners north.[17]

Communists and supporters of *tenentismo* were not alone in resenting Sobral's work. He successfully argued before Judge Octavio Kelly, of Rio's Second Circuit Court, that prison sentences should be given to six employees of the Federal District treasurer's office who had absconded with 500 contos de reis.[18]

Security forces themselves disliked Police Chief Fontoura's use of investigators to spy on army officers, and they criticized Sobral's efforts to control military authorities and the police. Sobral's intentions were to make sure that men carrying out arrests limited themselves to what he considered permissible under law. This is not to say that many an oppositionist journalist and politician would not dispute what Sobral found permissible during the state of siege, but it did mean that men who made arrests were not supposed to take the law into their own hands.[19]

Writing later to Minas politician Francisco Negrão de Lima, Sobral said: "If you are prepared really to rein in the police, . . . be prepared to face hateful onslaughts. . . . Every manner of foul play was used against me." Things got better, he added, "when they discovered that I knew how to assert myself and was familiar with the art of fearless counteroffensive."[20]

A key to Sobral's success was the confidence he inspired in President Bernardes and Justice Minister Affonso Penna Júnior. "I became," he has written, "the center of attention in Rio and had the complete support of the president and all the top authorities." At meetings held several times a week at Catete Palace, where the president and justice minister had their offices, he presented judgments about incarcerations carried out by the police and the military. The judgments, he wrote, were "so clear and impartial" that the president invariably agreed with them.[21]

The daily *O Paiz*, supporter of Bernardes, praised the "brilliance" and "dedication" of Sobral, but most of the Rio press condemned the president, the police chief, and the *procurador interino*. Sobral was furiously attacked in the *Correio da Manhã*, whose owner, Edmundo Bittencourt, had been jailed in 1922. The newspaper had been closed down for nine months, starting in 1924, for having allowed its printing press to be used to publish a pro-*tenente* weekly.[22]

Before leaving the presidency in November 1926, Bernardes appointed Sobral *procurador criminal da república* and found another position for Carlos Costa,[23] who had completed work that contributed to the sentencing, in 1925, of more than a hundred men implicated in the *tenente* uprising of July 1924 in São Paulo. One of the *tenentes*, Eduardo Gomes, was transferred from a São Paulo prison to one in Rio, the result of a plea made by his mother to Sobral.[24]

Sobral's promotion was scheduled to be observed at a speech-filled banquet attended by three hundred guests at Rio's Automobile Club. But Sobral believed hypocrisy and servility characterized the attitude of most of those who had signed up to attend the lunch. He arranged for a less ostentatious observance, one in which fifteen close friends met first at the graveside of his parents (his father had died in 1925) and, after leaving flowers, had a meal at the Confeitaria Colombo. There Benjamin Antunes de Oliveira Filho gave his recollections of life at the modest Porto Novo home of the Sobral family and told of the Christian faith and hard work of the youth who had become *procurador criminal da república*. Heráclito, during his response, became tearful, moved by the occasion's spirit of true friendship.[25]

4. Rough Days for the Procurador Criminal (1927–1928)

Washington Luiz Pereira de Souza, former governor of São Paulo, became president of Brazil in November 1926. As the official candidate he had been unopposed in the election, and he was regarded as a welcome change from Bernardes, especially after he let the state of siege expire at the end of the year and released the political prisoners. He retained Sobral as *procurador criminal da república* and appointed a new police chief of the Federal District, Coriolano de Góes, a thirty-year-old law school graduate and friend of Sobral.

The Supreme Court, responding in January 1927 to one of Sobral's appeals, sent the cases of forty-four Protógenes Conspiracy defendants back to the court of Sá e Albuquerque, and Coriolano jailed those of the forty-four that his policemen could locate. One of the forty-four was solicitor Eurico Peres da Costa, who called the Supreme Court's reversal of its 1926 position the result of an arrangement made by outgoing President Bernardes to increase the monthly pay of the court's ministers from 3 to 7 contos de reis.[1]

In denying a petition filed on behalf of Peres da Costa, the Supreme Court took into consideration Sobral's charge that the prisoner, late in 1924, had used scurrilous language when referring to Bernardes and his "Catete Palace gang," had praised the Gaúcho (Rio Grande do Sul) revolutionaries, and had acted to protect Protógenes against arrest. In response, Peres da Costa sent a message to Sá e Albuquerque that called Sobral a representative of the most tyrannical government ever seen in Brazil and that accused the Supreme Court of bowing to an order of the former president, thus bringing ruin to the once noble judiciary.[2]

In the meantime the revolutionaries who had taken control of the battleship *São Paulo* were tried before the Military Justice Council, with lawyers Justo Mendes de Moraes and Targino Ribeiro leading the defense team, and with a Military Justice *procurador* handling the government's case. In April 1927, when the Council rendered its verdict, nineteen of the defendants, including Edmundo Amorim do Valle, were present, and sixty-eight were absent. The absent Herculino Cascardo and Augusto do Amaral Peixoto were condemned to spend 11⅔ years in prison, but many received sentences of only two years, and many more, such as Amorim do Valle, were exonerated.[3]

Sobral, seeking five-year sentences for each of the Protógenes case defendants, found twenty of the forty-four, including Protógenes Guimarães and Ary Parreiras, in Sá e Albuquerque's courtroom in May 1927.[4] He was up against an unfriendly judge and a renowned defense team, in which Justo Mendes de Moraes and Targino Ribeiro had been joined by Levy Carneiro, former president of the venerable Instituto dos Advogados Brasileiros (IAB—Institute of Brazilian Lawyers).

The courtroom was crowded with spectators and the press when Levy Carneiro argued that the police investigators, despite "the most rigorous vigilance," had not uncovered a single fact to prove illegal activities. He accepted Sobral's assertion that a sort of "revolutionary mysticism" had prevailed in Brazil under Bernardes, but maintained that the sentiment, causing orderly people to consider "a revolutionary solution," was the result of "a series of government

acts" that had violated individual liberties and "debased the republican regime." He found no conspiracy in the technical sense—only
"a desperate desire for better days."[5] Judge Sá e Albuquerque agreed
and absolved all forty-four defendants. "I did not find," he said, "that
twenty or more people conspired"—the minimum number, according to the criminal code of 1890, to constitute "a conspiracy."[6]

Sobral turned again to the Supreme Court for a reversal. But before it heard his plea, he completed the accusation against those
he considered guilty of the uprisings in July 1922. His denouncement, submitted to the court of Sá e Albuquerque in September
1927, listed seventy-four army men said to have been rebellious in
the Federal District and in the state of Mato Grosso. It described
the evidence against them given in the testimonies of eyewitnesses,
and contained Sobral's conclusion that the discontented army men
had become overexcited by the presidential campaign of 1921–1922,
during which they had opposed the Bernardes candidacy, and had allowed themselves to be "dragged into the entanglement of intrigues,
petty and self-seeking." In February 1928, Sá e Albuquerque absolved twenty-one of these defendants and declared that minimum
imprisonments of only one year and three months should be served
by the other fifty-three. Sobral, disgusted with the judge's lack of
severity, appealed to the Supreme Court.[7]

Sobral's anger against *tenentismo* was aggravated by knowledge
of the fate of a Catholic priest and thirteen other men who had
been brutally killed after surrendering to Prestes Column revolutionaries in Piancó, Paraíba, in 1926, and by tales about the "Column of Death" of revolutionary João Cabanas, responsible for mur-
dering four foremen employed by a company that Cabanas had said
was mistreating its workers.[8] The *procurador criminal*'s indignation
was evident in his emotional oral appeal, made in May 1928 to the
Supreme Court, about the Protógenes conspirators:

> I am not concerned about the unjust attacks made against me in
> recent years nor about those that may be in store for me—coming
> from the demagogues of the press and Congress. Insults, slanders,
> threats. The more vehement they are, the more they proclaim my
> constancy, my fidelity, my effort to fulfill my duty. . . . I have
> given and shall continue to give all that is demanded by my con-
> science, revolted by these atrocious crimes against my country
> and humanity. . . .

In the courtrooms there have appeared hundreds of unfortunates, whose misery, ignorance, and failings, caused by the inferior condition in which they were born, led them to crime. The
public ministry, in carrying out its terrible but necessary and majestic mission to defend and restore juridical order, severely denounced the crimes and was unrelenting in demanding the fulfillment of punishments.

Should you be silent today? Just because you have, before you,
not miserable members of the lowest class, but graduates of
courses, protected by good fortune against hopelessness, and provided by the State with benefits and rank, for which they should
be grateful—men of intelligence, fully conscious of the crimes
they have planned. . . .

Is there one type of justice for the humble and unfortunate, and
another for the strong and fortunate?

Sobral went on to say that he knew of no crimes that, on account
of their consequences, called for greater juridical severity than
"these, born of ambition and flung against the entire collectivity in
an incredible contempt for the lives of fellow-beings and for the integrity of the nation."

What you are to judge now is one more episode in the tragedy that
began with the slaughter of passers-by, struck down in the streets
by the first shots from the fort that revolted on that morning of
July 1922 and that ended with the delivery of a ship of our navy
to foreigners.

Surely those accused today will not be found responsible for
the deaths strewn from south to north, for killings such as those
claimed by Tenente Cabanas, for the murders at Piancó, for the
destruction of landholdings, for the 100,000 horses and 30,000
head of cattle taken in the "civilizing" raids of Captain Prestes.

But today's defendants resolved to carry out similar iniquities.

The police, Sobral told the judges, had acted just at the right moment, preventing the Protógenes conspirators from unleashing bom-
bardments, burnings, sackings, insurrection by soldiers, and riot-
ing by the population. Justification of these plans, he said, had been
found in the revolts in Rio in 1922 and in São Paulo in 1924, carried
out by men who used, as "a mere pretext," their "false claim" that
the government had wounded military pride in June 1922 when it

had reacted against subversive views expressed by an anti-Bernardes wing in the army.

Sobral told of his confidence in the reports of the police investigators. But he added that if these reports were felt to be inadequate proof, one need only "turn to the abundant confessions, testimonies, interviews, photographs, and commentaries given in books and newspapers for over a year" to show that the defendants had been inspired by the same sentiments that had already led others to criminal rebellion. Judgments against the defendants, he concluded, were required for the sake of public peace, security of the institutions, and "equal justice for all."[9]

The Supreme Court spent several days in secret sessions debating the case, and on May 28, 1928, it ended public suspense by announcing that the presiding justice had cast a "vote of Minerva" (breaking a tie) that gave a majority to those who believed that all the Protógenes Conspiracy defendants should be absolved.[10]

"Despite every effort," the *Correio da Manhã* exulted, "the vile police of Bernardes" could not prevail. "The Supreme Court wrecked the rash scheme concocted by corrupt *bernardismo* and carried out by the *procurador criminal*."[11]

In June, Francisco de Assis Chateaubriand's anti-Bernardes *O Jornal* published a series of complaints against what it called the "reactionary tendencies" of Sobral. *O Jornal* also wrote that Sobral's "habitual negligence" resulted in delays of months, even years, so that defendants sometimes found themselves in jail, awaiting trial, for a longer time than they would have served if convicted. "A judicial observer," writing in *O Jornal*, listed specific cases of "negligence" and added that they contrasted sharply with the diligence shown by Sobral "in handling charges against the oppositionist press."

After the Supreme Court voted unanimously to censure the *procurador criminal* for taking too much time in bringing cases before judges, *O Jornal* wrote that its criticism had been confirmed.[12]

5. Jackson de Figueiredo (1891–1928)

Affonso Penna Júnior, Bernardes' justice minister in 1925 and 1926, admired the opinions given by Sobral and also those given by Jackson de Figueiredo, conservative lay Catholic leader. Jackson, who had campaigned for the election of Bernardes (a "practicing Catholic"), served as adviser of Penna, and, in November 1925, was appointed chief of censorship of the Federal District.[1]

When Sobral first met Jackson in the office of the justice minister, neither of these men of strong character found the other likable. According to Jackson, Sobral demonstrated a "conceited reserve" and regarded Jackson as impulsive and eager to dominate. However, in the course of exchanging opinions, they discovered they had much in common and became inseparable friends.[2]

Jackson de Figueiredo was born in the small northeastern state of Sergipe in 1891; he studied law in Bahia and was known there as a staunch advocate of materialism. After coming to Rio with scant resources in 1914, he received affection and help from Raymundo Farias Brito, an opponent of materialism. Jackson was moved by Farias Brito's eloquent advocacy of spiritualism and was attracted to his sister-in-law Laura, whom he married in 1915.[3]

Following the death of Farias Brito in January 1917, Jackson came under the influence of Catholicism, thanks in large part to Archbishop Sebastião Leme and Leonel Franca, Sobral's Colégio Anchieta roommate. His conversion became complete in 1918, and when he went late that year to the southern Minas town of Muzambinho to recover from the "Spanish flu," he persuaded Hamilton Nogueira, who was opening a medical practice there, to abandon agnosticism in favor of Catholicism.[4]

Back in Rio in 1919, Jackson became a schoolteacher. He was known for the polemic about literary criticism that he carried on in newspapers with Alceu Amoroso Lima,[5] owner of the Cometa Textile Company, but he turned now to writing about religion and politics with what one commentator has called "more heat and decision than any other Brazilian." At a time of discussions about postwar problems, new directions, and events in Russia, the books and articles of Jackson combated socialism, liberalism, Protestantism, scientism, demagoguery, and the "false notion of the equality of men." He condemned the international capitalism of Jews and Masons, "men unassociated with our traditions and Church." Defending a strong government with the moral authority for preventing disorder, he liked to say that "the worst legality is better than the best revolution."[6]

Jackson's views were reflected in the name A Ordem, which he gave to the Catholic journal he established in 1921 with the help of Hamilton Nogueira, poet Durval de Moraes, and Perilo Gomes, a young dentist who had been brought up in Brazil's northeast. Archbishop Sebastião Leme, advocate of an active Catholic laity, encouraged the organization by Jackson of the Centro Dom Vital in 1922, to hold meetings and persuade the Church's laity to emphasize liturgical piety, Catholic theology, and personal austerity. Jackson became the Centro's "perpetual president" and then founded the Livraria Católica, a bookstore where Catholics met.[7]

Jackson's interest in Sergipe politics and dislike of Sergipe Congressman Gilberto Amado were shared by Sobral and Justice Minister Affonso Penna Júnior. But Jackson's hope of becoming governor of Sergipe was foiled when Governor Maurício Graccho Cardoso, whom Jackson and the justice minister had been defending from the attacks of Gilberto Amado, made a deal with an ally of Amado. As a result, Bernardes put the governorship in the hands of a candidate agreeable to Amado and Graccho Cardoso, and Amado became a senator.[8]

Although Jackson was dissatisfied with Bernardes, he remained close to Affonso Penna Júnior. He accepted the unpleasant censorship post largely because of Penna's urging and held it only until November 1926, when Penna left office. He convinced Penna that anarchist José Oiticica should be set free, and he argued successfully in April 1926 that his friend from Sergipe, Pedro de Oliveira Ribeiro Sobrinho, should be placed in charge of the police department's Fourth Delegacia.[9]

Jackson's books and articles, written in the harsh and ardent style of a polemicist, and his Centro Dom Vital work gave vitality to conservative Catholicism. He was the subject of books about his political and religious beliefs by Perilo Gomes and Hamilton Nogueira. During the presidency of Washington Luiz, a man Jackson respected, Alceu Amoroso Lima's interest in Communist solutions gave way to the arguments of Jackson, who recommended reading the works of Jacques Maritain and Gilbert Chesterton. In 1928 Leonel Franca admitted Alceu into the Catholic Church.[10]

Sobral and Maria José chose Jackson to be godfather of Ruth, their third child, born in 1927. Quite often Sobral was present at the daily gatherings of Jackson and his friends at the Café Gaúcho. Among the participants were Centro Dom Vital cofounders Hamilton Nogueira, José Vicente de Souza, and Perilo Gomes (who was starting a career in diplomacy), political journalist Lourival Fontes (from Sergipe), and poets Francisco Karam and Augusto Frederico Schmidt.[11] Jackson wrote Alceu Amoroso Lima that Schmidt, a twenty-one-year-old businessman and manager of the Livraria Católica, was a deep-feeling Catholic who laughed loudly and interminably. But Alceu, ardent admirer of Schmidt's poetry, expressed the fear that Schmidt, "a bird who wants to set flight" and "would not be caged," might turn from the Catholic faith, attracted "as I once was" to the "sybaritic charm" of Communism, advocate of rapid solutions.[12]

Occasionally Jackson joined Sobral for the walks that Sobral enjoyed along Ipanema beach in the moonlight. Among the others who partook of the walks was José Barreto Filho, who had come from Sergipe to study law after publishing a book of poems in 1922, when he was fourteen, and who served as the youthful secretary of Rio Police Chief Coriolano de Góes from 1926 to 1930. "Jackson," Barreto said later, "was the greatest intellectual with whom I was ever associated."[13]

Opportunities to enjoy the company of Jackson were cut short on November 4, 1928. While fishing in Rio's Barra da Tijuca district, with his eight-year-old son and a son-in-law of spiritualist Raymundo Farias Brito, he drowned.[14] Sobral, writing in *A Ordem* about Jackson's life, stressed characteristics that he admired in himself. Jackson, he said, "had a horror of equivocal positions and ambiguous words. He liked positions that were clear and precise. He could not tolerate . . . mediocrity of the heart."[15]

6. The Downfall of the Procurador Criminal (June 1928)

In 1927 Sobral was an editor of *A Ordem* and was considered one of the stars of the Centro Dom Vital. He saw in his *procuradoria* work "a glory for the hosts of Catholicism" and a solid hope for improving the republic in an orderly, Jackson-like way. Blessed with fame, a satisfactory income, and good health, he was self-confident, believing in his ability to use arguments to humiliate the adversaries of the government. "No one," he noted later, "had any doubt about the brilliant prospects of my role in the nation's public life"—prospects that he attributed to his intelligence and a life of self-denial, hard work, and austerity.[1]

However, the young *procurador criminal* began to tire of self-denial and found it more and more difficult to turn his back on delights unbecoming to austerity. He attended fewer religious services. He even committed adultery, "hypnotized" by what he has called the seductive attractions of "an alluring woman, who was, to my misfortune, endowed with an exquisite and exceptional sensitivity."[2] She was the wife of a friend, Lieutenant-Colonel Paulo Gomide, former director of the government's telegraph operations.

Knowledge of the affair reached the inner circles of the government in 1928, creating what Sobral felt was a moral dilemma that his superiors could resolve by accepting or rejecting his offer to resign. In June he wrote the *procurador geral da república* (attorney-general) to say that he considered himself "unworthy to continue with the delicate task of being public accuser."[3] President Washington Luiz decided that the resignation should be accepted.

Following Sobral's brief note to inform the press of his departure from his position, the *Correio da Manhã* surmised that the immediate cause was the "laziness" about which, it said, the Supreme Court had spoken; and it added that his many serious failings made it hard for the top authorities to understand why the *procurador geral* had put up with him for so long.[4] *O Jornal* published an editorial signed by Assis Chateaubriand that spoke of Sobral's "alarming inability to comprehend the nature of his office." The editorial accused him of having ignored *O Jornal*'s revelation about an election candidate who had confessed to buying votes, and it accused President Washington Luiz of having paid no attention to *O Jornal*'s listings of examples of Sobral's negligence. According to Chateaubriand, Sobral was to be praised for having recognized his inability to do his job, and had, by submitting his resignation, offered a lesson to Washington Luiz about how he, too, could fulfill his duty.[5]

A Noite called Sobral one of the worst inventions of the past administration—an invention that reflected the vices of the times. "He transformed a post for defending society into a springboard for ridiculous personal exhibitionism. And when he presented his resignation, he ran to his friends asking them to persuade the president not to accept it."[6]

Later Sobral bitterly told Augusto Frederico Schmidt that no one spoke in public to deny the reports that he was a leprous dog.[7] In recollections that he eventually published, he explained that he avoided "the evil curiosity of newspapers and false friends" by finding refuge in the residence of an acquaintance in a town outside Rio. His move also reflected his reluctance to face his family in view of

the true reason for his downfall, and he contemplated never returning home. But Maria José, learning where her husband had gone,
went to find him and brought him back. She never referred to his
infidelity then or since.[8]

Sobral could count on a handful of true friends. They included
Coriolano de Góes, Affonso Penna Júnior, Alceu Amoroso Lima,
Pedro de Oliveira Ribeiro Sobrinho, and Jackson de Figueiredo.[9]
Jackson, finding Sobral devastated by his sin, asked him to call on
Archbishop Sebastião Leme.

The archbishop, who lived in a modest home, was compassion-
ate. He embraced Sobral in his large arms and said: "I perceive and
understand the torture of your soul. Don't worry about worldly insults. Your bishop has forgiven you and so you have nothing to
fear."[10]

Leme instructed Sobral to read the *Confessions of Saint Augus-
tine*. After plodding for a week through pages he found insipid and
dull, Sobral became engrossed. "How humble and small I felt. It was
then that I realized the full extent of my sins and the absurd vanity
associated with things that had been on my mind during the last
phase of my occupancy of the *procuradoria criminal*."[11]

7.   A Street Brawl Leads to More Woes for Sobral (September 1928)

André de Faria Pereira, the *procurador geral* of the Federal District,
became popular by trying to curtail the power of the Rio police, but
he alienated Justice Minister Augusto de Vianna do Castello. After
Vianna do Castello dismissed him for insubordination early in September, appeals court judges *(desembargadores)* criticized the justice minister, lawyers spoke at the Instituto dos Advogados Brasileiros to express alarm, and the opposition screamed.[1]

Adding to the fury of the opposition was the decision of the government to satisfy Police Chief Coriolano de Góes by naming Sobral
Pinto to replace Faria Pereira. Assis Chateaubriand told his *O Jornal*
readers that the "immoral appointment" reflected President Washington Luiz' backward mentality. *O Globo* lamented the return of
bernardismo, whereas the *Correio da Manhã* described Sobral as a
"sleepy-head" who had become well known for neglecting the duties
of his office.[2]

Congressman Adolpho Bergamini said that while legal circles in Rio were shocked by the dismissal of Faria Pereira, the public was stupefied to learn of Sobral's appointment. He spoke in Congress of Sobral's "sickly predilection" for presiding over tortures used to extort confessions from humble people, and added that Sobral's "trumped up" accusations had been filled with lies. Also he reminded his fellow-congressmen that Sobral had sought to arrest an illustrious member of their chamber, Azevedo Lima, whom he had accused of conspiring with Protógenes Guimarães.[3]

Sobral, at his investiture, promised to fight, with all the firmness he had shown earlier, for "the re-establishment of social discipline, so seriously threatened today." He emphasized the difficulties of the task and expressed the hope that the judiciary of Rio, "upright, brilliant, cultured, and courageous," would cooperate. The pro-government *O Paiz* wrote that he would, without doubt, "handle his new post with all the high purpose, efficiency, talent, and honor that are associated with his illustrious name."[4]

Sobral learned that three hundred of his friends and admirers had decided to offer him a congratulatory banquet at which he would be presented with the robe of his new office. This time he decided to accept the invitation because of the "perverse and satanic" attacks against him.[5]

On Saturday evening, September 22, three days before the date set for the banquet, Sobral had a rude surprise when he left the Livraria Católica in downtown Rio. He was met by Paulo Gomide, who had in one hand a letter to his wife from Sobral and in the other hand a riding whip to use against the man who had had an affair with her. After Gomide shouted, "Do you recognize this letter, you cur?" the two men scuffled briefly on the crowded street, with Gomide unable to make effective use of the whip. While Sobral defended himself with the aid of his cane, the combatants fell against a parked car and were separated by spectators. Sobral returned to the Livraria Católica, where, twenty minutes later, a police car brought Fourth Delegado Pedro de Oliveira Ribeiro Sobrinho. With Pedro and Jackson de Figueiredo, Sobral was driven home.[6]

The press on Sunday published front page photographs of the fracas along with sensational accounts that, in Sobral's opinion, presented him as a coward.[7] How, *O Globo* asked, could the "Don Juan," who had betrayed his friend Paulo Gomide, appear before judges as a prosecutor? The *Correio da Manhã* called the street brawl

appropriate for a *favela* (a slum or shantytown) and added that Sobral's appointment had been an insult to honest magistrates and an
affront to society.[8]

On Monday Sobral handed Justice Minister Vianna do Castello a
letter containing his offer to resign and his declaration that the dignity of his office had not suffered from the aggression, which he had
repelled with courage.[9]

Vianna do Castello spoke with Washington Luiz, who disappointed Sobral by deciding to accept his resignation. At the crowded
hotel suite of the justice minister, reporters learned that the authorities were forced to conclude that it was impossible to retain someone who had lost "indispensable social and moral esteem" and that
the choice of Sobral, a "wrongdoer" associated with the past administration, had perhaps been a mistake.[10]

Sobral, recalling later his "hours of indescribable agony," wrote
that he made no criticism of the government, although he felt that
Washington Luiz had acted toward him in a "cowardly, traitorous,
and inhuman" manner. Noting that he received expressions of support from only five of the three hundred persons who had been prepared to honor him at a banquet, he added that "an individual need
only undergo suffering and pain in order for everyone to detest him.
Men only remember us when we can be useful to them."[11]

8. A Polemic during the Old Republic's Collapse (October 1930)

Following his departure from government work, Sobral resumed the
private practice of law. He shared modest office space in downtown
Rio with Raymundo Lopes Machado and associated himself also
with Carlos Costa, who had brought him into the Bernardes administration in 1924 and was now practicing law in São Paulo.

Sobral abandoned his custom of having his work typed at the
Remington Typewriter School by Cecília Silva, a devout Catholic
he had known when they were youngsters in southern Minas. Instead, he dictated to her each morning at his residence. Such was
Sobral's esteem for her that he usually accepted her suggestions for
toning down aggressive expressions and for making other modifications, sometimes substantial. Cecy, as she was called, would return
each day to her home in a suburb after lunching at the Sobral Pinto
household, which included Heráclito's sister, Natalina (afflicted by

total deafness), and Maria José's mother, Luiza Azambuja. Cecy, who never married, was held in affection by the family.[1]

The advances of money that Sobral received from Affonso Penna Júnior were indispensable because, although lawyers Penna and Targino Ribeiro referred some clients to him, he had to rely on loans to support his family well into 1929.[2]

Money was scarce, especially after the financial crash of that year, and Sobral devoted considerable time to the cases of destitute individuals, in accordance with his belief that no one should be sent away because of an inability to pay legal fees. Better income providers were the clients he occasionally served who were connected with companies involved in disputes about the allocation of dwindling assets.[3]

Sobral agreed to give legal help to an adventurous *tenente*, Joaquim de Magalhães Barata, member of a short-lived revolutionary government of Amazonas in the mid-1920s who later escaped from prison and went to Uruguay. Back in Brazil in August 1930, he was soon arrested in the northern state of Pará for working for the overthrow of President Washington Luiz. After he got in touch with Sobral, Sobral wrote him that a reversal of the Military Tribunal's guilty verdict was unlikely and that they had best seek to delay the proceedings by submitting a habeas corpus petition to the Supreme Court.[4]

Politics were heated during the campaigning for the presidential and congressional elections of March 1930. Washington Luiz, who came from São Paulo, alienated Minas by naming a fellow-Paulista to be the official presidential candidate, whereupon Minas leaders, such as Arthur Bernardes, Affonso Penna Júnior, and the state governor, supported the oppositionist Aliança Liberal ticket, whose presidential candidate was Rio Grande do Sul Governor Getúlio Vargas.

Sobral sided with his Minas friends against the position of the president; but, after the official candidate was declared the election winner, he hesitated to share their enthusiasm for plans of *tenentes* and defeated politicians to launch an Aliança Liberal revolution to overthrow Washington Luiz. Writing a friend in September, he said that the government was directed by men without intelligence, culture, or morals, was unable to perceive Brazil's needs, and represented the worst plague that could befall a nation. But he called the antigovernment coalition a hodgepodge of politicians, revolutionaries, Communists, demagogues, and simple brawlers.[5]

Coriolano de Góes, supporter of Washington Luiz, was appointed to the Supreme Military Tribunal in September, and Sobral, pleased with the choice, applauded Coriolano's rectitude, scruples, firmness, fearlessness, and loyalty to companions. But it disappointed Sobral to learn that Pedro de Oliveira Ribeiro Sobrinho, another backer of the government, agreed to replace Coriolano as police chief. Pedro, who had recently become godfather of the Sobral Pintos' fourth child, was told by Sobral that the police had been turned into an instrument of brute force.[6]

More upsetting to Sobral were the pro-government articles of Centro Dom Vital President Alceu Amoroso Lima, published after the Aliança Liberal revolt broke out early in October. Sobral maintained, in letters to Alceu, Hamilton Nogueira, Perilo Gomes, and Schmidt, that each side in the conflict was guided by selfish materialism and disregarded the interests of the people.[7]

In particular, Sobral objected to the desire of Alceu and others to have the Centro Dom Vital declare itself for Washington Luiz. When Alceu, defending his position, cited Sobral's acceptance of Jackson's doctrine of legality while serving as *procurador*, Sobral replied that he had established his own doctrine a year before meeting Jackson. Bernardes, Sobral added, was a rigorous respecter of juridical formulas and was always guided by moral considerations. The problems in the 1920s, he wrote, concerned individuals who had rebelled, whereas in 1930 two oppositionist states, Minas and Paraíba, had arisen to defend their constitutional rights, flagrantly disrespected by a federal government that had refused to seat their congressmen, had denied their officials the use of the national telegraph service, and had, in other improper ways, penalized them.[8]

Alceu considered Washington Luiz a lesser evil than the revolutionaries, made up of "undisciplined" *tenentes* and "ambitious" politicians who had backed the unsuccessful presidential candidacy of Rio Grande do Sul Governor Getúlio Vargas. But he did at length give some satisfaction to Sobral, for he separated the position of the Centro Dom Vital from his personal view. The Centro, he wrote in *A Ordem*, should be guided by Jackson's recommendation that it place spiritual matters ahead of "direct participation in political struggles."[9]

After mid-October, when the revolutionaries were advancing on Rio, Sobral concluded that the uprising represented thunderbolts of divine rage, punishing Brazil for faithlessness and falling on men who had failed to check their ungovernable passions.[10] Upon reading a pro-government article by Schmidt, he scolded the poet for lacking political vision and told him to "listen to the public cry for justice." Accusing Perilo Gomes of disfiguring Jackson's admonition against revolution, Sobral told him that Jackson "opposed Caesarism" and that Washington Luiz had violated the legality that Gomes was defending.[11]

Hamilton Nogueira's articles, considered "wretched" by Sobral, expressed surprise at the support of the Aliança Liberal revolution by Bernardes, who, the physician said, had suppressed a movement "identical to the present one." He wrote Sobral that Brazil's spiritual life would best be served by avoiding material disorder, such as the revolutionaries had been stirring up for eight years. "Having lived at the side of Jackson, I cannot support indiscipline, confusion, and above all, doctrinal and moral deviation." Sobral, who had become eager to witness the defeat of Washington Luiz, told Hamilton that the president, a capricious despot, was practicing unprecedented violence, with the result that no solution could be found "in the deplorable legality that you and some friends of Jackson are preaching."[12]

On October 24, when the Washington Luiz government collapsed, Alceu took Police Chief Pedro de Oliveira Ribeiro Sobrinho into hiding.[13] Mobs of celebrating Cariocas (people of Rio) were threatening members of the fallen regime and were liberating prisoners and wrecking the installations of pro-government newspapers. Sebastião Leme, recently named cardinal, persuaded victorious military officers to consider the safety of Washington Luiz, and he accompanied him from the presidential palace to Copacabana Fort. There the fallen president found protection before going into exile.

PART II

Critic of Post-1930 Confusion (1931–1935)

1. Combating Liberalism and *Tenentismo* (1931)

The *tenentes* and the oppositionist politicians, responsible for the success of the 1930 revolution, parted company after the fall of the old regime. The *tenentes* felt that a return to traditional political ways would block radical reforms. They were encouraged by Getúlio Vargas, who was installed as head of Brazil's "provisional government" on November 3, 1930. Vargas, after calling for "an end of the profession of politics," closed Congress and scrapped the Constitution of 1891.

Men whom Sobral had prosecuted became heroes with great influence. One of them was Juarez Távora, the embodiment of *tenente* daring ever since 1922. As the new regime's "viceroy of the north," he appointed fellow-conspirators of the 1920s to administer the states in the north and northeast as representatives of Vargas and with the titles of *interventores*. Thus Herculino Cascardo, leader of the 1924 insurrection of the battleship *São Paulo*, was chosen *interventor* of Rio Grande do Norte. Protógenes Guimarães received the rank of admiral and was soon named minister of the navy. Ary Parreiras, his companion in the "Protógenes Conspiracy," became *interventor* of the state of Rio de Janeiro after serving on one of the commissions to investigate the sins of past administrations.

Adolpho Bergamini, denouncer of Sobral in 1928, was installed as mayor of the Federal District late in October by the generals who overthrew Washington Luiz before Vargas reached Rio. But the new mayor was an Aliança Liberal politician, and therefore a vicious campaign against him was carried out by *tenentes*, and he had to resign in September 1931. His replacement, medical doctor Pedro Ernesto Batista, was a favorite of the *tenentes* and had been an organizer, early in 1931, of the *tenentes'* 3 of October Club.

It was the legalists of the fallen regime who now received Sobral's help. One of his new clients, navy Commander Carlos Penna Botto, found himself defendant in a case of slander after his scathing confidential remarks about rebels on the battleship *São Paulo*, written in 1924, somehow reached the press.[1] Pedro de Oliveira Ribeiro Sobrinho, who moved to São Paulo to practice law, was defended by Sobral against *O Jornal*'s charge that he had stolen money from the Rio police department. Sobral was likewise anxious about the situation of Coriolano de Góes, who also settled in São Paulo; but Coriolano, less of a worrier than Sobral, was confident that the investigative commissions would accomplish little.[2]

Considering the diversity of the groups that had made the revolution, it was no surprise to Sobral to find post-revolutionary conditions confusing and even anarchical. On November 4, 1930, the day after Vargas became president, Sobral told Bernardes that the confusion was so great that it could be dissipated only by a ruler with absolute power. Unfortunately, he added, the revolution had succeeded too easily and speedily to allow the emergence of a great leader, one with exceptional vision and with the prestige that follows a series of victories in serious combats. The case of Brazil, Sobral told Bernardes, was unlike that of Italy, where Benito Mussolini, known to be "a man of exceptional qualities," had emerged after years of struggles during which he had formed a strong party to do away with anarchy and combat Communism.[3] Sobral told other friends that violent upheavals in Europe had sometimes produced excellent results but that the Brazilian upheaval had resulted in failure because of "the clash of different currents," the stupidity of the men in government, and the backwardness of the masses.[4]

In mid-1931 Schmidt's publishing firm distributed *Outubro 1930* by Virgílio de Mello Franco, who had worked for the revolution. Among the unfavorable reviews of the book was the one written by Sobral in an early number of *A Razão*, a São Paulo newspaper edited by Plínio Salgado and Francisco San Tiago Dantas, intellectual opponents of liberalism and the rapid reconstitutionalization of Brazil. According to Sobral, Virgílio's story was about "narrow, irresolute, and self-seeking aspects of the presidential campaign" and failed to address the true cause of the 1930 revolution: the illness of the entire national organism, a result of errors that had turned politicians away from the principles of Christianity.[5]

Continuing to write for *A Razão*, Sobral condemned "that miserable liberalism," which, he said, annihilated individual personality and was responsible for the rejection of "dogmatic morality, the only thing capable of coordinating the behavior of those who govern and those who are governed." Believing in mid-1931 that the new rulers had failed to carry out a single sensible step or reveal any vision, Sobral blamed "the anarchy" on the national mentality and concluded that the solution did not lie in the mere writing of a new constitution. In *A Razão*, he urged public figures to abandon cowardice and attack liberalism, which, he wrote, had been extolled down through the generations. This attack, he added, would require the use of blunt and vigorous language.[6]

Blunt and vigorous language characterized Sobral's political commentaries that appeared in *A Ordem* starting in March 1931. The request for Sobral's series of articles came from Alceu Amoroso Lima, who turned the bimonthly into a monthly with the help of Perilo Gomes.[7]

In *A Ordem*, Sobral quarreled with Magalhães Barata, the much-arrested *tenente* he had sought to help shortly before the revolution broke out. Magalhães Barata, having become *interventor* of Pará in November 1930, argued that "the imperious duty of the army is to rescue the unarmed nation, freeing it from political personalism."[8] Sobral believed that army men should devote their attention to the affairs of their profession, and he denounced the "military mentality" that pushed civilians out of the interventorships of Ceará and Bahia, replacing them with *tenentes*. He wrote in *A Ordem* that *tenente* João Alberto Lins de Barros, *interventor* of São Paulo, had, like his companions, "unleashed the revolution without knowing anything about the needs of Brazil." And he used *A Ordem* to object when the authorities decided to declare July 5 a holiday in commemoration of the revolt of 1922.[9]

Sobral's views provoked a response from *tenente* Severino Sombra de Albuquerque, a member of the 3 of October Club who was in Ceará receiving help from Padre Hélder Câmara to organize a fascist-inspired legion of workers. Readings of *A Ordem*, Sombra told Alceu, had convinced him and Dom Hélder and others that Sobral was a "man of yesterday" who was making a mistake in bickering about the high positions held by *tenentes*. Sobral called Sombra's letter to Alceu "positive proof of the ostensive, insolent, and unrestrained intervention of the *tenentes* in public administration." "Letters from the north," Sobral wrote Bernardes, "advise that all the garrisons obey Juarez Távora blindly and are in truth commanded by sergeants who tolerate superior officers only as long as they do not issue orders contrary to those of Juarez."[10]

2. Supporting Bernardes against Francisco Campos (1931)

Tenentes, wishing in 1931 to extend their influence to Minas Gerais, said that old Olegário Maciel, the state's "governor and interventor," was worm-eaten and unrevolutionary. In their endeavor to topple Olegário, they found themselves in an alliance with their former archenemy, Arthur Bernardes, who saw in the fall of Olegário an opportunity to restore the influence of the Partido Republicano Mineiro (PRM) and himself. Declining Vargas' offer of the ambassadorship to France, Bernardes prepared to participate in the anti-Olegário movement, a movement that was supported by two members of Vargas' cabinet. Justice Minister Oswaldo Aranha and Foreign Minister Afrânio de Mello Franco agreed with *tenentes* who argued that Virgílio, Afrânio's oldest son, would provide the Minas government with a revolutionary spirit and should replace Olegário.

Sobral gave advice and support to Bernardes. The advice, which was disregarded, was that the former president should stress, in his declarations, all he had done for Catholicism during his governorship of Minas, and should admit, in a press interview, that he had committed some errors while serving in a presidency that had been disturbed by an abnormal situation.[1] Sobral's support took the form of using his pen to attack the defenders of Olegário, especially Vargas' education minister, Francisco Campos, who had joined with Minas state cabinet secretaries Gustavo Capanema and Amaro Lanari to organize the pro-Olegário khaki-shirt Legião de Outubro (Legion of October).

Sobral told Bernardes and Alceu Amoroso Lima that Campos considered morality the equivalent of rationalism and that his promise of an educational reform to allow religious instruction in public schools was a mere political trick. In *A Ordem,* Sobral wrote that Campos, stirring up support for the Legião de Outubro, orated with a brilliance that hid his failure to understand Christianity.[2] But Cardinal Sebastião Leme and Alceu Amoroso Lima were backers of Campos' proposed reform, and the latter told Sobral that he ought not to be expressing doubt about the sincerity of Campos' promise to bring it about.[3]

Campos' promise was kept on April 30, 1931, by the issuance of an appropriate decree. Sobral, writing in *A Ordem*, saw some merit in the decree but called it "offensive to the rights of the Church" because it used the word "religious," without specifying Catholic, education, and thus opened the door to "other religions, mere representatives of error." He did admit, however, that Campos had made his Legião de Outubro attractive to the Catholics of Minas.[4]

The Legião gained the support of some prominent Partido Republicano Mineiro members, among them Wenceslau Braz, former president of Brazil. Another prominent PRM member who turned to the pro-Olegário Legião was former Minas governor Antônio Carlos de Andrada, who disliked both Bernardes and the criticism of himself to be found in Virgílio de Mello Franco's *Outubro 1930*. Sobral accused Braz and Antônio Carlos of scheming with the help of "the decrepitude and skullduggery of old Olegário," and suggested in *A Ordem* that Affonso Penna Júnior, friendly to both Bernardes and Antônio Carlos, could heal the "lamentable rift."[5] Writing to a friend, Sobral said: "Don't worry, the final victory will go, without the slightest doubt, to Dr. Bernardes." Bernardes, he added, was endowed with outstanding administrative vision, firmness, political shrewdness, psychological perceptiveness, and a Machiavellian ability to use, when necessary, force or seduction.[6]

In August, Bernardes decided to hold a PRM Congress in Belo Horizonte, the capital of Minas. Sobral, in his monthly commentary in *A Ordem*, praised the decision, calling it a noble step to bring about the coordination of political groups, useful for the achievement of normal political organization in Brazil.[7] But the PRM Congress had no such effect. It created havoc, designed to give Justice Minister Aranha an excuse to remove Olegário. The PRM Congress, assisted by noisy outsiders, became thoroughly offensive to the governor. Some of its participants discussed the new state cabinet they expected to install, while others increased the bedlam by kidnapping Olegário's agriculture secretary.[8]

At that point Aranha instructed the commander of the army regiment in Belo Horizonte to use his troops to depose the governor. The army troops, however, failed to carry out the order when they found that the state troops, on the instructions of state Justice Secretary Gustavo Capanema, were defending Olegário. Bernardes and some of his supporters were arrested by the Minas authorities.

Vargas completed the defeat of Bernardes and *tenentismo* in the state by resolving that Olegário should remain in office. When Olegário followed up this development by closing the state legislature, dominated by the pro-Bernardes PRM, Sobral assailed the act of "tyranny" and accused the ruler of Minas of breaking promises about maintaining a representative government. In reminding his readers that it was immoral for a ruler in Olegário's position to "go beyond the laws of reason and justice," Sobral made use of words written by his mentor, Antônio Vieira, a Portuguese Jesuit who had been a missionary in Brazil in the seventeenth century. "Our great Vieira," Sobral also pointed out, attributed the ills of the world to the failure of people to curb their appetites and ambitions.[9]

3. Critic of the Regime and of Its Paulista Opponents (1932)

Legal work, which Sobral frequently described as "arduous," included an important bankruptcy case in Rio state in 1932. "This horrible struggle for existence" did not prevent him from furnishing articles to *Política* (run by a São Paulo opponent of the 1930 revolution) and *A União* (a Catholic publication in Rio), as well as *A Ordem*.[1] In February 1932, the Centro Dom Vital published Sobral's booklet *Racionalismo, Capitalismo, Communismo*, which blamed rationalist philosophy for Communism and for "inhuman capitalism."[2]

Early in 1932 Sobral took over from Alceu Amoroso Lima a weekly column in *A Razão* of São Paulo. Shocked to find his work printed in the recently revised orthography, he wrote Plínio Salgado to denounce the "wretched" spelling reform by a "half dozen rash imbeciles"—a reform that he said was admired by "retarded mentalities" such as that of Colonel Manoel Rabello, recently named *interventor* of São Paulo.

Advising Salgado that his conscience would not allow him to have his work published with the new spelling, Sobral explained: "I respect tradition as a principal element of resistance against the horrible anarchy that is disorganizing the modern world."[3] When Alfredo Egydio de Sousa Aranha, financial backer of *A Razão*, visited Rio, Sobral persuaded him to allow his articles to be printed in the old spelling; but, not long after that, Alfredo became irritated to find that the articles berated Oswaldo Aranha, his famous cousin.[4]

A dispute about whether or not Sobral's criticism of Oswaldo Aranha constituted a "violent personal attack" was quickly eclipsed by the demise of *A Razão*, its installations destroyed during wild street demonstrations by young Paulistas who shouted "Death to Vargas!" and "Death to Aranha!" This turmoil of May 23, during which lives were lost, was mentioned in a letter that Pedro de Oliveira Ribeiro Sobrinho wrote to explain to Sobral that São Paulo was, at last, setting up a "relatively autonomous government." Sobral was pleased to hear from Pedro, who had been so upset by Sobral's "intransigent *bernardismo*" that he had been cool to his old friend.[5]

Sobral's *A Ordem* articles expressed sympathy for Paulistas who had complained for over a year that their state, following the 1930 revolution, had been dominated by outsiders: Vargas, Aranha, and the *tenentes*.[6] Sobral denounced Vargas for failing to give Brazil individual liberties, and he dealt so roughly with the *tenentes'* 3 of October Club that Jesuit Padre Antônio Fernandes, advocate of military participation in the government "during exceptional times," sent a plea from Recife to Alceu to have *A Ordem* stop featuring articles by "a member of a political party that favors the reconstitutionalization of Brazil."[7] Sobral, in his forty-page letter to the Jesuit Father, denied belonging to any political party or ever having voted, and he defended his interpretation of events "because mere narrative leads to immoral indifference between good and evil." Scoffing at Padre Fernandes' hope to have the 3 of October Club become a sponsor of Catholic ideas, Sobral cited influential club members, such as Herculino Cascardo, who, he said, were socialists or leftists, intent on inciting "ignorant members of the proletariat."[8]

The 3 of October Club did not believe that reforms, such as the pro-labor decrees of Vargas, would be enacted if Brazil returned to normal political institutions. It maintained its stance against elections in the face of Vargas' electoral reform of February 1932, which instituted the secret ballot, lowered the voting age from twenty-one to eighteen, extended voting rights to women, and took effective aim against electoral fraud. The 3 of October Club suffered a worse setback two months later when Vargas, in an impressive ceremony attended by his cabinet, the press, and foreign dignitaries, signed a decree calling for the election, in May 1933, of a Constituent Assembly. Sobral, in *A Ordem*, continued to argue that a constitution would be useless without a "transformation of the mentality" of Brazil's leaders, saturated with "the materialistic policy that has, like a leprosy, dominated the Brazilian soul for more than fifty years."[9]

Sobral had told Padre Antônio Fernandes in March 1932 that Vargas was "a mere plaything of intransigent military groups." But in June, after Vargas disappointed *tenentes,* he saw the president in a different light. He wrote in *A Ordem:* "Getúlio Vargas, equipped with a mental agility never before seen in Brazilian leaders, and assisted by a cold, impassive temperament, has known how to take advantage of the antagonism between the political wing that wants the country's immediate return to a legal regime and the militarist wing that struggles for a prolongation of the dictatorship." He added that Vargas relied on a political positivism that was decrepit and sterile because it ignored God, converting men into mere instruments of movements dominated by natural laws, such as those governing the behavior of the stars in space.[10]

São Paulo, demanding immediate constitutionalization of Brazil,[11] started its "Constitutionalist Revolution" against the Vargas government on July 9, 1932. The outbreak was supported by Bernardes in Minas and old Borges de Medeiros in Rio Grande do Sul, but the predominant political factions in those states kept them loyal to Vargas, and the outbreak by São Paulo was suppressed after about three months of warfare.

During the civil war, Sobral wrote in *A Ordem* of his admiration of the valor and "capacity for self-sacrifice" demonstrated by the people of São Paulo. However, he concluded then and later that the constitutionalization of Brazil had been merely a "pretext" used by Paulista leaders, whose objective had been to take over the nation. He felt it likely that a São Paulo victory would have the undesirable result of returning Brazil to its pre-1930 regime, which, he said, had been characterized by the same "satanic pride" displayed by its successor.[12] Writing late in 1932 to São Paulo lawyer Antônio de Queiroz Filho, he pointed out that many people, including himself, had disagreed with the ideology that had inspired the Paulista revolution, but he added that "nobody can claim that the victory of São Paulo would have been a greater evil than what now exists, terrifying us with its cynicism and ignorance."[13]

Following the military defeat of the insurgents, Vargas prepared to send federal assistance to São Paulo and send its leaders to exile in Portugal. He declared that the orderly Paulistas had been taken to a "sinister adventure" by an audacious group. Sobral, in *A Ordem,* accused Vargas of pretending not to know that all of São Paulo had arisen "as one man." He wrote that Bernardes and Borges de Medeiros, both now under arrest, were the leaders who had had the greatest prestige in their states. And he asserted that no person of good sense failed to realize that the 1930 revolution needed to be defeated. This, he went on to say, would have to be taken care of by time and new efforts.[14]

The opportunity for new efforts was at hand with the forthcoming May 1933 election of the Constituent Assembly, promised by Vargas in April 1932. Catholics would be able to contribute to the new order by working with, and following the orientation of, the Liga Eleitoral Católica (LEC—Catholic Electoral League), founded in mid-1932 by Alceu Amoroso Lima at the request of Cardinal Sebastião Leme and after Sobral spent a part of April working on the statutes.[15]

Late in 1932 Alceu was asked to give suggestions to a commission appointed by the government to write a draft of a constitution, to be submitted later to the Constituent Assembly. Again, Alceu sought the advice of Sobral.[16]

4. Sobral's Departure from *A Ordem* and *A União* (1933–1934)

Late in 1932, Alceu Amoroso Lima sought to become professor of political economy at the law school in Rio; but the *concurso* (contest), judged by a group of professors, was won by Leônidas de Rezende with the support of his influential fellow-Marxist, Professor Edgardo Castro Rebello.

Sobral, who received this news as an "unhappy surprise," helped Alceu prepare a thesis in 1933 to be judged by professors considering candidates for a new opening at the law school, the professorship of the introduction to the science of law. While sending Alceu studies about the nature of Marxism, Sobral told Henrique Hargreaves, a friend in Minas: "We are all absolutely certain of the defeat of Alceu because the Law School has long been dominated by Castro Rebello, a declared Communist, envious of Alceu's moral, intellectual, and social prestige."[1] When the contestants met to defend their theses before the *concurso* judges, leftist students in the audience shouted against Alceu (and hurled rolls of toilet paper into the air). They applauded Hermes Lima, who was declared the winner.[2]

Among those who heckled Alceu was Evandro Lins e Silva, a young law graduate who was furnishing articles about legal matters to *A Nação*, a pro-Vargas daily founded early in 1933 by Police Chief João Alberto Lins de Barros and run by José Soares de Maciel Filho. Because *A Nação's* founders had used dubious legal steps to take over the installations of *O Jornal*, Sobral accused them of perpetrating "the greatest scandal in Brazilian history." Warning Alceu and Leonel Franca against submitting articles to *A Nação*, Sobral described the new daily as run by "rogues" and "filthy revolutionary scum."[3]

Like *tenente* hero João Alberto, Alceu could have been a strong contender for a seat in the Constituent Assembly. But he chose, instead, to throw himself into his work as secretary general of the Liga Eleitoral Católica, while its president, Old Republic statesman Pandiá Calógeras, did little more than lend the LEC his famous name. Guided by Cardinal Leme and Alceu, the LEC sought to persuade political parties and Constituent Assembly candidates to accept its "minimum program," and it worked also to have as many of its followers as possible register to vote.

The "minimum program" had only three points: (1) the indissolubility of marriage and recognition of the validity of religious marriages, (2) religious education in public schools, and (3) the availability of religious services in the armed forces, prisons, and hospitals. Among the other points in the full program, whose acceptance was not required for LEC backing, were those calling for the promulgation of the constitution in the name of God, the ability of Catholic labor unions to operate like other labor unions, and the defense of private property. The LEC also favored "labor legislation inspired by social justice and the principles of Christianity."[4] Sobral helped Alceu distribute LEC bulletins and booklets, and he sent notices to parochial leaders urging them to increase the number of registered voters devoted to the LEC.[5]

Most of the parties and candidates accepted the minimum program. After João Alberto declared that "the Catholic Church is the greatest defender of the working class," Sobral asked, in *A Ordem*, whether the pro-Church declarations of João Alberto and other candidates were sincere or were made in order to gain the backing of the LEC.[6]

Plínio Salgado, head of the fascist-like Ação Integralista Brasileira (AIB), was a sincere Catholic. He expressed fervent support for the entire ten-point program of the LEC and asked it to declare the AIB its official party. Alceu and Leonel Franca would not agree. "Very well," Plínio said, "this time the victor will be the LEC; after that the Communists will win; and finally we shall triumph."[7]

Plínio's Integralistas, a national movement contending against local parties that had strong political backing, did poorly in the election of May 3, 1933. Although most of the winning parties had accepted the LEC's minimum program, Catholic leaders acknowledged that acceptance had frequently been given for tactical reasons and that only about 30 or 40 of the 214 *constituintes* elected on May 3 were practicing Catholics, the rest being indifferent.[8]

Diplomatic Cardinal Leme, disinclined to alienate leaders of the Provisional Government or others whose influence could be helpful to the Church, was effective in his new work of discussing the forthcoming constitution with many individual *constituintes* and with groups of them, and he was assisted by Alceu.[9] A problem lay in Sobral's attacks, in Catholic publications, against men whose goodwill was important for the cardinal.

When an unhappy reader of Sobral's articles in *A Ordem* suggested that Alceu and Sobral might not be in agreement, Sobral quoted praise from Alceu to show this was not true. However, in reply to another reader, Sobral admitted that his articles might be "a serious impediment to getting new subscriptions." He told him also that, in view of the cardinal's close relations with the Centro Dom Vital, these articles in the Centro's official organ might seriously interfere with the work that Leme was trying to carry out.[10]

In June 1933, following Alceu's suggestion that the Vargas regime be handled with less harshness in *A Ordem*,[11] Sobral said he would act on a "threat" made earlier in the year to discontinue his column,[12] preferring to do so than to pull his punches. Alceu sought to persuade him to change his mind, but Sobral replied that he had given his word about stepping aside and would not violate "family tradition" by falling into the weakness of breaking his word—something he had done once, leading to disastrous results in 1928. Explaining later his situation with *A Ordem* in 1933, Sobral wrote: "My frank, fearless, and virile language upset the country's rulers."[13]

No warning preceded Sobral's dismissal, early in 1934, from the political editorship of *A União*, a Catholic Church publication for the masses. Complaining bitterly to Alceu, Sobral said that the cardinal, "who always praised my articles in *A Ordem* and *A União* when we were together," failed to inform him of his disagreement with articles "that attacked government policy about São Paulo and the devious moves of Oswaldo Aranha." Instead, Sebastião Leme "summoned Osório Lopes, director of *A União*, in order to have him stab me in the back, thus providing me the greatest possible proof of the dislike and lack of esteem in which he holds me. What hurts and revolts me is that insidious attitude—that recrimination handled in an indirect manner."[14]

Months later Alceu suggested that Sobral, full of objections about how Ação Católica Brasileira was being run, call on the cardinal to discuss the matter. Sobral declined. "I am not," he told Alceu, "among those he has chosen to include in his circle of friends."[15]

5. "Incursions" into Ceará and Sergipe Politics (1934–1935)

The Constituent Assembly produced a new constitution in mid-1934. Alceu Amoroso Lima hailed it as a "complete victory" for the Catholics, in contrast to previous constitutions that had been "victories" for Masonry in 1824 and positivism in 1891. Besides incorporating the LEC's three minimum points, it provided for the existence of Catholic labor unions. Also, as Alceu pointed out happily in *A Ordem*, the new constitution was promulgated in the name of God, despite the juridical scruples of Raul Fernandes, Levy Carneiro, and a few others.[1] Sobral, who had been working with São Paulo's young LEC *constituinte*, Plínio Correia de Oliveira, gave most of the credit to Alceu. "Without you," he told Alceu, nothing would have resulted from the activities of Cardinal Leme and Rio Grande do Sul's Archbishop João Becker.[2]

The *constituintes* named themselves federal legislators, elected Vargas to be constitutional president until 1938, and called for elections on October 14, 1934, to choose a new Congress—along with state legislatures that would select the governors. Sobral, preparing to work for his favorite candidates in the 1934 elections, warned Alceu that the LEC's task would be more difficult than in May 1933, "when we used the element of surprise."[3] He told Ceará Congressman Luiz Cavalcanti Sucupira, an editor of *A Ordem*, that the LEC was being outmaneuvered everywhere, including Rio Grande do Sul, where, he said, *interventor* José Antônio Flores da Cunha was taking advantage of the "conceited naiveté" of Archbishop Becker.[4]

After telling Sucupira that "my warnings are always disparaged but are fulfilled 90 percent of the time," Sobral sent a plan to Alceu and Sucupira designed to renovate the LEC and give it a new president, Affonso Penna Júnior, who, he said, would make LEC President Calógeras seem like a mere "pygmy." He declared that Alceu's inertia in the case of Ceará amounted to capitulation in the face of orders being sent there by Vargas, and he added a warning: Cardinal Leme should not be deluded by the visits he received from Vargas, Foreign Minister José Carlos de Macedo Soares, and Justice Minister Vicente Ráo. "All this is in the program of political surgery that the rulers have planned in order to remove the gland of morality and civic idealism that is the LEC."[5]

Sobral's concern that Archbishop Becker was "favoring the political maneuvers of Getúlio Vargas" was expressed in a letter for Assis Chateaubriand, who had recovered *O Jornal* by making an alliance with Vargas. Alceu prevented Sobral from sending the letter.[6]

Although Alceu rejected Sobral's plan for revamping the LEC, he did follow his suggestion of sending a "word of order" to all Catholics in Ceará to support the LEC.[7] As Sobral saw it, the battle there was against "stupid" Juarez Távora and Colonel Filipe Moreira Lima, a socialist installed as *interventor* by Távora in August 1934. While Sobral called Moreira Lima a fanatic who had taken steps "to terrorize our people," Moreira Lima, in a letter to Bahia *interventor* Juracy Magalhães, called the LEC "a party of illiterate washerwomen and fanatical women," and of men "belonging generally to the neutral sex, uncombative representatives of a minority."[8]

Sobral was disappointed in the voting for Ceará federal congressmen in October 1934. But the election gave the LEC a slight edge in the state legislature, and so the LEC expected that its candidate, Fortaleza Law School Director Francisco de Menezes Pimentel, would win the governorship. In the ensuing turbulence, the LEC's foes sacked a newspaper, forced an LEC legislator to hide to avoid being kidnapped, and reportedly sought to poison other legislators. Only with the help of army troops and Vargas' dismissal of Interventor Moreira Lima was Menezes Pimentel finally able to assume the governorship in May 1935.[9]

Sobral's major political attention was focused on Sergipe. He told of his affection for Jackson de Figueiredo's birth state in a letter to medical doctor Augusto César Leite,[10] a leader of the LEC-backed União Republicana de Sergipe (URS). The URS, supported by the sugar aristocracy, sought to win enough state legislative seats in October 1934 to put one of its founders, army doctor Erônides de

Carvalho, in the governor's chair and thus defeat army Captain Augusto Maynard Gomes, who had been named *interventor* by Juarez Távora and wished to be the governor. Maynard Gomes, veteran of dramatic *tenente* episodes of the 1920s, found himself opposed in 1934 by a combination made up of the LEC, the conservative URS, Plínio Salgado's Integralistas, and a party headed by engineer Leandro Maciel.[11]

The conservative combination won sixteen of the state's thirty legislative seats and elected, as federal congressmen, Augusto Leite, Erônides de Carvalho, and Leandro Maciel (three of four seats from Sergipe). When the state legislature met, it chose Erônides de Carvalho governor and named Augusto Leite and Leandro Maciel federal senators.[12] At the request of one of Sergipe's *desembargadores* (top judges), Sobral wrote an opinion to define the authority of the new governor before the state received a constitution from its legislature, and the opinion was approved by fifteen of Sergipe's seventeen *desembargadores*.[13]

The legislature's gubernatorial and senatorial selections left vacancies in the federal Chamber of Deputies, and Sobral fought hard to have Sergipe's political leaders decide that two of them should be filled by state legislator José Barreto Filho and congressional *suplente* (alternate) Amando Fontes, a lawyer and novelist. Amando Fontes, like Lourival Fontes, a relative who directed federal propaganda, had belonged to the Jackson de Figueiredo group. José Barreto Filho had been the young secretary of Rio Police Chief Coriolano de Góes during the presidency of Washington Luiz.[14]

"You know," Sobral wrote Senator Augusto Leite, "of the ardor with which I have been helping Amando and Barreto save the honor of Sergipe against Maynard and his criminal partisans. I am bitter to learn that the candidacy of Barreto is threatened by Lourival Fontes, a turncoat." Sobral told Amando Fontes, who was certain to be named federal congressman, that Lourival was a rascal.[15]

Sobral was hurt to find that his intervention in Sergipe politics alienated Augusto Leite, who joined the anti-Barreto offensive, and that Amando Fontes was "left paralyzed" by that offensive.[16] But he persevered, calling Barreto Filho "the radiant symbol of Brazil's youthful intelligence." He asked Sergipe professor and poet Garcia Rosa to persuade young people in Sergipe to rally in favor of Barreto.[17] And when Augusto Frederico Schmidt criticized Sobral's intervention, Sobral upbraided Schmidt for degrading himself by seeking the prestige and social advantages that came from associating daily with men of "vulgar ambition" like Lourival Fontes and Francisco Campos, leaving him with little time for true friends like Sobral.[18]

José Barreto Filho gained his congressional seat late in July 1935, and Sobral followed the "victory" by exchanging enthusiastic correspondence with Pedro de Oliveira Ribeiro Sobrinho, the Centro Dom Vital's José Vicente de Souza, and Rubens Figueiredo Martins, brother of Jackson.[19]

The joy of victory was short-lived for Sobral, being followed by incidents that led him to conclude that the men he had supported would not act on behalf of a new type of moralizing politics. Why, he asked Erônides de Carvalho, had he sworn unconditional allegiance to Vargas?[20]

Sobral was distressed to learn in September 1935 that a lunch in Rio, honoring Bahia Governor Juracy Magalhães, had been attended by Senator Augusto Leite and Congressmen Amando Fontes and José Barreto Filho, along with Lourival Fontes. Their attendance revealed, he wrote Governor Erônides de Carvalho, that Sergipe politics were characterized by weak attitudes that were touched with disloyalty. He also told the governor to stop vacillating and to steer clear of Lourival Fontes, a "vial of poison," adroit but treacherous.[21] In a letter to José Vicente de Souza, he wrote that José Barreto Filho had been his last hope but that it had been dissipated with Barreto's "unforgivable" presence at "that imbecilic" gathering to honor "worthless" Captain Juracy Magalhães.[22]

José Barreto Filho and Amando Fontes went to Sobral's office to explain that press reports of the lunch had been misleading. But they irritated Sobral by refusing his demand that they publish a statement to that effect.[23] Writing Barreto in October, Sobral said he was definitely ending his "incursion" into Sergipe politics, whose directors, "uncouth, poorly bred, and full of vulgar ambition," made "the most nauseating impression."[24]

6. Family, Friends, and Work (1934–1935)

Sobral kept in close touch with his mother's sister, Virginia, and furnished fatherly advice, often stern, to Virginia's son Carlos. Above all, he was ceaseless in his attention to the education of his own children. He protested when he learned that his oldest, the ten-year-old Idalina, was required to read José Bento Monteiro Lobato's

História da Civilização, which he considered full of lies and false interpretations.[1]

The birth of Alberto in October 1932 and José Luiz in November 1934 brought the number of children to six and contributed to the need of a larger residence. Affonso Penna Júnior, wishing to have Sobral as his neighbor, invited him to acquire the large house on wooded property in the Laranjeiras district that adjoined the splendid Penna residence. Sobral had not finished paying off the loan made by Penna in the late 1920s. But Penna, a prosperous lawyer, advanced money for the house purchase, bringing the indebtedness to well over 100 contos. He told Sobral to repay him only when and as he could.[2]

Early in 1935 the Sobral family settled in their new home on Pereira da Silva Street. There Sobral enjoyed family gatherings in the large dining room. But he missed the old get-togethers with his friends. Writing to Pedro de Oliveira Ribeiro Sobrinho in São Paulo, he said that sometimes at night he felt like a hermit in a vast house where the silence was broken only by the croaking of frogs and the hooting of owls. "The Bohemian circle," he wrote another friend, had disappeared, leaving him without the "nocturnal discussions" he had cherished. José Vicente de Souza was engrossed in commercial activities and Wagner Dutra was "entirely absorbed" in the Catholic work he did for Alceu. Others, such as José Barreto Filho and economist Assede Karam, cousin of poet Francisco Karam, visited him no longer.[3]

Medical doctor Milton Fontes Magarão, another member of the old group, was practicing at a sanatorium near Petrópolis, where Philomena, daughter of spiritualist Farias Brito, was suffering from tuberculosis, squabbling with her doctors and nurses, and talking about committing suicide. Sobral, never forgetting that Jackson de Figueiredo had been very fond of her, sought to revive her spirits with his letters. And, as he kept receiving medical bills from the sanatorium, he appealed for donations from those who had been close to Jackson.[4]

Sobral enjoyed good health except for recurrences, several times each year, of agonizing neuralgic pains on the right side of his face. These afflictions would put him out of circulation for days on end, unable to eat, hardly able to talk, and with his hearing impaired. He told his sister, Natalina, that he was even considering having all his teeth pulled as a possible cure for the torment.[5]

In December 1934, Sobral was notified of his admission to membership of the Ordem dos Advogados do Brasil (OAB).[6] This long-contemplated official organization of Brazilian lawyers owed its existence to the approval that Justice Minister Oswaldo Aranha gave in November 1930 to a proposal of André de Faria Pereira, who had preceded Sobral as *procurador geral* of the Federal District and had been reappointed following the fall of Washington Luiz. During debates about the statutes of the OAB, Levy Carneiro was preeminent. He explained that the OAB, for registering lawyers so that they could practice, and for protecting their interests and ruling on professional ethics, would not be incompatible with the existence of the smaller, ninety-year-old Instituto dos Advogados Brasileiros (IAB), a cultural institution for studying juridical theses. Levy Carneiro, who had headed the IAB throughout most of the 1920s, was *consultor geral da república* in the early 1930s, and he became the first president of the Conselho Federal of the OAB. Targino Ribeiro was chosen president of the OAB's Federal District Conselho.[7]

Sobral, arguing before the Federal District Appeals Court on behalf of a client sent to him by Targino Ribeiro, was pleased that the court's *relator* of the case was Desembargador Álvaro Goulart de Oliveira. Goulart, with whom Sobral had worked as a young lawyer, had been a government *procurador* helpful to Sobral's handling of the estate of Farias Brito and had helped him also when serving in 1931 on the Tribunal Especial to investigate acts of the Washington Luiz administration. Now he backed Sobral's arguments to the appeals court, but a majority of the *desembargadores* disagreed with him.[8]

Sobral resigned from his position of secretary of the Centro Dom Vital, which had a membership of about five hundred in Rio and had affiliates in twelve other cities. Instead, he joined the administrative board of the Coligação Católica Brasileira, which was headed by Alceu. The Coligação was a blanket organization that incorporated the Centro Dom Vital, Ação Universitária Católica (founded in 1929 for university students), the Confederação Nacional de Operários Católicos (founded in 1932 for workers), and the Instituto Católico de Estudos Superiores (Catholic Institute of Advanced Studies, founded in 1932 to give courses). Sobral served as president of the Instituto and taught there.[9]

Centro Dom Vital members who gathered on November 4, 1935, for the annual observance of the death of Jackson de Figueiredo, listened in shocked silence to a talk by Sobral. It revealed that Jackson, in heart-to-heart conversations with him, had confessed to having been indecisive and full of doubts. José Vicente de Souza was quick to write to Sobral about his dismay. He also pointed out that Jackson's eighteen-year-old daughter Regina Figueiredo had been in the first row of the audience.[10]

Regina wrote Sobral on November 5, his forty-second birthday, to tell of her agony on hearing a talk that contradicted everything known about her father and that was inappropriate for the occasion. "My father was not full of doubts and uncertainties. . . . He never gave ground, felt fear, or fled from struggles." In closing, she said she considered Sobral a friend of Jackson, "whom you did not know how to understand."[11]

Sobral replied that his self-assurance did not allow the general disapproval of his talk to worry him, but that he was writing her to make sure that his talk did not leave Jackson's children with uncertainty about the extraordinary merits of their father. He explained that his purpose in disclosing confidences was to make it clear that Jackson's "saintly life" had been achieved in the course of "excruciating struggles" against temptations.[12]

General disapproval of his talk did worry Sobral. In a letter written on November 9, he told Alceu of his "hour of agony" and asked him to assure their Ação Católica companions that, in spite of the bad things attributed to him, he believed in the greatness of Jackson. Explaining his absence from a Centro Dom Vital meeting, he said that he had, for days, been tempted to resign from the Centro, leave off running the Catholic Institute of Advanced Studies, and abandon all Coligação Católica activity.[13]

The "hour of agony" passed because Perilo Gomes made it clear he would say nothing that might harm his friendship with Sobral, and because José Vicente de Souza told Hamilton Nogueira that he had not meant to offend Sobral when writing him on November 5.[14] After that, Sobral became vexed with Alceu for deciding, without consulting him, that the controversial talk of November 4 should not be published in *A Ordem*. "So you have joined with those" who think that "I dared, in the Centro Dom Vital itself, to vomit" on Jackson, Sobral wrote. Alceu replied that publication was impossible because it would open wounds and disastrously prolong a situation that, thanks to God, had been merely a passing one.[15]

A few months later, Sobral wrote fully about the matter to Pedro de Oliveira Ribeiro Sobrinho, the person who, in his opinion, had been beloved above all others by Jackson. Sobral admitted that he had prepared poorly and written poorly when trying to present, on November 4, the little-known tragedy that lay deep within "the agonized heart" of Jackson. Recalling his own suffering, caused in part by the letters from Regina Figueiredo and José Vicente de Souza, he told Pedro that he had concluded that his friends could best serve him and honor Jackson by maintaining "absolute silence" about his talk.[16]

7. Opposing the Aliança Nacional Libertadora (1935)

Alceu Amoroso Lima was pressed to give his opinion about Plínio Salgado's Integralista movement, whose members became known as "Green Shirts" on account of the uniforms they wore when parading belligerently on behalf of "God, Country, and Family." Setting down his personal view in *A Ordem* in December 1934, Alceu wrote that important Integralista leaders considered their movement as having been launched by Jackson de Figueiredo. Agreeing that they were right "up to a point," he wrote that Jackson was the first non-socialist or non-Communist to denounce the errors and evils of liberalism and advocate a regime of authority as a reaction against "the collapse that the democratic ideology brought to political practices." From a doctrinal point of view, Alceu saw no "irremovable impediment" to Catholics becoming Green Shirts. But he rejected three characteristics of Integralismo: the commitment to excessive power of the state, the use of violence, and the swearing of allegiance to the organization's National Chief, Plínio Salgado.[1]

Sobral accepted this view and limited his criticism of Alceu to the latter's increasing tendency to "turn to Vargas." Cardinal Leme and the Catholic Church, he told Alceu, were cooperating with Vargas' plan to use religion to keep the masses obedient and in misery. "Our pastors cultivate friendships with the powerful and rich and forget the masses who hunger and thirst for justice." Leme, he also wrote, had spoken highly of the "unbaptized" Herbert Moses, head of the Brazilian Press Association, and had honored other "such personalities, anti-Christian by race, thought, and example." Sobral found he had to agree with General Manoel Rabello's remark that Leme strove to establish confusion, although, Sobral added, it was painful to see the truth coming from such a satanic military fanatic.[2]

In November 1935, after Alceu was elected a member of the Brazilian Academy of Letters, Sobral noted "with horror" that Alceu had agreed to be honored at a large banquet to be attended by representatives of society and politics. Most of them, Sobral told Alceu, were unaware of the "magnanimous ideal that grips your soul and grips also the ardent breast of your companions of Ação Católica." These considerations, he explained, prevented him from adding his signature to those on the parchment with expressions of praise, to be presented to Alceu at the banquet.[3]

However, throughout 1935 Sobral and Alceu were in agreement about the danger represented by the Aliança Nacional Libertadora (ANL), a fast-growing leftist "Popular Front," organized early in the year in accordance with the policy of the Communist International to bring people together to fight fascism. Luiz Carlos Prestes, who had been in the Soviet Union since 1931 and was planning a clandestine return to Brazil, was named honorary president of the ANL, archenemy of the Green Shirts. Calling for a "popular government," the ANL opposed the Vargas regime, but Sobral believed that Vargas would not act energetically against it. Alceu assured Sobral that Vargas would do so.[4]

Sobral accused the ANL of promoting a "Communist poisoning of the hearts and brains of Brazilian workers," and he contended that the government was remiss in not cutting off its income. Most of this income, he maintained, came directly to the Federal District municipal government as payoffs by the czars of casino gambling and was distributed by Mayor Pedro Ernesto Batista.[5]

Alceu and Sobral shared a distaste for Anísio Teixeira, head of education in the Federal District. According to Sobral, Teixeira spread Communism among medical doctors, named Communists to municipal posts, and worked on Pedro Ernesto to cooperate with the remains of *tenentismo* as well as the ANL. Faced with the organization of the new Universidade do Distrito Federal by Pedro Ernesto and Anísio Teixeira, Sobral wrote Cardinal Leme to complain about the prevalence of "materialism and agnosticism" there and the appointment of law professors who, for the most part, were "absolutely inimical." As the cardinal was about to visit Rome, Sobral suggested that he obtain authorization for establishing a Universidade Católica.[6]

On July 10, 1935, Sobral wrote Alceu about steps, such as the dismissal of Anísio Teixeira and a ban on gambling, that Vargas ought to take if he were "really interested in crippling the ANL"; but he added that if Alceu gave these suggestions to Vargas, Vargas would ignore them. Sobral pictured Vargas as viewing the ANL as a strong social movement which did not depend on Anísio Teixeira or gambling money. "Vargas does not believe in men, considering them playthings in social movements which he seeks to dominate."[7]

On the next day, July 11, Vargas closed down the ANL, arguing that an ANL manifesto, issued by Luiz Carlos Prestes from a Rio hiding place on July 5, was subversive.

PART III

Opponent of the Post-1935 Repression (1936–1938)

1. Effects of the November 1935 Uprisings (1935–1936)

In the name of the extinct ANL a revolt by discontented civil guards and army sergeants occurred in Natal, in the far north, on November 23, 1935. Quickly it was followed by a rebellion led by Communist army officers in Recife, during which about sixty civilians were killed in street fighting. By November 26, both uprisings had been crushed, but Luiz Carlos Prestes and other Communists in Rio, unaware of these setbacks, ordered insurrections that took place at Rio's Third Infantry Regiment and at the army Aviation School near Rio and that cost about twenty-five more lives. By noon on November 27, these uprisings, too, had been subdued.

Police forces, supported by a state of siege that Congress voted on November 25, rounded up people they suspected of having favored the outbreaks. Jails in Natal, Recife, Rio, and São Paulo (where no outbreak had occurred) were filled with many hundreds of civilians who had been surprised by the violent turn of events. "Marxist" professors Castro Rebello, Leônidas de Rezende, and Hermes Lima found themselves in cells with journalists, medical doctors, lawyers, and students. So crowded were the Rio prisons that the Lloyd Brasileiro's old *Pedro I* was converted into a prison ship.

At the request of Affonso Penna Júnior, Sobral submitted a study to show that the executive needed no legislation beyond Law 38 of April 1935 to punish the subversives.[1] Congress, however, enacted Law 136 of December 14, 1935, to strengthen Law 38. Also, it voted a ninety-day extension of the state of siege and amended the constitution to assure the legality of dismissing subversive government personnel and to allow Vargas to declare, if he found it necessary, a "state of war" that would eliminate some remaining individual guarantees.

The situation of Mayor Pedro Ernesto became precarious. On December 1 his education secretary, Anísio Teixeira, lost his position. A telegram to Teixeira, in which Juracy Magalhães lamented his dismissal, was cited by Sobral when he scolded Alceu Amoroso Lima and Wagner Dutra for heaping praise on Juracy following religious services in Bahia attended by Cardinal Leme. After Leme delivered a pro-government speech, he, too, was criticized by Sobral, who warned that the masses, unable to tolerate the repression by Justice Minister Vicente Ráo and Rio Police Chief Filinto Müller, would throw themselves into the arms of Marxists.[2]

Sobral was pleased to find that Francisco Campos, Rio's new education secretary, was a sincere supporter of the Catholic program, and he went to Campos' home to congratulate him on his appointment. Campos was not able to find positions that Sobral sought to have filled by many of his friends who had come upon hard times; but the new education secretary delighted Sobral when he chose Affonso Penna Júnior to head the Universidade do Distrito Federal.[3]

It was also heartening to learn, in April 1936, that Padre Olympio de Mello was replacing Mayor Pedro Ernesto, who was imprisoned. The *padre,* together with Campos and Penna, asked Sobral to become secretary of the city's School of Education, but Sobral, although feeling that the salary would help him combat his "pauperism," declined with the explanation that he ought not to depart from the type of work in which he was engaged.[4]

Explaining to Alceu why he might seem to be failing to cooperate fully with the activities of Ação Católica, Sobral said he was exhausting himself in his legal work, needing an income of five contos a month on account of his large family.[5] The work paid off momentarily when he obtained, from the new mayorship, the extension of a bus concession for one of his clients, Viação Popular.[6]

Legal cases arising from the November 1935 uprisings were beginning to come Sobral's way, but his principles made it doubtful that these cases would provide much more than additional work. His principles were explained in a letter he wrote in January 1936 to the sister of the wife of imprisoned navy Captain Roberto Sisson, who had been secretary of the ANL: "In view of the exclusively political character of the case, in which I'll be defending one of the most vehement advocates of a philosophical-political system that I regard as fatal to the most sacred destinies of man, I would have no respect for myself if I gained any material advantage from handling the case."[7]

Throughout 1936 Sobral tried to visit the imprisoned Sisson but was prevented from doing so by Police Chief Filinto Müller, who complained about lawyers, saying that they worked mostly for socially prominent intellectuals who served Moscow. Sobral wrote, without success, to Justice Minister Ráo.[8]

To handle the cases of "subversives" like Sisson, Congress voted in August 1936 to create a National Security Tribunal (TSN—Tribunal de Segurança Nacional) to consist of two military officers, two civilians, and one professional magistrate, all to be appointed by Vargas. As soon as it was installed in a former schoolhouse in Rio on October 2, Sobral wrote its president, Frederico de Barros Barreto, demanding that lawyers be able to converse with their clients. Finally, early in 1937, the Ordem dos Advogados (OAB) and one of the TSN judges officially appointed Sobral to be Sisson's lawyer and Sobral was able to work with him.[9]

Sisson, deprived of his military rank by a decree of Vargas, made his own verbal defense to the TSN on May 7, 1937, in a speech about the poverty of the Brazilian masses. Later, when Sobral expected to address the TSN on behalf of Sisson, he was prevented from entering the courtroom because he refused to allow guards to frisk him, believing that such "searching" of his "person" demeaned his profession. Sisson was set free because he had been in prison longer than the 10½-month prison sentence he had received.[10] Later in 1937, he went to Uruguay.

A National Commission to Repress Communism was established early in 1936. One of its members, General Newton Cavalcanti, felt that repression was more important than observing judicial decisions (a view that Sobral hotly contested).[11] After being transferred to an army command in the northeast, Newton Cavalcanti had medical doctor Sebastião da Hora arrested in the state of Alagoas on charges that lacked any foundation, and Sobral, who became the doctor's lawyer on Sisson's recommendation, obtained his freedom in 1937.[12]

In 1936, when the Tribunal de Segurança Nacional (TSN) was being formed, Francisco Campos joined with Congressman Adalberto Corrêa, president of the Commission to Repress Communism, in approaching Sobral about his becoming one of the TSN judges.

Their approach, Sobral reported later, was made after Vargas concluded that Sobral's being a "soldier" of the cardinal was enough to offset the scandal of 1928.[13] "I replied in the negative," Sobral also reported, and he might have added that he had no esteem for this "exceptional" tribunal that was not a part of the established judicial system.

Other developments in 1936 were Vargas' decree in March of a "state of war" and a law by Congress for the creation of five agricultural-penal colonies. Later in the year, Adalberto Corrêa helped persuade Congress to extend, by a 158–46 vote, the "state of war," and to suspend the immunities of its own members. He believed that the regular courts acted too slowly to allow efficient repression of subversion and found himself in a dispute with Sobral, his former candidate for a TSN judgeship.[14]

Sobral, condemning Congress for passage of the "monstrous law" that created the TSN, told Francisco Campos on September 1, 1936, that the victors had been Vargas, "that Satan in human form," and Congressional President Antônio Carlos, "that old prostitute." He pictured Antônio Carlos as having joined forces with Vargas, thus contributing to the obliteration of the prestige of Minas.[15] But, even while Sobral wrote Campos about "the spectacular triumph of Antônio Carlos," it was becoming clear that Minas Governor Benedicto Valladares, working with Campos and backed by Vargas, was achieving his aim of destroying Antônio Carlos politically. On September 1, Antônio Carlos was forced to resign as leader of the Minas congressional bloc. After that he lost the presidency of Congress.[16]

2. Ex officio Lawyer of Harry Berger (1935–1937)

The Rio police, looking for the leaders of the Communist uprisings of November 1935, made an important arrest a month after the uprisings when they found two Germans, Harry Berger and his wife Elise. Berger, whose real name was Arthur Ernst Ewert, was a large, active Communist who had worked for the Comintern (Communist International) in Latin America and China. Like Luiz Carlos Prestes, who had been in the Soviet Union in the early 1930s, Berger and a handful of other Comintern militants had come to Brazil in the first half of 1935 with false passports to organize the revolution. Berger was among those who had brought their wives. Prestes had come with his companion, Olga Benário, a militant German Communist he had met in Russia, and she became known in Brazil as Olga Benário Prestes.

The police picked up information about Communists and their plans for Brazil from papers found at the Bergers' residence. But they could get nothing out of the Bergers. Lieutenant Euzébio de Queiroz Filho, head of a tough force known as the Special Police, urged his men to use severe torture to break the Bergers' vow of silence.[1]

Savagery did not succeed in persuading the Bergers to talk and resulted in a habeas corpus petition submitted on the Bergers' behalf by Senator Abel Chermont. It told of electric shocks applied to their heads, burns from lighted cigarettes and cigars, prevention of sleep, and painful and indecent treatment of the nude Elise in front of her husband. But First District Federal Court Judge Edgard Ribas Carneiro, after examining Harry Berger's torso, denied the petition. He described Berger as insensitive, unable to laugh or cry, and added that he was a faker who lied about being given poisoned water and about being unable to speak Portuguese.[2]

After the capture of Prestes and Olga on March 5, 1936, Prestes was put in the well-guarded room that the Bergers had occupied at the Special Police barracks. A place beneath a noisily used staircase at the barracks was chosen for holding and torturing Berger. It was too small to allow him much movement and lacked a bed and hygienic facilities. His wife Elise was transferred to the jail which held Olga Benário Prestes, who was pregnant, and, in August 1936, the two women were deported to Germany, where they were imprisoned by the Nazis.

Later in December 1936 the TSN (Tribunal de Segurança Nacional) called on the Federal District Conselho of the OAB (Ordem dos Advogados do Brasil) to name lawyers to defend political prisoners who would not cooperate with the TSN by naming their own lawyers. The OAB agreed to try to find lawyers to act in an ex officio capacity (not named by the defendants) but made it clear that it was not budging from its contention that the TSN was unconstitutional.[3]

Sobral, having returned from a vacation spent with friends in southern Minas, was well rested when he was approached by the OAB's Targino Ribeiro about handling the cases of Berger and Prestes, the two most notorious prisoners. In accepting, Sobral told Targino of his resolve to demonstrate that his clients were members of the human family whose errors were no greater than their willingness to make sacrifices on behalf of "benevolent truths."[4]

When Sobral met Berger in the office of Special Police com-

mander Euzébio de Queiroz Filho, the prisoner said he had no reason to trust Sobral and wished to be represented by Justo Mendes
de Moraes, whom he had known before the uprisings. As Justo had
already told Sobral he would not represent Berger, Sobral suggested
a meeting at which Justo would recommend Sobral to Berger. Berger
agreed and asked for the presence of a translator who knew German
or English, whereupon Sobral offered the services of young Gabriel
Costa Carvalho, who had been working at his law office.[5]

The meeting with Justo Mendes de Moraes never took place because TSN Judge Raul Machado failed to act on Sobral's petition to
allow Berger to attend. As Raul Machado was in charge of studying
the Berger case, he received no end of petitions from Sobral, some of
them telling him that it was his duty to have the ailing prisoner held
in a more suitable place. Only in that way, Sobral wrote, would support be given to Vargas' assertion that prisoners were being handled
in a manner reflecting Christian principles of civilization.

Raul Machado, a poet who hoped to be elected to the Brazilian
Academy of Letters, was considered by lawyer Evandro Lins e Silva
to be an ultra-reactionary, fearful of anything like the Samba or
Communism that might, in his opinion, cause the "degeneration" of
the family, art, or religion.[6]

Natalina scolded her brother for becoming Prestes' lawyer. Never,
Sobral wrote in reply, had he felt so completely Christian as when
he had accepted the assignment. He explained that no one should be
without comforting support and defense, and added that Prestes had
demonstrated praiseworthy disinterestedness in 1930, when he had
remained faithful to his ideas—"erroneous ones it is true"—rather
than be seduced, like Vargas and others, by selfish considerations.
Sobral sent copies of this letter to Cardinal Leme, Penna, and Alceu
and told them of his hope of support from friends in the face of all
the criticism he was receiving.[7]

A disagreement between Alceu and Sobral about the Spanish
Civil War had developed, with Alceu attacking the Marxists and Sobral maintaining that the Spanish clergy had failed to oppose the
corruption of the selfish ruling classes.[8] Upon learning that Sobral
had accepted the task of defending Prestes and Berger, Alceu backed
him in public but wrote him that he did not approve. While admitting that Sobral was demonstrating disinterest and generosity, in
keeping with his spirit, "so noble and chivalrous," he faulted him
for giving encouragement to the supporters of "the iron gauntlet of

Stalin" and thus weakening Brazil's existing social order, in which the Church enjoyed complete liberty and in which the "abandoned and proletarian classes" were being helped. According to Alceu, Vargas had provided a great service to Brazil in reacting against Prestes and his companions in rebellion, and Catholics should show their appreciation by remaining at his side.

Alceu called Prestes a criminal who would, when released, continue to strive to implant a cruel, bloody, Russian-type regime. Insisting that "we do not have the right to be naïve," he wrote that defending Prestes would require defending Prestes' goal because the two were "indissolubly linked." Besides, he argued, Brazil did not lack lawyers who were devoted to Communism, and Prestes could find one who would defend his cause more effectively than Sobral.[9]

Sobral wrote with some understanding of the Communist cause when he drew up, on Berger's behalf, a *defesa prévia* (preliminary brief). Written without the cooperation of his client, who believed him to be a police agent, the brief presented a sympathetic view of the loathed German Communist. Trying to demolish Judge Ribas Carneiro's caricature of Berger, he wrote that a less superficial view would reveal emotions beneath the granite-like exterior. He called Berger a simple worker for an ideal in a struggle caused by the failure of the ruling classes to correct the unjust distribution of the riches produced by work. The brief said that Communism contained many truths and one overwhelming lie, materialism, and concluded that the problem would not be solved by repression, organized by a *tribunal de exceção*, the TSN.[10]

On January 28, 1937, the day before the presentation of the brief, an American lawyer, David Levinson, reached Rio with a power of attorney on behalf of Prestes and Berger signed by American lawyer Theodore Draper. He also brought an authorization to represent Berger signed by Berger's sister Minna, a trained nurse with the Red Cross in London who was calling on influential people there in pursuit of help for her brother.[11]

By February 10, when Levinson visited Sobral, the press had been describing him as a Comintern agent, and he had held a press conference in his Hotel Glória suite—resulting in what he called "malicious and unashamed perversion and falsification" of his statements.[12]

Sobral liked the Philadelphia lawyer, who asked to be permitted to tell Berger of Minna's thoughtfulness and to discuss defense ideas with the prisoner, in the presence, if necessary, of Judge Raul Machado. Sobral, petitioning Machado for the meeting, told of his own need of it on account of Berger's hostility to him.[13]

On the following day, however, the Rio police told Levinson he could avoid arrest only by returning to the United States on the next available steamer, and TSN President Barros Barreto told the press of having asked Police Chief Müller to prevent Levinson, "a dangerous person," from seeing any political prisoner.[14] To no avail, Sobral sent appeals on behalf of Levinson to Judge Raul Machado and Interim Justice Minister Agamemnon Magalhães. He told the latter that the real reason for the order to Levinson was to withhold from him the nauseous sight of Berger under the stairs in filthy clothing. Levinson, upon returning to the United States, discussed publicly his experience in Brazil.[15]

Following Levinson's departure, Sobral sent Raul Machado a newspaper article about a man who had been punished, by a fine and prison sentence, for treating a horse so badly that it had died. In his accompanying letter, he quoted legislation forbidding that animals be kept in places that were unsanitary or that "restricted respiration, movement, or rest or deprived them of air or light."[16] The lawyer's request for a change for Berger was forwarded by Machado to Müller, but no action was taken.

"You cannot," Sobral wrote Prestes' mother in Paris, "imagine my distress. Harry Berger, with expressions of rage, considers my visits as the efforts of a scurrilous humbug." When Sobral brought Berger letters that Minna had addressed to her brother in care of Sobral, Berger remarked that he could not recall Minna's handwriting and dismissed them as fakes. The letters revealed that Elise Berger, who was held in deep affection by her imprisoned husband, had written Minna from Germany to say that things were going badly for her.[17]

London attorney P. R. Kimber, engaged by Minna to do what he could for Berger and Elise, wrote Sobral about information that, he said, seemed "almost incredible." Kimber cited a report by an American lawyer who had been in Rio in March 1936 that said that the Bergers had been forced to endure limb twistings, electric shocks, and beatings in the nude. "For three weeks Berger was not allowed to sleep." If the details in such reports and in Senator Chermont's habeas corpus petition were true, Kimber concluded, Brazil's authorities in charge of prisoners were too barbarous to be considered civilized. In reply, Sobral defended his country, which, he wrote, had no "social castes" or race or class hatred. "Please tell *The*

Times that Brazil should be viewed from a broad perspective and not from one police case."[18]

On May 7, 1937, the TSN held a "solemn session" to hand down its verdicts about the "red chieftains." The crowd of spectators heard *relator* Raul Machado discuss papers found at the Prestes' residence and declare that the five judges had reached unanimous decisions in the dozens of cases, disagreeing only about former mayor Pedro Ernesto, who would be jailed for the 3½ years voted by the majority. Prestes drew a 16½-year sentence. Berger, as Sobral cabled Minna, was sentenced to 13½ years and was becoming "weaker and weaker."[19]

Following the TSN's "solemn session," the police prevented Sobral from communicating with Prestes or Berger. Incensed, Sobral complained to the OAB, but TSN President Barros Barreto told the OAB's Philadelpho de Azevedo that the TSN could do no more than recommend that lawyers be able to consult clients. Philadelpho asked Interim Justice Minister Agamemnon Magalhães to have the TSN recommendation made effective.[20]

Fortunately for lawyers and political prisoners, José Carlos de Macedo Soares, of São Paulo, took over the justice ministry on June 3, 1937. He wasted no time in taking steps to allow the presidential election campaign to go forward in an atmosphere of democratic liberties. After a well-publicized visit to Rio's prisons, he ordered Police Chief Müller to release 308 political prisoners in Rio who had not been formally accused of any crimes. Congressman Adalberto Corrêa criticized the new minister and expressed surprise that Müller was not resigning.

When Macedo Soares consulted federal legislators he found little support for a further extension of the state of war. Congressmen favoring Armando de Sales Oliveira, São Paulo's opposition candidate for president, adamantly opposed any extension and so did many backers of northeasterner José Américo de Almeida, the "official candidate." With Vargas' approval, the state of war was allowed to expire on June 18.

3. Berger Becomes Deranged (June–November 1937)

Alceu Amoroso Lima, a close friend of Justice Minister Macedo Soares, arranged for Sobral to speak with him at the ministry. Sobral was so persuasive that Macedo Soares went at once to visit

Prestes and Berger. As a result Alceu was able to assure Sobral that, on June 13, Prestes would be moved to the Casa de Correção (correctional prison) and Berger put in the room that Prestes would vacate. Both, Alceu also reported, would be allowed to read books and the *Jornal do Commercio*, converse privately with their lawyers, and exchange letters with their families.

"From now on," Sobral wrote Minna Ewert, "the physical sufferings of your brother will end completely. Dr. Macedo Soares is a practicing Catholic."[1]

The promised changes, however, did not occur. Sobral, explaining the setback in one of his letters to Prestes' mother, Leocádia, wrote of the delay in the construction of special cells for Prestes and Berger at the Casa de Correção. He mentioned also the opposition to Macedo Soares' wishes that had developed in government circles, and the ill will created there and in the press by the campaign on behalf of Prestes and Berger in France, England, and the United States. The campaign, Sobral told Leocádia, "hurts my work."[2]

The campaign, which Leocádia said was arousing "great emotion" in Europe, provoked inquiries and protests against the Brazilian government. It was assisted by Minna, who stirred up British legislators as well as the Salvation Army and the Red Cross. The Howard League for Penal Reform, headed by a British lord, advised Sobral of the "considerable public interest" in England about Berger's condition.[3]

After Minna visited Paris to seek support from the French government, Macedo Soares warned Sobral against her anti-Brazilian propaganda, made in collaboration with Lady Astor and Lady Hastings. He called Minna an intelligent agitator, highly respected by the Comintern.[4]

Sobral pleaded with Cardinal Leme to use his influence with Vargas to secure the transfer of Berger, "almost dead," and freezing in the Rio winter weather. He explained to the cardinal that the military supported Police Chief Müller, who was immovable in his determination "not to allow Berger to slip from his claws alive." A few days later Sobral himself sent an appeal to Vargas in which he described Berger as "reduced to the condition of a rabies-infected animal."[5]

Among those who attacked Macedo Soares for softness on Communism was the Catholic *A União*. Sobral, reacting, told the newspaper's Osório Lopes: "Instead of blaming Macedo Soares, who is acting with honor and in a highly Christian way, you should blame us Catholics who have not known how to fulfill the duties of our religious conscience in the case of the suffering masses."[6]

Finally, on July 18, Prestes was transferred to one of the thickly walled new cells, and a few days later, Berger was put in the room vacated by the Cavalier of Hope. Although Prestes found his new cell much smaller than the room he had left, and although Berger remained at the mercy of the Special Police, Sobral was pleased. In reply to an inquiry from the Salvation Army, he wrote that Berger's undernourishment would be remedied if the justice minister's orders about food were observed.[7] Prestes, at least, seemed likely to receive adequate food and other considerations because Casa de Correção Director Carlos Lassance respected the rights of prisoners.

Berger, after his transfer, became less suspicious of his lawyer and agreed that Minna's letters were authentic. Sobral, furnishing him fruit and clothing he had requested, learned that the Special Police would not let the prisoner see his lawyer alone, write to his family, have reading material, or receive the food recommended by Macedo Soares. In exasperation, Sobral wrote Alceu: "Tomorrow, when Brazil sees itself immersed in hatred and blood, of which you and I will be the first victims, Brazilian Catholicism, now inattentive to this endless martyrdom of Berger, will say that our decapitators are barbarians."[8]

With the time approaching for the Supreme Military Tribunal (STM) to act on the appeals of the "thirty-five extremist chieftains" from the sentences decreed by the TSN in May, the STM ruled that each appellant would be allowed fifteen minutes to address the judges.

Such was the public interest in, and fear of, the "dangerous Reds" that traffic was not permitted in the neighborhood of the Tribunal on September 8 when the prisoners were brought there. Berger was so bent and emaciated that Rodolfo Ghioldi, an Argentine Communist in a paddy wagon with him, would not have recognized him had not Berger spoken. Berger told Ghioldi that he did not expect to survive the tortures and that, if he did, it would be without his sanity.[9]

Sobral objected to being frisked and therefore was not present when the "chieftains" made their short speeches, messages for the public. Berger's straightforward message, given in English and translated, was a refusal to deny his belief in Communism or his mission on behalf of Brazil in 1935. He praised the Brazilian people and the world proletariat and expressed faith in "the final victory, freeing humanity from hunger and oppression," but added that a "barbarous death" might prevent him from witnessing it. His mind, he said, could not resist the "electrical applications."[10]

On the next day Sobral asked the Military Tribunal for permission to give the court an oral appeal that was technical, for he wanted the judges to accept his contention that Berger and Prestes should each receive "a single punishment" for acts springing from one originating fact rather than consecutive punishments for more than one crime.[11] Such arguments, however, had already been presented in papers presumably studied by the Military Tribunal.

On September 12, the STM confirmed the sentences handed down in May for Prestes, Berger, and most of the "Red chieftains." A few military rebels had their sentences shortened. The great legal victor of the appeals was Mário Bulhões Pedreira, whose brilliant arguments secured the acquittal of the popular Pedro Ernesto. Sobral wrote Mário, his law school classmate: "The enthusiastic applause reaching you from everywhere was won by the magnificent work of your great intelligence."[12]

Journalist Rubem Braga published a sarcastic article, "Sobral Pinto, the Monster," that discussed politicians calling each other Communists, and "the industry of combating Communism." It was, Braga wrote, fortunate for TSN prosecutor Hymalaia Vergolino and the authorities that two "legitimate" Communists, Prestes and Berger, were available. They had to be judged and that meant giving them a lawyer. Levinson appeared but was expelled. Senator Chermont appeared but was jailed. Then, Braga continued, the authorities turned to Sobral with a plan to have him handle the defense in a way to bring about convictions. But what did anti-Communist Sobral do after reciting a prayer and crossing himself? "He said a Communist could be a person. What heresy! . . . He even said that what was being done to Berger was worse than any Communism. . . . Disclaim him, good Catholics of Brazil. He is a strange case: a human being. A monster."[13]

The transfer of Berger to the cell adjoining that of Prestes in the Casa de Correção on October 3 gave Sobral so much joy that he felt he must be in dreamland. Good-hearted prison director Carlos Lassance provided the special food needed by Berger and allowed him to read newspapers and books, see his lawyer alone, and correspond with family members. At long last Sobral was able to hand the prisoner a letter that Elise had written her husband. In this, the first Berger had seen from her, she wrote of her loneliness in a Berlin prison and of her dream of being with him "in some corner of Brazil, perhaps in a correctional colony, clearing the virgin forest, working hard but usefully, sharing our fate together."[14]

Sobral told Lassance that Berger, in accordance with a resolution of the commission to execute a recently enacted new state of war, would be transferred to an island prison camp and that before he was transferred he should be examined by a medical doctor with a knowledge of German. Something, Sobral said, had gone wrong with his client's mind. "He is positively abnormal."[15]

For Berger's mind the curtain fell on November 10, 1937, when Vargas and the military, canceling the presidential election, gave Brazil the dictatorship of the Estado Novo (New State) along with a new constitution that declared the country to be in a state of emergency.

Police Chief Müller, who called Sobral the link between Prestes and unarrested Communists, dismissed Lassance and had him arrested for being "lax" in guarding Prestes. In his place he installed Lieutenant Vitório Caneppa, who told Sobral that he followed only the orders of Müller and Israel Souto, the *delegado da ordem política e social*. Caneppa reduced the rations of food in the Casa de Correção and showed no laxity. He abolished privileges that Lassance had allowed Prestes and Berger. Sobral complained to Leocádia Prestes in December 1937 that he was unable to communicate with his imprisoned clients, who by then had become quite numerous.[16]

"Everything was carried out against Berger," Prestes has written. During entire nights Prestes heard, from the adjoining cell, the wild screams of the tortured German.[17] As a transfer to a prison camp would put the prisoner beyond Müller's claws, it was out of the question.

4. The Development of Affection between Prestes and Sobral (March–May 1937)

After the Rio police located Prestes and Olga on March 5, 1936, Olga and their maid were locked up in the Casa de Detenção (Detention Prison), and Prestes was taken to police headquarters, where he was identified by Lieutenant Colonel Oswaldo Cordeiro de Farias, who had rebelled with him in the 1920s. Interrogated by Delegado Eurico Bellens Porto, he said his political philosophy had been expressed in his manifesto of July 5, 1935, a long document ending with a call for "All Power to the Aliança Nacional Libertadora." He would say nothing about the 1935 insurrections then or a few days later, when he was interrogated by Judge Barros Barreto at the Special Police barracks.[1]

In January 1937, after ten months of isolation, Prestes received a copy of the charges that TSN Procurador Hymalaia Vergolino had prepared about his involvement in the 1935 insurrections. Later in the month, in the office of the Special Police commander, he met Sobral and made it clear that he would not authorize his ex officio lawyer to defend him.[2]

Late in February Prestes appeared before a Military Justice Special Council to answer the charge of deserting the army in 1924. Spectators, curious to observe a figure so long out of public view, found that he wore a black beard and spoke with vigor: "I am a Communist! I am director of the Aliança Nacional Libertadora! . . . I ask the Council how I can choose a lawyer of my entire confidence. . . . I would expose him to threats and harassments." Prestes spoke of the elderly Senator Chermont, arrested and "subjected to violent mistreatments in the garage of the Special Police." The presiding officer said Prestes was discussing the TSN, not the council he was facing. Smiling ironically at the mention of the TSN, Prestes said: "What justice! A tribunal that was created during this year of terror which found me in prison cannot be recognized by me."[3]

During the same last days of February 1937, Olga Prestes wrote from a Berlin prison to Paris to inform her mother-in-law, Leocádia Prestes, of the birth in the prison of Anita Leocádia Prestes on November 27, 1936. Leocádia wrote her son in care of Sobral to give him the news, and she included a copy of Olga's letter.[4] TSN Judge Raul Machado was able to arrange for Prestes to receive the letters, but otherwise, Sobral told Leocádia, he limited himself to issuing directives that the police ignored.[5]

Leocádia saw a newspaper photograph of Prestes at the Military Justice Council and was shocked by his thinness and shabby clothing. With Lygia, one of her daughters, she assembled a collection of new clothes and mailed them, together with toiletries and chocolate, for Sobral to deliver. Prestes received the articles after Sobral battled "ridiculous" roadblocks for a month and after Lieutenant

Queiroz and three subordinates broke up the bars of chocolate and soap and made sure that neither they nor the clothes contained hidden messages or steel files.[6]

On April 9 Prestes was notified that his final written defense should be presented to the TSN in three days. Sobral, explaining in an official statement to Raul Machado why Prestes would not comply, quoted Bukharin's condemnation of bourgeois justice and pointed out that the Brazilian Constitution prohibited citizens from being judged in accordance with laws, such as the one creating the TSN, that postdated the alleged crimes.[7]

Prestes studied a copy of Sobral's statement and then wrote a long memorandum to let him know that he completely disagreed with much of it. He explained that Communists, such as Dimitrov in Leipzig, and he himself at the military tribunal, were willing to defend themselves before bourgeois tribunals. "Judges of the reaction tremble, like the invertebrates of the Getulista gang, lest my word, and through me the word of my Party, reach the ears of the people." If, however, he were to submit a statement to the TSN, he would, he said, be simply participating in a farce during which the men in power would publish isolated phrases. Noting Sobral's quotations from Engels and Bukharin, Prestes accused him of becoming misled by theories. Communist revolutionaries, Prestes explained, never forsook reality to dwell in ivory towers.

Prestes' memorandum was more than a refutation of thoughts expressed by Sobral. It was a revolutionary call for liberty that denounced, in a lively manner, the "sordid politics" of Mayor Olympio de Mello, the "ignorance of the Hymalaia Vergolinos," the "venality" of judges, the "scurrility" of journalists, and the "mud" of Getulismo.[8]

Prestes sought to hand his memorandum to Sobral when they met in Lieutenant Queiroz' office on May 4. Queiroz, who had an assistant at his side, said this could not be done before Müller had censored what had been written. Prestes, observing that at least the oral word was permitted him, began reading the memorandum aloud. But Queiroz, after hearing caustic expressions about Brazilian authorities, ordered Prestes to stop reading and give the memorandum to him. Prestes, claiming to own it, started tearing up the pages and was pounced on by Queiroz' assistant and soldiers who had been loitering nearby. The sheets, many of them torn, were seized, and Prestes was returned to his imprisonment room. When Sobral lectured Queiroz on the seriousness of the incident, the lieutenant said he was obeying orders and could not allow Prestes to slander his Special Police and the Brazilian authorities.[9]

After the Tribunal de Segurança Nacional's "solemn session" of May 7 that imposed a 16½-year prison sentence on Prestes, Sobral obtained Prestes' authorization to submit an appeal to the Supremo Tribunal Militar, which was not a "court of exception." Sobral wrote Leocádia of Prestes' change of attitude toward him, evident in recent meetings and after the letters from her began to pour in.[10]

Prestes, however, was becoming indebted to Sobral, and this he found so embarrassing that he proposed an end to Sobral's visits. Opening his heart while conversing with Sobral late in May, he expressed his immense gratitude for what his lawyer was doing for him and especially for Leocádia, evidently at a cost to Sobral's professional work and standing. Prestes made it clear that he understood that Catholic sentiments were guiding Sobral but added that he was uncomfortable, even humiliated, to receive alms from someone whose position about "the social problem" made them adversaries.

Prestes said he would have preferred, had the authorities allowed, to express his thoughts in writing, and he went on to say that an end to Sobral's visits would be painful. They were his "only oasis" of intellectuality and human comfort. Courteously he mentioned the mutual affection that had developed and said there was nothing personal about his decision. He wished to spare Sobral the harassments mentioned in one of the lawyer's petitions to the authorities.

Prestes had spoken with care and calm, but his emotion was evident. Sobral, replying with firmness, said that his own constant references to Christian charity were not meant to disturb Communists, but, rather, bourgeois reactionaries. That charity, he added, was not synonymous with alms but was a sublime concept expressing the equality of people. He insisted that his visits were simply the fulfillment of his duty and should arouse no feeling of humiliation in Prestes. If, Sobral said, they should later face each other as foes, he would never be so infamous as to remind Prestes of what he was presently doing as ex officio lawyer of Communists.

Sobral placed in Leocádia's hands the decision about ending the visits. He told her it involved more than a Catholic lawyer and a Communist revolutionary. "Between the two is a mother's heart, suffering and shedding tears."[11]

Leocádia replied that her son's scruples made him wish to spare Sobral from disgraceful scenes, such as the one when Prestes' torn pages had been seized. But, she wrote, a suspension of the visits would harm the cause Sobral had been handling with dedication. She asked him to continue with the visits because the fight should go on until victory was won over enemies who found in slander and brutal acts their only recourse.[12]

5. The Indefatigable Leocádia Prestes (June–November 1937)

If Prestes had presented no defense to the TSN, Sobral told the Supremo Tribunal Militar, it was because, after the defendant had been held in strictest isolation for almost a year, his lawyer had suddenly been given three days to answer charges contained in fifty volumes that the government had assembled during twelve months. To this explanation, contained in the appeal of May 24, 1937, Sobral added that the TSN should not have classified as a second crime Prestes' alleged planning for a new revolt after 1935. To back his contention about a single crime, Sobral described Prestes as guided by Communist doctrine that viewed the achievement of national liberation and democracy as part of a single plan that would culminate later in the dictatorship of the proletariat.[1]

Prestes and his mother objected to the appeal. Leocádia wrote Sobral that none of her son's manifestoes had called for the dictatorship of the proletariat. She asked Sobral to fortify the appeal by arranging to have the Military Tribunal (STM) read, "at its first session," letters she had sent him for forwarding to the TSN and STM. They complained that Prestes had been condemned without being heard and without any public debate; and in one of them she asked the STM judges to have the Brazilian government persuade the Germans to free Olga and her baby. The letters were added to the STM's collection of documents.[2]

Leocádia also wrote Sobral about his assertion that his work was hurt by the Communists' campaign against Brazil. The "international campaign," she reported, was spontaneous, was not Communist, and did not discredit Brazil. She pictured Brazilians as having gained enormous international prestige for their country with their struggle for liberty—a struggle that had aroused more foreign support than anything previously undertaken in Brazilian history. She listed notables in Europe and the United States, among them religious leaders, who had come to the defense of her son.[3]

Olga, writing Prestes on May 15, told of their blue-eyed baby girl and of the daily half hour Olga was allowed to spend in the prison courtyard. "I'm always thinking about us," she wrote after being touched by the sight of a family of birds in a nest in a courtyard tree. The letter, together with a lock of the infant's hair, was received by Sobral from Leocádia, and, after the Brazilian police studied the letter (which they translated from French), both were delivered to Prestes. By then, July 16, Prestes was in the special cell at the Casa de Correção under the benign supervision of Carlos Lassance.[4]

Leocádia, who continued indefatigable, informed Sobral that although she was sixty, her heart remained strong whenever she dealt with the rights of defense and the principles of justice and liberty. She sent letters and a useful document to the lawyer who had been named by the Military Justice Council to defend Prestes against the desertion charge.[5] She went to Germany in July in a vain effort to see Olga and the baby, and, after that, started to work on what became a spirited international campaign to prevent her granddaughter from being separated from Olga and placed in a German-government-run orphanage upon reaching the age of ten months, in accordance with German regulations. She sought help from Orlando Leite Ribeiro, a Brazilian diplomat who had once been close to Prestes. And she wrote Justice Minister Macedo Soares, saying that if Anita had to be separated from Olga, let her come to her grandmother in Paris. A plea from Rio Grande do Sul, signed by Leocádia's mother, was also sent to the justice minister.[6]

Prison Director Lassance and Sobral spent all of September 17 calling on notary publics, hoping to find one willing to record a statement by Prestes that he was the infant's father. All of them, Sobral told Leocádia, feared becoming victims of a campaign, "like that made against me, in which they would be called Comintern delegates, in the pay of Stalin." Only on September 21 was Sobral successful in obtaining the required document.[7]

On September 8, with the Military Tribunal about to hear declarations from the "Red chieftains," Prestes managed to get in a fight with guards who frisked him at the Tribunal. Special Police commander Queiroz had warned the men to take care lest the prisoner succeed in entering the courtroom with the bloodied face of a mistreated martyr, but the warning went unheeded and Prestes was hit on the nose.[8] He screamed and was brought before the judges with blood on his face. Raising a clenched fist he declared the frisking unnecessary because he had come from jail. The presiding judge said the prisoners had been called to present their defenses, not to provoke confusion. Another judge sent for a doctor.[9]

Prestes, the first to give an oral defense, said he had just emerged from a round of boxing. He assailed the tortures, the beatings, the "Tribunal of Repression," and the "campaign of slander." To explain his differences with points made by Sobral to Raul Machado, he read a rewrite he had made of pages seized by the Special Police on May 4, and he was allowed to finish although he exceeded the fifteen-minute time limit. In conclusion he said that the "revolutionaries of 1935" had received no money from Pedro Ernesto or Russia but had used funds that Aranha and Vargas had supplied Prestes in 1930 when they wanted him to support their "assault on the power."[10]

After the STM upheld the TSN sentence against Prestes, Sobral promised Leocádia that he would submit further appeals. But supporters of the Cavalier of Hope expressed dissatisfaction with Sobral's handling of the case and sent emissaries to Sobral to suggest that he be joined in the defense by two lawyers, one able to present the true thinking of Prestes and the other having enough renown to gain sympathetic decisions from judges.

Sobral told one of the emissaries that if Prestes and his mother felt it would be helpful, he would withdraw, but that if he continued it would be only as ex officio lawyer and not as a participant in the suggested threesome. The matter was closed after Prestes and then Leocádia rejected the idea of naming new lawyers.[11]

Leocádia, appreciative of the consideration being shown by Prison Director Lassance, received a rude shock with the onset of the Estado Novo dictatorship in November and the replacement of Lassance by Müller's man, Vitório Caneppa. Sobral, writing her on December 4, said he had been unable to see her son since November 8. Among the new rulings that he reported was one depriving the prisoner of newspaper reading and another requiring that Leocádia's letters to her son be sent directly to the prison and not to Sobral.[12]

6.   Defending Barreto Leite, Graciliano Ramos, and Others (1936–1937)

Before the imposition of the Estado Novo added to Sobral's work, he was already busy on behalf of about thirty men accused of supporting subversive ideas. Prominent among the civilians were Alagoas educator and writer Graciliano Ramos and Rio journalist João Batista Barreto Leite Filho. Among the military men, all of whom lost their army rankings soon after the 1935 uprisings, a prominent client was former Second Lieutenant José Gutman.

In the course of defending a former sergeant, Sobral denounced excessive use of *prisão preventiva* (preventive imprisonment) for locking up people not yet accused but suspected of having broken the law. Quoting legal authorities, Sobral pointed out that *prisão preventiva* should be applied only when it was "perfectly" demonstrated that the suspected individual might flee from justice, become an active disturber of the peace, or seek to destroy evidence.[1]

Another former sergeant defended by Sobral was Azôr Galvão de Souza, who, on the night of the November 1935 uprising at the Aviation School, carried out the commands of his superior, army Captain Agilberto Vieira de Azevedo, until he realized that the commands were those of a rebel leader. In June 1937 Sobral persuaded a judge of the Tribunal de Segurança Nacional (TSN) to order the freedom of Azôr, but influential First Aviation Regiment Commander Eduardo Gomes had the ex-sergeant reimprisoned. Despite a Supremo Tribunal Militar (STM) ruling that Azôr was being held illegally, the former sergeant remained *incomunicável* in the prison of the Aviation Regiment. Sobral, after accusing Lieutenant Colonel Eduardo Gomes of acting above the law, drew up a strong case with help from the Aviation School commander, who did not believe Azôr had been guilty. The TSN, however, condemned Azôr in October 1937 to 7¼ years of imprisonment.[2]

Sobral, who put much effort into the case of Azôr, could not agree with the stiff sentence, or that his client had violated the article of Law 38 of April 1935 that made it a crime to try, "by violence, to alter the Constitution or the form of government established by it." What he did argue, in appeals made on behalf of Azôr and others, was that Vargas had violated Law 38 on November 10, 1937, and had affirmed, as some of Sobral's clients had done earlier, that the 1934 Constitution "did not correspond to Brazilian social realities or take care of popular aspirations." Furthermore, Sobral maintained that the disappearance of the 1934 Constitution meant the disappearance of the article of Law 38 that referred to altering that constitution.[3]

These arguments, along with the story of Azôr's improper imprisonments, were given in Sobral's appeal, copies of which he sent to Alceu and the cardinal to buttress his denouncements of the Vargas regime and the recently decreed Estado Novo. However, neither the TSN nor the STM was moved by the arguments.[4]

In the case of Lieutenant José Gutman, whom Sobral served in an ex officio capacity, it was well established that he had been in the thick of the rebels' fight of November 1935 to take over the Third Infantry Regiment and had been shouting *vivas* for Prestes while ordering his men to seize a legalist colonel. Gutman, who made it clear to the TSN that he wanted to be held responsible for his acts on behalf of "the liberating movement," was placed in a cell in the Casa de Detenção, lest, in the Casa de Correção's large and crowded Sala da Capela (Chapel Room), he disrupt the lives of prisoners who disagreed with his campaign to boycott the TSN.[5]

Like others in the Casa de Detenção, Gutman informed the Ordem dos Advogados do Brasil (OAB) that he wished to defend himself before the STM, a court of "regular justice." But, after the TSN sentenced Gutman to an eight-year prison term, he and Sobral found themselves unable to appeal to the STM. They were told that, in accordance with TSN regulations, the intention to appeal should have been expressed within five days of Gutman's receiving notice of his sentence. Without success, Gutman and Sobral pointed out that the prisoner, being held in strict seclusion, had been out of touch with his lawyer and the *Diário de Justiça*, whose reporting about the sentence, they also argued, did not constitute proper notification. As Sobral told Gutman's brother a year later, the outlook was dismal for the former army officer, who, "with arms in hand, had tried to overthrow Getúlio Vargas."[6]

The case against journalist João Batista Barreto Leite Filho was curious because it relied on a letter of October 26, 1935, that the journalist had written Prestes to persuade him to abandon his plans for an insurrection. The letter, with views held by Brazilian Trotskyites, resulted in the prompt expulsion from the Communist Party (PCB) of Barreto Leite and all others who shared his ideas.

Barreto Leite was arrested in January 1936 on a *prisão preventiva* order because the letter, which police had found in Berger's papers, did reveal that the journalist had been moved earlier by party loyalty to cooperate, although reluctantly, with ANL orders to seek understandings about a "Popular Front" with opposition congressmen and associates of longtime conspirator Carlos da Costa Leite. After Barreto Leite spent months aboard the prison ship *Pedro I*, he was transferred to the Casa de Correção's Sala da Capela, where he played bridge with Herculino Cascardo, Hermes Lima, and Trotskyite Febus Gikovate.[7]

Barreto Leite got in touch with Sobral in 1937, and in June of that year Sobral appealed to TSN Judge Luiz Carlos da Costa Netto, an army colonel, to end the *prisão preventiva* of his client, whose seventeen months without work had left him in "extreme penury." Sobral argued that the code of military justice did not allow the use of *prisão preventiva* unless the accused person had confessed or been shown clearly by at least two witnesses to have committed a crime.[8]

To demonstrate that Barreto Leite had made every effort to prevent "any sort of armed violence," Sobral quoted from his client's famous letter to Prestes:

> [The planned] revolt will not have the participation of even a tiny fraction of the masses, . . . and will end up, whether you wish it or not, harming the masses. . . . Do you want to participate in this? . . . Should we allow the prestige and personal decision of one man to determine the class policy of the revolutionary vanguard of the proletariat? That is *Prestismo* in its most wretched form.[9]

Late in June, before action was taken on the appeal, Justice Minister Macedo Soares canceled many *prisão preventiva* orders. Thus Barreto Leite was set free along with another of Sobral's civilian clients, Pedro Bona, a resident of the state of Maranhão, whose sin consisted of having been a member of the ANL.[10]

Novelist Graciliano Ramos had not been a member of the ANL and was carrying out his work as director of public education of Alagoas when he was arrested in the state capital, Maceió, in March 1936 on the orders of General Newton Cavalcanti. As education director, Graciliano had failed to give teaching jobs to favorites of influential men and had sought to bring the pay of rural teachers into line with the pay of teachers in Maceió. The term "dangerous Communist" had been applied to him by some of his enemies and was repeated by the general. After his arrest he spent time in Rio's Casa de Detenção and then with degenerate common criminals at the Correctional Colony on Ilha Grande, the island between Rio and São Paulo state. From that distasteful setting the former education director was transferred, thanks to appeals by his wife and friends, to Rio's Casa de Correção, where he enjoyed the company of civilized fellow-prisoners, most especially Hermes Lima.[11]

There, late in 1936, Graciliano's wife brought him a paper to sign appointing Sobral to be his lawyer. Learning that his literary friend José Lins do Rego had suggested Sobral, Graciliano told his wife that the famous defender of Prestes and Berger was too important to touch the case of a penniless, insignificant wretch like himself. "I won't sign. Dr. Sobral must be rich and I don't even have the money to pay for stamps needed for documents. Leave me in peace. I can't get along with people like that. Tell José Lins to go to the devil."[12]

But Graciliano signed, not wanting to disappoint unknown friends who were seeking to free him. He found Sobral, who visited him a few days later, "a thin man of medium height with an energetic countenance, a strong mouth, and terribly sharp eyes. . . . The lawyer sat down, . . . opened his briefcase and began to ask questions. It was the first interrogation to which I had been submitted."

Graciliano asked Sobral how he proposed to prepare a defense without the existence of any accusation.

"They are idiots," Sobral replied. "If I were chief of police you would be involved in a proper legal case."

"And where, doctor, would you find any material for it?"

"In your novels, man. With the laws they are making now, your novels would provide enough to convict you."

During subsequent visits by Sobral, Graciliano changed his opinion of the lawyer. "I discovered he was also poor. And for this reason he wished to set me free. Our ideas differed. Of little importance. Sobral Pinto, a man of perfect charity, wanted the freedom of a creature who, in my opinion, was a useless animal, and who, in his opinion, was a son of God."[13]

Sobral's petition, submitted to the TSN in November 1936, told of his client's undeserved tribulations at the Correctional Colony "with the most discredited scum of society." It reminded the TSN that no charge had been brought against Graciliano, and it urged the TSN to undertake, without delay, investigations to clarify the situations of prisoners like Graciliano, who had never considered participating in subversive movements. Receiving no reply from the TSN,

Sobral addressed Police Chief Müller in January 1937 in order to point out that his client's release was required "in accordance with the criteria established by the federal administration for handling improper jailings."[14]

Later in January Graciliano Ramos was set free. He remained in Rio, where he was named inspector of secondary education and received prizes for his literary works.[15]

7. Condemning Church Support of the Estado Novo (Late 1937)

In 1937 Sobral told Alceu Amoroso Lima that of all the men in political circles, none had been closer to him during the past six years than Francisco Campos. "A simple nod by me and I'd be in the Consultoria Geral da República to collaborate with Campos."[1]

Collaboration, however, was not on Sobral's mind in October 1937 when Campos worked to give impetus to the plan of Vargas and military leaders to cancel the presidential election and promulgate a new, authoritarian constitution. Campos had been drafting such a constitution at the request of Vargas.

Sobral, avoiding election politics, had declined invitations to sign declarations in favor of either of the leading presidential candidates, but he believed that the election to choose a successor for Vargas, "principal cause of our moral and religious ruin," would have "miraculous effects" on Brazil. Throughout October he argued heatedly in Campos' office.[2]

Putting his thoughts on paper, Sobral wrote Campos on November 6 to express amazement that a man of Campos' intelligence and education ("you are probably the most able man in Brazil") should display so much skepticism about the nation and its people and should demonstrate "alarming opportunism, placing yourself at the orders of Vargas, that great corrupter of souls." He asked Campos if Brazil had not gone far enough on the road to corruption, placing Minas in the hands of Benedicto Valladares and the presidency of the Chamber of Deputies in the hands of Pedro Aleixo. Worse than "the presence of these insignificant little figures is the instability" caused by the "deliberate neglect" of the 1934 Constitution by the men in government.[3]

On November 9 Campos took over the justice ministry. His chief of staff (chefe de gabinete) became Francisco Negrão de Lima, who had earlier undertaken a secret mission for Vargas and Valladares to persuade governors to adhere to the planned coup. The coup took place on November 10 when Congress was closed by the Federal District police. Vargas became head of the Estado Novo, and most of the governors became *interventores,* accountable to a powerful central government.

Eulogies to Vargas appeared in the press, now controlled by the Departamento de Propaganda e Difusão Cultural, which Lourival Fontes had been running. One of the eulogies, published in all the Rio dailies on orders of the chief of police, called Vargas the great "guide to Brazilianism, the creator of nationalism, who has just saved Brazil." Sobral, calling this adulation the worst infamy in the annals of Brazilian political life, assigned the responsibility to Campos, who, he told Augusto Frederico Schmidt, was using Bolshevik methods to alienate new generations from religious, social, and political traditions.[4]

Sobral kept after Church leaders to resist the Estado Novo. In one of his letters to the cardinal, he called Vargas an atheist and a liar. In another he described Vargas' method of corrupting men as leaving them unable to appreciate their own corruption and servility. Maintaining that he could cite "thousands and thousands" of examples, Sobral limited himself to two: he denounced the recent justice minister, José Carlos de Macedo Soares, for his role in bringing about the dictatorship, and Labor Minister Waldemar Falcão for a role that would eliminate the Church as a "social force among the working masses."[5]

Sobral promised Alceu, the head of Ação Católica Brasileira, that he would provide him and the cardinal with all the evidence needed to show that "the Church in Brazil has never been as threatened as at present." He noted that the *"Carta Constitucional"* (new constitution) contained none of those articles that the Church had found satisfying in the 1934 Constitution. And he warned against supporting the Estado Novo in exchange for favors.[6]

Alceu replied that the 1937 Carta Constitucional contained some excellent things and could in no way be considered "the expression of a totalitarian state." Noting that the abuse of power had occurred under even the most liberal constitutions in the world, Alceu wrote that, paradoxical as it might seem, an authoritarian constitution could result in curbing abuses of power that "have been plentiful in our political history."

Alceu's principal message was that Ação Católica Brasileira

should not be political. Also he appealed for "the unity of our forces."[7]

Sobral, rejecting Alceu's appeal, wrote him that Campos and army Chief of Staff Pedro Aurélio de Góes Monteiro sought to handle Brazil as if it were a mental case needing years of treatment, and he declared that the silence of Ação Católica was worse than desertion. "Our capitulation," he insisted, would result in "irremediable harm" to the consciences of the common people and the minds of "the new generations." "I feel ashamed to find it necessary to say things so disagreeable to those I love and admire so much, such as Dom Leme and you."[8]

Alceu's reaction was to repeat that Ação Católica was doing exactly the right thing in shunning politics. The political situation, he argued, was "merely one more episode in the revolutionary sequence" begun in 1922 and taking place also in other countries as a result of "historic causes that transcend the strict limits of our case." "I see the experiment of an authoritarian state in Brazil not as a victory for oppression against the law, as you seem to think, but as a link in the chain of events in which we are involved and the consequence of the errors and abuses of the democratic state." His attitude, he said, did not make him a "systematic backer" of Vargas— whose offer of the post of labor minister, he revealed confidentially, he had recently declined.[9]

Early in December Alceu wrote Sobral to accuse him of being in "revolt" against the cardinal and of aggravating a schism among Catholics. Faced with these charges, Sobral bowed to the wishes of Cardinal Leme and Alceu. On December 6 he gave the cardinal his "unrestricted submission" in order to prevent "indiscipline and rebellion" from occurring in the flock of His Eminence, and he agreed to make his act of compliance known to everyone who had been shown copies of his recent letters to the cardinal. While admitting that the "final word" about the position of Ação Católica was in Alceu's hands, he added that Alceu's arguments had convinced him that Alceu was wrong.[10]

Sobral did not regard his submission as a reason to refrain from disagreeing with the way Ação Católica was being run by Alceu. Writing Cardinal Leme on December 9, he asserted that Ação Católica had, in over one year, accomplished practically nothing, and that its directors were never asked to meet for discussions about the position that Ação Católica should take "in the face of the Brazilian social situation."[11]

Nor did Sobral let up on his attacks against the Estado Novo. He wrote Campos that Vargas and General Góes Monteiro regarded Brazilians as unintelligent savages and that Campos, inspired by Bolshevism, racist fascism, and Portuguese corporativism, ignored the Church's view of the civilized character of Brazilians. Sobral accused Campos of favoring the oppression of justice and the law. "As long as you are dominated by this pagan mentality, I shall oppose you vigorously."[12]

Henrique Dodsworth, a former congressman who had become mayor of the Federal District, asked Alceu to be *reitor* (president) of the Universidade do Distrito Federal. Alceu told Sobral he would accept if it suited the cardinal, whose decision would be "final," but that he wished also to have Sobral's opinion.[13] Sobral replied that Alceu, as a member of the National Council of Education since October, had found himself able to serve the federal government and could logically accept the municipal post offered by Dodsworth, "your friend since boyhood," especially as the cardinal had made it clear, in a telegram to Labor Minister Waldemar Falcão, that the new federal regime had the support of the Catholics. However, Sobral added, if his own wishes were to prevail, men of the "moral and intellectual stature" of Alceu would abstain from cooperating with the "usurpers."[14]

On assuming the presidency of the university, Alceu gave an interview which, as reported by *O Globo* on December 30, blamed the university's outgoing administration for its failure to progress. An attack on former *reitor* Affonso Penna Júnior was uncalled for, Sobral wrote, and he pointed out that Penna, under the Estado Novo, was suffering intense financial difficulties because he rejected advantages that might be had if he abandoned his convictions.[15]

8. Defending Captain Cortez and Mary and Mário Pedrosa (1938)

Following the implantation of the Estado Novo, Sobral worked on additional cases arising from accusations against people suspected of favoring Communism. Among his military clients were former sergeants and corporals who had been attached to barracks in Mato Grosso before being expelled from the army and threatened with prison sentences. With the authorities claiming they had violated an article of Law 38 forbidding the transmission of propaganda in favor of subversion, Sobral argued that remarks reportedly made during private conversations did not constitute transmitting propaganda. However, seven of the eight young defendants in the case were sentenced to serve between one and three years in prison.[1]

A more distinguished defendant was former navy Captain Amarilio Vieira Cortez, who had served the navy for twenty-five years and become chief of the division of tactics of the navy's aviation staff. Loathing the Green Shirts, he had joined the Aliança Nacional Libertadora (ANL) in May 1935 and for two months had held a nonexecutive post in the organization. Sobral in his *defesa prévia* (preliminary brief), presented to the TSN in December 1937, quoted words of praise of Cortez expressed by the defendant's superior, Fábio de Sá Earp (chief of staff of naval aviation), and by dignitaries who, incidentally, had been prosecuted by Sobral in the 1920s: Admiral Protógenes Guimarães (the ailing former governor of Rio state), navy Commander Ary Parreiras (former *interventor* of Rio state), and Colonel Gustavo Cordeiro de Farias (*chefe de gabinete* of the army staff).[2]

In his *razões finais*, submitted in January 1938, Sobral remarked about how Vargas, having promised to defend the liberal Constitution of 1934, had taken advantage of martial law and the Supreme Court's disregard of individual rights to carry out a *golpe* (coup) and implant "the most dreadful of dictatorships."[3] TSN Judge Alberto de Lemos Basto, a navy captain, deleted this part of Sobral's presentation because it violated a TSN internal regulation prohibiting defense arguments from offending the authorities or the judiciary. Sobral, in response, sent the judge a stinging letter saying that never, in his twenty years of legal work, had any magistrate made a deletion from any of his defense arguments.

"Your career," Sobral told the judge, "had been exclusively military and you found yourself unexpectedly, and without preparation, elevated to the judiciary." Sobral maintained that the deleted sentences contained "one of the most essential arguments for the defense," and that if Basto were a career magistrate he would be acquainted with the definition of *golpe* given by the Italian authority Brunialti and would know that the word dictatorship was appropriate for a situation in which the will of the rulers was not restricted by the judiciary. Basto replied that Sobral's protest and "lessons about morality and the law" contained nothing that would affect the case.[4]

Late in January 1938, Cortez was sentenced to serve 10½ months of imprisonment for violating a clause of Law 38 that prohibited "the promotion or direction" of associations which sought to subvert social or political order. In appealing the sentence, Sobral explained to Basto that Cortez' superior, Sá Earp, had described Cortez as having taken steps to repress the Communist uprisings.[5] Basto denied the appeal.

Sobral was hopeful of the outcome of a further appeal because the TSN *relator* would be Dr. Pedro Borges, a trained magistrate. He asked Borges to reinstate the words deleted by Basto, calling them "the best that can be invoked" in favor of the client. And he wrote that "the only reason" for sentencing Cortez had been a conversation in which Cortez, prior to learning of the closing of the ANL, had reportedly recommended a "political connection" with conspirator Carlos da Costa Leite.[6]

Pedro Borges, in writing "Denied" on the appeal, added a comment supporting Basto's observation that the deleted passage did nothing for the defense. "The papers about the case," Borges also wrote, "cannot include attacks on the regime and its top representatives."[7] A bitter Sobral, in a personal note to Borges, said that the current regime "that you praise" was guilty of doing away with federal justice, "to which you brought so much honor until November 10, 1937." Sobral also wrote about the deletion to Philadelpho de Azevedo of the local section of the OAB, saying that if the OAB did not forcefully remedy the situation it would become impossible for lawyers to carry out their arduous mission.[8]

While working without success on the case of Cortez, Sobral handled the case of Mário Pedrosa, who, as the leader of the Brazilian Trotskyite movement, had denounced Stalinism and called Prestes a "raving *caudilho*." Unlike Cortez, Mário Pedrosa was abroad. Having found the Brazilian repression intolerable, he went to France after the Estado Novo came into existence and there, and a little later in the United States, helped organize the Trotskyites' Fourth International.[9]

To clear the name of Mário Pedrosa, accused in Brazil of promoting revolutionary ideas, Sobral worked with Mário's wife, Mary Houston Pedrosa, a shorthand typist for a municipality in Rio state, and Mário's seventy-four-year-old father, sugar mill owner Pedro da Cunha Pedrosa, who had been Paraíba's vice governor before serving in the Senate during the Old Republic. Sobral's arguments, presented to the TSN in December 1937, described Mário as an intelligent young student of Brazil's social problems who had written in favor of Marxism but who, unlike Vargas, had never ordered the use of violence to alter the Constitution.[10]

In January 1938 a police raid on a Niterói property of the family of Mary Houston Pedrosa located a shed full of Trotskyite documents. Mary, found at the Rio residence of her mother, Arinda, was arrested, along with her sister Celina, Celina's husband, and Arinda. The four children, who included the Pedrosas' two-year-old daughter Vera, were not taken.[11]

At about the same time the Rio police arrested bookseller Pasquale Petracconi and his employees. The press was told that he was a friend of Mário Pedrosa and that the Red propaganda found at his office in downtown Rio had been "radiated" all over Brazil, captivating uneducated individuals who were too weak to resist the "ravenous tentacles" of Communism. The Houston family's Niterói shed was called the "general barracks" of the Rio state "extremists."[12]

Sobral wrote Justice Minister Campos to complain that the arrests had left Arinda's four grandchildren alone (the oldest was fifteen) and to point out that Celina's husband had nothing to do with Marxism. He wrote that Mary had dedicated all her time to raising Vera and caring for a husband whose life in hiding had made him unable to find employment. Arinda and Celina, he wrote, were incapable of disturbing public order. Citing his own experience in the 1920s and later, he told Campos that in 80 percent of the cases the arrests provided no benefits to public order but, on the contrary, created "an environment of general ill will toward the government."[13] Soon after the letter was written Mary's mother, sister, and brother-in-law were released, but Mary remained behind bars.

Sobral, drawing up a brief in favor of Mary in February 1938, wrote that she had done nothing illegal and needed to be at her job to support her daughter and herself. A month later he sent a copy of the brief to Negrão de Lima, *chefe de gabinete* of Campos. In an accompanying letter he called the detainment of Mary "mere persecution" and expressed outrage at Article 170 of the 1937 Constitution, which allowed the police to arrest whomever they wanted without the judiciary being able to curb their acts. "If things continue in this way, I shall not be surprised to find myself in a cell at the Casa de Detenção accused of being one of the most dangerous Communists."[14]

Former Senator Pedro da Cunha Pedrosa, calling himself too feeble to appear before the TSN, submitted his testimony in June in a letter to Sobral. He described Mary as a "sort of hostage," held to get "my poor Mário" to turn himself in. The former senator declared that Mário had not been close to Petracconi, the Italian bookseller who had simply asked Mário to translate books, and he pointed out that a codefendant of Mário's, seized in the Niterói shed, had made it clear that the papers found there had not belonged to Mário.[15]

TSN Judge Basto, considering the evidence presented against Petracconi and his employees, reprimanded the police investigators for submitting reports that were filled with sensational conclusions not substantiated by facts. In June and July 1938 the TSN absolved Petracconi and his employees, along with Mary Houston Pedrosa and Elias and Aristides Lobo, brothers who had been doing work for Petracconi.[16]

Mary joined her husband in Washington and worked there for the Pan American Union. After she returned to Brazil in 1941, Mário decided to follow her example, but he was arrested upon reaching Rio. With the intervention of Mário's father and the help of a letter from the Pan American Union, expressing views of the U.S. secretary of state, arrangements were made with Filinto Müller and others for Mário's return to Washington.[17]

Petracconi, after settling in São Paulo in 1938, expressed his gratitude to Sobral in a letter inquiring about legal fees. Sobral replied that Petracconi owed him nothing. The outcome of the Petracconi case, Sobral wrote, could be attributed to Augusto Frederico Schmidt's handling of it with Negrão de Lima and Campos. "If I agreed to intervene with Campos to request a declaration of innocence . . . , it was because Schmidt said that I alone could obtain such a declaration from him. Although I believed that Schmidt had already taken care of everything, I did not want to refuse the favor he asked."[18]

PART IV

In the Aftermath of the 1938
Uprisings (1938–1941)

1. Defending Raymundo Padilha and
Lanari Júnior (1938)

Following the establishment of the Estado Novo, discontented Paulistas started plotting its overthrow. They were joined by Green
Shirts (members of Ação Integralista Brasileira), who were furious
because the Estado Novo had outlawed their organization along
with all political parties in December 1937.

A plan to have an uprising in Rio on the night of March 10–11,
1938, was hatched by Colonel Euclydes Figueiredo (a leading fighter
for the 1932 Paulista revolt), Octavio Mangabeira (Washington Luiz'
foreign minister), and General João Cândido Pereira de Castro Júnior
(opponent of the government's intervention in Rio Grande do Sul in
1937). The plan became known to authorities and, although it was
abandoned, conspirators Mangabeira and Figueiredo ended up in a
prison hospital. Castro Júnior, the cautious general who had been
chosen by Mangabeira to head the military movement, was arrested,
but soon he was released because of insufficient evidence against
him.[1]

Two of Sobral's early Integralista clients were navy Captain Jatir
de Carvalho Serejo, who had started to lead sailors in revolt on the
night of March 10, and his fellow-conspirator, Arnoldo Hasselmann
Fairbairn, the navy lieutenant who had persuaded Serejo to discontinue his move in view of the abandonment of the plan for the insurrection. Defending the pair, Sobral told the TSN that "Getúlio
Vargas has made criminals out of those who tried to defend the
1934 Constitution, which he suppressed." Accusations, he said, were
being brought against military men simply because it was suspected, without any proof, that they had been "thinking of partici-

pating in some uprising that never occurred." Serejo and Hasselmann were held but briefly.[2]

When an uprising did occur in Rio on the night of May 10–11, Hasselmann was wounded in an unsuccessful struggle to take possession of the navy ministry building and, as result of his action, was given a ten-year prison sentence. Also on that night in May, Colonel Figueiredo's associate, army Lieutenant Severo Fournier, led thirty-five Green Shirts in an unsuccessful "mission" to kidnap Vargas at Guanabara Palace. Fournier, who was eventually captured and locked up, had left papers about the plot in a car he had abandoned. Found by the Rio police, the papers contained many names which were helpful in the round-up of almost fifteen hundred considered to have been sympathetic to the uprising.[3]

Among those who were arrested was Bank of Brazil employee Raymundo Padilha, who had organized Green Shirt parades in Rio state. He had played no role in the uprisings, having gone into hiding in February in southern Minas. There on the night of May 10–11, he had been amazed to hear a radio broadcast from Rio saying that he was leading ten thousand men from Minas to Rio. Arrested by the Minas police three days later, he was shipped to Rio state and spent time in prisons in Petrópolis and Niterói.[4]

Padilha turned to Sobral, who became also the lawyer for the Mineiros who had helped Padilha hide. An appeal for a transfer of Padilha to Rio's Casa de Correção was denied by the TSN and so was the habeas corpus petition for his freedom presented in July. In September Padilha was sentenced to a three-month jail term for associating with an illegal organization.[5]

Another arrested in Minas after the May insurrections was engineer Amaro Lanari Júnior. He had rejected an appeal to participate in an Integralista plot in Minas, but conversations about the plans, incorrectly reported by the interrogators of the Green Shirt who had tried to involve him, led to his being given a four-month prison sentence. After a majority of the TSN confirmed the sentence, Sobral was retained by Lanari Júnior's father, a resident of Rio who, like Padilha, had belonged to the Câmara dos Quarenta (Chamber of Forty), top organ of Integralismo. Sobral drew up a petition to the TSN that pointed out that the defendant, at liberty in March and May, could have cooperated with the Integralistas' plans but did not do so.[6]

In September, a few days after the petition was submitted, a new

approach was used because lawyer Evandro Lins e Silva won a startling victory at the Supreme Court for one of his clients by claiming that a *sursis*, or *suspensão condicional* (conditional suspension
of the punishment), should prevail in accordance with a decree of
1924.

In congratulating Evandro, Sobral wrote: "As you know, *suspensão condicional* is based on very special circumstances" in which
the crime is considered to result "from events foreign to, and beyond the will of, the criminal, . . . an unfortunate, abnormal incident in an otherwise correct and honest life." In prior discussions
Sobral had disputed Evandro's contention that a *suspensão condicional* was appropriate for a political crime. Now Sobral praised his fellow lawyer, saying he had astutely won the notable Supreme Court
verdict by arranging to have its judges devote their attention exclusively to the question of the non-retroactivity of a decree-law, thus
overlooking what Sobral continued to feel was "an insuperable difficulty." He told Evandro that although he had not played any role
in Evandro's pro–*suspensão condicional* campaign, he would, like
other defense lawyers, take advantage of the victory in cases where
the new Supreme Court decision was applicable. He promised also,
in those cases, to let clients know that Evandro was responsible for
their being set free.

In a note to the elder Lanari, Sobral called Evandro the chief of
the pro–*suspensão condicional* campaign and added that its successful conclusion would bring "immediate freedom" to Amaro Lanari
Júnior.[7]

Writing again to his client's father on October 12, Sobral said that
he was withdrawing from the case of Cassio Lanari, another of the
elder Lanari's many sons. At the same time he placed in the hands
of lawyer Mário Bulhões Pedreira the appeals of Raymundo Padilha
and the Mineiros who had hidden him. As Sobral explained to the
elder Lanari, he had felt earlier that the TSN judges wished to avoid
becoming "mere instruments of the present hangmen of liberties"
but that the decisions in TSN Cases 600 and 606 had convinced him
otherwise and he would no longer handle TSN cases.[8]

2. Colonel Figueiredo, General Castro, and Youthful Integralistas (1938)

Case 600 arose from the activities of a group of eighteen of Sobral's Integralista clients, many of them medical students. All had taken a ferry from Niterói to Rio on the night of May 10 and been ordered by the uprising's leadership to join others in the capture of Góes Monteiro (army chief of staff), Colonel Canrobert Pereira da Costa (*chefe de gabinete* of War Minister Eurico Gaspar Dutra), and General Almério de Moura (head of the First Military Region).[1]

Only one of the eighteen had done any capturing, being part of a group that had taken Colonel Canrobert Pereira da Costa for a wild automobile ride in his pajamas and then deserted him and the car. The other seventeen, Sobral argued, had agreed to collaborate with the plans for May 11 but, "when faced with dramatic reality," had decided not to carry out their assignments.[2] Like the assault groups chosen to seize the war and justice ministers, they had done nothing.

As Sobral had frequent occasion also to point out, the charges against those assigned to kidnap pillars of the regime were based on lists found in the car abandoned by Lieutenant Severo Fournier and did not correspond to facts. Several young men accused of trying to break into General Góes Monteiro's residence had been a long way from there, mingling with a group of twenty that took no action in the neighborhood of General Almério de Moura's home.[3]

The five-year prison sentences handed down by TSN Judge Pedro Borges were considered excessive by Sobral. He told Judge Raul Machado, *relator* of the appeal, that some Communist military men, who had opened fire against government forces in November 1935, had received similar sentences.[4]

Early in October Raul Machado persuaded the full court to uphold the judgments given by Pedro Borges. Sobral, dismayed, wrote Machado to express amazement that anyone, especially a man with the heart of a poet, could have been so cruel as to favor such a "monstrous error." "How could you impassively cast the vote which imprisons, for years and years, young students who did nothing, and heads of families who limited themselves to crossing the bay?" Sobral pointed out that the police had not caught his clients enticing others or arguing for some future action. "If you continue on this path of severity, use will be made of the death penalty, decreed on

May 18, 1938, and, with this, we shall have definitely entered the realm of red terror."[5]

A few days after the TSN confirmed the sentences of the young Green Shirts it shocked Sobral again, this time with its decision about General Castro Júnior, one of the defendants in Case 606.[6]

Following the events of March, General Castro Júnior had kept in touch with Colonel Euclydes Figueiredo despite the latter's confinement in a prison hospital. He had sent word to assure the colonel that he would be set free, along with Octavio Mangabeira, so that he could play an important military role in uprisings to start late on May 10; but the arrangement for the escape had not succeeded.[7]

With the failure of the conspiracy on May 11, Figueiredo's legally trained son Guilherme lost track of his father for three months. And in the meantime it became known that among the papers in the car abandoned by Lieutenant Fournier was a detailed plan for the insurrections, its pages covered with comments that Figueiredo had written while in the prison hospital.

Guilherme finally found his father in the Casa de Correção. Preparing to defend him, he turned to Sobral for assistance. "I'll teach you some things about the technique of defense," Sobral said, "and you will speak as your father's defender." Although Sobral was named lawyer for Figueiredo and seven others in the case, important written defense arguments for Figueiredo were signed by Guilherme.[8]

Guilherme found the TSN a "sinister place," frequented by members of the tough Special Police, and with a judge who "had already made up his mind." He complained also of being given only fifteen minutes for oral arguments, but he made up for the restriction by submitting, with Sobral's help, a long brief that mocked the prosecution's references to mysterious, conspiratorial visits to the prison hospital and that sought to throw doubt on the authenticity of notes written by Figueiredo on the plan to guide the uprising. The TSN, however, ordered Figueiredo to spend $4\frac{1}{3}$ years in prison for having played a role in planning the revolt and for having persuaded fellow-officers to adhere to it.[9]

General Castro Júnior, considered by the plotters to be the movement's overall military leader, spent the early morning hours of May 11 at his residence simply awaiting the outcome. Later, at the TSN, he was absolved by Judge Antônio Pereira Braga in the first ruling about his case.[10]

Sobral praised Braga's decision and set out to win a confirmation at the TSN's second judgment, to be rendered by the full court. He wrote the *relator*, Colonel Costa Netto: "With the information that makes up Case 606, you cannot possibly get the Tribunal to condemn General Castro Júnior." How, Sobral asked, could the general's call on Colonel Eduardo Gomes on the evening of May 10 be held against him when Gomes himself had categorically asserted that it had not been made to persuade him to join the uprising? "You heard from a friend that General Castro Júnior sounded out army companions . . . but you know that such tales usually have no basis. Two military men told me that the failure of the May 11 movement resulted exclusively from the lack of participation by General Castro Júnior."[11]

On October 10 the TSN sentenced General Castro Júnior to 1⅓ years in prison. Sobral, writing on the 11th to one of the young Green Shirts who had taken the ferry from Niterói, said he was "overcome by the most bitter disappointment" and was "definitely retiring" from TSN cases. "The consideration and esteem that all of you never failed to show me will remain as a consolation in these days when I feel an immense wave of sadness that increases, without ceasing, in my oppressed and tortured heart."[12]

Some of Sobral's desolation was evident in a letter he wrote the next day to Aníbal Freire, the Bernardes finance minister who had recently agreed to become *consultor geral da república*. He told Freire that he used to admire him but saw him now as a supporter of "the political organization that has transformed penal justice into mere courts of the police." He wrote that when he contemplated "the new principles that rule the world," he grieved for his seven children, the youngest not yet two years old. "I could not read your speech of yesterday without my eyes becoming filled with tears."[13]

3. Good-bye, Romano, Old Friend (June–December 1938)

Among the suspects rounded up by the Rio police after the uprisings of May 1938 was Alexandre Hirgué, a businessman from Bessarabia (Romania) who was accused of having had close relations with one of the Integralista rebels and of being, at the same time, a Moscow agent responsible for arranging that Brazilian coffee, exported to Turkey, be transshipped to Stalin's "paradise." The press, using sensational headlines, urged the authorities to deport the "obnoxious nabob."[1]

Hirgué's imprisonment was handled by Antônio Emílio Romano, who had been a dedicated assistant of *procurador* Sobral in the 1920s and become by 1938 the head of *segurança política* (political security) of the Rio police. Romano, *O Globo* reported in March 1938, had commanded the invasion of the Rio residence of Green Shirt Chief Plínio Salgado, leading to the discovery there of arms, munitions, and radio transmission equipment.[2] A pillar of the Estado Novo police, Romano kept his distance from Sobral.[3]

Hirgué was thrashed at night by policemen on orders of Romano and was led to expect that worse treatment was in store for him and his wife, who, like Hirgué, was held *incomunicável*.[4] Romano, responsible for torturing prisoners, including Communist Carlos Marighella in 1936, took care in 1938 to have another victim, bleeding from torture, share for a while a cell with Hirgué.[5] There, according to an investigation carried out a little later, Romano and two associates, one a young policeman and the other an acquaintance of Hirgué, offered to save the Hirgués in return for 500 contos. Hirgué, the investigation showed, wrote out a check for 200 contos and addressed an appeal to his partner in the Turkish Coffee Monopoly for more money.[6]

Late in June 1938, Police Chief Müller dismissed Romano. In his place he appointed Joaquim Antunes de Oliveira, brother of Sobral's friend Benjamin.[7]

Romano turned to Sobral for help and found his old chief willing to serve as his lawyer. In August, after Romano and his two codefendants in the extortion case were arrested in accordance with a *prisão preventiva* order of the First Criminal Court, Romano's wife came to Sobral's home to point out that their financial situation was bad and to try to explain why her husband, during the Vargas regime, had displayed some lack of gratitude to Sobral for help given by him in 1928.[8]

Romano was in the prison of the Military Police cavalry barracks when Filinto Müller let it be known in a press interview that he had decided to dismiss Romano upon learning that he had "ruthlessly beaten and tortured prisoners" at the police headquarters "at night when I was not present." It was after that, the police chief added, that the extortion case had come to his attention.[9]

The criminal justice system found Romano guilty of extortion, whereupon Sobral wrote one of the judges: "I am sad that you are so severe with Romano. During three years, when I was *procurador criminal da república*, he was often at my home and merited my complete confidence. I never saw any trace of covetousness in him." Sobral told of his recommendation of Romano given in 1928 to Pedro de Oliveira Ribeiro Sobrinho of the Fourth Delegacia Auxiliar. "I want to save the probity of my former assistant, whose principal crime is to have served with vigor the *caudilhismo* that has besmirched our once glorious country."[10]

Sobral wrote Justice Minister Campos to complain of unfair treatment of Romano and Hymalaia Vergolino, who had been dismissed as *procurador geral* of the TSN. To serve Vargas, Sobral wrote, these men had created waves of hatred and slanders against themselves. "*Caudilhismo* has forgotten the oceans of services of every sort that these men carried out for Getúlio."[11]

Romano, whose transgressions excited the press as much as dubious charges against Hirgué had excited it earlier, announced that he was turning to new lawyers because Sobral had neglected his case.[12]

Writing Romano on December 1, Sobral described his old friend as trying to hurt him in order to reduce "the bloodthirsty ire of your cruel hangmen." He recalled the appeal for help he had received from Romano, in agony about the public destruction of his honor, and the visit of Romano's wife, during which he had promised her he would charge no fee. He was, he wrote, absorbing the expenses connected with his work even though Romano had recently received all his back pay in a lump sum. Sobral pointed out that as recently as November 26, during a two-hour conversation, Romano had approved Sobral's plans for appealing the case.

"Your present behavior does not surprise me. It reflects the logic of your life. You do not place your trust in justice, but rather, in obtaining protection. Justice is moral force. The other reflects the realm of brute force, the realm in which you became an important figure and in which you also collapsed." Sobral said that Romano could not harm him, although he was trying to do so to benefit himself. "My conscience is clear and I bow to my religion, which obliges me to forgive you, wishing you happiness and a rapid end to these sad days."[13]

In the face of press reports about Romano's switch of lawyers, Sobral explained to the Ordem dos Advogados (OAB) that he had spared no effort on behalf of his client and continued to believe in his denial of the extortion charge. This was not to say, Sobral pointed out to a friend, that he lacked knowledge of Romano's defects. "Life, and, above all, my profession, have taught me to know men."[14]

4. Disagreeing Again with Alceu (1938–1939)

In mid-July 1938 the *Jornal do Brasil* described "the delightful banquet" at which the Japanese ambassador honored visiting Japanese Admiral Shinjiro Yamamoto and "the most distinguished representatives of Brazilian Catholicism." The distinguished Catholic representatives, men of prestige in Brazilian affairs, were reported to have enthusiastically applauded the speech of welcome to the admiral, delivered by a Brazilian bishop who declared: "We acclaim the noble empire of Japan."[1]

Alceu Amoroso Lima, one of the banquet's guests, received a letter in which Sobral wrote of the grief he felt about the affair, "starting with names of those said to be legitimate representatives of Catholic thinking in Brazil."[2]

Sobral appreciated that the bonds of affection and admiration between Alceu and himself could not be broken by disagreements and that Alceu understood that Sobral, in expressing himself frankly, sought to be useful. In this spirit Sobral told Alceu: "The whole nation will suppose that Brazilian Catholics consider Japan to be the international defender of Christian principles of peace and that . . . the director of Catholic Action in China is a liar and slanderer for denouncing Japan as hostile to humankind." He accused Alceu of ignoring Japanese atrocities against Chinese Catholics and of cooperating with the campaign of the "unscrupulous" Japanese ambassador to place the Brazilian Church at the service of Nipponic imperialism. About that imperialism, Sobral wrote, Alceu should speak with the *Jornal do Commercio*'s Elmano Cardim, whose refusal to be bought by the Japanese ambassador had led to police censorship that prevented the newspaper from voicing its opinion of Japan.[3]

In a twelve-page letter to the Japanese ambassador, Sobral explained his absence from the banquet by saying that pagan Japan was committed, like Germany and Italy, to an aggressive imperialism and that the Yamamoto "mission," far from signifying appreciation of the religious truth of the Church of Jesus Christ, was a part of the program to expand that imperialism. Japan, Sobral wrote, sought to gobble up Formosa, Korea, and China and infiltrate Brazil, "to the natural resentment of Brazilians." He added that at the banquet the only true representative of the thinking of Brazilian Catholic laity had been Alceu Amoroso Lima.[4]

Alceu, replying to Sobral's criticism of his attendance, said that Sobral was too much inspired by "a political spirit." Sobral, stung by the charge, wrote: "According to you and Dom Leme, I am always wrong. The two of you believe that I do not see men and things of this world from the viewpoint of the Church." As a reward for "all my dedication to the Church, all my sacrifices, the leader of Ação Católica Brasileira tells me that, on account of my diabolical political spirit, my 'eyes are always on the human aspects' as though you have your eyes only on the *supernatural* aspects. . . . No, Alceu, I am not a traitor to the *spirit of the Church*. . . . Where in the Yamamoto episode can you find 'political' interest on my part? The one who has been animated by a political spirit is you, not I."[5]

Late in July, Ação Católica Brasileira sponsored a talk by Yamamoto entitled "Catholicism in Japan." Sobral, learning from Hamilton Nogueira about the talk, told Alceu that Yamamoto had for the most part used it to defend Japanese foreign policy and to describe the Nipponic empire as a democracy. Could this defense of a pagan government, Sobral asked, be considered beyond the realm of what Alceu called politics?[6]

Alceu accused Sobral of "aggravating resentments."[7] It was urgent, Alceu told him in 1939, to concentrate on organizing Ação Católica Brasileira, and it was best not to make judgments about Getúlio Vargas and his companions, who were simply transitory figures. "A campaign against them only helps the game of our enemies, the ANL people."[8]

Sobral, unconvinced, faulted Alceu and biology Professor Hamilton Nogueira for helping the Church "glorify" Vargas by appearing in his company at a ceremony at which Universidade do Brasil Reitor Raul Leitão da Cunha praised "the admirable educational plan being carried out by the government." Both Alceu and Hamilton, Sobral reminded the former, were critical in private of the government's educational ideas, and he suggested that the two of them were becoming involved in political matters.[9]

At the same time, Sobral criticized Alceu for praising the authoritarianism of Portugal without appreciating that it was not carried out to benefit Christian morality in the family.[10] As for Brazilian government authoritarianism, Sobral described Alceu's capitulation to it as having become "absolute." When he made this charge he was feeling resentful because of Alceu's failure even to discuss with him a decision of Church leaders that denied his wish to publish a preface in a brochure containing a speech by Alceu.[11] Sobral complained, as he had done earlier, that Leme, Alceu, and Leonel Franca had reduced him to a mere decoration in Ação Católica, and he argued the organization's initiatives should be in the hands of more than three people.[12]

In response, Alceu pointed out that Pope Pius XI had made it clear in 1930 that Ação Católica was subordinate to the Church hierarchy. "The initiatives of which you speak," Alceu wrote, "must be rigorously within the general lines that determine our activity."[13]

5. Returning to TSN Cases (1939–1940)

Francisco Campos, observing the Estado Novo's first anniversary, gave a speech disparaging Brazil before November 1937. Sobral, perhaps more indignant than surprised, wrote the justice minister to express amazement that he had described "the Brazil of yesterday" as a "no man's land" of irresponsible institutions. "What exists now," Sobral added, "is a nation whose elites are robbed of their natural ascendancy over their fellow citizens—a robbery carried out so that half a dozen men can place their ambition above the well-being of every Brazilian." The Estado Novo, he said, was nothing *novo* but merely a transfer to the whole nation of "the dictatorship of positivism, mixed with the *caudilhismo* that Júlio de Castilhos brought to Rio Grande do Sul when the Brazilian Republic was getting started."[1]

With the TSN running out of cases, Vargas and Campos gave it new meaning by making it, and not the regular justice system, responsible for judging crimes against the *economia popular*.[2] Issuing Decree-Law 869 on November 18, 1938, they listed as crimes: charging interest rates above 1 percent per month, curtailing production in order to raise prices, charging prices above those officially set, discouraging competition by entering into sellers' alliances or by reducing prices below production costs, stipulating sales prices to be used by wholesalers or retailers, and forcing sellers to abstain from offering the merchandise of rival producers.[3]

Campos, defending the new law in an interview, attributed the difficulties in obtaining convictions in the regular courts to the "juridical formalities" found there. Decree-Law 869, he said, would reduce by almost 100 percent the possibility of "chicanery" by lawyers and the delays of judgments. Sobral told the OAB that it should vigorously object to Campos' remark about lawyers; and, in his own "vehement protest" sent to the justice minister, he called Campos' statements incredible—especially in view of the behavior of the TSN, "a mere police court."[4]

Sobral's withdrawal from TSN cases did not mean that he expected his office companions, Raymundo Lopes Machado, Wilson Salazar, and Gabriel Costa Carvalho, to follow his example to the detriment of their incomes and reputations.[5] Before leaving on vacation late in February 1939, he offered them guidance on TSN cases. He also drew up a paper with arguments that could be used in the defense of mining school student Cassio Lanari and Cassio's uncle, Gil Guatemozim, neither of whom had furthered the Integralista uprising of May 1938. And he worked on the case of one of his old clients, the Pequena Cruzada group of nuns, whose orphanage building in Rio had been collapsing, leading to controversies with the contractors.[6]

Sobral's vacation, his first in three years, was spent relaxing, as in 1936, at the *fazendas* of two friends in southwest Minas: José Tocqueville Costa Carvalho, of Muzambinho, whose younger son Gabriel was an affectionately regarded office companion, and Lindolpho Pio da Silva Dias, who continued to hope for commercial success from the bauxite at his *fazenda* near Poços de Caldas.[7]

Upon returning to Rio, Sobral found that the financial situation of Affonso Penna Júnior had worsened. Already Sobral had reduced his own indebtedness to Penna from over 100 contos to 40 with the help of a loan of 60 from the Sul America financing firm, and he asked Benjamin Antunes de Oliveira Filho to find him another lender so that he could pay off Penna in full. But Sobral was too poor a credit risk for this. As he wrote Augusto Frederico Schmidt and Waldemar de Moraes, friends since the days of Jackson de Figueiredo, he could not keep up with payments due on borrowings he had already made nor on payments due for the schooling of his children.[8]

More cheerful news came from the TSN, thanks to Luiz Rosati, father of Renato Rosati, a student from Niterói sentenced to spend 3¼ years in prison. Luiz turned to men of influence to exert pressure on TSN judges. Sobral, agreeing with the elder Rosati's method, remarked that in view of "the merely political character" of the TSN, it was important to have people close to the government let the TSN know that the administration favored a shorter sentence for Renato. He discussed legal arguments with Luiz Rosati.[9]

Renato's sentence was reduced to one year, and he was set free, having already been held longer than that.[10] Sobral, deciding to return to TSN work, secured reviews of the sentences of all those whose cases were similar to that of Renato, and these clients were liberated in January 1940.[11]

Sobral's return to TSN work allowed him to play a useful role as a defense lawyer in a case that originated in São Paulo against former governor and presidential candidate Armando de Sales Oliveira and others said to have been active in São Paulo in planning for revolts in 1938. Some of the defendants, like Armando Sales, had been ordered to leave Brazil and had joined Octavio Mangabeira in Paris late in 1938. It was on behalf of three others, still in Brazil, that São Paulo lawyer Luiz Corrêa de Brito turned in April 1940 to Sobral, his friend from school days.[12]

The case involved forty-five machine guns that had been in the possession of Nelson Ottoni de Rezende. After Nelson had been taken from his home in São Paulo city for questioning by the police, his wife, Pola, had become worried that the guns would be found where they were kept, at the Rezendes' country place, and she had persuaded their nephews Urbano and Renato Rezende Barbosa to hide them. Despite the hiding, the arms had been discovered by the authorities, and so, when lawyer Luiz Corrêa de Brito appealed to Sobral, Nelson and his nephews were in prison in Rio, awaiting a ruling of the TSN.[13]

With the help of a letter from the São Paulo Institute of Engineering, Sobral obtained the release of the three defendants from prison. And then he submitted a brief to point out to Antônio Pereira Braga, the judge chosen to make the court's initial decision, that in 1936 the São Paulo state government had asked Nelson Ottoni de Rezende to keep automatic rifles on hand in case of a Communist uprising or an Integralista revolt.[14]

Braga in August 1940 surprised Sobral by finding Nelson and his nephews guilty. Sobral, explaining the decision to São Paulo lawyer

Luiz Corrêa de Brito, said that Pereira Braga had been determined to "find a scapegoat to prevent complete ridicule from falling on the São Paulo police, who have been berated by public opinion for the way they handled the so-called *Conspiração Armandista*."[15]

For the 2ª Instância (second stage) judgment by the full TSN, Sobral gathered more evidence about the authorization of São Paulo state for Nelson to possess arms.[16] While doing this he found that Nelson's wife Pola and friends of her husband were blaming his "incapacity" for Pereira Braga's decision. When two men came to his office to suggest that Mário Bulhões Pedreira be called in to help with the defense, Sobral asserted that he would not handle the case if they lacked complete confidence in him, in which case they should turn at once to Mário. One of the men rather furiously declared that the case needed better handling, but Pola dropped the idea of turning to Mário.[17]

Her decision was vindicated in September 1940 when a majority of the TSN absolved Nelson and his nephews.[18]

6.   A Physical Scuffle with "Horse Trainer" Caneppa (1938)

The Comintern and other organizations campaigned to have Prestes' daughter, "a beautiful little girl with big blue eyes," placed in the care of Leocádia in Paris instead of in a Nazi orphanage. Leocádia, reporting to Sobral in April 1938 about the campaign's "victory," expressed alarm about her son because a month had passed since she had heard from him.[1]

Sobral, who had not seen Prestes since late 1937, made his third attempt of the new year on May 6, but, after an hour's wait at the Casa de Correção, was told that prison director Caneppa was too busy to see him. He wrote Leocádia that Caneppa simply ignored an order to allow his visits, issued in January by the justice ministry's Negrão de Lima, and, in order to punish Prestes for protesting cruel treatment of Berger, was denying him reading material and access to his cell's patio for thirty days.[2]

At his office on May 31, Sobral found a letter from Prestes telling of his need to discuss with him the appeal to be made to the Supremo Tribunal Militar (STM) for a revision of its decision of December 1937.[3] After arriving home that evening, Sobral was visited by a relative of Hasselmann who sought his help for the arrested navy officer. At the TSN the next morning Sobral received an authorization from Judge Alberto de Lemos Basto allowing him to see Hasselmann. To a note on a card for Caneppa, whom Sobral had seen only once, Sobral attached the judge's authorization along with the letter from Prestes.[4]

With these papers, on that afternoon of June 1 Sobral went to the room that, on his May 6 visit, had served as the prison director's waiting room. He was unaware that the room had become Caneppa's office. Because of his myopia he believed he was presenting the papers to a clerk, and he apologized when he found he was dealing, instead, with Caneppa himself. The director, after reprimanding the doorman for having allowed Sobral to enter unannounced, looked at the papers and told Sobral he could see Hasselmann but that a visit to Prestes would require an "express authorization of the TSN." Sobral replied that the TSN was unlikely to furnish one because the Prestes case was in the hands of the STM.[5]

Caneppa, on his feet, repeated in a harsh tone that without a TSN authorization Sobral could not see Prestes. In an equally unfriendly tone, Sobral reminded Caneppa of Negrão's directive of January. Sobral, retreating to a chair near a door, was followed by Caneppa, who lectured him about his need to show greater courtesy to himself, the director. That courtesy, he maintained, had been lacking when Sobral, in January, had written Caneppa to protest against his letters to clients being opened and read "by anyone, no matter who," words not proper for a reference to the director. A lack of courtesy, Sobral replied, was being demonstrated by Caneppa, acting as though he were dealing with a subordinate.[6]

Caneppa, enraged, called Sobral a liar, whereupon Sobral said the liar was Caneppa.[7] The two men glared at each other. Caneppa, tall and athletic, made a gesture as though he were going to strike Sobral. After Sobral reacted, to ward off a possible blow, Caneppa seized the lapels of Sobral's jacket. While Sobral resisted, one of his legs hit the director.[8]

Bureaucrats and inspectors, about eight in number, rushed into the room and forced Sobral into an adjoining room, used by secretaries and clerks. In the doorway between the rooms, Caneppa shouted: "Arrest that man!" Someone else shouted that Sobral had come "to insult the director in his office."[9]

Sobral, after being searched by investigators, spent two hours on a sofa in the secretaries' office, and then a police *delegado* arrived with a notary. The *delegado* was Paulo João Miranda Netto, an old acquaintance of Sobral, and he agreed that Sobral could continue smoking while he recounted, as did others, testimonies for the notary to record. "You can imagine the series of untruths they built up," Sobral later wrote the OAB, and added: "They wished to impute to me no fewer than four crimes in order to make bail very onerous or else to charge me with resistance in order to make bail impossible."[10]

At 11:30 P.M. Miranda Netto set bail at slightly more than one conto. Sobral, short of cash, was allowed to telephone Benjamin Antunes de Oliveira Filho for the bail money.[11] Then he was escorted to a district police station, and there, shortly after midnight, the money arrived and he was set free.[12]

Press and radio reports about the "clash" of June 1 brought Sobral telegrams and letters of support.[13] Carlos Costa, the *procurador criminal* of Bernardes (and uncle of Sobral's law assistant Gabriel Costa Carvalho), wrote to Caneppa to accuse him of abuse of power, and he advised Sobral that if he were the judge in the case he would denounce Caneppa for such abuse.[14]

Sobral on June 2 dictated a detailed account of his version for the OAB and sent copies to Francisco Campos, Judge Raul Machado, and Cardinal Leme. In a note to the cardinal he confessed to his failure to mention that he had called Caneppa a liar to his face. The omission, he said, would help in his defense against the charge of having disrespected the authorities and was probably permissible in view of the injustice of the case of the police against him.[15]

The case of the police suffered a setback because government attorney Ananias Serpa (the denouncer of Antônio Emílio Romano) concluded that Sobral had shown no lack of respect for Caneppa and had attacked no one physically. In accordance with this finding, First Criminal District Judge Emanuel Sodré ordered that the case be closed.[16]

Earlier, while the press was commenting on the "incident" of June 1,[17] the *Jornal do Commercio*'s Elmano Cardim told Sobral that a member of the police censorship had "formally prohibited" his daily from printing anything that favored Sobral. Indignant, Sobral complained to Francisco Campos about this plan of "arbitrary authorities" to ruin his reputation. His law office, he wrote, had become transformed into a "vast juridical polyclinic" to which "hundreds and hundreds" of fellow citizens turned for help that he furnished, usually without charge, to their persecuted friends and relatives.[18]

Still trying to fulfill Prestes' wish of late May for a visit, Sobral found that the switch of the Prestes case to the Supremo Tribunal Militar (STM) left the TSN unable to issue the authorization demanded by Caneppa. The STM, however, sent Campos an official document declaring that Sobral's clients were to be able to confer with their lawyer in accordance with the Code of Military Justice. After that, Sobral received a copy of a document issued in August by Negrão de Lima to Caneppa authorizing Sobral to see his clients "under the supervision of Caneppa."[19]

Sobral wrote that a "savage" such as Caneppa should not supervise a high-caliber lawyer. He accused Negrão of trying to humiliate him with supervisions by "that tamer of horses" who had been rebuked by the *promotor público* and the judge of the First Criminal District. On same day, August 5, 1938, he wrote Campos of the indignation and revulsion he felt at discovering that Campos, the minister of justice, was supporting, instead of dismissing, the man who "never was more than a handler of horses and who uses brutality and coarseness to resolve everything."[20]

Campos issued a new directive to Caneppa which conformed to the wishes of Sobral and the STM, and, as a result, on August 12 Sobral had his first visit of 1938 with Prestes. He wrote Leocádia that her son was in good health and spirits. They had, Sobral wrote, discussed the final appeal, to be made to the STM, and had spoken also about government plans for agricultural penal colonies and the possibility of Olga joining her husband at one of them.[21]

Prestes, with the help of friendly Casa de Correção guards, carried out at this time a correspondence with some Brazilian Communist Party members who avoided arrest and sought to keep the party alive. He signed his letters "Bento."[22] He signed as "Vila" when he wrote four long letters to ailing prisoner Severo Fournier, who had tried to lead Green Shirts in the attack on Guanabara Palace on the night of May 10–11. The question of individual leaders, Prestes told Fournier, was less important than the need of all Brazilians to support democracy, nationalism, and the well-being of the people. Arguing that even Vargas should be supported if he would turn to such a program, Prestes rejected conspiracy, saying it would result in a civil war or in a coup, with the replacement of one dictator by another. The ANL, he also wrote, had not favored a dictatorship of the proletariat but was struggling for a bourgeois, or capitalist, democracy, which would bring better conditions to the people and would eventually lead to socialism.[23]

Early in November 1938, Leocádia, little Anita, and Prestes' sister Lygia went to Mexico, following the example of Minna Ewert, sister of "Harry Berger." The active Minna, who was seeking to have Mexican President Lázaro Cárdenas arrange for Berger to live in exile in Mexico, wrote Sobral that she had had no news of her brother since reading in 1937 that he had been sentenced, but that his wife, Elise, carrying out garden work as a prisoner in a concentration camp at a German castle on the Elbe River, wrote her twice a month.[24]

Sobral, with further help from the STM, visited Prestes late in September 1938, but the visit seemed likely to be the last because the forthcoming judgments by the STM were expected to close the appeals process unfavorably and end his missions. The clients for whom he presented arguments on October 3 and November 28 included Agildo Barata, who had led the Communist rebellion at Rio's Third Infantry Regiment on November 27, 1935. Agildo's wife told Sobral that her husband was held in such strict isolation at the Casa de Detenção that she could not acquaint him with her arrangement to have Sobral act in the place of Agildo's regular lawyer, who had gone to Europe.[25]

Sobral argued that Prestes' pre-revolutionary exemplary conduct should be taken into consideration, that Berger had not been shown to have committed any crime, and that Agildo Barata had not been one of the "heads" of the November 1935 movement. He also pointed out that what had been considered criminal in November 1935 was considered meritorious on November 10, 1937. "And what about those who sought on October 3, 1930, to modify the Constitution of 1891?"[26]

The STM denied Sobral's final appeals. Leocádia, learning from the Brazilian press that Judge Joaquim Pedro Salgado Filho had voted in her son's favor, called his voice the only honest one and his vote "a consolation" for her heart.[27]

7. Berger and Prestes (1939–1941)

Sobral, unable to see his most notable Communist clients, spent the first half of 1939 appealing to authorities for better prison conditions for Prestes, "isolated and allowed no reading material," and for Berger, "a miserable mental case." Arguing that the principles of humanity and Christianity should prevail, he informed Campos that Berger needed treatment in a mental hospital, and he offered to raise money for such treatment by turning to Minna for a contribution and by using some of the money that Leocádia sent him from time to time to put at the disposal of her son. "Surely," he told Campos, "Prestes will not object."[1]

The government responded by sending three psychiatrists to examine Berger. Sobral noted in September 1939 that they had agreed with his contention that therapy would be ineffective in Berger's jail cell. He kept after Campos. "You have," he wrote, "the obligation to take immediate steps to restore reason to a man who lost it because indescribable tortures were inflicted, year after year, by agents of the government of which you are a part." He added that the ANL people supported Prestes but did not hide "their antipathy for the cause of Harry Berger, especially in this era of nationalist policy that regards foreigners as enemies."[2]

Sobral's scoldings of Campos also dealt with an extramarital love affair of the justice minister. He told him that at his age, forty-eight, it was inexplicable that he "turn to the most funereal of treasons, the deliberate abandonment of what you wrote in the Carta Constitucional about the family being 'based on indissoluble marriage.'" Discussing his own infidelity of the 1920s, he wrote: "I did not give heed to the wise words of Affonso Penna Júnior nor the affectionate advice of Pedro de Oliveira Ribeiro Sobrinho, nor the savage warnings of the romantic Jackson! Had I done so, how different would my life have been! What a useful man I would be today for my country and fellow citizens!"[3]

Campos, who was frequently on leave from his post for reasons of health, did not follow Sobral's recommendation for the possible restoration of Berger's mentality; and in March 1941 Sobral addressed Negrão de Lima to say that Berger had become completely insane, a blessing for the prisoner, "sparing this member of the human family" the knowledge that "the rulers of Brazil reduced him to the condition of a hydrophobic animal."[4] Late in June 1942 Berger was transferred from his cell to Rio's Judiciary Insane Asylum, described by João Batista Barreto Leite Filho as a filthy, repulsive place, lacking medical attention.[5]

In the case of Prestes, Sobral was unable to persuade the authorities to accept Leocádia's recommendation that her son be permitted a small phonograph to satisfy his craving for music.[6] But a development in 1939 gave promise of renewed visits by Sobral. The Cavalier of Hope refused in April to accept the services of the lawyer named to defend him against the old charge of desertion from the army, and the Military Justice Council agreed in mid-June with the defendant's wish to have Sobral represent him.[7] Accordingly, on June 28, 1939, Sobral made his first visit since September 1938. But it was an unsatisfactory one. Three guards were present and, as Prestes explained later, "incidents almost broke out because I used expressions that, in the opinion of one of the guards, were not to be uttered there."[8]

Leocádia, who had not heard from her son in months, urged Sobral in late August 1939 to give publicity to the "infamy" that would be responsible for Prestes' "slow death."[9] Sobral, seeking to relieve her, reported in September on his only visit to the prisoner in 1939, the unsatisfactory one of late June. Prestes, he said, had been in good health and had demonstrated his usual vigor and haughtiness. He added that her request about publicity showed her lack of understanding of the Brazilian situation and of the dangers for him as Prestes' lawyer. He mentioned the censorship, the worst ever experienced in Brazil, as well as the suspension of individual rights and "the state of emergency," written into the Constitution.[10]

Not until April 1, 1940, was Sobral able to discuss the desertion case with his client. It was a good two-hour talk, but after it took place the police released sensational reports accusing Prestes of ordering the murder of a young Communist woman, Elza Fernandes, early in 1936, and strict isolation was ordered for the prisoner.[11]

Eventually, in June 1941, War Minister Eurico Gaspar Dutra wrote a letter, requested by the Military Justice Council, authorizing Sobral to have two more discussions with Prestes about the desertion matter "under the same conditions in which the first took place."[12]

The Military Council, in the next month, absolved Prestes of the desertion charge. Sobral, calling the decision a "soothing balm" for Prestes' "tormented soul," prepared for the government's appeal for a different decision by listing arguments that had convinced the Council. According to one of the victorious arguments, the application of the term "deserter" on June 4, 1931, had been technically improper because, according to army regulations, Prestes should have been allowed eight days in which to report to the war ministry after being told to do so in a *Diário Oficial* notice of May 28. Of greater importance, according to Sobral, was the need to understand that "desertion is for those who fear risks in military life." Sobral, maintaining that Prestes had merely changed his post in the 1920s, quoted a Federal Supreme Court justice, Viveiros de Castro, who had declared it absurd to think that a revolutionary should recognize the authority of a government military region commander.[13]

8. The Case of the Elza Fernandes Murder (1940–1941)

The arrests of Communist Party (PCB) leaders in Rio in March and April 1940 were the most significant since the capture of Prestes, Berger, and others about four years earlier. Torture of newly arrested PCB members and the threat of torturing the young daughter of an arrested couple led to further arrests, and, in April, to sensational publicity about the murder of Elza Fernandes by Communist leaders in February 1936.[1]

Elza had been the companion of PCB Secretary General "Miranda" (known more formally as Antônio Maciel Bonfim or Adalberto Fernandes). Following the arrest of "Miranda" and Elza in January 1936, she had been released so that the police might learn something new by following her. Soon the PCB secretariat, fearful of what the police might find out, had seized her and held her captive.[2]

Despite her captivity, PCB secretariat member "Martins" (Honório de Freitas Guimarães) had kept reporting to the hiding Prestes that Elza's knowledge about the party and its unarrested leaders made her such a danger that she should be killed. "Martins," a PCB leadership rival of "Miranda," had persuaded the hesitant secretariat to adopt this solution by telling it that Prestes favored "extreme measures," and then he had obtained Prestes' approval of the decision to kill the young woman—a decision, Prestes had written, "reached by the National Secretariat."[3]

Still, secretariat member "Bangu" (Lauro Reginaldo da Rocha) had demurred "because the execution might result in the separation of the Party from the masses and because the girl is in our hands securely."[4] Prestes' response had been vehement: "Is she or is she not a great danger to the Party, a person entirely at the service of the adversary . . . ? Fully conscious of my responsibility, I have, from the outset, given you my opinion as to what to do with her." He had written that the secretariat seemed to consist of "fainthearted people, incapable of a decision, frightened in the face of responsibility. Either you agree with the extreme measures, in which case they should be resolutely carried out, or you disagree, and you should, in that case, courageously defend your opinion. . . . A leadership has not the right to vacillate on questions that concern the defense of the organization itself."[5]

Secretariat members had vacillated no more. They had strangled Elza with a rope and buried her body. At Prestes' request, "Martins" had returned the correspondence to him.

The exhumation of Elza's remains in 1940 and the confessions of some of those who had participated in the strangling were reported in the press under inflammatory headlines in April, together with accusations placing much of the responsibility on Prestes. Captain Felisberto Batista Teixeira, head of the DESPS (Delegacia Especial de Segurança Política e Social), declared that "the Communist danger in Brazil has never been greater than at present."[6]

On the night of May 13–14, 1940, Prestes was taken from his cell to police headquarters to face some of Elza's executioners and to hear readings of their declarations and excerpts from his letters, seized at the time of his capture in March 1936. Prestes refused to sign any document or say anything about the case.[7]

On October 9, 1940, a TSN officer came to Prestes' cell with an order that he name a lawyer and prepare his defense. Prestes sent word to Colonel Augusto Maynard Gomes, the TSN judge handling the case, that Sobral would be his lawyer; and Sobral, after that, asked the judge to overcome the obstacles "always created" by Caneppa to his wishes to visit his client.[8] Colonel Maynard Gomes, the replacement for Colonel Costa Netto on the TSN, had been *interventor* of Sergipe after the 1930 revolution but had been defeated for the governorship in 1935 by the political combination actively backed by Sobral.

Prestes' defense argument, presented to Maynard Gomes on November 5, 1940, explained that the TSN lacked competence to rule on the case because the laws governing the TSN authorized it to deal with cases concerning the security of the nation and its institutions, and cases about the *economia popular*. "The murder, real or supposed, of a girl, a minor, who lived in obscurity, can in no way be shown appropriate for the TSN or covered by Law 38." The disappearance of Elza had been handled earlier by the regular justice system in a case that had been handicapped by insufficient evidence about the cause of her disappearance but that the regular justice system had claimed was within its competence. Now the defense for Prestes maintained that the Supreme Court should settle the conflict between the TSN and regular justice, each claiming competence.[9]

The hearing before TSN Judge Maynard Gomes was for the defendants in the Elza Fernandes case. The lawyer of "Bangu" pleaded that the court allow the appearance of his client—the secretariat member who had been accused of vacillation by Prestes in February 1936 and who had been the only member of that secretariat who had remained silent in 1940. The silence had cost him all his fingernails and toenails. Savage beatings and the use of a blowtorch on his body had left him in such bad shape that the request for his appearance was denied in accordance with the practice of keeping physical wrecks, overcome with pain, out of sight.[10]

Prestes spoke at the hearing. He observed that the date was the "twenty-third anniversary of the liberation of the Russian people," and he launched into an angry protest against the "inhuman" isolation he had suffered. The press, reporting on his remarks, wrote that he maintained that he could not have written the letters to the secretariat about Elza because of his *incomunicabilidade*.

Neither this argument, repeated later by Jorge Amado, nor Jorge Amado's claim that the letters were forgeries, has stood up.[11] More recently Sobral objected to the prosecution's use of only "one part" of one of Prestes' letters, and Prestes has described that letter as simply one in which he "recommended punishment for traitors." Prestes has also stated in more recent times that, before he was heard by Maynard Gomes, he was assured by Sobral that he would be absolved but that when Sobral told him that the others would be convicted he was unwilling not to share their fate and created such a scene in the courtroom with his praise of the glorious Russian Revolution that Colonel Maynard Gomes changed his mind about absolving him.[12]

The colonel handed down thirty-year prison sentences for Prestes and four former secretariat members who had carried out the murder, and a twenty-year sentence for "Bangu." Prestes is reported by Jorge Amado to have written Leocádia: "This sentence frees me of the last remains of pride or vanity that I still possess and throws me into the immense sea of the most humble and wretched. And this, sincerely, does not displease me."[13]

An appeal to the full TSN, presented on November 25 to Judge Raul Machado as coming from Prestes, contained a quotation from Antônio Vieira, the Jesuit father so much admired by Sobral: "God judges with understanding whereas men judge in accordance with their wishes." The appeal described the police as having spent much time secretly accumulating information while Prestes, in isolation and allowed no newspapers, had no idea what was being prepared against him. On the night of May 13–14, the appeal said, Prestes was suddenly presented to "some old companions of struggle whose faces showed the sufferings they had endured. Shadows of men, not men." And it was then, the document went on to say, that he was accused of ordering the murder.

The appeal pointed out that the authority of the men in the Communist Party in 1936 did not come from the defendant but from the appropriate Party organs. "Where can there be found proof of any mandate of the defendant to authorize such a murder?" Also it observed that during the 1930 revolution some valorous army men had been killed "in purely individual attacks" that had come to be regarded as heroic because that revolution, unlike the movement of 1935, had ended in victory.[14]

The appeal was ineffective, as were subsequent efforts by Sobral to "unify" sentences in order to have them run concurrently. And so the 30-year sentence remained added to the earlier 16⅔-year sentence.[15]

For more than ten months after mid-April 1940, when the police began filling the press with stories about Elza Fernandes' murder, Sobral's letters to Leocádia about the matter disappeared from the postal system. Furthermore, a cable of November 11, sent by a distressed Leocádia about Mexican reports of the shooting of Prestes by the Brazilian authorities, never reached Sobral, causing Leocádia to blame him for failing to reply.[16]

Leocádia, writing Sobral on December 30, 1940, accused him of having capitulated, "deserting the cause."[17] Sobral, pained, asked José Eduardo de Macedo Soares in February 1941 to find a copy of A Noite's final edition of April 17, 1940, with much about Prestes, because Sobral's copy, used in April 1940 to supplement his letters to Leocádia, had not been received by her. Next, Sobral turned to a friend of Foreign Minister Oswaldo Aranha in order to gain access to the diplomatic pouch to get his explanation and the old A Noite articles to Leocádia.[18]

Why, he asked Leocádia, was she trying to hurt the one person who had never failed to seek to help her son? Turning to the pro-Prestes protests that she said were arousing the continent, Sobral asked her whether anyone had made more courageous pro-Prestes protests than he. The only difference, he wrote, was that the foreign protesters mentioned by her ran no risks, whereas his protests could put him in prison, "as has happened once." While he found the foreign protests admirable for advancing principles of the protesters, he called them "a constant source of sufferings for your son." They remained, he said, unknown to the Brazilian people, and, at the same time, they irritated the Brazilian authorities, causing them to act "still more vigorously" in repressing Communism.[19]

PART V

Dealing with the Economia Popular and Matarazzo (1940–1944)

1. Early Polemics in "Pelos Domínios do Direito" (1940–1941)

In May 1940 Sobral accepted the request of Elmano Cardim that he write a weekly column for the *Jornal do Commercio*. Recalling that Ruy Barbosa had described *The Times* of London as "a monument to the civilization of Great Britain," Sobral observed that, in the case of Brazil, the same could be said of the *Jornal do Commercio*.[1]

Starting on May 25, 1940, the column appeared each Saturday under the heading "Pelos Domínios do Direito" (For the Rule of Law). Sobral received no pay for the work and absorbed incidental costs, such as taxi fares to the newspaper, until early in 1942, when Cardim arranged a monthly stipend of 200 milreis (about eleven dollars).[2]

The column allowed Sobral to bring before the public the opinions he held about government decrees, legal cases, and the role of the law, and led to polemics. While he was defending Nelson Ottoni de Rezende's right to possess machine guns, he used the column to attack the 1ª Instância decision of TSN Judge Antônio Pereira Braga that found Nelson and his nephews guilty of violating national security laws. A guilty verdict, Sobral wrote on August 31, 1940, could not be based on the mere possession of arms but required that the possessor be found to have had the intention of using the arms against the nation's political or social order. "It is impossible to accept the view that Judge Antônio Pereira Braga has been upholding at the TSN. In a country like Brazil, not well policed, especially in the interior, the possession of arms is the only way for people to defend themselves and their property."[3]

Sobral returned to the subject in columns published in September and October.[4] He was stimulated by articles in the *Jornal do Commercio* written by Pereira Braga, who maintained that "the possession of arms is an infraction of common law and the possession of weapons of war is an aspect of that violation, transferred from common law to special laws that define political crimes."[5] After Braga wrote that Law 38 "does not in a single place speak of parties and much less of militant parties," Sobral's typist Cecy found that the law contradicted the judge's statement, and therefore Sobral wrote Judge Raul Machado that Braga had, for four years, been applying Law 38 "without ever reading it in full!"[6] But Raul Machado backed Braga's position in the polemic. Sobral, surprised, wrote Machado: "My articles are clear, precise, coherent, and reveal a perfect understanding of the material." He asked Machado to compare his articles with those of Braga, "lacking all these characteristics and stuffed with contradictions and incoherences."[7]

The heat of the polemic was reflected in remarks at the courthouse, where Braga told Sobral that he would vanquish him in the manner used by a cat which "yesterday, at my home, destroyed five rats"—leading Sobral to rejoin that the cat had sought to duplicate the feat in Sobral's yard but had been torn to shreds there by a dog.[8]

After Nelson was exonerated by the full TSN, Sobral wrote a São Paulo lawyer: "The same judges who absolved Nelson of the accusation of possessing forty-five machine guns condemned, a few minutes later, a nineteen-year-old because he possessed a Mauser pistol." The two military judges, he wrote, "are totally destitute of juridical knowledge. The decisions of the full court depend on imponderables, unpredictable and dangerous for lawyers."[9]

Unlike the exchanges with Judge Pereira Braga, Sobral's dispute with São Paulo journalist and lawyer Plínio Barreto, also carried on in the press, reflected mutual admiration. Plínio Barreto, whom Sobral had not met, had been an executive of the anti-Vargas *O Estado de S. Paulo.* After the daily's Júlio de Mesquita Filho had been forced to leave Brazil with Armando de Sales Oliveira, Plínio Barreto had carried on as editor-in-chief until the state government had taken over the newspaper in April 1940. The high regard that Sobral had for Plínio was evident in his denouncement, in 1939, of a police raid of Plínio's office during which Plínio's correspondence with a client was stolen. He called Plínio "one of Brazil's most patriotic, honorable, and intelligent lawyers."[10]

Plínio, after the takeover of *O Estado de S. Paulo,* published a column about legal matters for the Chateaubriand chain, and from it in

April 1941 Sobral learned that Plínio could not understand why the new penal code provided special immunity from *injúria* (libel) and *defamação* (defamation) for lawyers and prosecutors arguing cases. Plínio wrote that "any case can be debated perfectly well without the need to libel or defame." He deplored that "lack of discipline in language" shown by "lawyers without breeding."[11]

Replying in "Pelos Domínios do Direito," Sobral wrote that lawyers could be regarded as lacking moral fiber if they did not reveal, when necessary, "all the indignation felt in the face of the immense vileness of their adversaries." He agreed with Plínio that lawyers should not resort to *calúnia*, which he defined as making false charges, but he defended "the use of facts offensive to reputations and the use of words offensive to personal dignity."[12]

An admiring letter from Plínio, written on July 30, raised Sobral's self-esteem and was followed by a response in which Sobral poured out his feelings. "Recently I have started to feel that I am becoming considered as of some worth in legal circles of this capital and in the small circle of men of spirit." Contributing to this, he wrote, were his handling of difficult legal cases and his weekly articles, "which a small number of men of letters find, to their surprise, are written with discernment and agreeable fluency."

> However, God knows I have no illusions about the harshness of my future. Daily I see an increase in my almost insuperable difficulties. Except for a blessed and peaceful home, made happy by the joviality of seven healthy children . . . , and an office with five unselfish associates . . . , everything in my personal and professional life is infernally hard work. Were it not for my being always willing to engage in struggles of whatever sort and having the satisfaction, even in defeat, of using every means within my reach, I would consider myself a failure in view of the frequency of my setbacks. . . . I have never had a minute of rest. . . . In twenty-three years of professional life only three cases have rewarded me with more than ten contos. . . . Occasionally I find clients blessed with a sense of gratitude, but much more frequently, after I have served them disinterestedly, they abandon me. Others, whose honor and liberty I have saved without charging even a penny, invent reasons for disparaging me.

Denying that his "bitter confession" was a result of cowardice or discouragement, Sobral told Plínio that he found struggles "a stimulus" for his "virile energy." Denying also that he was complaining, he wrote that he considered himself well rewarded because he, his family, and office companions had never lacked the "daily bread" mentioned in the Lord's Prayer. "And if that is not enough, I have a new blessing: your letter, which brought me much happiness, not on account of the good things you say about me but because it shows that I was able to please and do justice to one of the lawyers who have known best how to work on behalf of the Law."[13]

By this time Sobral's full life included lecturing three days a week at the Universidade Católica do Brasil, which had opened on April 1, 1941. Following the appeals of Leonel Franca, head of the new university, and of Alceu, head of the Universidade do Distrito Federal, Sobral had agreed to become the first tenured professor of penal law of the Universidade Católica and to give courses there in penal law and the introduction to the science of law.[14]

So upset was Sobral by the "leftist ideology" of some of the Universidade do Distrito Federal professors appointed by Alceu that he described the matter as more serious than anything else he had ever discussed in his long relationship with his friend.[15] Another professor who alarmed Sobral was Francisco San Tiago Dantas, advocate of a science of law that would not be indifferent to the wishes of leaders of governments. San Tiago Dantas, whose law lectures deeply influenced students at the Universidade do Brasil and the Universidade Católica,[16] delivered his opinion in October 1941 in a major address in which he said that a political regime should give birth and strength to a new system of positive law because "the Law is the fashioner of innovations and political creations which have only ephemeral life and meaning if they do not produce a juridical order through which these innovations and political creations become a part of the life of societies."[17]

Sobral, replying to San Tiago Dantas in "Pelos Domínios do Direito," asserted that a system of law had to subordinate itself to the precepts of morality, and, through morality, to the principles of religion. He expressed regret that this concept was being replaced by steps that made the legal system a mere technique at the service of politics and governments. Sponsors of the new orientation, he told his readers, failed to understand that a system of law had meaning and value in itself. Its inherent moral principles "make it the only adequate means of honorably defending human beings."[18]

Sobral sent a copy of his article to Leonel Franca. "If," he wrote, "you had held faculty meetings, as I kept imploring, San Tiago would not have made a public scandal with his address." Sobral pointed out that most of the professors opposed San Tiago's view and that, at a faculty meeting, Franca could have acquainted him with appropriate principles enunciated in Church literature, such as the Code of Canonical Law.[19]

2. Observations about the Early Years of the War (1939–1941)

Following the outbreak of World War II in Europe in September 1939, Sobral filled letters to friends with condemnations of German materialism, disgust with the decadence of the French, and praise of the character of the British.

In one of his letters to Francisco Campos about the mistreatment of Prestes, written in December 1939, he said that his only consolation from following world events was to have found, in the conduct of British leaders, a "reconciliation with human nature, something I do not see in public men in Brazil." He told Campos that the honor of Brazilian citizens, like that of all Christian people, depended on the bravery and resistance of "that sentry that God placed between the Atlantic and the North Sea."[1]

Sobral went on to tell Campos of his pleasure to find that English statesmen, while their country was in a life-and-death struggle, allowed freedom of expression. He wrote that Prime Minister Neville Chamberlain, "instead of reducing the country to silence," handled press criticism by speaking in Parliament to defend the government's position. Chamberlain's recent speech, Sobral wrote, filled him with "immense relief" and the conviction that England would win the war, "resulting in a complete transformation of our public life." How different from "your speech of November 10, obliterating all our past and denying all the greatness of the Brazilian nation."[2]

After France fell to the Germans in mid-1940, Sobral wrote Luiz Corrêa de Brito, the São Paulo lawyer of Nelson Ottoni de Rezende, that he had never had any illusions about France: "The writings of men in politics and the military who carried on the war of 1914 in the French sector reveal a character so mean and petty that no one familiar with these writings can have any doubts about the incredible decadence of France." Sobral, who somehow found time to do a lot of reading, quoted a Polish author who had written in 1935 that France, afraid of the strength of Germany, would make every sort of concession and would sacrifice allies, such as Poland, Czechoslovakia, and Romania. Sobral told Luiz Corrêa de Brito that his hope lay in England. The war, he predicted, would be won by whoever dominated the seas. "Until now, Germany has not been able to sweep England from the seas."

In another letter to Luiz Corrêa de Brito, this one written late in 1940, Sobral decried Germany's failure to consider moral and spiritual values. He also told him that the Catholics, who ought to be the trailblazers of civilization, failed to understand the risk that could result from the defeat of "all moral values."[3]

With the approach of 1941, Sobral took heart from a joint resolution of English church leaders. Quoting from it in his "Pelos Domínios do Direito" column, he wrote: "A permanent peace in Europe will never be possible unless the principles of the Catholic religion become the fundamentals of national policy and social life." It was gratifying, he told his readers, to find that Christian principles, which seemed to have become completely buried, "begin now to revive with unaccustomed and irrepressible vigor."[4]

Sobral was displeased to find what he called "illusions about France" in José Barreto Filho, the Jackson de Figueiredo admirer who had served as congressman from Sergipe. "Don't lose time," he wrote Barreto in February 1941, "with Pétain, Weygand, Laval, and France." The "rottenness" of France, he told him, was well known to all who understood the situation in Europe. His own long-held opinions about France, he added, had once been considered "scandalous" but were now proving to be correct.[5]

A couple of months later Sobral was writing about the "indescribable elation" that filled him when he read the "virile" speeches of Winston Churchill. He informed an acquaintance that "these speeches convince me of the continued existence of vigorous and wholesome seeds of moral independence, alive and able to multiply in the future." Churchill's speeches, Sobral pointed out, were addressed to the British but were an inspiration to all men throughout the world who understood the meaning of human dignity.[6]

After the Japanese attack on Pearl Harbor in December 1941, led by Admiral Isoroku Yamamoto, Sobral told his "Pelos Domínios do Direito" readers that the Japanese government and Admiral Shinjiro Yamamoto, who had visited Brazil in 1939, had used statements about fraternity among men to mask military plans that were acts of treason. He printed his letter of July 1938 to the Japanese ambassador to Brazil and quoted from a recent Tokyo broadcast announcing that Isoroku Yamamoto, glorified in Japan as the planner of the surprise attack on Pearl Harbor, promised to dictate peace terms to the United States in the White House itself.

Sobral told his readers that fraternity among men had always been the ideal of the Church of Jesus Christ and had reached its peak during the "golden period of the Middle Ages." Never, he wrote, had that ideal been accepted by the Empire of the Rising Sun, which, "guided by the destructive principles of its purely pagan policy, has become, in the last fifty years, the most resolute pioneer of an implacable economic imperialism."[7]

3. Immigrants and Missionaries (1939–1943)

Sobral battled the Brazilian government's increasing tendency to restrict immigration and expel "undesirable foreigners."

Seeking in 1939 to save one of his foreign clients from expulsion, he had a stormy session with Justice Minister Campos, during which Campos told him that his freedom to enter the minister's office did not give him the right to tell the minister he was being untruthful. Following the incident, Sobral wrote Campos that his visits honored the minister and were a way of serving his country. "I could frequent the offices of all the ministers who serve our dictator but none of them deserves my esteem. You were the exception because I supposed that you did not judge men on the basis of their fame or importance . . . but on account of their respect for moral values." Observing that he had upset Campos, Sobral added: "Do not worry, I shall not return to your office." A little later Campos ruled in favor of Sobral's client and therefore received a warm thank you note in which Sobral expressed pleasure that their many divergences had not destroyed a close relationship based on a "capacity for reciprocal understanding."[1]

Sobral had some success in a couple of cases about which he wrote to Vargas. The president, dealing with one of these in mid-1941, was careful not to overrule the police who had persuaded him to sign an expulsion decree. He sent the case back to the police department so that it could be the one to propose revoking the decree after consulting the new Delegacia de Estrangeiros, created to handle cases of foreigners.[2] Vargas also heard from Sobral about Constantino Arza, a Spanish worker being deported from Argentina. Arguing that Brazil should let Arza find asylum, Sobral wrote the president: "Arza will probably be shot by the present Spanish government." This, Sobral wrote, had usually been the fate of "Spaniards expelled from Brazil who are Communists or otherwise foes of Franco, . . . and I know your government is opposed to sending them to Spain." Alexandre Marcondes Filho, in charge of the Brazilian justice ministry at the time, arranged for Arza to find asylum in Uruguay after going ashore in Rio.[3]

In "Pelos Domínios do Direito" in September 1941, Sobral reviewed legislation about the admission of foreigners into Brazil. Requirements about passports, he wrote, had been instituted in 1926 and were ratified in the 1934 Constitution, which otherwise reflected "the principle of Christian fraternity" and left it up to *legislação ordinária* to decide about foreigners who "might harm the Brazilian community." The 1937 Constitution, Sobral wrote, disregarded Christian fraternity and made the admission of foreigners dependent on the approval of specific cases instead of making it the general rule. Decree 3,175 of April 5, 1941, confirmed the constitution's principle and was modified by a ruling of April 25 that limited the issuance of visas to foreigners who were technicians in industry, commerce, or agriculture, or who had exceptional scientific or artistic merits, or who would invest over 200 contos in industry.[4]

Sobral, in his article, pointed out that the new legislation created, "for the Catholic Church in Brazil, one of the most serious problems in its entire history. . . . Priests, monks, and missionaries, born abroad, to whom Brazil owes in large part its moral grandeur, its spiritual unity, and its participation in Western civilization, can no longer enter Brazil." Sobral called on the justice ministry to revise the legislation.[5]

Sobral's view brought him into conflict with the archbishop of Belo Horizonte, Antônio dos Santos Cabral, who wrote the American ambassador in Rio of the need to prevent the entry into Brazil of missionaries from the United States, saying that they brought Protestant ideas. Sobral wrote the archbishop that missionaries from the United States included splendid Catholics such as those who were "civilizing immense regions in Mato Grosso and Paraná," and the Sisters of Notre Dame, of Cleveland, Ohio, active in Rio Grande do

Sul and the city of Rio de Janeiro. Sobral called Brazil's 1941 legislation about immigration much more serious than the matter raised by the archbishop. He charged that the Catholic leadership in Brazil was remiss in making no effort to have the "odious" legislation modified by the government of Vargas, who, he told the archbishop, "is extolled by you with so much praise."[6]

Vargas, in the latter half of 1941, had been elected to membership in the Brazilian Academy of Letters, an event that Sobral called "the most heartbreaking of all the unhappy surprises of the last ten years." Praising Afrânio Peixoto for being one of the three Academy members who had voted against Vargas' admission, Sobral wrote him that the outcome had been "a humiliation imposed on our men of letters, who, in incomprehensible resignation, did not know how to carry out their duty of preserving the message of austere virility and serene independence that all men of letters have the obligation to make known."[7]

Alceu Amoroso Lima, in a confidential letter to Sobral, explained that his own vote in favor of the admission of Vargas was the result of his obeying, with great reluctance, the wishes of Cardinal Leme, who maintained that a blank vote by Alceu would be harmful to the work of the Church and Ação Católica in Brazil. So painful for Alceu was this demonstration of his obedience that he followed it by seeking peace in a church in Ipanema, where, he informed Sobral, "I cried as I have never cried before. . . . While this wound is so painful, I need your prayers more than I ever have."[8]

Sobral planned to present his views about foreign priests and about Vargas to the archbishop Santos Cabral personally in Belo Horizonte during a trip he would make to Minas, occasioned in part by an invitation to address young Catholics in Juiz de Fora. As he wrote Henrique Hargreaves, lawyer in Juiz de Fora, his sister, Natalina, had been born there, and he looked forward to being again in the industrial city, "the Manchester of Minas," which he had not visited since 1928. He told his law office companion, Wilson Salazar, that the trip would do him good because his work had worn him out.[9]

Partially responsible for his exhaustion was the work brought on by the unexpected death of Cândida, his father's sister, in December 1941. As requested by some of his many cousins, he agreed to handle the estate—charging no fee in view of all that "Aunt Candóca" had done for him in his youth. It was no small task and included devising a formula for the equitable distribution of the large estate among his cousins and their spouses, some of whom were quarreling with each other.[10]

In Belo Horizonte late in February 1942 Sobral was given a reception by the Minas Institute of Lawyers. His trip included a call on Francisco Campos, who was recovering from poor health at the Fazenda do Barreiro, one of his large landholdings in the state. Campos' hospitality was lavish but time-consuming, and it, combined with stormy weather and the need to get to Juiz de Fora, left Sobral unable to carry out plans to see the archbishop in Belo Horizonte and lunch there with the Lara Rezende family.[11]

Sobral was active in combating views that appeared in the press in opposition to his own views about foreign priests. One of two articles that stirred him in January 1943 was an interview given by Brazilian Bishop Carlos Duarte Costa to journalist Joel Silveira and published in the popular weekly *Diretrizes*. Sobral informed Joel Silveira that *Diretrizes* should have disapproved of the bishop's remarks instead of contributing to "this campaign that could have disastrous results for the Nation's spiritual unity." He cited the civilizing work done in the past by foreign priests, and the benefits presently being brought by them to interior communities. He also deplored Bishop Costa's "fantastic" description of Ação Católica Brasileira as "a political party within the Church" made up of the sympathizers of fascism.[12]

More time-consuming was a quarrel that Sobral got into with *Diário de Notícias* columnist Osório Borba after the latter maintained that a German Jesuit teacher in Porto Alegre, Max Schneller, was poisoning Brazilian students with pro-German, anti-Jewish ideas. Borba's article of January 17, 1943, "How a German Teaches History in Brazilian Schools," attacked not only numerous points in a book by Schneller but also attacked Alceu Amoroso Lima, described by Borba as a supporter of fascist pedagogy because Alceu had criticized American educator John Dewey.[13] Sobral, in a letter to Borba, defended Alceu and sought to demonstrate that Schneller was not a pro-Nazi, pro-fascist racist. As for Schneller's account of the entry of the United States into World War I, an account challenged by Borba, Sobral quoted a paragraph, written by the "generous" and "intelligent" mutual friend of himself and Borba, journalist João Batista Barreto Leite Filho, that expressed ideas similar to those of Schneller. "I disagreed with Barreto Leite's opinions," Sobral wrote, "but I certainly never thought of classifying them as pro-Nazi." Nor, Sobral also wrote, could anyone conceive of Barreto Leite as advancing fascist ideas in order to "poison our young people."[14]

In his *Jornal do Commercio* article of February 27, 1943, Sobral maintained that members of religious orders could not be classified as foreigners or nationals, for they were apostles of the truth, true international teachers of the love of God. He argued that Catholic missionaries should receive "privileged treatment" by the laws and that, since missionaries from abroad were not subjects of foreign governments and could not be considered foreigners, it was senseless to apply, in their cases, Decree 383 of April 18, 1938, that prohibited foreigners from becoming involved in public affairs. Turning to the decree's ruling prohibiting foreign societies in Brazil from receiving contributions from foreign persons, groups, or governments, he wrote that the religious orders had nothing to do with foreign entities. "Money from the Holy Father or the superiors of the religious orders is collected from the faithful of the Church of Jesus Christ and is not used to benefit Italian culture in Brazil."[15]

Clearly not all activities of foreigners in Brazil were admirable. Sobral made this point in a column in June 1943 criticizing the decision of Paulista Appeals Court Desembargador Raphael de Barros Monteiro that absolved a couple of Japanese immigrants.[16] After Sobral sent a copy of his column to the *desembargador,* another member of the São Paulo Appeals Court, J. C. de Azevedo Marques, denounced Sobral for criticizing "São Paulo justice." Sobral wrote Marques, accusing him of trying to transform the debate into a regionalist question, whereupon he found himself opposed also by São Paulo law professor Noé Azevedo, who wrote in São Paulo's *Folha da Manhã,* and by São Paulo Appeals Court President Manuel Carlos de Figueiredo Ferraz, who wrote in Rio's *Jornal do Commercio.*[17]

Sobral's "overture" to Ferraz was a letter denying that he had intended to attack the Paulista judiciary, and explaining that Pedro de Oliveira Ribeiro Sobrinho, of São Paulo, could testify about Sobral's disinterestedness and refusal to harm gratuitously any fellow-being. The letter described its author as a frank, independent, militant lawyer, whose weekly articles, often misunderstood, brought him "moral compensation," and whose life was beset with poverty and the task of maintaining a household of no less than fourteen persons. After Ferraz did not reply, Sobral wrote Pedro that he was hurt, and informed another Paulista that he was "outraged" at the "slanderous" positions taken by the *Correio Paulistano* and *O Estado de S. Paulo* "without reading my articles."[18]

A little later he described himself as "appalled" to learn that the São Paulo judiciary viewed his position as having been dictated by his desire to have a Supreme Court vacancy filled by Carioca Desembargador Edgard Costa instead of one of the Paulista aspirants, Desembargadores Marques and Ferraz and Professor Noé Azevedo. Commenting on this explanation, Sobral said that it demonstrated that his disinterested purpose had been debased, "made into mere instruments of niggardly individual interests."[19]

4. Economia Popular Cases (1940–1942)

According to Article 3 of Decree-Law 869 of November 1938 about the *economia popular*, it was illegal to "make an agreement for the purpose of establishing a fixed resale price."

Sobral wrote in "Pelos Domínios do Direito" that the decree meant to say a price that would provide excessive profit. He cited legislation authorizing the formation of *sindicatos* or associations for the defense of the professional interests of their members and added that those interests included "reasonable and honest profits." He argued that unless associations could establish sales prices and expel members who failed to observe them, no syndical economic life could be organized. These rights, he warned, were being threatened by the excessively rigorous thinking of the TSN.[1]

Sobral was asked by an acquaintance whether sixty-eight of the eighty-eight bakeries in Recife and nearby Olinda were violating the law in forming an association to save the industry from "economic ruin" caused by the "disloyal competition" of those who failed to uphold standards about hygiene and sellers' commissions. He replied that he did not feel that the association violated Law 869 but that the TSN, in dealing with *economia popular* legislation, "has no logic, no direction, and no constructive purpose." "Its judges never had the opportunity to study the complex problems of industrial and commercial alliances from either the legal or the economic angle. They regard our defense arguments as purely formalistic manifestations of a juridical Byzantinism, completely anachronistic and sterile."[2]

Paulo Uras and others, founders of the São Paulo Syndicate of Retailers of Scientific Goods and Instruments, ran into trouble in 1940 because they sought to fix prices for the sale of dental products. Uras, as secretary of the *sindicato*, had signed its papers about prices and about the expulsion of a seller who had violated its pricing policy. Sobral, after receiving the case from São Paulo lawyer Souza Netto, told TSN Judge Raul Machado, who would render the 1ª Instância decision, that the founders of the *sindicato* had no speculative intention or potential to control the market but simply wished to "standardize" sales prices as a protection against importers who did dominate the market and dishonest merchants who lowered prices in order to raise them onerously after forcing competitors into bankruptcy.[3] Raul Machado, unconvinced, sentenced Uras and another São Paulo retailer, Onofre Grasiano, to 2-conto fines and six-month jail terms.[4]

The choice of Colonel Augusto Maynard Gomes, former *interventor* of Sergipe, to be *relator* for the 2ª Instância ruling by the full TSN, worried Sobral, who understood that the colonel, ignorant of the law, was not inclined to overrule the findings of trained judges such as Raul Machado.[5] As Sobral feared, the full TSN confirmed the guilt of Uras and Grasiano, even though Sobral, in a new argument on behalf of Uras, explained that the secretary of the *sindicato* sold only articles used in photography and did not deal in dental products.[6]

Sobral prepared to submit habeas corpus petitions to the TSN and later, if necessary, to the Supreme Court. The sisters of Uras, contending that the defense was being mismanaged, gave Sobral little peace until November 1940, when the TSN ruled favorably on the Uras habeas corpus petition. Onofre Grasiano, less fortunate, turned to another Rio lawyer.[7]

Sobral came to feel that the TSN, considering appeals, sometimes reversed its earlier decisions in political cases, which were often made under pressure for speedy judgments about groups of defendants.[8] But he found reversals by the TSN much less frequent in *economia popular* cases, and, as a result, submitted many habeas corpus petitions to the Supreme Court. When he submitted such a petition on behalf of José da Motta Assumpção, found guilty by the TSN of usury in a real estate deal, he had poor luck because Supreme Court Justice José Linhares, chosen to be the *relator*, opposed having the Supreme Court (STF) grant habeas corpus petitions in order to annul TSN decisions. Writing STF Justice José de Castro Nunes, Sobral declared that the failure to grant such petitions removed all possibility of overturning "monstrosities" like the one inflicted by the TSN on Motta Assumpção. He also wrote to STF Justices Laudo de Camargo and Aníbal Freire to explain that the views of the TSN and its new member, navy Captain Alfredo Miranda Rodrigues (replacement for navy Captain Lemos Basto), undermined property rights and were "anarchist" and "Bolshevist."[9]

Although this appeal, made to the Supreme Court in January 1941, was rejected, a different habeas corpus appeal, submitted by Sobral in July, received a favorable response from the same court. However, the client and his daughter had become so annoyed at Sobral and at what they called his procrastination that Sobral was calling them "insolent beyond all limits." Speaking on the phone to Motta Assumpção in July in a vain effort to get two contos the client owed him, Sobral heard him say the delay in the submission of the successful appeal had caused him "incalculable harm." Sobral retorted, "You are all alike! Quite to be expected now that you have been freed of the condemnation," and hung up the phone.[10] A more pleasant experience was provided by São Paulo financial broker Antônio de Almeida, accused of charging more than 12 percent annual interest in discount operations. Sobral, after persuading the TSN to absolve the broker, received a warm letter of thanks and a check for three contos. He sent one of the contos to Múcio Continentino, the lawyer who had introduced him to Antônio de Almeida. And he wrote the broker: "I assure you that it is seldom that a lawyer, after the complete success of a case, receives such generous expressions from his client."[11]

The *economia popular* case of São Paulo banker José de Sampaio Moreira did the most to build up the folklore about Sobral and elicit amazed comments about his principles in handling legal fees. While the wealthy banker was in prison in São Paulo, two of his relatives came to Rio to find a suitable lawyer, but neither knew what the other was doing. One, following the recommendation of Foreign Minister Aranha, engaged the services of Mário Bulhões Pedreira for a fee of between 100 and 200 contos. The other, at the suggestion of Plínio Barreto, called on Sobral, who agreed to take the case for a 5-conto fee. The visitor, expressing surprise at such a low figure, acquiesced after Sobral said indignantly that anyone who charged more would be guilty of exploitation.[12]

After the two Paulistas compared notes, they called on Mário Bulhões Pedreira, who proposed that he and Sobral handle the case jointly. Sobral, declining the suggestion, expressed his wish to withdraw. A TSN presentation, he said, was not one to be handled by two lawyers. "This man," Mário replied, "is wealthy and wants to have two good lawyers." Sobral finally agreed to the wish of his friend but made it clear that he would accept no fee. Mário felt certain that the client, after a favorable TSN verdict, would be eager to reward each lawyer.[13]

Mário was right. The check that Sobral received after Sampaio Moreira was acquitted was for 50 contos. Sobral, writing the banker on December 31, 1941, insisted that the word he had given about no fee was his word of honor. He said: "I only agreed to appear as your lawyer on account of a fraternal plea from Mário. I established the condition that I was to receive no fee. But I cannot fail to recognize the kindness of your offer." Sobral explained also that his role had been limited to two rather brief discussions with Mário. "The only person who handled your defense and its orientation, with his usual proficiency and exceptional talent, was Mário."[14]

Mário, after receiving a copy of the letter, sent Sobral a blank check and asked him to write in the amount. Evandro Lins e Silva, who handled the case of Sampaio Moreira's codefendant, learned that Sobral, in returning the check to Mário, expressed indignation at the idea that he might ever alter his given word.

"You need a caretaker," Evandro told Sobral. "I understand very well your not charging a poor person who cannot pay you, but you should accept the fee from a wealthy man." Evandro concluded that poverty was a vocation of Sobral.[15]

Debtors found the economia popular legislation useful for making trouble for those to whom they owed money. Alfredo Fayad, a successful businessman in Catalão, Goiás, was a victim of such troublemaking on a grand scale (the man owing money to Fayad used corrupt local authorities and false testimonies to claim ownership of Fayad's properties). Sobral accepted the case in 1940 at the request of a close relative of Francisco Negrão de Lima, but, after two TSN decisions went against Fayad, he almost withdrew in the face of Fayad's criticism of his handling of the case. He told an intermediary to advise Fayad: "I do not give him the right to find fault with my legal action. I do not allow any client to do that."[16]

Sobral submitted a habeas corpus petition to the Supreme Court, and he wrote each STF justice about the "scandalous" TSN rulings.[17] The STF's judgment, given in January 1942, favored Fayad; and Sobral, considering the "magnificent outcome," and the wealth of the Fayads, decided to raise his fee from two contos to four for a case that had cost him more work than any other related to the *economia popular* legislation.[18]

5. Judge Miranda Rodrigues Breaks Relations with Sobral (December 1941)

A "Pelos Domínios do Direito" column published late in December 1941 discussed the tribulations of Catholic padres judged by the TSN. It mentioned Padre Sebastião Carlos, "dragged before the TSN for asserting in a sermon . . . that in religious matters it is more important to obey God than men," and Padre João José Azevedo, accused of a crime because, in a church service, he insisted that his "spiritual authority" be recognized by a government agent.[1]

Sobral's article objected chiefly to the TSN's 1ª Instância judgment, made by navy Captain Alfredo Miranda Rodrigues, sentencing Luiz Santiago, a priest in Paraíba, to twelve years in prison for disparaging Protestants so eloquently that someone killed a Protestant worshipper. Miranda Rodrigues, agreeing with Prosecutor Eduardo Jara, claimed that Luiz Santiago, stirring up violent opposition to Protestants, was the intellectual author of the crime.

Evidence against the man accused of the actual shooting was so weak that Miranda Rodrigues absolved him and concluded that "it is impossible to name the material author or authors." Therefore, Sobral wrote in his column, Miranda Rodrigues was guilty of violating the juridical precept that held that it was never possible to decide about the intellectual author without knowing who had been the material author. How, Sobral asked, was one to know what had inspired the material author? Sobral argued that Miranda Rodrigues' decision had been based on suppositions, and he maintained that Luiz Santiago, as a good Catholic, was imbued with Christian fraternity and only sought to show Protestants the errors of their ways.

Even though Luiz Santiago was acquitted in the 2ª Instância judgment by the full court, Sobral accused the court of being disrespectful of the sacred mission of the apostles of Jesus Christ. In his article he warned the TSN that it would become a "Tribunal de Insegurança Nacional" if it did not prevent itself and each of its members from being "a constant threat to the divine role of the priest of Jesus Christ."[2]

With a note expressing esteem for Captain Miranda Rodrigues, Sobral sent him a copy of the article. Miranda Rodrigues returned the article and, in an accompanying letter, said he had no interest in Sobral's opinion about any matter, religious or otherwise. "For a long time I have been aware of your animosity toward the TSN. This also is of no interest to me. But I must warn you that when the matter reaches the personal realm of ridiculing people, as is your habit, the solution will be found in another realm, very different from the columns of the *Jornal do Commercio.* Any explanation from you, made personally or through an intermediary, will be useless because now I have this opportunity to break off relations, all of which, including those of mere courtesy, I find distasteful."[3]

Sobral returned the letter with a note calling it boorish. "Your threats," Sobral wrote the navy captain, "only make me laugh!"[4] In a letter to Augusto Frederico Schmidt, Sobral said: "The ignorant and ridiculous military man" might, "in this regime without guarantees, make use of violence against me." Sobral added: "You know I am afraid of nothing and no one, and shall continue undaunted in the face of any sort of risk."[5]

During his oral defense of his Goiás client, Alfredo Fayad, at the Supreme Court (STF) on January 14, 1942, Sobral criticized TSN Judge Alfredo Miranda Rodrigues for his rude reaction to lawyers and columnists who disagreed with his decisions, and he declared that the TSN, in decisions about usury, acted as if the STF's authority did not exist.[6]

TSN President Barros Barreto, present as an STF member, defended Miranda Rodrigues for his forceful reaction to "insults" in a letter received from Sobral, and he asked STF President Eduardo Espínola to order Sobral to stop speaking. Eduardo Espínola, according to *A Noite's* account, agreed with the request, saying that Sobral had gone too far in his statements in the courtroom. Sobral, before leaving the speakers' rostrum, said he had told the truth about Miranda Rodrigues, whereupon Barros Barreto said the Sobral–Miranda Rodrigues quarrel had been started by Sobral. Sobral promised to demonstrate later to each STF justice that Barros Barreto was wrong.[7]

Sobral's letters to the Supreme Court justices were accompanied by copies of the respectful note he had sent to Miranda Rodrigues with the article about the Catholic priests, and by copies of the violent response from the captain, who was described by Sobral as having been "petulant" and "impertinent." He told STF President Eduardo Espínola of the revulsion he had felt when Barros Barreto, "disrespecting the truth" in a public STF session, had declared that the captain had done no more than strike back against an insulting letter from Sobral. Also he informed Espínola that his article about the priests had brought him favorable messages from Cardinal Leme, Alceu Amoroso Lima, and former Senator Pedro da Cunha Pedrosa.[8]

After *A Noite* reported on the STF session, Sobral called its version false in his letters to his sister Natalina, STF Justice Francisco Tavares da Cunha Mello, and the OAB's Targino Ribeiro, who refused to handle any TSN cases.[9]

At the request of TSN President Barros Barreto, STF President Eduardo Espínola issued a public reprimand of Sobral citing his breach of courtesy in the courtroom while defending Fayad. Sobral, in his petition to Espínola to withdraw the reprimand, wrote that he had declined insistent pleas that he become a TSN judge, preferring to plead the cases of defendants, and, while vigorously doing so on January 14, had used expressions which were strong but which lacked any intent to hurt the TSN, "and much less Captain Alfredo Miranda Rodrigues." He reviewed his reasons for objecting to the twelve-year sentence imposed on Padre Luiz Santiago and said that his article on the subject had been "purely doctrinal." Also he pointed out that the Supreme Court, on January 14, had been judging a TSN decision (about Fayad), which meant that Barros Barreto, according to legislation, had been present without the right to participate in the judgment or debate.[10]

Eduardo Espínola canceled the reprimand in a ruling that revealed that Barros Barreto, having learned that Sobral had had no intention of offending a TSN member or its president, agreed with the cancellation.[11]

Pleased with Espínola's "courageous" and "morally noble" decision, Sobral discussed the incident in his weekly column. He cited a legal authority who justified criticisms of judicial rulings as long as they refrained from attacking the judges themselves. A week later Plínio Barreto, in his "Vida Forense" column, agreed with Sobral's position.[12]

6. Sobral Breaks Relations with All the TSN Judges (July 1942)

In March 1942 TSN Judge Augusto Maynard Gomes returned to Sergipe to become its *interventor* again. The colonel's replacement on the TSN was Erônides de Carvalho, the medical doctor and army captain who had defeated him for the Sergipe governorship in 1934.

Sobral's past relations with Erônides had been friendly, and, in May and June 1942, he wrote the new TSN judge, asking him to oppose the lawsuit that TSN President Barros Barreto was arranging to have brought against greengrocer Augusto Pereira. Sobral explained to Erônides, chosen to pronounce the 1ª Instância judgment, why the accusation against Pereira was "entirely unjust." "But," he added, "you are a medical doctor and therefore unfamiliar with the lofty functions of the judiciary."[1]

TSN President Barros Barreto, a customer of the small shop of Augusto Pereira, had been in the habit of accepting only the fruit and vegetables that were in the best condition and had taken his time to pay for them, leading Pereira to feel justified in charging prices higher than those on the government's price list. Pereira was seeking payment of approximately 300 milreis owed for purchases made in April and May 1942.[2]

Barros Barreto claimed that his orderly, Military Police soldier José Pio da Costa, was the purchaser, and he arranged to have three price commission inspectors find that Pereira's prices violated regulations.[3]

Pereira, at the suggestion of lawyer Cunha Vasconcelos, spoke with Sobral, who told him the case appeared hopeless, being one in which justice could not be expected to prevail. Pereira, rejecting Sobral's proposal that he flee, authorized Sobral to defend him. Sobral agreed, and it was decided that Cunha Vasconcelos would later establish an appropriate legal fee, bearing in mind the financial situation of the defendant.[4]

Pereira was jailed on a *prisão preventiva* order. Sobral, in letters to Erônides, called Pio da Costa, the complainant, a straw man. He refused to believe that a soldier, earning 344 milreis a month, spent so much on fruit and vegetables. He cited also the cost to Pereira of the credit extended to the purchaser.[5]

Sobral asked Erônides to allow him to interrogate the soldier making the accusation and the price commission members, and to ex-

amine the handwriting of Barros Barreto in order to show that nota-
tions, in a purchase record book that Barreto had turned over to the
soldier, had been written by Barreto. The requests were rejected.[6]

A conversation with Judge Raul Machado persuaded Sobral that
the TSN judges regarded his defense of Augusto Pereira as inspired
by personal animosity toward Barros Barreto. He wrote Raul that
the case was one in which Barros Barreto took advantage of his position to persecute a creditor, and he copied Raul with one of his letters to Erônides—a letter in which he complained that the DIP (Department of the Press and Propaganda), run by Lourival Fontes, had
forbidden any mention of the case in the press.[7] Thus the *Jornal do
Commercio* could not allow "Pelos Domínios do Direito" to comment on it.

Learning that all the TSN judges felt that Pereira should be convicted, Sobral told Erônides that Francisco Campos had not placed
economia popular cases in the hands of the TSN in order to allow
the court's president to free himself from his creditors. "There are,"
he wrote, "abuses that go so far as to threaten the whole system of
government. Barros Barreto's conduct is one of these."[8]

On June 11, Erônides sentenced Augusto Pereira to spend 3½
months in prison and pay a half-conto (500-milreis) fine. The censors whom Sobral had mentioned gave no trouble to the *Correio
da Manhã* for praising the decision and condemning "sharks" like
Augusto Pereira. Sobral, responding, wrote *Correio da Manhã* director Manoel Paulo Filho, with whom he had not spoken since
the daily had attacked him in the 1920s. He told what he knew
about "the case of the greengrocer" and said he would appeal to the
full TSN and then probably submit a habeas corpus petition to the
Supreme Court.[9]

The TSN delayed so long in arranging for a 2ª Instância hearing
that Sobral complained, calling it the longest in the six-year history of the TSN. What Sobral did not know was that, during the
delay, men connected with the TSN negotiated with his imprisoned
client, offering to reduce his sentence to thirty days and thus set
him free if he would sign a letter, addressed to Erônides, blaming his
predicament on Sobral's poor defense and Sobral's desire to use the
case to disparage Barros Barreto.[10]

At last a *relator* was named: navy Captain Alfredo Miranda Rodrigues, who had broken with Sobral after receiving Sobral's article
about his twelve-year sentencing of Padre Luiz Santiago. And so, on

July 17, Sobral appeared before the full TSN, where Antônio Pereira Braga presided because Barros Barreto disqualified himself. Sobral read an appeal (prepared in writing "to avoid the excesses of improvisation") that demonstrated that the purchaser had been Barros Barreto and not the soldier. He declared that notes in the purchase record book were in Barros Barreto's handwriting and argued that written prices there constituted no proof about final prices because lower prices had sometimes been agreed upon later. And he cited a legal authority who had asserted that government ceiling prices could be exceeded for goods of exceptionally high quality. Sobral's presentation was followed by judges' remarks that struck him as hateful and unjust, made with the purpose of "splattering mud" on his "untarnished professional honor."[11]

Indignantly Sobral strode out, thus missing the high point of the session, the reading of a letter from his client to Erônides de Carvalho. In it Augusto Pereira said that Sobral, instead of protecting the defendant's interest, had given vent to the passion with which he hated "his enemy," Barros Barreto. The letter also accused Sobral of having one other interest, the receipt of a 5-conto fee, and said that Sobral had promised, in return for such a sum, to obtain an acquittal.[12]

Sobral's reactions were given in harsh letters to Augusto Pereira and to the civilian TSN judges who had participated in the session of July 17. He told the grocer that his "iniquitous, miserable, and slanderous letter," signed to gain his immediate freedom, aroused Sobral's pity, not ire. "You were in a dismal prison and did not perceive that they wished not only to cover you with dishonor but also to soil the professional reputation of your lawyer, who, in the forceful defense of your disregarded rights, had no hesitation in facing every risk and in sacrificing the future of his activity at the TSN." Sobral wrote that, before the case, neither Barros Barreto nor Erônides de Carvalho had been his personal enemies. "Today, exclusively on your account, they both honor me with their impotent hatred."[13]

Sobral opened his letter to Raul Machado by informing him that he was breaking forever their personal relations—relations that had become affectionate during six years. He accused Raul of having violated his obligations as a friend and as a judge, and he called it incredible that Raul had supported, if only by his silence, the "satanic plot" to "liquidate" Sobral, "carried out in your presence by diabolical minds."[14] Likewise Sobral wrote bitter letters to Judges Pedro

Borges da Silva and Antônio Pereira Braga informing them of the end of his personal relations with them.

Sobral's break with Antônio Pereira Braga ended twenty years of personal relations. He wrote Braga to tell him that, as acting TSN president on July 17, he should have prevented the reading of Augusto Pereira's "revolting" letter and should have praised the virility of Sobral's Herculean endeavor "to free an unprotected man of the people from the cruel, implacable claws of someone all-powerful." Sobral had, he wrote Braga, been fortunate in his unplanned departure from the courtroom before the reading of the grocer's letter. Otherwise, he said, he would have created a scene that would have had dire consequences, with Braga using "in a vigorous manner" police powers against Sobral.[15]

In letters written early in 1943 to Porto Alegre lawyer Adroaldo Mesquita da Costa, Sobral notified his Gaúcho Catholic friend that, on account of his break with all TSN judges, he was transferring to Evandro Lins e Silva the defense of Oscar Leopoldo Becker, accused of criticizing Rio Grande do Sul authorities. The "so-called case of the greengrocer," he told Adroaldo, had provoked an enormous repercussion in all of Brazil and been the subject of an article written by José Eduardo de Macedo Soares.[16] Sobral's book about the case, published in 1942, contributed to the repercussion.

Early in 1943 Sobral was asked about *economia popular* cases (under Law 869 of November 1938) by the Washington-appointed Morris L. Cooke Commission, studying the economic impact of the war on Brazil.[17] He replied that the TSN, since its inception late in 1936, had dealt with about 2,400 cases, and, since the promulgation of Law 869, had handled about 1,500 cases. He guessed that about 50 percent of these 1,500 cases had to do with infractions of Law 869.[18]

Some usury cases, Sobral reported, were judged simply on the basis of the legally established interest rate ceiling. But, he added, "all the remaining economic questions brought up by Decree 869" were subject to divergent interpretations, which was not surprising because the TSN had not a single judge equipped to handle the economic questions that needed to be addressed.

Sobral wrote that those responsible for starting *economia popular* cases were the TSN president or the Rio police chief or the *delegados de polícia* of local communities. The aggrieved party usually petitioned the TSN president (in Rio) or the local police *delegado* (outside Rio), and the recipient of the petition, if he felt the case merited consideration, would order a police investigation. What followed, according to Sobral's report, was a demand for a declaration from the defendant, who was frequently arrested, and then the gathering of testimonies from witnesses of the plaintiff by the police, who seldom heard defense witnesses. Concluding that in practice the accuser had all the rights and the defense none, Sobral reminded the Cooke Commission that since November 10, 1937, the police had been able to arrest whomever they wanted, ransack homes, and make searches and seizures, without the accused having access to any TSN judge for the purpose of submitting objections. Witnesses for the plaintiffs, Sobral explained, did not testify before the TSN, and their testimonies were recorded without the presence of the accused or his lawyer, neither of whom was allowed to interrogate them.

Sobral pointed out that according to Decree-Law 474 of June 8, 1938, testimonies favoring the accuser were to be considered truthful unless proven false at the TSN trial; but, he added, the same decree-law allowed no more than two defense witnesses at the TSN hearings, and each was given no more than fifteen minutes. In the 2^a Instância, he wrote, the defense situation was worse because of the limitation of thirty minutes for the oral defense. He cited a case involving 180 defendants, where the 38 defense lawyers, finding themselves with less than one minute each, were told by the judge to choose six from their group to speak, thus allowing five minutes per speaker.

Sobral reported that in about 20 percent of the *economia popular* cases the defendants were absolved, whereas in about 50 percent they were found guilty. About 30 percent of the cases, he said, were set aside because of situations in which the police could not reach conclusions.[19]

7. Sobral versus Matarazzo (1936–1944)

In 1936, lawyer Targino Ribeiro was handling the legal defense of Julietta Naegeli Beaufort, who was on the verge of losing her property in Rio to Indústrias Reunidas F. Matarazzo because of the failure to repay 370 contos she had borrowed from the São Paulo industrial giant in 1929. The loan had been used to complete construction of an apartment building on land owned by Julietta in Rio's Glória district.[1]

Targino Ribeiro, declaring that a conflict of interest prevented him from continuing to represent Julietta, turned the case over to Sobral in December 1936, by which time two court decisions had been handed down against her. Targino told Sobral that he was giving him nothing more than a corpse ready for burial. Although the lawyer's fee had been set by Targino at three contos, Sobral reduced it to two contos in view of the unfortunate situation of the client.[2]

Sobral studied documents. They showed that in the 1920s the Naegeli family business matters had been handled by Julietta's husband, Max Naegeli. He had signed an agreement allowing Indústrias Reunidas F. Matarazzo to use, starting on January 1, 1926, his Patent 10,663 for producing artificial silk, in return for which he was to receive 5 percent of the profits attributable to the use of his invention. When the 370-conto loan agreement had been signed in 1929 it had been stipulated that the artificial silk royalties were to be applied against the loan. Naegeli's invention had, since January 1, 1926, been used continuously by the Viscoseda Matarazzo plant in São Caetano, São Paulo. Unfortunately for the Naegelis, Patent 10,663 had been declared invalid, starting in 1927, by the First District Federal Court of Rio, and the Matarazzo firm, citing this decision, paid no royalties.[3]

But, Sobral discovered, the Supreme Court (STF) had reversed the District Court decision in October 1935 and, on May 22, 1936, had rejected an appeal against the 1935 ruling. Thus the patent had been given validity until its expiration on December 24, 1934.[4]

Sobral also learned that Julietta, after spending two years in Europe recovering from an illness, had returned to Rio in 1932 to find that her husband had squandered the family assets and left the Glória district apartment building heavily mortgaged. In 1933 she had canceled the power of attorney that she had signed in his favor in 1924. And, in 1934, she had obtained a separation decree that left her with three children to support and the rights to Patent 10,663 and to a small aniline plant in Rio's São Cristóvão district. The documents showed that this plant had been pledged as security for the loan.[5]

In May 1937, at the Câmaras Conjuntas de Aggravos (Joint Chambers of Torts) of the Appeals Court in Rio, Sobral argued that Julietta had been abandoned by a husband guilty of debauchery and wasteful spending; she was, he wrote, devoting what was left of her strength to the effort of saving the modest aniline plant, "worth no more than 200 contos." He cited the STF's 1935 and 1936 rulings on the patent's validity.[6]

After the Câmaras Conjuntas agreed that royalties from Mata-razzo, from 1926 through 1934, were owed to Julietta, Sobral sent a friendly note to Targino: "When the coffin that you gave me to bury was opened at the cemetery for the last blessing, it was found to contain not the corpse of Julietta Naegeli Beaufort but that of Indús-trias Reunidas F. Matarazzo. I won by a 5-0 vote." Targino replied that he had presented the coffin to Sobral, knowing that "only you have the ability to bring about the miracle of resurrection."[7]

When Horácio Lafer, São Paulo industrialist, visited Sobral's office in 1938, Sobral casually mentioned the case of Julietta and was in-formed by his visitor that Viscoseda Matarazzo had undoubtedly made fabulous profits between 1926 and 1934. Similar information was received by Julietta's son Max Naegeli Júnior from Ciccilo Mata-razzo de Nicola, a cousin of Francesco Matarazzo Júnior. Francesco, known as "Chiquinho," had recently inherited the management of the huge enterprise along with the title of count, bestowed on his father by Mussolini. His cousin Ciccilo, who had been dismissed by Chiquinho from the management of Viscoseda, told Max Naegeli Júnior that the income figures reported by Viscoseda were false, having been reduced to save taxes.[8]

In discussing the case with friends, Sobral spoke of his determi-nation to obtain justice for his client. Occasionally he also pointed out that the large sum involved made the case his single opportunity to liquidate his debts and put his finances on a sound basis. He ex-plained that although the 2-conto fee was the only one he had men-tioned, he knew very well that Julietta and her children "will not forget what I have done for them." Thanks to Ciccilo Matarazzo de Nicola, whom Chiquinho Matarazzo had dismissed, Sobral was able to tell his São Paulo friend Pedro de Oliveira Ribeiro Sobrinho that he had documents showing that Viscoseda's annual profits some-times exceeded 20,000 contos; and he informed Procurador Geral da República Gabriel Passos that Matarazzo owed thousands of contos to Julietta.[9]

Sobral's chief objective was to obtain, through the courts or an out-of-court agreement, a good look at the Viscoseda Matarazzo books. The strategy of Matarazzo was twofold: (1) to prolong for many years a judicial settlement by flooding the courts with appeals and claims that the patent had not been used; and (2) to carry out discussions about a possible "friendly settlement" that would not require Viscoseda Matarazzo to open its books. Matarazzo knew, as

Sobral wrote Lafer, that Julietta and her children were in a hurry for a resolution of the case.[10]

In 1939 Sobral came to feel that an out-of-court solution, being sought by Max Naegeli Júnior, was not possible and that Matarazzo was simply causing Sobral and his client to lose precious time. Still, he did not close the door, recognizing that a negotiated settlement would be to his client's interest even if she had to surrender "a part of her just claims." Agreeing to make another trip for discussions in São Paulo, he told Max Naegeli Júnior that these trips interfered with much he had to do in his Rio office. And he added: "A man of my nature, in the habit of fighting, is not transformed overnight into an able and patient negotiator."[11]

With Sobral insisting that no settlement would be possible without an examination of the Viscoseda books, negotiations failed, and on December 14, 1939, Sobral petitioned Rio's Third District Civil Court to order the examination.[12]

Sobral's petition included estimates of the profits of Viscoseda, and therefore Indústrias Reunidas F. Matarazzo threatened to sue Sobral for the crime of "stealing commercial correspondence" from its files.[13] Matarazzo's lawyer Oliveira Filho consulted Mário Bulhões Pedreira about going ahead with the suit and learned that Mário backed Sobral unconditionally and considered his probity beyond reproach. Mário also told Oliveira Filho that Sobral's combativity was such that a suit accusing him of theft would be likely to have serious consequences for the Matarazzo firm and its lawyers. Sobral, thanking Mário for his support, said that "these thieves, who live by stealing and cheating and plundering the whole world," were going to be given a lesson, "perhaps for the first time in their lives."[14]

In January 1940, Judge Narcélio de Queiroz of Rio's Third District Civil Court ruled favorably on Sobral's petition for an examination of the books. However, in February the judge shocked Sobral by ruling that the examination should be carried out in São Paulo. Sobral then turned to the 5ª Câmara of Rio's Appeals Court and, in March, obtained a decision calling for the examination to take place in Rio and include the books for 1935 (because artificial silk sold in 1935 had been produced in 1934). Third District Civil Court Judge Narcélio de Queiroz, in charge of executing the examination, accepted the new decision.[15]

Such was the influence of the Matarazzo firm in São Paulo that it persuaded a judge there, Castro Rosa, to rule against any examination of the books. Following this setback in March 1941, Sobral wrote Judge Narcélio de Queiroz that justice in Rio de Janeiro was being "paralyzed in its sovereign decisions by a mere adjunct judge of São Paulo." He expressed sorrow that a São Paulo judge was participating in a disgraceful conspiracy, and pointed out that Castro Rosa had issued his ruling after receiving a simple petition (accompanied by no documents) and without calling for a single testimony.[16]

The decision of Castro Rosa resulted in a conflict of jurisdiction case to be decided by the Supreme Court (STF). Sobral submitted arguments to the *relator*, STF Justice Francisco Tavares da Cunha Mello, and to the two *procuradores gerais da república*, Luiz Gallotti and Gabriel Passos, because their opinions were being sought by the STF.

Sobral maintained that a conflict of jurisdiction did not exist in view of the difference in hierarchy of the judicial authorities that were involved. He asked: "How can a judge in São Paulo consider himself competent to intervene in a case begun in the judiciary of Rio by the Matarazzo firm itself and which in this judiciary has been acted on at all levels and whose final ruling is already being carried out?"[17]

Newspapers, apparently inspired by the Matarazzo firm, maintained that it would be illegal and scandalous to have books moved to Rio from the domicile and commercial center of the firm. Sobral, in letters to Supreme Court justices, argued that the judicial decisions reached in Rio were legal, and he pointed out that the so-called conflict of jurisdiction case "represents the twentieth or thirtieth effort by the Matarazzo firm" to prevent execution of a unanimous decision reached in May 1937.[18]

The conflict of jurisdiction case was won by Sobral with only two Supreme Court justices (Castro Nunes and Laudo de Camargo) voting against him.[19] Then, in October 1941, the Matarazzo firm started two more legal cases to prevent examination of the books in Rio. One was an argument presented to the Rio Court of Appeals explaining why it should, by an *ação rescisória*, annul its previous decision. The other, more serious, was a *recurso extraordinário* (extraordinary appeal) delivered to the STF and based on the Commercial Code's Article 19, which forbade that books of commercial firms be transferred from the firms' domiciles for the purpose of examinations made in litigation.[20]

Sobral, turning to Affonso Penna Júnior for help, called the *recurso extraordinário* more disturbing than any of the other onslaughts by the Matarazzo group. He suggested that Penna provide a legal opinion in which it be shown that the Commercial Code, in its Articles 18 and 19, referred to two types of examinations of books and that Article 19 dealt with a type not applicable to the case. Penna wrote an opinion that Sobral, in one of his letters to Pedro de Oliveira Ribeiro Sobrinho, called "a marvel." It handled the Commercial Code as Sobral had suggested. And it declared that the Rio Appeals Court had been "inspired by a prudent will to provide justice" and had violated no regulation.[21]

Again Sobral wrote the STF justices individually. In January 1942, the court resolved, by unanimous decision, to disregard the Matarazzo firm's *recurso extraordinário,* and Sobral was thus able to turn to the firm's appeal to the Rio Court of Appeals for the annulment of its previous judgment.[22]

So much publicity had filled the press in an apparent effort to influence judges that Sobral received advice from a veteran of the bench, who declared that such publicity was ineffective. Sobral replied that the publicity came neither from himself, with his "horror" of discussing cases in "improper" places, nor from his client, who could not afford to pay for publicity, struggling, as she was, "with financial difficulties that depress her." The tone of the publicity, he wrote, made it clear that it was the work of Matarazzo, who asked "all the commercial associations" to carry out a press campaign.[23]

Desembargadores of the Rio Appeals Court, considering the Matarazzo firm's appeal for the annulment of its earlier judgment, received written opinions from Sobral, and, on behalf of Matarazzo, from lawyer Gama Cerqueira and the *procurador geral* of the Federal District.[24] The court's decision in March 1942 went against Matarazzo[25] and was followed in June by an appeal to the Supreme Court by the Matarazzo firm, which contended that the Appeals Court had acted improperly. Sobral demonstrated that the Appeals Court's decision was in accord with a decision already given by the Supreme Court.[26]

In 1943, following the death of Julietta, Sobral learned that Francesco Matarazzo Júnior and his lawyer Oliveira Filho were working with Hugo Ribeiro Carneiro, a Carioca businessman, for an out-of-court settlement with Max Naegeli Júnior. Sobral wrote to

Carneiro and Carneiro's accountant to say that the Matarazzo family was simply carrying out Machiavellian plans not only to retard the solution of the case but to avoid paying what it owed, and was seeking to give Sobral the impression that it had found a way to exert pressure on the examiner of the Viscoseda books.[27]

During 1943 and later the examination of the books went slowly. In March 1944, Sobral wrote the examiner that the documents presented by the company in May 1943 had been falsified and were not, as the company had claimed, true translations of originals written in Italian. Discussing the originals, obtained in January 1944, Sobral wrote: "You discovered that the documents exhibited in May were false. . . . You are in a position to assert that they were not such as to reveal faithfully the original inventories." The Matarazzo case, he told a friend in March 1944, had reached its zenith and was contributing to days in which he was "overwhelmed with work and worries."[28]

Odette, sister of Max Naegeli Júnior, was becoming critical of the way Sobral was handling the case, and this led to Sobral's withdrawal. The withdrawal did not mean that a speedy conclusion was reached. Nor did it mean that Sobral's work was forgotten when the victory over the Matarazzo firm was achieved in 1951 by lawyer Jorge Dyott Fontenelle. Sobral received half a million cruzeiros (about seventeen thousand dollars of the 1951 variety). The payment helped him and his law partners purchase office space for the firm on Debret Street in downtown Rio and allowed him to purchase a house to be used by his secretary Cecília Silva (Cecy) and her sister for the rest of their lives.[29]

PART VI

Giving Attention to International Matters (1942–1943)

1. Brazil Breaks Relations with the Axis (January 1942)

The Vargas government, after receiving assurances of considerable economic assistance from the United States, acceded to the wishes of the State Department and broke diplomatic and commercial relations with the Axis nations (Germany, Italy, and Japan). The break, announced by Foreign Minister Oswaldo Aranha on January 28, 1942, was welcomed by Communists, whose support of Germany during the Hitler-Stalin Pact (1939–1941) had abruptly ended when Germany had invaded Russia.

Brazil's break with the Axis had been foreseen by Sobral, who had speculated on January 24 about the possibility of the transfer of clients from the prison camp on Fernando de Noronha Island, whose location off the northeast coast would become of strategic importance, especially with the United States planning large-scale military operations at bases on the coast.[1]

Sobral also foresaw difficulties for clients belonging to the German colony in Brazil and asked Itiberê de Moura, lawyer in Rio Grande do Sul, not to delay in sending papers needed in Rio for the defense of two such clients. Writing on January 29 to José Vicente de Souza, Sobral said: "All Germans are going to be regarded with suspicion from now on. As you realize, where passion reigns, serenity disappears. Faithful, however, to my Christian principles, I shall work for these Germans as I did for the Integralistas and the Communists; I shall not abandon them."[2]

Anti-German passion turned into a wild frenzy because, starting in February, German submarines torpedoed Brazilian ships. In March, when it became known that fifty-three lives had been lost aboard the *Cairu*, Cariocas stormed through Rio's streets, intent on attacking German-owned stores, and similar reactions occurred on a large scale in the far south.

In "Pelos Domínios do Direito" in April, Sobral wrote that Brazil, "because of its raw materials and geographic position," had become, for the first time, the object of attention of powerful foreign countries. Brazil's support, he said, had been sought by two opposing ideological movements, one consisting of the Axis nations, presenting themselves as the pioneers of a new social order, and the other made up of Axis adversaries, inspired by the principle of liberty.

Within Brazil, Sobral wrote, two different explanations of the war had emerged. According to one current, the fighting was the result of a conflict of economic interests between Germany and England, whereas the other current, rejecting the economic explanation, saw the fighting as a conflict between opposing political mentalities and felt that "a victory of the German-headed bloc would have the worst consequences for the world."[3]

Expressing his personal view, Sobral said he had never doubted that the fate of human liberty depended on a victory by the English. The Brazilian government, he declared, should "imitate the virile, arduous example of the republican governments of 1908 and 1926 for the honor of our civilization." His references were to a proclamation of the juridical equality of nations made by Ruy Barbosa in 1908 when Affonso Penna was president, and to Brazil's departure from the League of Nations in 1926 when Bernardes was president—a step taken in defense of Brazil's aspirations after Germany was awarded a council seat at the League to the exclusion of Brazil.

Asserting that Brazil had reached "the most serious hour in its history," Sobral told his *Jornal do Commercio* readers: "No longer is there room in the administration for men who do not believe in the austere principle of liberty, now being defended by the adversaries of Germany, Italy, and Japan. Decision-making positions must be in the hands of men who are resolute, forceful, and possessed of broad vision." He also condemned the principle of nonintervention. He wrote that nations had the duty to intervene quickly on the side of countries being attacked unjustly, and he maintained that Christian principles made it clear that "neutrality of nations" during wartime was harmful to "the fundamental truth of human fraternity."[4]

Early in March *Diretrizes* writer Francisco de Assis Barbosa came to Sobral's office, seeking an interview. Sobral told him that he was unwilling to give any sort of interview to any publication and would send him a personal letter explaining his reasons. After he delayed writing the letter, Augusto Frederico Schmidt phoned him, insisting that he write it and adding that it would be published in *Diretrizes* with a preface by Schmidt, praising Sobral. Sobral then wrote Francisco de Assis Barbosa to say that, upon receiving this news from Schmidt, he had decided not to write the letter.[5] Thereupon Barbosa sent Sobral a letter that Sobral felt was meant to hurt him. He answered it by denying charges he attributed to Barbosa and by explaining his reaction to the news from Schmidt. "One of the things that upset me the most is publicity full of praise." Barbosa ended the incident by saying he understood how Sobral felt. "You did well to fly the white flag," Sobral answered. "You have brought me happiness."[6]

Diretrizes, being run by the able Samuel Wainer, published a "Declaration of Principles," signed in May by approximately one hundred intellectuals.[7] It described the war as "the historic clash" between regimes of oppression and the progressive forces favoring democratic liberties. It expressed complete support for "nations that struggle for their liberty and independence" and denounced "bad Brazilians who seek to place us on the side of totalitarians." War Minister Eurico Gaspar Dutra, who considered the Declaration an expression of discontent with the Estado Novo, told Vargas emotionally that its signers, some of them Communists released from jail, were using "the excellent pretext of the war" to spread "Communist propaganda."[8]

In "Pelos Domínios do Direito," Sobral explained why he had refused to sign the "Declaration of Principles." He wrote that each of the warring groups claimed to be fighting for "the liberation of the world," and therefore "to struggle for the principle of a generic liberty, separated from the philosophic fundamentals that justify it," would be a disservice to "true human civilization." The Declaration, he said, contributed to the confusion about ideas and doctrines.[9]

According to Sobral, the Declaration's signers had the most contradictory points of view. "Some of them are completely antagonistic to our reason for living and acting. Everything we do is linked indissolubly to the existence of a supernatural life. The list of signers contains over a dozen who consider the supernatural life a simple chimera. For us the existence of the war is subordinated to the existence of a much more important question: should the world be governed by the Spirit of God or by material force?"

"Thus our interest in the victory of Great Britain is not based on a preference for the English over the Germans, the Russians over the Italians, or the Americans over the Japanese. All men are brothers. As we see it, the cause of the English is the intransigent defense of the worth of the human person, one of the cornerstones of the Christian social structure."[10]

A pro–United States parade, planned by students for July 4, shook the Vargas administration because Police Chief Filinto Müller, who opposed the parade, did not wish to take instructions from Acting Justice Minister Vasco Leitão da Cunha, supporter of the parade, and therefore Leitão da Cunha ordered forty-eight hours of house arrest for Müller. Dutra led the camp supporting the police chief and Aranha led the camp supporting Leitão da Cunha, who also received encouragement from the ailing Francisco Campos and from the DIP's Lourival Fontes. Vargas accepted the resignations of Campos, Müller, Leitão da Cunha, and Lourival Fontes.[11]

Sobral wrote Campos that his departure left the cabinet without any strong cultural force and added that it was Campos' "love of intelligence" that kept them together despite Campos' view that Sobral's belief in the supernatural was mere fantasy. "Of all the public men in Brazil, only two have spiritual rapport with me: you and Affonso Penna Júnior. . . . Needless to say, I am at your side at this moment when you are cast aside by . . . that tremendous source of disintegration, Getúlio Vargas."[12]

Vargas, according to Sobral's letter to Campos, had strengthened his own position by overthrowing all the great political and moral personalities, including "the two most outstanding political forces of the last years of the First Republic," Borges de Medeiros and Arthur Bernardes. Vargas, Sobral added, had jailed the prestigious Pedro Ernesto Batista and humiliated Antônio Carlos de Andrada, replaced as Chamber of Deputies president in May 1937 by "the simple-minded and inexperienced Pedro Aleixo."[13]

Another who lost his position in the July 1942 shuffle was Captain Felisberto Batista Teixeira, head of the Delegacia Especial de Segurança Política e Social (DESPS). Thus it was to Major Atilio Denys, the captain's successor, that Sobral turned with a request that he be allowed to converse with Honório de Freitas Guimarães ("Martins"), who was in the Casa de Detenção serving a thirty-year jail sentence for the murder of Elza Fernandes. Maria Emília Carneiro Leão de Barros Guimarães, wealthy mother of Honório, was hoping that Sobral might act as lawyer for her forty-year-old son, who had been known as *o milionário* in Communist circles and had helped strangle Elza Fernandes after persuading Prestes of the need to eliminate her.[14]

Sobral, who had just made his final break with the TSN, argued that Honório de Freitas Guimarães should get a new trial in the regular court system because the Elza Fernandes case was not an appropriate one for the TSN, but this argument had not been accepted when Sobral had presented it on behalf of Prestes.[15]

2. Preparing to Attend the American Catholic Seminar (July–August 1942)

Late in June 1942, Cardinal Leme's office advised Sobral about the plans of the National Catholic Welfare Conference, of Washington, to hold an Inter-American Seminar of Social Studies in the United States in August and September. Alceu Amoroso Lima asked Sobral to be one of the three Brazilian participants, but Sobral declined. Although travel expenses would be paid by the Welfare Conference, he felt he could not cope with the loss of income resulting from an absence that would last at least four weeks.[1]

In the official invitation, received by Sobral on July 8, Archbishop Edward Mooney of Detroit wrote that fifty Latin American Catholics and an equal number representing the United States and Canada would seek to reach conclusions about "The Americas in the Crisis of Civilization" by discussing inter-American social and economic problems, the postwar world, and the future of Catholic social action in the Americas.[2]

Commenting on the invitation, Sobral wrote in his "Pelos Domínios do Direito" column that he had little prestige in Ação Católica Brasileira and that his lack of administrative responsibility in the organization left him unfamiliar with its activities in its different regions. Brazil's delegates, he wrote, should be Alceu and two others, "true interpreters of Ação Católica Brasileira."[3]

Several Catholics, such as former Senator Pedro da Cunha Pedrosa, urged Sobral to accept Mooney's invitation. Sobral, after receiving their appeals and reflecting on the material sent by Mooney, wrote Sebastião Leme to ask what he should do. He mentioned his precarious financial situation but questioned his right to decline the opportunity to serve the Church of Brazil and enrich his own experience, allowing him later to assist, under Leme's guidance, their brothers in the Faith.[4]

Leme, in a telegram, urged Sobral to accept the invitation and thus give luster to the Brazilian representation. At Leme's request, Sobral met with him on July 29 and was told that the Church would make certain that his absence from the practice of law would not be a financial strain on his family. Sobral wrote the cardinal the next day: "You have removed all the difficulties of a long absence. . . . I shall depart with tranquillity and confidence."[5]

Sobral wrote to Brazilian archbishops about his need to receive, before his departure in three weeks, reports from their districts about Ação Católica activities and Catholic social assistance. Also he asked Pedro de Oliveira Ribeiro Sobrinho to make arrangements for him to visit former President Washington Luiz, whose "noble silence" in New York "is a character lesson that this man has been giving our country, where a lack of fiber is the rule."[6]

In thanking Archbishop Mooney, Sobral told him that Brazil was a poor country and that the Church was not highly regarded among its rich men—nor by its intellectuals, who considered the Faith incompatible with reason. Freemasonry, he reported, had been influential in the last days of the empire and had been followed by the influence of naturalism in much of the period of the republic. Writing about the "Catholic restoration, begun twenty-five years ago," he called its progress slow, but said that some good results could be seen fairly recently: "the founding of the Catholic Institute of Advanced Studies ten years ago, and the founding of the Catholic University two years ago."[7]

Sobral agreed to let *Diretrizes* publish his written answers to questions, and therefore its August 13 issue contained what it called his "sensational interview" about the coming "Catholic Congress of Washington." In an introduction, the weekly said that Sobral, "unusual, brilliant, and frank," worked in a small office on the second floor of an Assembléia Street building. "On the wall, over the head of Doctor Sobral Pinto, is a picture of Churchill."[8]

In his replies to questions, Sobral revealed that his fellow delegates would be José Vieira Coelho, a Catholic University law professor, and Armando Câmara, a Porto Alegre professor of the philosophy of law. "We are going to the United States," he said, to react against what Jackson de Figueiredo had called the predominant evil of the world, the desire for material things. The riches of the world, Sobral wrote, should be made available to all members of society.

For *Diretrizes'* readers, Sobral listed "the fundamental points for Catholic social life": the teaching of religion, the indissolubility of marriage, the incorruptibility of justice, the independence of the judiciary, protection of the right to work, and the fight against immorality. Catholics, he wrote, could disagree among themselves but could never cast doubt on the dogmas of the Immaculate Conception, the infallibility of the Pope, the creation of the world by God, and the existence of the Holy Trinity. Likewise there was to be no dispute about the preaching, passion, and resurrection of Christ, His ascension into heaven, the communion of the saints, the forgiveness of sins, the resurrection of the dead, the final judgment, the reality of hell, the eternal life, and the authority of the Catholic Church. Asserting that nothing should damage the principle of human fraternity, Sobral wrote that no possibility existed for a conciliation between Catholicism and the totalitarian regimes.[9]

Asked if Brazilian Catholics were prepared to deal with the problems of a postwar world, Sobral replied in the negative. "Leading members of Catholicism, justly alarmed by Communist atheism, throw themselves blindly into the ranks of social authoritarianism. Many in our midst favor a victory by Franco, Salazar, and Hitler, and by Japan over China."[10]

Sobral mailed a copy of the *Diretrizes* interview to Father Raymund A. McGowan, leading organizer of the forthcoming American Catholic Seminar. He also sent him copies of some of his weekly articles in the *Jornal do Commercio,* which he described as Brazil's equivalent of *The Times* of London.[11]

In one of these articles, Sobral stressed the importance of being truthful in order to overcome the obstacles to inter-American cooperation. Setting what he felt to be an example of honest reporting, he wrote that "in Brazil today, generally speaking, no profession is organized in a Christian way; in the liberal professions (medicine, engineering, legal work, and teaching), as in the fields of technology (industry, commerce, and the crafts), the role of the Church is practically nil."[12] In another article, he described Brazilian Catholics as not noticing that the nation's workers were without housing, schools, hospitals, and laws for protection against injustices imposed by the powerful. Recalling that statesmen of the First Republic had considered the social question "a question for the police," he added that the best Catholics were becoming more enlightened. He cited the Círculos Operários, founded in Rio Grande do Sul by Father Leopoldo Brentano, S.J., and later incorporated into Ação Católica. These Círculos, Sobral wrote, were inspired by directors who knew that the achievement of social justice should be taken from the hands of the unbelievers.[13]

Before leaving for the Catholic Seminar, Sobral praised the *Correio da Manhã* for what he said was its courageous campaign against gambling. In a letter to the daily's Paulo Filho, he said that Orlando Ribeiro Dantas, founder and owner of the *Diário de Notícias*, was no longer alone in his "gigantic" effort to defy the dangerous seductions of those who, "with their casinos, are bringing perdition to the Brazilian family."[14]

3.   The American Seminar and the Death of Cardinal Leme (1942–1943)

The sessions of the Inter-American Seminar of Social Studies were held in Washington, Chicago, Detroit, Niagara Falls, Buffalo, New York City, and, at the close, again in Washington. Visits were made to religious, cultural, and social organizations. Sobral, who headed the Brazilian delegation, was well impressed by the spirit of Father McGowan and noted that the meetings were marred neither by pride nor "mental reservations."[1]

Sobral participated in the discussions, such as those following an address by the United States secretary of agriculture and following a talk by Armando Câmara about "the degradation of the concept of Law."[2] More importantly, he played a leading role in the task, assigned to the Brazilian delegation, of drawing up a summary of the conclusions reached during the four weeks of discussions.[3]

The summary of conclusions pointed out that only Catholics, defenders of the eternal values, could establish "the spiritual unity of the continent." It called for an examination of the unjust conditions in agricultural labor, and, for workers in general, the application of Christian social justice, "flagrantly disrespected even by Catholics."[4]

According to one of the conclusions, Catholic universities should play an important role in reviving correct concepts of the Law, "whose disfigurement was one of the factors responsible for the intensification of the crisis." The creation of an inter-American juridical institute was recommended, and Franklin D. Roosevelt's warning against postwar "vengeance by the victors" was to be heeded.[5]

Another document, the "Declaration of Principles" of the Seminar, asserted that the crisis of civilization was the result of a false concept of man and the disregard of his origin, destiny, and mission on earth, errors that dated back to the breakdown of Christian unity and the rebirth of paganism. The Declaration's statement about democracy, reached after much debate, said that the only true democracy was "organic democracy," featuring autonomy not only for governments but also for families, industries, professions, the Church, and cultural societies.

"Our chief aspiration," the Declaration said, "is the achievement of social peace by the suppression of the class struggle." Because "God gave the earth and its riches to all of humanity," a world economic organization was to be set up to subordinate economics to the common good and arrange for a distribution of riches that would allow every nation and family to live prosperously. The countries of the Americas were to provide special guarantees for blacks and Indians, and were to give postwar help to Europe, remembering contributions made by their mother countries in the past.[6]

A third document, the Closing Resolution of the Seminar, stated that the participants were to continue the work that had been started and were to develop a close collaboration among the Catholics of the American nations. To help bring this about and to handle suggestions, a permanent organization was to be established, and, in the meantime, coordination was to be in the hands of the Social Action department of the National Catholic Welfare Conference.[7]

Sobral returned to Brazil by plane on September 22 and lost little time in calling on Cardinal Leme. Finding him gravely ill, he gave him only a brief oral résumé.[8] On September 26 he sent Father McGowan the first of his articles about the seminar and a promise to distribute copies of all his articles on the subject to all Latin American participants. Informing the Father that he was not able to put all his writing into English, he recommended the establishment of a translation service in Washington. In response to McGowan's suggestion that a second seminar be held in the future in Rio, Sobral spread what he called appropriate "propaganda" among Brazilian Catholics. He arranged for A Ordem to include, in each number, a section about Catholic Pan-Americanism, and he advised Armando Câmara to do likewise in his publication in Porto Alegre.[9]

Alceu Amoroso Lima presided at the September 30 meeting of the national directorship of Ação Católica Brasileira, where Sobral gave an account of the activities of the Brazilian delegates and read the Closing Resolution. A motion, introduced by Alceu, praised the "brilliant" participation of the Brazilian delegation and proposed that its three members become "a permanent commission of international relations of Ação Católica Brasileira," subordinate to the directorship, to handle responsibilities called for in the Closing Resolution. Alceu's motion, adopted unanimously, was forwarded to the cardinal, who gave his approval in his last official ruling. He died on October 17.[10]

Already in August, before departing for the United States, Sobral had published in his weekly column a tribute to Dom Sebastião Leme, saying that the cardinal had invariably provided an angelic calm, a consoling and virile refuge from "my indescribable agonies." In this tribute Sobral had recalled that during the scandal of 1928, when his soul had been devastated by a "deadly hurricane of despair" following his "failure to observe the sacred duties of a Christian husband," he had turned to Dom Leme, as suggested by Jackson de Figueiredo, and received his forgiveness. "Dom Leme comforted my soul by giving me the honor of becoming one of his chosen soldiers to participate in the battle for the salvation of souls. . . . I never saw him disconcerted."[11]

Writing in a less personal vein in October, Sobral recalled that in July 1922, when Carioca political foes were threatening President Epitácio Pessoa after the shooting of *tenentes*, the revered Archbishop Leme rode in an open car beside the president through the downtown streets in a demonstration of support that made it improbable that anyone would dare attack the president. Sobral recalled also that, during the centennial observations of Brazil's independence, held later in 1922, Dom Leme had organized the Congresso Eucarístico do Centenário, resulting in a religious ceremony that was, "in the opinion of everyone, the great event of the Centenary. The Bishop defeated the Constitution's agnosticism."

Sobral wrote about the "charitable" and "noble" role of the cardinal in 1930, when he protected President Washington Luiz, being deposed by the revolution. And he expressed admiration for the activity of the cardinal during the debates about the 1934 Constitution, when Leme had arranged personally, "through his authorized lay representatives," to bring an end to the paganism that, for forty years, had "opposed the yearnings of the Nation."[12]

In July 1943 the Vatican revealed that Dom Jayme de Barros Câ-mara, bishop of Belém, would succeed Leme as archbishop of Rio. Sobral sent telegrams at once to Dom Jayme, pledging his own obedience and that of the Catholic Institute of Advanced Studies. But it was not until mid-September that Dom Jayme assumed his new post.

So warm had been the relations between Alceu and Leme that it can be said that Alceu was more than Leme's right hand in the task of inspiring lay Catholics to play an influential role in the work of the Church. Soon there was evidence of the sharp contrast between these relations and Alceu's relations with the new archbishop, who, Ralph Della Cava has written, dismantled the ecclesiastical organization that Dom Leme had set up.[13]

It is important to point out that the ecclesiastical organization that Dom Leme had set up reflected his close ties to intellectuals. He made the connection of the Catholic Church with intellectuals through Jackson de Figueiredo and brought the intellectuals into the pastoral work, while giving attention also to government leaders. Dom Jayme, who had received his training in Rome and who came to Rio from the north, was not considered an intellectual, and he, unlike Dom Leme, concentrated on bringing the common people into the pastoral work. In de-emphasizing the role of intellectuals he hurt some feelings. Sobral came to feel that Archbishop Jayme was suspicious of Catholic lay leaders, especially Alceu and himself, and was demanding that they be excessively servile to the hierarchy even when debating matters of a temporal nature.[14]

Another matter was the situation of Ação Católica Brasileira, which had shown signs of languishing even before the cardinal's death, and was beginning to receive, in 1943, a new orientation based on European principles advocated by Belgian Father Joseph Cardjin, who felt that it was not possible to reform individuals spiritually without a reform in the thinking of the social groups to which the individuals belonged. Plínio Correia de Oliveira, who had worked with Sobral in the Liga Eleitoral Católica (LEC) ten years earlier, led a group that left Ação Católica in 1943 because it opposed the new orientation. Ação Católica, according to Emanuel de Kadt, was becoming "an organization impressive on paper but virtually nonexistent in reality."[15]

Sobral, writing Alceu on November 12, urged him to put up with the tribulations caused by Dom Jayme and Father José Maria Moss

Tapajóz. "The crisis in the ranks of the Church in this archdiocese is too serious for us to be thinking about our personal susceptibilities, our wounded pride, and our undeserved humiliations, imposed by the ecclesiastical authorities. . . . We must overcome the crisis of Ação Católica not with human responses but with divine ones. And the only response possible for us is voluntary humiliation. Only with enduring patience, complete submission, and the most faithful loyalty in the face of unjustly authoritarian superiors can we demonstrate that we are worthy of participating in the ecclesiastical hierarchy as members of Ação Católica."[16]

Sobral tried to make it clear that his recommendation was not a betrayal of the memory of "our unforgettable" Sebastião Leme. Never, he told Alceu, was he able to talk about Leme without tears coming to his eyes. "What has happened recently is a warning from Heaven. We have been forgetting the paths of thorns that make up the Church of Jesus Christ.

"And so, instead of breaking with the archbishop, our duty is to get close to him even if this costs us indescribable sacrifices." "Your suffering," he told Alceu, "is a result of your virtues, of your immense effort to have the Church of Jesus Christ respected in the Brazilian community"—very different from "my humiliation" of 1928, "a result of wickedness."[17]

4. Questions Raised after Brazil's Declaration of War (1942–1943)

The further torpedoing of Brazilian ships and particularly a German U-boat attack that drowned about six hundred people in mid-August 1942 led to Brazil's declaration of war against Germany and Italy. The announcement, made after a cabinet meeting on August 22, was greeted with enthusiasm throughout Brazil.

Sobral, while corresponding with Jorge Amado, wrote: "When general mobilization is decreed, I shall present myself to provide what service I can." He said that if his physical condition did not permit him to serve as a common soldier in fields of battle, he could become a garbage collector or vehicle driver in Brazil and thus release, for the fighting, younger men "better at handling weapons."[1]

This attitude was inspired by his determination to contribute to the defeat of forces opposing democracy, liberty, justice, and the principles of the Church, especially fraternity. Concluding that few Brazilians had a correct understanding of why Brazil should be in the war, he presented his arguments in his weekly columns and in his letters.[2]

In September 1942, he wrote João Batista Barreto Leite Filho, columnist for the Chateaubriand newspapers, to object to one of his articles, "a monstrosity bearing the pompous title of 'a realistic interpretation of the crisis of our times.'" It was altogether wrong, Sobral said, for Barreto Leite to defend the idea that each nation should be guided by its own concrete interests without concern for the universal principles of justice and signed treaties. He asked his former client how he could so ardently favor Germany's defeat if he believed in the foreign policy that Germany had adopted, and he accused him of having embraced a dangerous economic interpretation in earlier articles that had called England the champion of ignorance, backwardness, and barbarism. "Get rid of that Marxism that prevents your heart from flying to more lofty heights."[3]

After Barreto Leite acknowledged flaws in what he had written, Sobral wrote that the matter could be considered closed but that he preferred "to prolong such a pleasant discussion."[4]

Prolong it he did in a letter of great length that opened by describing Brazil as moved by moral and juridical idealism when it entered World War I, and describing the idealism of Woodrow Wilson as decisive in bringing about the participation of the United States in that war. As for World War II, Sobral told Barreto Leite that Brazil had entered it "with no clear idea of what we want to do." The Brazilian dictatorship, he wrote, had silenced all pronouncements by men who were intelligent, sincere, and patriotic.

"We live in ignorance and believe only that the paralyzation of commercial activity and of much industrial activity has brought on a crisis of catastrophic proportions. . . . Communists, Integralistas, and Getulistas have proclaimed since 1939 that the war is a continuation of a struggle between British and German imperialisms." A better understanding, according to Sobral, would take into consideration Britain's effort to prevent the war by offering to ally itself with Russia—an effort that had been thwarted by Soviet Communism, which wished to expand by having the democracies and the Nazi-fascists exhaust themselves combating each other.

Turning to the Catholics, Sobral maintained that their support of General Franco had been erroneous but natural on account of the

Spanish republican government allying itself with Communists and anarchists and receiving support from the atheistic Soviet Union. He was pleased to report that Catholics in the United States and Brazil disapproved of Franco's policy of executing Communists, and displeased to report that Italian Catholicism, forgetting human fraternity, had made it possible for Italy to conquer Abyssinia.

"Those chiefly responsible for the present calamity in the world are the Catholics because they continue to betray the most imperative duties of their faith." At Church services, Sobral said, Catholics received, full of penitence, the Holy Communion; but, hours later, in their professional activities, they ignored human fraternity, the fundamental principle of faith in Jesus Christ.[5]

Writing Alceu Amoroso Lima in October 1942, he criticized Ação Católica for issuing a manifesto putting itself officially at the side of Vargas, as head of the nation at war.

"I was not consulted," he complained to Alceu, "and I should have been because I am a member of one of the directive organs." Loyalty to his brothers in the faith, he wrote, would not allow him to remain silent even though by speaking out he could be criticized again for being "too political" or be mistakenly accused of being influenced by his dislike of Vargas.

Pointing out that the statutes of Ação Católica made it an organization "to spread and consolidate the kingdom of Jesus Christ," he argued that its leaders should not tie it officially to a declaration of war made simply in the name of the interests of one nation, no matter how respectable those interests might be. "Ação Católica is a movement of universal apostleship, within the Church, for spreading the Faith. How can it be transformed into a purely national movement subordinated to the temporal and political aims of a particular nation?" He argued that if such a transformation were legitimate, the directors of Italian and German Catholic Action could behave in a similar way, and the world would witness three Catholic Actions, all organized to spread the faith but becoming supporters of warfare instead of preaching Christian fraternity.[6]

Sobral's correspondence with Jorge Amado took place in the latter part of 1942 after the novelist sent him two copies of his book *O Cavaleiro da Esperança*, one for Sobral and the other for Prestes, the subject of the book. Sobral said that the book's "exaggerated praise of my work and person" was accompanied by "insolent attacks on, and unjust evaluations of, my brothers in Faith and beloved friends. . . . The lovely rose you offer me is on a stem full of sharp thorns." Citing a remark of Jorge Amado that made Catholics seem like hypocritical profiteers, Sobral wrote that he was reminded of the position assumed in 1937 by journalist Rubem Braga, who had praised Sobral in the course of making "gratuitous attacks on Brazilian Catholicism." From Amado's book, Sobral quoted:

> While Jackson and all the Leonel Francas, Bernardeses, and their friends prayed in regal chapels in the palaces of Rio de Janeiro, asking that a bandit assassinate Prestes, sick people, pale-faced women, and enslaved men, in the hovels of the poor, in the hiding places that had been used by runaway slaves, implored to the heavens and to their various gods—white, Indian, black gods made from a mixture of religion and superstition—for the victory of the Cavalier of Hope.

Sobral wrote that in those days he had been close to Bernardes, "one of the most ardent patriots . . . , with a fiber in every way equal to that of Prestes." Bernardes, Sobral continued, had rejected the delights of being an ambassador to a country of his choosing in order to struggle for the principles of democracy. Jackson de Figueiredo, Sobral told the novelist, was one of the great defenders of the Christian principle of order and had never lived in palaces. "None of us, in fulfilling our duty, was happy about the task of opposing disorder because we could never forget that we were combating our fellow-citizens. We never disrespected our adversaries. We considered them wayward but never accused them of being profiteers or hypocrites."[7]

Recalling those "sad days," Sobral wrote that Padre Leonel Franca had lived, withdrawn, in his convent, preparing his notable religious talks. "He never betrayed his sacred priestly duties by praying for the death of Luiz Carlos Prestes. . . . It is important, my dear Jorge Amado, to bring an end to the myth of Bernardes and his associates placing a price on the head of Prestes." According to Sobral's recollection, Bernardes, his justice minister, and his military ministers had never deviated from recommending strict obedience to the precepts of legality, "which, in those days, was in effect in the nation." Excesses, Sobral admitted, had been committed, "as in all moments of disturbances of order," but never with the knowledge of the leaders of Brazil. "I ask you to correct, in the new edition, the injustices you have inflicted on good, worthy, honorable, and sincere men."[8]

More than three weeks passed before Sobral received a reply from Jorge Amado, who had been imprisoned after returning to Brazil from exile in Uruguay and Argentina. The reply admitted that the book contained unjust attacks on some of Sobral's friends. And it reflected the "extended hand" policy of Communism when it proposed that "we forget our ideological differences" and work together "against the demonic forces of Nippo-Nazi-fascism."[9]

Sobral's response was to express admiration for Jorge Amado for revising his judgments about men Sobral respected, but to declare that no regime of the Right or Left, restricting the liberty of the Church, could count on his collaboration. He wrote that Amado, misinterpreting the objectives of Sobral's post-1935 work, had given it political meaning, whereas Christian ideals and a concern about souls and personal sufferings had inspired his defense of Communists and Integralistas, accused and judged "with total neglect of the principles of full and free defense." Jorge Amado had written Sobral: "While attacking some Catholics, I remain apart from the idea of attacking Catholicism." Sobral told the novelist that his own philosophy was the opposite: "In attacking Communism, I never thought of attacking Communists. I consider them my brothers in Jesus Christ."[10]

Sobral wrote that it was impossible for him to collaborate, in matters of politics or public life, with Jorge Amado and his friends, "more or less orthodox supporters of Russian Sovietism, atheistic and anti-Christian." "It is clear that at the time of postwar reconstruction, the Brazil that you wish for must be far different from the Brazil about which I dream." As for joining forces to defend Brazil against Nazi Germany and fascist Italy, Sobral replied in the affirmative, "as long as the collaboration is restricted to the military field."[11]

Copies of the Jorge Amado–Sobral correspondence were sent by Sobral late in November 1942 to Catholic friends mentioned in Amado's book and to people chosen by Amado to receive his appeal for "national union," among them Álvaro Lins, director of the literary supplement of the *Correio da Manhã*, and poet Augusto Frederico Schmidt. Sobral wrote Lins and Schmidt that Amado was directing his appeal to intellectuals, in accordance with the "extended hand policy." "I cannot agree with that policy," he told Lins, and he told Schmidt that he was leaving no doubt about his position "in this hour of confusion and scurrility."[12]

On November 23, 1942, Sobral advised Alceu Amoroso Lima

about the proposal of Jorge Amado, "so unexpected, with its message of the *extended hand*, used by the French Communists starting on April 17, 1936."[13] After reading Sobral's response to Amado, Alceu wrote the novelist to reject "an impossible alliance between positions that are substantially irreconcilable." "A common enemy," Alceu told him, was not enough to surmount the barrier of principles "between true Communism and true Catholicism."[14]

Luiz Carlos Prestes had spoken in July 1942 about the need for "national union" when he had seen Blas Roca, a Cuban Communist leader who had visited the prisoner with diplomat Orlando Leite Ribeiro, friend of Vargas and Prestes, as arranged by Foreign Minister Aranha. According to Prestes' message, reported in the international (but not Brazilian) press, every Brazilian patriot had the duty to end disputes of an internal character and to contribute to the effort to defeat the Axis powers.[15]

Prestes, Sobral wrote Leocádia in November 1942, had told Blas Roca of his fond hope of embracing her. Leocádia had applied for a visa, but, as Sobral also wrote her, the situation in Brazil was such that both Sobral and Prestes felt her presence in Brazil would only add to the many worries that tormented her son's soul. This was not to deny that the departure of Müller from the police department had been helpful. Major Alcides Etchegoyen, the new police chief, gave Sobral permission to visit Prestes once a week.[16]

Economic mobilization for the war effort was placed in the hands of João Alberto Lins de Barros. When a new government regulation, calling rent increases a cause of rising prices, gave João Alberto the authority to control the rents of business properties, Sobral, in his weekly column, complained of this interference with property rights and contracts. The regulation, according to Sobral, infringed civil law and gave João Alberto powers that exceeded those in the law defining his job of coordinator of economic mobilization.[17]

When the war brought Allied bombings on Rome in July 1943, Sobral wrote an article condemning this method of warfare. Finding that Brazilian censors prevented its publication, he sent copies to the British ambassador in Rio, the papal nuncio, and others. He told the ambassador that if Britain wished to bring liberty and peace to the world in the postwar era, it was indispensable for it to be faithful, during the fighting, "to the undeniable imperatives of the moral forces on which the spiritual civilization of the West is founded."[18]

"I cannot understand," Sobral wrote Schmidt, "why a poet of your talent does not feel revulsion at the bombings from the air on non-military zones." German barbarism, Sobral said, had been condemned for the bombings of Warsaw, Belgrade, Rotterdam, London, Coventry, Birmingham, and other cities, "where factories keep on producing war equipment, but when the English and North Americans, having become dominant in the air, bomb cities under the same pretexts used by the Germans, men like yourself, who are enlightened, say it is all right."[19]

After novelist Afrânio Peixoto's support of the bombings appeared in O Globo, Sobral wrote him that such bombings, "now considered licit acts of war," had been rightfully condemned earlier by the United Nations, when it had called them typical of the German mentality. "I wanted to use the bombing of Rome to demonstrate this contradiction but, unfortunately, government censorship prohibits any criticism of the bombardment of the Eternal City."[20]

5. The Law Office: An "Affectionate Family" Loses Raymundo (1943)

Carioca lawyers were busy early in 1943 with trials in the military justice system to judge officers and employees of Condor Airlines, which, as a subsidiary of Germany's Lufthansa, was felt to have helped wartime aims of the Nazis. Sobral, having committed himself to defend a minor Condor employee, Aulette Albuquerque Silva do Valle, rejected an appeal of former Sergipe Governor Graccho Cardoso that he defend Condor director Ernest Holck. Following his recommendation to Graccho Cardoso, Evandro Lins e Silva became Holck's lawyer.[1]

On behalf of Aulette, Sobral wrote General Manoel Rabello, a member of the Supremo Tribunal Militar who was gaining prominence as president of the anti-fascist Sociedade Amigos da América, which was attracting Communists along with liberal opponents of Vargas.[2] Sobral told the general that Aulette, jailed on the charge of treason, had held such a minor job at Condor and had so few acquaintances that he "could not have obtained political or military information of interest to the German government or its agents." Brazilian military men, Sobral wrote, had sought to reveal their patriotism by "hurling into the fire" everyone who was called a traitor, without proper examination.[3]

"Aulette is as much a traitor as you and I are Communists. I don't know whether the Head of State has received a report about your Communism. As for me, I can assure you that Lourival Fontes received from Getúlio Vargas a report drawn up by Filinto Müller containing sentences from my letters and articles to demonstrate my orthodox Marxism." Sobral said that what saved him was "the warfare between the then Police Chief and the then DIP director." He added that Aulette was unable to count on such factors in the top echelons to assist him.[4]

Aulette was absolved and only then was a legal fee discussed. Sobral explained that his principal desire had been to prove Aulette's innocence, and he left the amount up to Aulette, who agreed on 10,000 cruzeiros (about 570 dollars of the 1943 variety), which meant that 4,800 cruzeiros were still owed after considering payments already made.[5]

There followed the matter of an indemnification payment by Condor to Aulette, who had worked fewer than ten years for the company and thus had no tenure (estabilidade) rights. One of Sobral's partners, Wilson Salazar, helped secure 11,000 cruzeiros from Condor, and, at Aulette's request, passed on the full amount to the client, making no deduction for legal fees still owed.[6]

In the law office, a few days later, Aulette told Wilson Salazar he could not pay what he owed because of payments he had to make to his father and brother. Still later, when Sobral was "in difficulties about a bill" owed by the office, Wilson asked Aulette to return and settle his account. Aulette returned, squabbled with Wilson, and then wrote the law firm a rude letter, attacking Wilson.

"In your ingratitude," Sobral wrote Aulette, "you had the unspeakable effrontery to threaten my office companions. They are more than my friends. They show me filial affection. . . . We are a united family." Sobral recounted what the firm had done for Aulette and mentioned visits to the Casa de Detenção by Wilson. "Let me say that Evandro, who took the Holck case that I rejected for your sake, received a 15,000 cruzeiro fee. . . . My reply to your letter is simply this: Do what your conscience dictates. If you think the payment of 4,800 cruzeiros is an extortion on my part, forget about it."[7]

Sobral's firm, the "united family," had recently lost its longtime associate, Raymundo Lopes Machado, who felt he was worth more than he was receiving.[8] In reply to his observations about the firm's reduced income, Sobral wrote him: "The disaster of my financial life and the progressive decline of my law office, to which you referred in your letter, are not caused by the facts and circumstances you mention. Clients leave me because, instead of my being their instrument against justice, I seek always to be an intransigent defender of the truth. Do not accuse me of being oblivious to the tempest that envelops me. My apparent lack of concern reflects my conviction that I must inspire confidence in those who depend largely on me. . . . I have little more than ten cruzeiros in my pocket. But I do not despair or worry. God will help me."[9]

Sobral wrote his young partner Gabriel Costa Carvalho: "It was not I who broke the friendship; it was Raymundo. He acted like my enemy and pretended to be acting in the name of friendship. But I, sincere and loyal as always, would not permit this sham to continue. Please never allow me to utter again the name of this former friend." Thanking office assistant Francisco Monteiro Filho for his support, Sobral wrote that he could not reflect on the defection of Raymundo without intense suffering. "Let us never speak again of the episode or of the principal person involved."[10]

Sobral established new formulas for calculating monthly remuneration for Gabriel, Wilson, Monteiro, and Henrique (another assistant): they were to receive fixed amounts (800, 400, 250, and 200 cruzeiros, respectively), to which would be added percentages (15, 15, 3, and 2) of the firm's total fees in excess of 1,000 cruzeiros per month. The lawyers could also receive fees from their "personal clients." In July, Monteiro left the firm, and this gave Sobral the opportunity to bring in José Tocqueville de Carvalho Filho, brother of Gabriel.[11]

Compensating for Aulette's conduct about fees was the attitude of Max Hamers. While Hamers was held at the Ilha Grande prison camp in October 1943, Sobral spoke on his behalf to the Rio police, which had received a new chief, Nelson de Mello, a colonel who demonstrated his democratic inclinations by refusing to give trouble to the oppositionist Sociedade Amigos da América.[12] Sobral convinced the colonel and his secretary, Luiz Carlos de Oliveira, that Hamers should not be considered a culprit but, rather, a victim of the episode that had landed him in prison. Nelson de Mello told Sobral that Hamers would be set free at once, and he kept his word. Spontaneously Hamers paid Sobral 25,000 cruzeiros.[13]

Writing Hamers, Sobral said: "Your gesture captivates me because I see in it the unmistakable evidence that you and your family are pleased with what I did. My profession brings me indescribable setbacks but I do have the consolation of feeling that my efforts often result in gratitude shown by clients who are especially noble."[14]

6. Prestes' Situation at the Time of Leocádia's Death (1943)

Although Sobral, starting late in 1942, could visit Prestes for one hour each week in the visitors' room of the prison, Prestes was being allowed no other regular visitors, and, in his cell, was monitored by guards every fifteen minutes. Sobral was convinced that the strict isolation of Prestes, not practiced against any of the other rebels of 1935, violated penal legislation.[1]

In discussing Prestes' situation with Prison Director Caneppa, Sobral was turning to a friend, the result of a change in relations that had followed Caneppa's apology in 1942 for the disagreeable incident in 1938. Sobral wrote Leocádia in February 1943 that Caneppa, if he had the authority, would be the first to alter the severe imprisonment rules that left her son with no distraction except for rigorously censored reading.

"My recent talks with you," Sobral wrote Caneppa, "convince me that the prison regime of Luiz Carlos Prestes has been maintained against your will." Sobral told Caneppa that he had in mind asking the judiciary and higher authorities to allow Prestes the company of other prisoners and the opportunity to do some work in prison outside his cell, but, he added, he did not wish to make the requests without first giving Caneppa the opportunity to make them, in accordance with Caneppa's expressed wishes in mid-1942.[2]

In April 1943 Sobral received a letter from Mexico in which Prestes' sister Lygia revealed that Leocádia was seriously ill. In reply to Lygia's questions, Sobral wrote that he had no material that would allow appeals from the sentences that had imprisoned her brother. The Elza Fernandes murder case decision, he said, had been based on reports obtained by the use of pressure and violence, but the TSN considered the matter closed.[3]

The Left, Sobral reported to Lygia, felt that the future belonged to it and was closing ranks around Vargas in a National Union movement in the belief that Vargas, an opportunist, would bring the Left to power, whereas the ruling class, disliking Russia, was doing its best to prevent Vargas from supporting the Left. Vargas himself was described by Sobral as following his usual practice of letting the two currents oppose each other in order to decide later which side could best satisfy his personal designs. "Meanwhile, your imprisoned brother, isolated from the outside world, emerges in the eyes of the whole world as the Brazilian expression of the great ideal of the workers of the world—an ideal created and sustained by Soviet Russia."

Sobral told Lygia that professional ethics did not allow him to act outside his capacity as Prestes' lawyer, and therefore he did not provide Prestes with information about the agitations of the world nor provide leftists with the thinking of Prestes. But the thinking of Prestes was among the subjects discussed in his correspondence with Lygia. "Your brother," he told her, "does not favor backing Vargas unless Vargas gives positive demonstrations of having modified the political line of his government. The first of these demonstrations would be immediate freedom for all those who struggle against fascist and Nazi regimes, regardless of the names or disguises under which the regimes appear."[4]

Lygia had inquired about pension payments that Leocádia, widow of an army officer, had received for twenty years until 1932, when they had inexplicably stopped coming. Therefore in May Sobral obtained some necessary information about Prestes' father, written by Prestes in seven lines on a piece of paper.[5]

A police inspector, present at Sobral's meeting with Prestes, told Sobral he could not leave without showing him the paper. Sobral, declining, told the inspector to get in touch with Caneppa; but, as Caneppa was unavailable, it was Francisco Chagas, the director's assistant, who came to the visitors' room. Sobral described himself as a man who always acted correctly and who was now being offended unjustly. Chagas let Sobral have his way.[6]

Remaining disturbed by the incident, Sobral wrote Caneppa of his determination to allow no abuse of his right to be free of censorship of his professional correspondence. He told him of the "insolent" conduct of a guard who had tried to provoke trouble in the visitors' room by aggressively wiggling a long pole pointed in the direction of Sobral and Prestes. The guards at the visits, Sobral wrote, should behave with courtesy.[7]

In his office, Sobral received a visit from Roberto Sisson, who had returned from exile. The former secretary-general of the Aliança Nacional Libertadora (ANL) showed him a copy of a printed open letter, addressed to "the honest men of 1935," about a "National Union for the Defense of the Nation, under the leadership of the President of the Republic." He asked Sobral to deliver the copy to Prestes; but Sobral delivered it instead to Caneppa and explained to the latter that he was doing this because the matter was not among those covered by his professional relations with Prestes.[8]

With Leocádia on the verge of death, former Mexican President Lázaro Cárdenas sought unsuccessfully to have Vargas grant permission for Prestes to visit her. Following her death in July 1943, the funeral of "La Madre Heroica" might have touched off a demonstration against Brazil's embassy in Mexico had not one of Cárdenas' generals declared that the ambassador was not responsible for Vargas' failure to respond to Cárdenas' request.[9] In Brazil, Sobral was permitted to place a brief notice about Leocádia's death in the *Jornal do Commercio* without any reference to her son, whose name the DIP would not allow the press to mention.[10]

Leocádia's death, Sobral wrote Caneppa, made it all the more urgent to ease the situation of the "tormented prisoner." "I have the firm conviction that you want things to be different." Caneppa agreed to Sobral's loaning Prestes his copies of French translations of philosophy books by Hegel after Sobral pointed out they had been written over one hundred years earlier "before any systematic presentation of Communism had been made."[11]

A lack of letters from Lygia worried Prestes, and he fell into a depression after Sobral, following an exchange of cables, learned that her health was "precarious." Prestes himself, as Sobral informed Justice Minister Marcondes Filho, had for months been suffering from stomach pains that were becoming worse.[12] And then, as 1943 ended, Sobral fell victim again to excruciating neuralgia in his face. Unable to use the phone on January 1, 1944, to wish a good year to Alceu Amoroso Lima, Sobral wrote his friend a few days later to explain that the pain had been terrible.[13]

7. The Manifesto of the Mineiros (October 1943)

The Manifesto of the Mineiros, a well-circulated printed political declaration expressing direct opposition to the Vargas dictatorship, was dated October 24, 1943. It evolved from drafts made by Virgílio de Mello Franco (who had been denied the Minas interventorship by Vargas in 1933), Odilon Braga (who had resigned as agriculture minister in November 1937 to protest against the installation of the Estado Novo), and lawyer Dario de Almeida Magalhães. Other anti-Getulistas actively engaged in bringing the Manifesto into existence were Affonso Arinos de Mello Franco (Virgílio's brother), Pedro Aleixo (former head of the Chamber of Deputies), and Luiz Camillo de Oliveira Netto, the foreign ministry library executive whose work for the Manifesto and its circulation equaled that of the zealous Virgílio de Mello Franco. The ninety-two Mineiros who signed it included many of Sobral's friends, among them Affonso Penna Júnior and Arthur Bernardes.[1]

The Manifesto declared that "a people reduced to silence and deprived of the faculty of thinking or expressing itself is a corroded organism. . . . If we fight against fascism at the side of the United Nations so that liberty and democracy may be restored to all people, certainly we are not asking too much in demanding for ourselves such rights and guarantees."

The reaction of the Vargas government was to arrange to have many of the signers lose their jobs. Judges were removed, professors (such as Olavo Bilac Pinto) were dismissed, as were legal consultants of banks. Pressure was exerted on private companies to dismiss signers.[2]

The federal government persuaded the state of Minas Gerais to take over the Banco Hipotecário e Agrícola de Minas Gerais, remove anti-Getulista officers, and compensate stockholders by paying only the nominal value of the shares, far below the market value. The takeover punished the bank's Vice President Affonso Penna Júnior, its director, Pedro Aleixo, and its anti-Getulista president, Estevão Leite de Magalhães Pinto (not a signer of the Manifesto).[3] Sobral, speaking with Affonso Penna Júnior, learned of the fate of other signers, such as Affonso Arinos de Mello Franco, removed from his legal consultancy at the Bank of Brazil.

Sobral, writing Affonso Arinos, condemned the "brutal and boorish violence" of people who felt that "the best way to dominate adversaries" was "to harm their economic interests." "These men forget that material possessions, which mean so much to them, mean nothing to men like you who live . . . for great achievements of the spirit."

"You, Odilon Braga, Pedro Aleixo, Gudesteu Pires, Daniel de Carvalho, José de Magalhães Pinto, Affonso Penna Júnior, Estevão Pinto,

Dario de Almeida Magalhães, Luiz Camillo de Oliveira Netto, and
so many others, who are now suffering from raging attacks on your
personal honor and economic possessions, . . . constitute the wholesome seed of public liberties, now planted in the fertile soil of our
Nation, soon to sprout . . . and become like a gigantic, spreading
tree, whose shadow will safeguard . . . the irrepressible dignity of the
Brazilian citizen."[4]

It was, Sobral told Affonso Arinos, the duty of "all of us who suffer
for the cause of democracy . . . no longer to have any contact with
men who are unconditional devotees of brutal force and who ambi-
tiously seek acceptance among the people by using the disguises of
syndicalism, cooperativism, social democracy, and corporativism."
"The hour, my dear Affonso Arinos, is one of decision."[5]

Soon Sobral learned that Affonso Arinos was writing no more for
the pro-government *A Manhã*, directed by poet Cassiano Ricardo,
member of the Brazilian Academy of Letters.[6]

Luiz Camillo de Oliveira Netto lost his position at the foreign
ministry library and set to work making his home an oppositionist propaganda center.[7] The letter he received from Sobral told him
that his punishment brought him honor. "Without vacillating for a
single second, you preferred to be faithful to the true imperatives
of your civic conscience, despite knowing that, from now on, everything at your home is uncertainty and anxiety. . . . I am totally at
your side, disposed to face all tempests. Your fate is my fate."[8]

Adaucto Lucio Cardoso, another signer of the Manifesto, was dismissed from his legal adviser post at the Lloyd Brasileiro shipping
company.[9] Sobral, informed of this development, wrote Adaucto
that if the government had any idea of the value of the human person, it would never have deprived him of something he had obtained by twenty-five years of uninterrupted work, begun in humble
posts.[10]

PART VII

Battling Cassiano Ricardo and the DIP (1943–1944)

1. The Polemic with Cassiano Ricardo (September–October 1943)

In August 1943 the Instituto dos Advogados Brasileiros (IAB) observed its centennial. Justice Minister Marcondes Filho, presiding over the meetings, turned down the request of some of the lawyers to hold three plenary sessions to discuss theses, critical of the Estado Novo, that had found approval in sessions of the commissions. After the minister's refusal, many disgruntled lawyers abandoned the meetings; and on September 2 a group of them gave a lunch to honor Pedro Aleixo, who had been among those who had left the meetings.[1]

Sobral, delivering the principal speech at the lunch, described Pedro Aleixo as one of the idealists of a new generation who had sought to install, in the 1934 Constitution, a regime of organic democracy with limits on the executive power.[2]

In *A Manhã* on September 5 Cassiano Ricardo published an article that Sobral considered a "scurrilous attack" against those who had attended the lunch.[3] Cassiano, unaware that Sobral had been the speaker,[4] mentioned none of the lawyers in his article, in which he defended the Vargas regime and said that liberals who complained of "a lack of representation" had no right to describe themselves as heroes in the combat against fascism, which had recently collapsed in Italy. "Were not these liberals, some years ago, principally responsible for the invasion of our land by fascism and Nazism? Did any of them, at the proper time, give a speech against Mussolini and his aberrant concept of the state?"[5]

Cassiano asserted that totalitarianism was associated with the philosophy of bourgeois liberalism, and he listed "totalitarian char-

acteristics" of pre–Estado Novo regimes: the lack of true representation, the domination of power by political parties, the lack of
human rights, and the acts of violence carried out by administrators because they lacked the constitutional authority they needed.
He wrote that the Estado Nacional (new name for the Estado Novo)
had given Brazil the habeas corpus and had, in the words of Francisco Campos, been concerned about individual rights in schools,
families, and workplaces—not as an abstraction.[6]

Sobral used his *Jornal do Commercio* columns to reply "with the
greatest vigor" to Cassiano's "attack on the unselfish admirers of
Pedro Aleixo."[7] The resulting polemic was notable for lengthy quib-
bling about minor points by both participants, some misrepresen-
tation of Sobral's positions by Cassiano, and some self-glorification
by Sobral. Among Sobral's positive contributions was his paragraph,
published on September 18 in his first reply to Cassiano, explaining what he meant by the "really democratic" practices that he said
ought to prevail in all nations. They should, he wrote, provide direct and periodic participation of the citizenry in the formation of
governments, provide continuous supervision of government acts
by "adequate, honest, and efficient public notice," and provide also
strong judiciaries in order that the rights of citizens (including property ownership) be protected. "These principles apply to all epochs
and countries. They are eternal, like truth itself."[8]

Cassiano, writing in *A Manhã* on September 29, said that jurists,
practiced in the science of turning white into black, should be well
aware that "truth is relative."[9] In Cassiano's opinion, "the truth
proclaimed by juridical monism does not always correspond to social and human truth." Condemning lawyers for "taking us to 'aca-
demic abstractions' and 'legal bureaucracy,'" Cassiano pointed out
that Friedrich Engels had observed that such jurists "are idiots and
scream 'legality is killing us' while we, Bolsheviks, live and prosper
thanks to the laws that they themselves enacted."

According to Cassiano, the regime established in November 1937
had removed the juridical fiction of democracy, replacing it with social democracy, "the Christian and modern concept" that "springs
from our own roots" and not from ideas expressed by Pope Leo XIII
or by Jacques Maritain, or by French, English, German, or Russian
socialism.

Cassiano's article, called "The Apostle and His Errors," said that
Sobral had demonstrated how often "a jurist who calls himself the

apostle of truth can be the victim of self-deceit and therefore betray his mission." Sobral's first mistake, according to Cassiano, was to believe that anyone might cast doubts on his "shining moral honor." Who, Cassiano asked, had denied Sobral's description of himself as "decent," "upright," "free," "honest," and "sincere"? Noting that Sobral had called the lunch for Pedro Aleixo "a decent manifestation of some free men to honor another free man," Cassiano asked, "Are we not all free men in Brazil?" He accused Sobral of implying that a lunch was "decent" only if organized by the opposition.[10]

"Cassiano Ricardo can be sure," Sobral wrote on October 2, "that we shall never forget his chivalry in giving us the splendid and honorable name of apostle. To demonstrate our gratitude, we shall, with compassion, inform him about some historic truths." Sobral wrote that if Cassiano would turn to the Larousse *Grande Dictionnaire* and other works he would learn that Engels had died in 1895 and could not have used the term Bolshevik, which began to circulate in 1903. Sobral also wrote that it was inconceivable that a member of the Brazilian Academy of Letters and director of an important daily should preach that truth was inaccessible and multiple, thus confusing the idea of "truth" with the idea of "fact."[11]

Sobral wrote that if Cassiano would read all that Sobral wrote, he would discover a lawyer who toiled long hours and "never betrayed the duties of his vocation." To help Cassiano understand this reference to Sobral's virtues, Sobral quoted paragraphs from letters of praise received from Plínio Barreto and Supreme Court Justice José Linhares. He described himself as struggling intransigently—not as a politician, which he was not, but as a serene friend of the truth—for organic democracy, the only democracy able to do away with exclusivism, imposition, and oppression.[12]

Returning to the fray on October 9, Sobral insisted that it was not he, but Cassiano, who was unclear about defining his position. According to Sobral, the term social democracy, advocated vaguely by Cassiano, had been described by Pope Leo XIII as reducing all citizens to a single "level of equality," abolishing property rights, and turning instruments of production over to state ownership—concepts completely at variance with those of "organic democracy," which had been described by Leo XIII as maintaining property rights and class distinctions, thus providing "the human community with a form and character in harmony with what had been established by God." Cassiano, Sobral wrote, favored a democracy that used the pretext of defending the common man as an excuse to place the common man in the deadly grip of the agents of the regime.

It was not fair, Sobral wrote, to say that the defenders of human liberty were guilty of favoring political liberalism. "The very essence of political liberalism is the tendency to liberate man from his subordination to God and act as though no relation exists between political order and religious order."

To demonstrate that his own efforts on behalf of "a truly authentic legal system" were appreciated, Sobral quoted from a letter in which Alceu Amoroso Lima had written him: "Like Afrânio Peixoto, I believe that no writer in Brazil today deserves as much respect as you on account of your intellectual and moral qualities."[13]

Cassiano, in his article of October 10, repeated adjectives of self-praise used by Sobral in September and noted that more recently Sobral had added new "trophies" to his formidable collection, such as "faithful to his duty" and "*intrépido*" [dauntless]. Agreeing that these words were applicable to Sobral, Cassiano asserted that among them the most appropriate was the vivid, martial word "*intrépido*," demonstrated in the rapidity with which Sobral accepted the title of apostle and demonstrated also in his failure to hesitate before making use of sophisms, evident in his discussion of "whether Engels was a Bolshevik when he was born." Cassiano argued that Sobral, calling himself a friend of truth and not a politician, had implied that all politicians were untruthful, and he replied that this view was unfair to a politician who had attended the "banquet" in honor of Pedro Aleixo: "Arthur Bernardes, as far as I know, never had the habit of turning against the truth."[14]

Cassiano argued that when Brazil copied foreign constitutions, as in 1891, it failed to be faithful to its destiny, and only when the Estado Nacional appeared in 1937 was it saved from "juridical falsehood, electoral falsehood, and ideological falsehood. . . . This is the truth for which I struggle, for the love of the truth and not of the Larousse *Grande Dictionnaire*. . . . But Sobral, instead of replying to me, uses the opportunity to make propaganda in favor of his masculinity and evokes the testimony of Plínio Barreto." Cassiano quoted from Plínio Barreto's review praising Cassiano's book, *O Brasil no Original*.

Sobral, Cassiano went on to say, was the one who was keeping silent on the main issue, "unbecoming for a person who declares himself to be crowned with the halo of fearlessness." To get Sobral to turn from "sophisms" and "evasions" and, instead, comment on Cassiano's contention about "all of us being free in the regime of liberty in which we live," Cassiano sought to provoke Sobral by listing reasons why Sobral must be in favor of social democracy.

According to Cassiano, social democracy was the only alternative for a person who could not favor Communism, Nazism, or bourgeois liberalism (considered atheistic by the Church). Maintaining that Ruy Barbosa, Alceu Amoroso Lima, and Belgian Cardinal Désiré Mercier had all spoken well of social democracy, Cassiano told his *A Manhã* readers that Sobral, without knowing it, was a "fervent adept" of the Vargas regime, "which is a social democracy. If I am wrong, let him move his lips, giving proof of his intrepidity."[15]

2. The DIP Intervenes against Sobral (October 19, 1943)

In Sobral's opinion, the article published in *A Manhã* on October 10 was a challenge hurled at him by Cassiano Ricardo, who had been "decisively destroyed" by Sobral's arguments published on October 2 and 9. "He defied me to define, if I am really a man of courage, the regime currently in effect in Brazil."[1]

That the definition would get him and the *Jornal do Commercio* into trouble with the DIP (Department of the Press and Propaganda), Sobral had no doubt, and he believed that Cassiano had been aware of this in making his challenge. "He never imagined that I would accept the challenge. . . . But I, faced with the alternatives of falling into discredit or being harmed, did not vacillate."[2]

In his column of October 16, Sobral wrote: "Shielded by the purity of our life, we now respond, with virile and Christian austerity, to the heartless provocations." The Carta Constitucional of November 1937, he declared, "does not provide the organic democracy described in the juridical thinking of the Christian world." Sobral quoted from a Christmas Eve message of Pope Pius XII condemning the use often made of positivism and utilitarianism, and calling for the rejection of all measures that might damage the liberty, property, honor, progress, and health of individuals.[3]

Sobral pointed out that the 1937 Constitution had been described as dictatorial by Francisco Cavalcanti Pontes de Miranda, a leading jurist "well regarded by Brazil's rulers." To enlighten Cassiano, enthusiastic about the Brazilian roots of the 1937 Constitution, Sobral mentioned Pontes de Miranda's observation that the 1937 document had been drawn up under the influence of European authoritarian socialism. To enlighten Cassiano still further, Sobral reproduced the correct wording of the sentence of "revolutionary" (not "Bolshevik") Engels that had mocked "politicians" (and not "jurists," as maintained by the "intellectually dishonest" Cassiano).

Having quoted authorities to show that the Estado Nacional was undemocratic, Sobral went on to liken his own situation to that of men who had perished in the arenas of the Roman Empire while lifting up prayers on behalf of their executioners. "In order to win we do not kill; we die." "While we are involved in bitter struggles that have brought us poverty, Cassiano Ricardo takes the opposite course, applauding unconditionally the people who are in charge. We accept with Christian resignation the sanctions of Cassiano's unfairly used power. It will not be the first time that, protected only by the moral shield of our invincible blamelessness, we will have imitated the example of Jesus Christ, who remained imperturbably silent in the face of accusers who knew that they were slandering their victim."[4]

Sobral's character, however, was not well suited to remaining imperturbably silent in the face of accusations. He would, in the course of making further charges against Cassiano, assert that it was the *A Manhã* columnist who caused a problem with the DIP (Department of the Press and Propaganda). Cassiano, according to Sobral, was so dismayed by the "calm and austere *intrepidez* [dauntlessness]" of Sobral's article of October 16 that he rushed to see the DIP director, army Captain Amilcar Dutra de Menezes, and persuaded him to forbid that the *Jornal do Commercio* publish any more of Sobral's replies.[5]

On October 19, *Jornal do Commercio* Director Elmano Cardim was called to Dutra de Menezes' office and told that Sobral had violated DIP regulations in discussing the nature of the Brazilian regime. Cardim explained that Sobral, unwilling to be a coward, had simply replied to a challenge and that if anyone deserved a reprimand it was Cassiano Ricardo. But the DIP director ordered Cardim to refrain from publishing further articles by Sobral about the nature of the political institutions in effect in Brazil.[6]

Sobral, learning of this development, sent Dutra de Menezes a letter in which he spoke of his desire to see legal order restored in Brazil in accordance with Christian truth. He added that if he were not so determined to struggle for his convictions he could have been a TSN judge, the director of the College of Law and Economics of the Federal District University, the *procurador geral* of the Public Servants' Welfare Institute (IPASE), or legal consultant of the Patrimony of the Brazil Railway, as the director of the DIP could verify by checking with Francisco Campos, Henrique Dodsworth, and others.[7]

For almost four years, Sobral wrote, he had refrained from writing anything in his columns that would present difficulties for the *Jornal do Commercio* or the DIP. His article of October 16, he argued, had been forced on him by a "journalist of the government who was clearly aware of the vileness he was carrying out in placing me in this dilemma . . . in front of the entire Brazilian nation!" Sobral asked Captain Dutra de Menezes to compare Cassiano's articles, "full of the words of an unthinking man seeking only to please the powerful," with the articles of Sobral, "full of ideas."

Sobral explained to the captain that he was not glorifying his own conduct on account of vanity but because it was necessary to focus on his example to demonstrate that "it is possible to maintain a decent and upright position despite all obstacles." He asked the DIP director whether he could fail to support a good man who toiled unselfishly from dawn until nightfall.[8]

Sobral was so confident in the effectiveness of his appeal that he was not disturbed to read, on Saturday, October 23, *A Manhã*'s announcement of the scheduled appearance on Sunday of Cassiano Ricardo's "The Man Who Dressed Himself in the Hide of a Jaguar." He felt certain that the DIP, having muzzled his *Jornal do Commercio* articles, would not permit Cassiano to "carry out the unspeakably monstrous cowardice" of publishing another provocation.[9]

It was therefore a shock to find Cassiano's new article in Sunday's *A Manhã*. It listed once again Sobral's words of self-praise, but this time it suggested that "honest" was not an appropriate term to describe a man who had omitted the date of a letter of adulation to give the misleading impression that it had been written recently. If, Cassiano now wrote, Sobral were a man of greater modesty and courtesy and were more respectful of the truth, an exchange of views with him about modern concepts of democracy might be possible. But "how can I have a discussion with a person who, not even knowing me, considers me his personal enemy?"[10]

To get Sobral "to open his lips," Cassiano said he had presented, in a lighthearted way, the challenging idea that Sobral might be an adept of social democracy if he could not support any of the alternatives. But, he added, Sobral had greeted this "friendly invitation" by calling it a "brutal and monstrous challenge," leading Cassiano to fear he was dealing with a pathological case.

"To pretend to be valiant . . . , he dresses in the hide of a jaguar . . . and exclaims that he must die, 'sacrificed' like the ancient Christians in the Roman arena. . . . But what does the 'valiant man' do at the crucial moment? He calls for Pontes de Miranda to help him and says that it is Pontes who once criticized the 1937 Constitution." Cassiano suggested that Sobral, lacking the courage to speak for himself, might be seeking to be "sacrificed" by an ambassadorial appointment, perhaps to the Vatican, for repeating words that Pontes de Miranda had expressed before being named ambassador to Colombia.

Cassiano accused Sobral of having misinterpreted Pope Leo XIII and of having falsely portrayed Pius XII, the current Pope, as an opponent of the Brazilian regime. In truth, Cassiano wrote, it was the new Brazilian regime that, thanks to the vision of Vargas, had freed Brazil from the liberalism and totalitarianisms that the Pope condemned.

After citing Archbishop Jayme Câmara's praise of the Vargas labor legislation, Cassiano launched into a glorification of the Estado Nacional. He asked how it could be called a dictatorship when it had a constitution that placed limits on government power, and he asked if any laws protecting the honor, liberty, property, and health of individuals had been suspended. As in the case of all countries at war, he said, Brazil had to place restrictions on freedom of expression. But he reminded his readers that Brazilians were free to hold "free banquets at which free men could freely manifest free thoughts."

In the final words of his article, Cassiano wrote that if Sobral became an ambassador, he would take flowers to the docks to see him off.[11]

3. Ineffective Appeals by the Silenced Columnist (October–November 1943)

On Monday morning, October 25, Sobral sent a telegram to Elmano Cardim asking him to obtain the permission of the DIP director for the publication of an article, for which Sobral alone would be responsible, in reply to Cassiano's article of the 24th. He told Cardim that at 6 P.M. he would inquire about the DIP's decision.[1]

Sobral also persuaded Herbert Moses, president of the Brazilian Press Association (ABI), to send a message to the DIP director in support of Cardim's mission.[2] And, before he went to the DIP at 6 P.M., he paid a call on the police chief, Colonel Nelson de Mello, about whom he had heard good things but whom he had never met. Explaining that he harbored no plans for "agitation, indiscipline, or rebellion," he asked the colonel to inform government authorities of his "noble intention" of carrying on a debate on a purely cultural plane.[3]

At the DIP, Sobral found Captain Amilcar Dutra de Menezes determined to speak at length to persuade him that he should support the Vargas regime, defender of the interests of the "popular masses."[4] After Sobral several times reminded the captain of the only question he wanted answered, the captain observed that his visitor was stubborn and turned to what Sobral had published on October 16. That article, he told Sobral, was worth "three hundred articles" by Cassiano Ricardo, and therefore Sobral had no need to reply to what Cassiano had written on the 24th. However, he did express a willingness to let Sobral write his proposed article and submit it to him for examination.

Sobral retorted that he would allow no one to exercise censorship over what he wrote. The DIP director then asked his visitor what he would discuss when he wrote about Cassiano's article of October 24; and, after hearing Sobral mention the themes he had in mind, he called them out of bounds because they concerned "the nature of the regime." That being the case, Sobral said he would publish a note for his readers, saying he could not reply to Cassiano because of the DIP's prohibition. But Dutra de Menezes forbade the note, saying it would give the impression that the DIP was engaged in pre-publication censorship, which was not the case.

During a discussion about Dutra de Menezes' failure to prevent the publication of Cassiano's article of the 24th, Sobral was shocked to hear the DIP director declare that on the 23rd he had found himself obliged to deal with twenty-four matters of much greater importance. Sobral observed that further conversation would be useless and was preparing to leave when Dutra de Menezes remarked: "I am pleased to have made your acquaintance because you give me the impression of being intelligent and knowing how to argue. What is your impression of me?" Sobral said he had a good impression of the captain as a person and the worst impression of him as the DIP director. He added that he would seek fair treatment by appealing to all the cabinet members, and, if these appeals failed, would appeal to the head of state.[5]

Visiting with Cardim on the next day, Sobral learned of a DIP directive against the publication of any of his articles without prior submission to the DIP.[6] Therefore on the 27th he wrote Herbert Moses to say that prior censorship had brought his "Pelos Domínios do Direito" articles to an end, and he wrote Dutra de Menezes to say that Cassiano, in his "cowardly article of October 24," had been wrong in supposing that Sobral imagined inexistent dangers. He also wrote Nelson de Mello to thank him for his understanding "in this moment of intense suffering in my patriotic heart."[7]

After dictating these letters to Cecy, Sobral went to his office, where he found replies from three of the eight cabinet ministers to whom he had sent telegrams on the 26th. Transport Minister João de Mendonça Lima suggested that Sobral deal with President Vargas, to whom the DIP reported. Education Minister Gustavo Capanema pointed out that the matter did not concern his ministry. Foreign Minister Oswaldo Aranha said that if the matter depended on him he would make sure that Sobral could defend himself and discuss Brazil's juridical and political problems.[8]

As requested by Sobral, the *Jornal do Commercio* published, on October 30, his letter to Cardim advising that his column had been interrupted and expressing his gratitude for Cardim's support of "my unyielding and constant work on behalf of the restoration of juridical values."[9] A communication from Nelson de Mello, in reply to one of Sobral's messages, spoke of Sobral's merits but described the case as beyond the police department's jurisdiction.[10] Another communication told of a plea made to the DIP director by the Centro Dom Vital and Alceu Amoroso Lima to allow Sobral to express himself freely, under his own responsibility, in the weekly column that, "with so much justification, has become famous in Brazil."[11]

One of Sobral's appeals had been sent to Colonel Luiz Carlos da Costa Netto, the former TSN judge who had been appointed superintendent of the government's Patrimônio da União, which included the dailies *A Manhã* and *A Noite*. The colonel replied that Cassiano would write no further on the subject about which he and Sobral had clashed. Sobral, in a telegram to Costa Netto, said he was hurt by the colonel's "incredible" message. Declaring that he had no fear of Cassiano's articles, Sobral explained, "it is Cassiano Ricardo who is terror-stricken by what I write. My appeal of honor was for your intervention to restitute my right to publish a reply—a right that Cassiano Ricardo took from me by going to the director of the DIP."[12]

This accusation was denied in a letter that Cassiano wrote to Affonso Arinos de Mello Franco with a copy to Alceu Amoroso Lima.[13] In it Cassiano affirmed that he had published his article of October 24 "after having personally verified that Sobral Pinto would suffer no restriction on account of his latest article. Sobral Pinto had until then received no warning from the DIP. I satisfied myself on this point because of my desire for Sobral Pinto to be at liberty to say and write whatever he wanted so that I could act with a similar lack of constraint." Cassiano assured Affonso Arinos that he had had nothing to do with the resolution of the authorities to "bring an end to the polemic," and he expressed his belief that the regime should not fear the discussion, such a discussion being permitted by the constitution and being the best way to overcome the ideas of "those who consider the regime antidemocratic." Cassiano told Affonso Arinos that on October 26 he had learned (a) that the polemic was not to continue because of the "factious and oppositionist" way it was being carried out, and (b) that the prohibition would be against each of the contestants and not just against Sobral Pinto.[14]

Sobral, after learning from Luiz Camillo de Oliveira Netto about Cassiano's letter, wrote to Cassiano on November 10, with copies for Affonso Arinos and Alceu. He accused Cassiano of lying and told him to confess that on October 18 he had gone to Dutra de Menezes and given him Sobral's article of the 16th, with pencil markings, leading the DIP director to give his order to Cardim on the 19th. Sobral added that Cassiano, in view of his connections, must have known about Sobral's letter of the 20th to the DIP director, written to persuade the latter to extend his prohibition to Cassiano. Sobral accused Cassiano of trying to confuse Affonso Arinos by stating that the DIP did not intervene until the 25th, whereas it had done so on the 19th. He told Cassiano to behave in a virile manner by arranging for Sobral to reply to Cassiano or else by breaking relations with *A Manhã* and with "a juridical order that seeks to take you along the path of grief, dishonor, and spiritual treason."[15]

Sobral, preparing a booklet about his conflict with Cassiano and the DIP, assured Cassiano that the letter he was writing him would become known to "all our fellow citizens. I want everyone to know that I am engaged in this struggle without the slightest bitterness in my Christian heart."

The letter described its author as an optimistic, tolerant, understanding, friendly, even playful person who avoided, as much as possible, any publicity about himself. "It is people like you who force me to appear in public as sad, cranky, serious, pessimistic, and despairing. The requirements of the struggle for the reign of truth make me, during the combat, tough and intransigent." In closing, Sobral asked Cassiano not to think he wished ill for those he opposed. "What they bring out in me is pity." He told Cassiano that, being a Catholic who recognized that he and Cassiano were brothers in Jesus Christ, he did not regard him as worthless.[16]

4.   Responses to Booklets about Cassiano and the DIP (Late 1943–Early 1944)

In mid-November 1943, Sobral told Alceu that the struggle for the right of free discussion about doctrinal matters was so important that he was turning for help to the principal cultural institutions as well as the top government authorities. Writing to Affonso Arinos de Mello Franco, he said he would not rest before obtaining victory, and he added that he could not accept Affonso Arinos' view about the conduct of Cassiano Ricardo. "Thank God I have the documents needed to refute the falsehoods spread by Cassiano."[1]

By early December Sobral's collection of documents about his struggle with Cassiano and the DIP had been published in a 115-page booklet whose appendix quoted men who had praise for "Pelos Domínios do Direito."[2] He sent a copy to Getúlio Vargas along with a lengthy telegram that reminded the president of his words to the nation on September 7, when he had said that "no people affected by the difficulties of the war have greater liberty to enjoy life, prosperity, and the pursuit of happiness than the Brazilian people." To demonstrate the untruth of those words, Sobral (1) outlined his problem with the DIP, whose decision, he said, was not based on Brazil's being at war, and (2) cited the acceptance of public criticism by British authorities in 1940, mentioning also a recent declaration by Britain and the United States about the value of honest criticism. Sobral explained that Vargas' transport minister had advised him that he could get relief from acts of the DIP only by turning to the president of the republic.[3]

The telegram to Vargas was published as a small second booklet that Sobral sent, along with the larger one, to people of influence, among them the DIP director and officers of the Instituto Brasileiro de Cultura.[4] Copies sent to Catholic Monsignor Benedicto Marinho were accompanied by a warning that "the restriction against the ideas of a legal critic can be turned tomorrow against the priest of Jesus Christ."[5]

Affonso Arinos phoned Sobral on December 8 to say that he had a message from Nelson Baptista, secretary of Amilcar Dutra de Menezes, asking Sobral to be at the DIP director's office at 10 A.M. the next day. Sobral told Affonso Arinos of his surprise at the indirect way the request had been made. A more direct approach, he added, would have been used by anyone conversant with courtesy and loyalty and would have allowed Sobral to explain the inconvenience of the hour, when he would be at home "carrying out urgent professional work." He told Affonso Arinos that Dutra de Menezes was eager to disparage him, as revealed on October 25 when he had spoken about twenty-four matters of much greater importance.[6]

After he refused to act on the message received through Affonso Arinos, Sobral found three messages sent to his office from Nelson Baptista, who insisted that he visit Captain Dutra de Menezes on the morning of December 9. Sobral directed an office companion to inform Baptista that he had to handle two cases at court. In any event, he wished to have a reply to his appeal to Vargas before dealing further with the DIP.[7]

Nelson Baptista managed to find Sobral in the court on the afternoon of December 9 and told him that his appeal to the president had been forwarded to Dutra de Menezes. He added that the DIP director, having an appointment with Vargas at 2 P.M. that day, had been hoping to discuss the matter with Sobral in the morning. It now being too late for them to meet before the director's meeting with Vargas, Nelson Baptista left it up to Sobral to decide when Dutra de Menezes and Sobral would converse.

Sobral agreed to see Dutra de Menezes at 4 P.M. on December 10. At the meeting, which was brief, the DIP director continued to forbid Sobral to publish anything about the political themes raised on October 24 by Cassiano. He said Sobral could attack Cassiano personally, and Sobral said he had no interest in that.[8]

Sobral was pleased that Desembargador J. C. de Azevedo Marques, who had denounced him in June for criticizing "São Paulo justice," wrote to thank him for the booklets.[9] But other letters of thanks included comments to which Sobral took exception. A letter from lawyer José Pimentel was criticized by Sobral for reflecting the pessimistic view of writer Monteiro Lobato about what could be accomplished in the way of "holding back the process of moral decomposition."[10]

When Clementino Fraga, of the Brazilian Academy of Letters, expressed the belief that Cassiano had not been involved in the DIP ruling against Sobral, Sobral, rather weakly, defended his charge by calling Fraga's attention to Cassiano's falsification of the statement by Engels and telling him that anyone who would stoop to such "scurrility" was "capable of every sort of outrageous conduct."[11]

Cláudio de Mello e Souza, another member of the Academy of Letters, irritated Sobral by defending the PEN Club, described by Cláudio as a "universal association of writers" that favored liberty of expression but opposed the use of the pen to advance political, sectarian, or religious ideas. Sobral told Cláudio that "everyone should struggle, . . . with tolerant charity, for the victory of his ideas," and he added that the rise of modern totalitarian states had been assisted by the "cultural mentality of which the PEN Club is today the most active expression." For these reasons, Sobral wrote, he had advised Hermes Lima of his refusal to accept an invitation to give a speech, to be sponsored by the PEN Club at the Brazilian Academy of Letters, about law in the postwar world.[12]

Exhausted from "excessive work," Sobral took a vacation that lasted throughout most of February 1944. After visiting Plínio Barreto and his family in São Paulo, he relaxed with the Lindolpho Pio da Silva Dias family in Poços de Caldas.[13]

5. Comments on Agamemnon Magalhães and Cassiano's New Post (March 1944)

Upon his return to Rio, Sobral found that Agamemnon Magalhães, authoritarian *interventor* of Pernambuco, was carrying on his feud with newspaper magnate Assis Chateaubriand by publishing articles that seemed to demand refutation. As Sobral wrote Agamemnon, he would have denounced his views in his *Jornal do Commercio* column but could not do so because it had been silenced by the

Estado Novo "which you and others established with the violent coup of November 10, 1937." To give Agamemnon "exact knowledge of the present situation in Brazil," he sent him the two booklets about Cassiano and the DIP.[1]

Agamemnon's articles railed against the Chateaubriand Diários Associados media empire, calling it "the worst of the trusts." This "trust of associated newspapers and radio stations," he wrote, opposed the labor ministry and social reforms while seeking to impoverish the northeast by campaigning against the government's sugar policy. Concluding that "the State cannot permit, without risk to its stability, the existence of a power that opposes its own power," Agamemnon declared that the only solution was a government takeover of the trust.[2]

Sobral told Agamemnon that "the worst of the trusts" were the government bodies which had simply seized, overnight, the Brazil Railway, *A Noite, O Estado de S. Paulo,* and "hundreds of other private establishments." He mentioned the recent fate of Affonso Penna Júnior, deprived of a bank officership and falsely charged with acting immorally. Untruths coming from the DIP, he said, could not be answered, whereas the citizenry was free to disprove untruths expressed by the Chateaubriand chain.[3]

To show that the media were far weaker than the government, Sobral wrote that Cassiano Ricardo, with newspapers and a radio station at his disposal, found himself "discredited in the opinion of all good men" by Sobral's defense, "now becoming known to all our fellow-citizens." He also pointed out that Chateaubriand's campaign against Indústrias Reunidas F. Matarazzo had been unable to prevent that firm from obtaining astronomical profits at its four hundred plants, whereas the government could, if it wished, take over "this most powerful industrial organization of South America and leave its directors without legal recourse."

Sobral told Agamemnon that only Soviet Russia had adopted his idea of "an absolute monopoly of publicity in the hands of the sovereign state" and that even Nazi Germany had not gone that far. "I would be pleased if you would make my words public and allow me to document my assertions. That would constitute one of the most stirring chapters of the battle I have been carrying out, for over eight years, for the prevalence of Law in Brazil."[4]

Militant lawyer Adroaldo Mesquita da Costa, Catholic friend of Sobral in Rio Grande do Sul, had been siding with Agamemnon

Magalhães and was therefore condemned in articles by Chateaubriand that Sobral considered unfair. Sobral, reprimanding Adroaldo
for his position and Chateaubriand for his words about Adroaldo,
told Chateaubriand that his articles brought tears to his eyes. "I find
you insulting, unnecessarily and in the most excruciating manner,
my friend Adroaldo, for whom I have great affection and who is one
of Brazil's most outstanding Catholic intellectuals."[5]

The press in February 1944 disclosed that Cassiano had been appointed a member of the Conselho Federal do Comércio Exterior. To
warn the other Conselho members of the danger he saw of having
Cassiano in their midst, Sobral wrote a letter to each one, and he
wrote Cassiano that he was doing this as part of his program to obtain redress for "the violation of my rights" by the DIP caused by
"your cold and cruel provocation."[6]

In his letters to the Conselho members, Sobral pointed out that
the Conselho, as a result of Decree-Law 74, of December 16, 1937,
had acquired much importance, becoming "the vigilant sentinel of
the Nation's economic life." The decree-law, he also pointed out, required that the Conselho members, appointed by the president of
the republic, be men of "spotless reputation." Thus, he said, he was
required to make it known that the Conselho was threatened by
the recent appointment of Cassiano, whose statements "cannot be
given the slightest credit" because, "if it is to his interest, he will
not hesitate to carry out the most unforgivable intellectual frauds.
. . . If he needs to wound an adversary who catches him flagrantly
adulterating texts, he will not vacillate in saving his immeasurable
vanity by the use of the most underhanded methods; he will drag, to
especially dangerous and vexing situations, the adversary who has
defeated him intellectually."[7]

Sobral offered to provide documentary proof of "the fraudulent
and underhanded acts" of Cassiano Ricardo and asked the members of the Conselho to read his two booklets. He told them that
when the DIP had "stifled" his "virile [varonil] voice" as a result of
his reply to Cassiano's challenge, Cassiano had spurned the "correct and loyal" course of placing himself at Sobral's side and had
"cold-bloodedly and firmly supported the DIP." "I denounce," Sobral
concluded, "all these dangerous characteristics of this writer, thus
warning you against the possibility of a disastrous role by him in
the Conselho Federal do Comércio Exterior."[8]

6. Rejecting the Charge of Persecuting Cassiano (May–July 1944)

In April 1944, reports reached Brazil that the Argentine government had closed the Buenos Aires oppositionist daily, *La Prensa*. Rio's *O Globo* published indignant protests by prominent Brazilians, among them Cassiano Ricardo, who declared that the act against *La Prensa* was "a blow to all journalists at this moment when the spiritual values of democracy are the greatest force we have in the struggle against the totalitarian beast."[1]

Sobral wrote Cassiano to tell him that his declaration would not accomplish his wish to deceive public opinion once again. "In the course of your role of disservice to democracy you committed a sin that is far more harmful than the step taken by the Argentine government against *La Prensa*." Sobral accused Cassiano of disparaging "the virile character of Brazilians" by subscribing to Francisco Campos' remark that "in Brazil nothing has any consequence" and of therefore believing no one would remember his sins of September and October 1943. Campos, Sobral told Cassiano, had come to recognize the error of his hasty remark and had observed later: "In Brazil nothing has any consequence except when Sobral Pinto is involved."[2]

José Eduardo de Macedo Soares' condemnation of the Argentine government was praised by Sobral for its virility. In his letter to the founder of the *Diário Carioca*, Sobral told of the dismay felt by all who had read Cassiano's declaration. "In order not to permit Cassiano Ricardo to place himself, sneakily, among the pioneers of Brazilian press freedom, I immediately sent him a letter putting him in his place." He furnished a copy for Macedo Soares.[3]

During June and July, Sobral and Cassiano exchanged letters, with Cassiano describing himself as persecuted by Sobral. Cassiano repeated that he had had nothing to do with the DIP ruling that had silenced Sobral, and he added that he had discontinued publishing anything that might be considered a continuation of their polemic. Sobral called the second claim untrue. "Under your direction," he wrote, "*A Manhã* never ceased publishing articles and editorials that described Brazil as 'a completely free democracy.'" He wrote that Cassiano's situation was the distressing one of being "a journalist at the unconditional service of the present regime."[4]

How in the world, Sobral asked, could Cassiano, a man occupying high positions, be so "mentally cross-eyed" as to claim to be persecuted by Sobral, a modest lawyer with no publicity organ and without government influence? "Now you assume a childish stance and invite me to your office, a place filled with violence and lies, in order to assault me physically because, according to your understanding, only in such an encounter can I demonstrate to my fellow-citizens that I am really a man of courage! How far have you fallen!" Sobral explained that he had initiated a doctrinal polemic and not a boxing match, and added that "all my fellow-citizens, including you, are aware that I do not cultivate the vile trait of fear."[5]

In letters written late in July to all members of the Academy of Letters, including Vargas, Sobral called Brazil a dictatorship in a straightforward manner. Cassiano, he said, should have obtained the restoration of Sobral's rights or else ceased asserting that Brazil was a democracy. In the latter case, Sobral maintained, Cassiano should have preserved his fidelity to democracy by breaking with the government, or, if such a step had not suited his interests, at least stopped calling the regime democratic.

Sobral told the Academy members that the "democracy" supported by Cassiano was the "democratic Caesarism" advocated by positivists like the Venezuelan author Laureano Vallenilla Lanz, or was the "*caudilho* state, extolled by so many Hispanic-American thinkers" and mentioned by the English publicist Cecil Jane. These regimes, Sobral declared, did not represent "Christian democracy, respecter of individual liberties and the dignity of citizens."[6]

Sobral addressed Vargas as a "man of letters," "illustrious Academy member," and "artist with words" possessed of a "literary sensitivity." He told him and other Academy members that "my religious conscience does not allow me to act with cruelty toward anyone, and much less be a persecutor of any individual."[7] And he added that Cassiano had not the slightest reason for complaining that Sobral had ever said anything against his person,[8] a statement that Cassiano might have considered at variance with Sobral's warnings to the members of the Conselho Federal do Comércio Exterior.

In writing Cassiano, Sobral now said: "I have no desire to cause you to lose your reputation." Denying that he was applying Nazi methods of persecution, Sobral described his goal as the Christian one of liberating Cassiano from the errors to which he had fallen victim.[9]

7. Jacyra, the Indian Girl from Amazônia (March–April 1944)

Jacyra, a five-year-old Indian girl from the Amazon region, was living in Rio's Ipanema district in 1944 because she had been adopted by medical doctor Doracy de Souza and his wife.

With the school year about to start in March, the doctor's wife went to the school of the Sisters of Notre Dame, on nearby Barão da Torre Street, to enroll Jacyra. After she explained that Jacyra was a dark-skinned Indian, she was asked to bring the child to the school, and, when she did so, a nun pointed out that the girl's color would be likely to cause her difficulties because the other girls were white and had parents who preferred that they not associate with dark-skinned schoolmates. It was suggested that Jacyra be enrolled in a different school, run by the same Catholic sisterhood and attended by students of all colors. Jacyra, who had been hoping to join her friends at the school on Barão da Torre Street, was crushed, and her adoptive parents and some of their relatives were angry.[1]

Medical doctor Maurício de Medeiros, a *Diário Carioca* columnist and friend of Jacyra's adoptive father, started a campaign against the Sisters of Notre Dame on March 7 with an article that described the decision to reject the girl as having been made by a racist from the land of Hitler. He wrote that it was a mistake to allow foreigners with such a mentality to educate Brazilian children and that the government should cancel the license of the school, "whose moral principles are in conflict with those of our country."[2]

Journalist Rubem Braga, writing also in the *Diário Carioca*, asserted that the nuns of Notre Dame, mostly foreigners, had rejected Jacyra because she was an Indian and that the case was being brought to the attention of the Serviço de Proteção aos Índios and the education ministry. He recommended that the school director be tried in court and her "Nazi school" be closed at once.[3]

In *O Globo*, Dr. Doracy de Souza, Jacyra's adoptive father, contributed to the campaign by publishing a letter about the incident in which he wrote: "You can imagine our indignation," especially when the nun's decision was made known in the presence of Jacyra.[4] Maurício de Medeiros, publishing a second article on March 11, said: "If our laws prohibit foreigners from owning newspapers and other press organs, how can we permit foreigners to own our educational facilities, that have a much greater impact?"[5]

In the *Jornal do Commercio* Sobral published a letter to Maurício de Medeiros to defend the nuns of Notre Dame, who had been receiving Sobral's guidance for ten years along with his help in raising money for the school. He said that the school had been organized by sisters who had originally been associated with Catholics of Cleveland, Ohio, and that Maurício de Medeiros, if he were to investigate impartially, would learn that Mother Firmina, the "saintly director" of the school, was a United States citizen, and that the nun who spoke with Sra. Doracy de Souza on her second visit was a Brazilian whose only concern was to avoid difficulties for Jacyra. "The quiet, hardworking, humble, generous, self-sacrificing" staff of the school, Sobral wrote, was made up of four United States citizens, three Brazilians, one Belgian, one Pole, and one Dutch nun, along with four Germans who had been forced to flee from the pagan Nazi government.[6]

Sobral sent Archbishop Jayme de Barros Câmara a copy of this letter together with a warning that the press campaign against foreign Catholics had become "extreme." He suggested that Dom Jayme organize a Secretariat of the Press to reply quickly to accusations against the Church and its priests.[7]

Maurício de Medeiros noted the mention in Sobral's letter of a police report alleging the doctor-columnist's Communist affiliation in 1936 and got back at Sobral with an indirect reference to Sobral's adultery in the 1920s: "As a confessed atheist I do not have virtues to compare with those of Sobral, but I am not guilty of having willfully violated a single one of the Ten Commandments." Maurício de Medeiros also judged it improper for a good Christian to "flaunt his own virtues so frequently." *Diário de Notícias* columnist Osório Borba, finding in Sobral's' letter to Maurício de Medeiros a reference to Borba's January 1943 "unjust campaign" against Max Schneller, initiated a new polemic with Sobral about the foreign Jesuit teacher, who by this time had died.[8]

Rubem Braga, writing at far less length than Borba, took up the Jacyra case again in the *Diário Carioca*.[9] Addressing Sobral on March 18, he said:

> Oh my dear monster, with so much thirst for Truth and Justice: Stick with your "saintly and meritorious" Catholic Sisters from North America, Holland, Belgium, Poland, Germany, and Brazil, associated with the upper crust of Ipanema; but please let

someone speak in defense of that little Indian. . . . For in truth I tell you, Oh Sobral: that little Indian driven from the portals of a school, that child who comes from the Amazon forests to be rejected by your illustrious Catholic institution, is worth more than all the nuns put together.

Ah, Sobral, your great God did not create Paradise for white people. . . . Ah, you don't have to tell me, for I know that my destiny is the great Inferno with 100,000 devils. Very well: so be it! But I tell you, Sobral, that in the midst of my tortures, I'll have the wicked consolation of thinking about how the little Indian girl Jacyra plays on the swings of Heaven while you, wearing your eyeglasses and a graduation ring, together with the nuns of Ipanema, are wailing, oh, oh, oh, in the provisional furnaces of Purgatory. And when your order of transfer comes and you reach the gates of Heaven, it is possible that Peter, the fisherman, will receive you with these words: "My dear Sobral, my dear Sisters, won't it be possible for you to remain a bit longer there below? Jacyra is so happy, enjoying herself so much! You might frighten her with your presence: she would stop playing and huddle in a corner because, poor thing, she is an Indian and you are all so white, so inflexible, so important, so exclusive!"

And, from within, the innocent little Indian can be heard calling to Peter: "Saint Peter, do you or don't you want to fish for *pirarucu* today?"

And Peter is going to learn to fish for *pirarucu* [Amazon fish] because Peter is a fisherman and is a poor Jew and is not bothered by the girl's being an Indian. And in truth it is better to fish for *pirarucu* and *piau* with a clear soul than to fish for souls for the Lord with hypocrisy.[10]

Sobral, also on March 18, prepared a long letter for Maurício de Medeiros that he hoped to have published in the *Jornal do Commercio*. In it he declared that he was not hurling back, in retaliation, "the slimy, greenish mud that you—with your inopportune invocation of the Commandments of God—sought to heap upon my poor and modest name. Christians do not seek vengeance; they pardon."

It is my duty to forgive the perverse reminder that you, in the form of crafty insinuation, allowed yourself to express about a bad sin of mine . . . which political hatred, cruel and ruthless, did not hesitate to make public in 1928. . . . Why do you thrust again the dagger of your malice into an old wound . . . , risking the revival of cruel sorrows that are not mine alone but are principally of others, innocent victims of my faults? I did not concern myself with your private life. Nor did I throw any doubt on your being a saint—such an exceptional one that you consider yourself to have the right to flaunt publicly your absolutely clear conscience, totally without sin.[11]

But, Sobral added, Maurício de Medeiros' statements made it permissible now to point out that the columnist's claim to have violated none of the Ten Commandments was "tremendously blasphemous," reflecting the sin of ostentation "inspired by satanic pride," and was false because his atheism was in violation of the First Commandment.

Responding to the charge that he himself was guilty of ostentation, Sobral wrote that nobody, reading Saint Paul's account of his sufferings and "heroic feats, performed for the Christian faith," would say that "the great Apostle was guilty of the sin of ostentation. . . . He sought to persuade Christians to fulfill heroically the duties of the Faith. No lesson equals that of an example. The Apostle revealed what he had done in order to strengthen his fellow Christians."[12]

8. The DIP Ends the Debate about Jacyra (March–April 1944)

On Saturday night, March 18, Sobral was at the *Jornal do Commercio*, correcting proofs for the publication of his latest letter to Maurício de Medeiros, when he was told that the DIP had phoned to advise of a new ruling preventing publication in the press of anything about the case of Jacyra.[1]

Writing on Monday to DIP director Amilcar Dutra de Menezes, Sobral pointed out that the Rio press, starting on March 7, had been full of "terrible" onslaughts against the nuns of the school and that, when the "enemies of the Church" had occupied the field alone, the DIP had remained in slumber. "When one man comes forth to face the satanic rage of the adversaries of Jesus Christ and his disciples, the DIP's inertia is replaced by a zeal to force total silence upon the press." Sobral wrote that his inability to respond to the "cruel" attacks published on March 15, 17, and 18 would give readers the impression that he had deserted the struggle, believing himself vanquished.[2]

Some reason, Sobral wrote, could be given for halting the polemic with Cassiano Ricardo because the theme was a political one, distasteful to agents of the authorities. But he maintained that the text of Decree-Law 1,915 of December 27, 1939, creating the DIP, provided no justification whatever for the new DIP ruling. "I cannot conform to it. . . . The truth, Sr. Director, causes no fear in men of the Church."[3]

Sobral learned that the DIP based its prohibition on the decision of the education ministry to undertake a "rigorous investigation" of the Notre Dame nuns. Therefore he wrote the education minister, Gustavo Capanema, to advise that the decision to investigate had been the result of the "cruel" campaign of "anti-religious demagogues," such as Maurício de Medeiros *(Diário Carioca),* Osório Borba *(Diário de Notícias),* Rubem Braga *(Diário Carioca),* and Arthur Ramos *(Folha Carioca).* Calling the Church sisters the descendants of the Christians of the first centuries who had defied the power of Rome and the obstinate hatred of pagans and Jews, Sobral said that they wished to win a victory "in the realm of public opinion." For this reason he called it urgent for the education minister to obtain a reversal of the DIP ruling, "issued without any legal basis."[4]

In a letter to Archbishop Jayme de Barros Câmara, Sobral said the nuns were entirely in the right and therefore a public debate would be useful. Stressing that "nothing can hurt us worse than silence," he asked Dom Jayme to arrange to end the intervention of the temporal powers in matters of concern to the religious conscience of Brazilians. Dom Jayme invited Sobral to the Palácio São Joaquim, where, on March 24, Sobral reiterated these views.[5]

"I need to be with you," Sobral wrote Alceu Amoroso Lima on March 22 in a letter about how attacks came "from every direction." Because Alceu spent much of his time in Petrópolis and was in Rio only during hours when Sobral was busy with his legal practice, Sobral said he found himself "isolated," unable to open his "troubled heart." He told his friend that he disliked speaking about his "anguish" to people at his office or home lest he needlessly burden them with his worries.[6]

Dom Jayme, Sobral informed Alceu, liked the idea of a press secretariat to defend the Church in the Rio press, and awaited an appropriate organizational plan, to be submitted by Sobral. "Obviously," Sobral told Alceu, "I cannot present the plan without first submitting it to you for your consideration."[7]

Sobral hoped that Alceu, leader of Brazil's Catholic laity, would persuade Capanema and Dutra de Menezes that the DIP directive should be withdrawn, and he turned also for help to the *Jornal do Commercio*'s Elmano Cardim and the ABI's Herbert Moses.[8]

The response of Capanema to Sobral's wish was a telegram in which the education minister shocked him by advising of having learned from Dutra de Menezes that the debate about the nuns had been "suspended at the request of His Excellency the Archbishop of Rio de Janeiro."[9] Sobral, who received the telegram on the 25th, wrote Don Jayme to point out that on the 24th, when they had conversed, the archbishop had said he had no knowledge about the DIP regulation.

Explaining that the official news from Capanema put him in a difficult position, Sobral told Dom Jayme that probably someone had used the archbishop's name at the DIP. Catholics, he told Dom Jayme, should not make agreements with the DIP, which had arbitrarily prevented publication in the Rio archdiocese of a collective pastoral letter by São Paulo Catholics in opposition to gambling and legislation that disrespected the sanctity of the family. "To turn now to the DIP to end a press discussion about Jacyra, which may be inconvenient to Catholics, is to recognize the legitimacy of an organ that allows itself to establish rules governing what is said by Brazilian bishops about customs and morals."[10]

Sobral advised both Capanema and Dutra de Menezes that he disapproved of the "position of the person who spoke in the name of the Archbishop." "I must point out," he told the DIP director, "that when the Sister directing the Colégio Notre Dame got in touch with me, she told me that the father of a pupil had suggested seeking intervention by the DIP to bring an end to the unjust campaign that was distressing the nuns. I replied that . . . such an intervention might be obtained and that prohibitions of this sort were being put into effect daily." But, Sobral continued, he had told the sister that protection by the DIP should not be accepted, and she had agreed with him.[11]

Father José Távora, asked by Dom Jayme to investigate Capanema's statement about the request for the DIP ruling, reported early in April that no ecclesiastical authority had been involved. Sobral told Dom Jayme of his elation at this news and sent copies of Távora's report to Capanema and Dutra de Menezes. He asked the DIP director to provide publicity about the unjust anticlerical character of the campaign against the nuns, and he wrote severely to Capanema, telling him that the unreliability of official government statements was even more serious than the "odious disrespect of my rights."[12]

Writing to Alceu a few days later, Sobral congratulated him for his article about liberty because it showed that he was no longer satisfied to remain the philosopher, enumerator of moral truths, but had decided to carry out the mission of demanding that the truths be given practical application. The public power, Sobral also told Alceu, was using censorship to smother all truths that threatened its stability.[13]

9. "The Eviction of Dr. Sobral Pinto" (May–October 1944)

Soon after Sobral moved into the modest three-room office on Rua da Assembléia in 1929, he was in arrears on rent payments. But the head of the commercial firm to which the payments were due was a friend who did not insist on prompt payments.

The firm went bankrupt three years after Sobral moved in, and therefore the rent became payable to Desembargador Luiz Guedes de Moraes Sarmento, owner of the building. The *desembargador* told Sobral not to worry about the rent he owed the extinct firm. And he put up rather graciously with the tardiness of Sobral's payments during the next twelve years. So did Moraes Sarmento's son-in-law, Humberto Duarte, who handled the *desembargador's* business affairs after the latter's illness in 1943.[1]

Moraes Sarmento died in January 1944. As soon as Sobral learned that the executors of the estate had sold the building to the Banco Nacional de Depósitos, he told Humberto Duarte that he would seek a loan to permit him to liquidate the arrearage of nine months.

In May 1944, press reports about the inauguration of a branch of the bank on the building's ground floor revealed that TSN Judge Erônides de Carvalho, unfriendly to Sobral, was a director of the bank. Furthermore, late in May Sobral received official notice that the bank had become administrator of Moraes Sarmento's estate. He sent José Tocqueville de Carvalho Filho to speak with the bank's secretary, Otacílio de Lucena, and thus learned that what the bank wanted was the May 1944 rent, payable on June 10, and that back rent was another matter, having to do with the estate.[2]

Sobral sent for the May 1944 receipt, applicable to the rent he was going to pay, but the bank administrators sent him, instead, a receipt for the unpaid August 1943 rent. This convinced him of the "malice" of the administrators, and he sent Tocqueville de Carvalho Filho to the bank again, this time to tell Otacílio de Lucena that he would quickly borrow the funds necessary to pay his full indebtedness and would move out because he could not be a tenant of Erônides de Carvalho. "I could not appear," he wrote later in the *Jornal do Commercio*, "to have any personal obligation to the TSN judge who made a highly abusive accusation against me when I defended greengrocer Augusto Pereira—an accusation that he knew was totally false and that he made in order to please Frederico de Barros Barreto, president of the court."[3]

A 15,000-cruzeiro loan that Sobral hoped to receive from a friend on Saturday, June 10, did not materialize, and therefore that day passed without any rent payment. On Sunday, lawyer Dario de Almeida Magalhães came to Sobral's home to tell him that the bank planned to start legal eviction proceedings against Sobral the next day. Filling Sobral with gratitude, Dario signed and handed him a blank check.[4]

At the bank on Monday, Sobral offered to pay off his ten-month arrearage. But the late payments were rejected, and so he initiated a law case at the Twelfth District Civil Court to have the payments accepted.[5] On the same day an eviction suit against him was presented to the First District Civil Court by Erônides de Carvalho, Otacílio de Lucena, and lawyer Epitácio Pessoa Cavalcanti de Albuquerque, as directors of the bank and attorneys for the estate of Moraes Sarmento.[6]

Sobral wrote Supreme Court Justice José Linhares that the purpose of the accusation was to have him considered "a swindler" by the judiciary, and he asked Linhares for permission to use, in his defense, a letter of praise that Linhares had written in 1942. Sobral also defended his honor in a letter to the OAB (Ordem dos Advogados do Brasil).[7] And he sent Evandro Lins e Silva a copy of his legal defense together with a request for his written testimony ("to show that my financial difficulties are largely the result of the philosophy I have adopted about being a lawyer")[8] After José Linhares agreed to Sobral's request, Sobral told him that his real opponents in the case were Erônides de Carvalho and Epitácio Pessoa Cavalcanti de Albuquerque (son of João Pessoa, the running mate of Vargas who was murdered in 1930)[9]

Sobral was grieved by the role played by Humberto Duarte and his brothers-in-law. "Why," he asked Moraes Sarmento's son-in-law, "did you turn over to the building's new owners, and without any advice to me, the unpaid receipts, making the eviction suit possible and thus damaging my personal honor in the eyes of an uninformed public?" He said he would leave the building as soon as he was absolved.[10]

At the Twelfth District Court in September Sobral won his case against the estate of Moraes Sarmento. Therefore, a little later, at the First District Court, Judge Emanuel Sodré dismissed the accusation against him. Sodré, who had dismissed charges brought against Sobral in 1938 for offending Caneppa, now ruled that Sobral had done his best to make full payment in June 1944 and had presented testimonies demonstrating "the high opinion" in which he was held by fellow lawyers. Judge Sodré also pointed out that Sobral might have made use of a recent decree-law allowing him to offer the court only 20 percent of what he owed but that he had presented the full amount because he considered the decree-law contrary to property rights.[11]

Sobral wrote Sodré of his gratitude for the decision but took exception to some words in it about how a high level of morality did not depend on a person's believing in the supernatural. He wrote Sodré that the high level of morality displayed by the judge and his illustrious father, Senator Lauro Sodré, was not a testimony in favor of agnosticism or the positivism of Auguste Comte but had been established and strengthened by the presence of Christianity, "which has been contributing continuously to the civilization of our Nation."[12]

On Sunday, October 1, the *Correio da Manhã* displayed prominently "The Eviction of Dr. Sobral Pinto," a *matéria paga* article (published in return for a payment). It presented the arguments given at the Twelfth District Court against Sobral, accused of having broken a verbal agreement made with Moraes Sarmento.[13] Sobral, after reading it, concluded that Moraes Sarmento's son, who was unjustly blaming him for press reports about the estate's courtroom defeats, had "allied himself with Erônides de Carvalho and Epitácio Pessoa Cavalcanti de Albuquerque, servants of justice who seek to disparage my honorable and honest poverty."[14]

A letter from Sobral in the *Jornal do Commercio* on Sunday, October 8, called the *Correio da Manhã* publication a "new public humiliation, an appalling revelation of a hatred that I do not deserve and that will certainly increase the already maddening difficulties with which I have been struggling in these last nine years because I have always placed the common good of my country ahead of my personal interests."

His maligners' publication, Sobral wrote, made the public aware of his poverty but at least had the merit of showing that "penury does not dismay me." He wrote that he would not retain, in his Christian heart, any memory of the wrongs inflicted on him by his "triumphant persecutors." Should these people suffer setbacks in the future, they should, he said, feel free to turn to him for his "disinterested assistance."[15]

PART VIII

Reacting to Catholic Conformity and Coriolano's Repression (1944–1945)

1. "The Brazilian Nazi Boy" (March–April 1944)

The case of "The Brazilian Nazi Boy" was made public in the *Diário de Notícias* on March 12 by Osório Borba, who seized upon the pro-Nazi sentiments of an eight-year-old to condemn the teaching at the Rio boarding school run by the Benedictine monks of São Bento do Alto da Boa Vista. Borba reported that Sra. Branca Fialho, the adoptive mother of the boy, Ubiraci, was submitting a complaint against the monks to the National Department of Instruction because she was so disturbed by his displaying swastikas (sometimes on toy planes), shouting *vivas* for "the great German Reich," and decrying the "injustice" of an entire world making war on one country.[1]

Borba sought to stir up Rio by writing: "These remarks by an eight-year-old boy are enough to reveal that he was attending one of those factories for making little Hitler fanatics—a factory operating in our very capital under the cross of Christ and at the service of the swastika cross and under our alarming complacency toward the educational fifth column."[2]

Sobral, in a letter to Borba, published in the *Jornal do Commercio* on April 16, defended the renowned Benedictine monastery. He wrote that it was imperative that Borba, having permanent space available in Rio's best-selling daily, reflect on the wisdom of Father Antônio Vieira, who had written that people should refrain from expressing judgments based on passionate impulses inspired by their own wishes. "As you are filled with implacable hatred for the priests of Jesus Christ, everything about them is distorted by the blackness of your anticlerical passion."[3]

Surely, Sobral wrote, Borba was aware of the great services rendered to humanity by the Benedictines during fourteen centuries. "Against these giants of civilization, who saved the treasures of ancient wisdom, you raised your hate-filled voice solely on the basis of the testimony of a child of eight years!" The source of Borba's accusation, Sobral contended, had been casual conversation about the boy picked up at a bookstore. He asked Borba if he was not aware of the danger of relying on declarations of children, often at odds with their teachers and parents, and he pointed out that Ubiraci, a particularly unreliable child, had left the school after being disciplined by the monks more than one hundred times in one year. Surely such evidence could not be used to persuade Brazilians "to demolish the virtuous monks of São Bento, all of them described by you as Germans and supporters of Nazism."

Instructing Borba about the Benedictine Order and the "magnificent Rules of São Bento," Sobral wrote that its monks were not permitted to leave the Order and had allegiance to no nation—only to the monastery's community. He listed nineteen monks of the Rio Benedictine Abbey who had come from Brazilian families, many of them "traditional and respected," and he added that many Brazilian medical doctors, lawyers, and engineers were preparing to become Benedictine priests, among them a grandson of former Brazilian President Affonso Penna. He asked Borba to note that Father Vicente de Oliveira Ribeiro, director of the São Bento boarding school, had, as an athlete in 1924, brilliantly defended Brazil at the Olympic Games in Paris. "He would never permit that the Monastery's educational faculty, dedicated to teaching young Brazilians, become a school of hate."

Sobral recalled that the famous lawyer Evaristo de Moraes had been one of those who had studied at the São Bento school at no cost, learning there his admirable debating style—a style he had used later when attacking the Church. Sobral had been close to Evaristo de Moraes in his last years when he had expressed regret at having made the attacks. "I had the pleasure of hearing him tell of his repentance about many things that he had written and express the hope that they be buried in oblivion."[4]

In reply to this letter, Borba published an article, "O Brasileirinho 'Nazista.'" Sobral, he complained, reacted to commentaries that were based on indisputable facts as though they were inspired by a "preconceived purpose of combating the Church or religion, and were associated with mysterious 'anticlerical' campaigns." As a result, Borba wrote, Sobral had attacked him personally, "whereas I never referred to Sobral Pinto in any way that did not reflect the greatest respect for his person even when our divergences were great and when his interpretations of my positions and statements were blatantly unjust."[5]

Denying any connection with a preconceived sectarian campaign, Borba explained that his wish was to contribute to the antitotalitarian struggle by presenting comments inspired by facts. "I cannot accept the dogma, apparently held by Sobral Pinto, that no Catholic can make a mistake and that all priests refrain from politics and are incapable of serving fascism. Facts constantly betray this sham of the infallibility of all Catholics." Borba reminded his readers that on November 11, 1937, the Rio press had published declarations of twenty Brazilian bishops applauding Integralismo, which, Borba wrote, had been an orthodox fascist movement notoriously associated with German fascism.

Borba denied having said that all the São Bento monks were pro-Nazi Germans. "I only referred to the 'school of foreign monks' and I do believe they are mostly foreigners." Denying also that he had relied on "the testimony of an eight-year-old child," Borba wrote that the reports of the swastikas and pro-Nazi exclamations had come from the boy's adoptive mother, "an illustrious teacher," and from former magistrate Octavio Tarquinio de Souza, "who later told me I had reported the story faithfully."[6]

Vicente de Oliveira Ribeiro, the former athlete who headed the São Bento boarding school, wrote a letter to Borba to praise and support the "convincing letter" of Sobral, "who spontaneously came to our defense." In it the headmaster told of his surprise at learning that Dona Branca Fialho had turned to the National Department of Instruction without having discussed the problem with himself, "a Brazilian and friend of the family," or with one of the other monks. But he expressed satisfaction to know that the "grave insinuation" would be handled by the Department, made up of people familiar with the monastery, its traditions, and responsibilities.[7]

Borba, Dom Vicente wrote, should not be surprised that the schoolboys played at war games in which swastikas and Vs for Victory marked toy planes that were shot down by marbles. The boys, he wrote, had become familiar with slogans, including "Heil Hitler," from bellicose stories in Globo Juvenil and the monthly Gibi, publications for children that were not allowed at the school but were read elsewhere. As described by Dom Vicente, boys sometimes shouted German slogans to irritate the school's head of discipline, an anti-Nazi German who had been in Brazil seventeen years. "He is the only German because the three others who were born in Germany are naturalized Brazilians. The prior, school director, two teachers and an assistant for discipline are native Brazilians, and it is an evident exaggeration to assert that the boarding school is 'a school of foreign priests,' as you wrote on March 12" in an article that "has brought the school a lot of phone calls from parents" proposing the issuance of "a collective declaration" refuting Borba—a proposal that Dom Vicente said he had rejected as unnecessary.

According to Dom Vicente, the eight-year-old Ubiraci had received 112 reprimands in one year, making him "the worst of the boarders," and, after being withdrawn from the school, was reported to have declared that his compassion for Germany had not been acquired at the school. As for the school being a factory for making "young fanatics of Hitler," Dom Vicente pointed out that the school had been exhibiting anti-Nazi films supplied at his request by the United States Bureau of Coordination of Inter-American Affairs.

In conclusion, Dom Vicente invited Borba to visit the school; and he told him that if he would "publish this letter in the *Diário de Notícias*" he would be grateful.[8] The letter appeared in the newspaper on April 27.

Borba at this time was furthering his campaign against the "educational fifth column" in articles that renewed his polemic with Sobral about the history book of Father Max Schneller, the foreigner who had been teaching young Brazilians before his recent death. In the *Diário de Notícias*, Borba condemned what he called the book's racism, anti-Semitism, defense of German expansionism, and Nazi-like objections to the treaty that had followed World War I. He called the book "pro-German and pro-Hitler" and said that the author's reactionary position, revealed in his unsympathetic opinion about the French Revolution, had led him to justify totalitarianism.[9]

In the *Jornal do Commercio*, Sobral quoted historians whose views were similar to those of Schneller. Neither those historians nor Schneller's book, he wrote, were anti-Semitic or pro-Nazi, and he pointed out that Schneller, a noble Jesuit, had been a Swiss and not, as Borba had written, a German. He referred ironically to "the enlightenment" that the French Revolution had brought to Borba and attributed Borba's failure to renew his criticism of Alceu Amoroso Lima to his inability to describe Alceu as "a German monk preaching insolent Nazism in this land of savages."[10]

2. The Church and the Law (April–August 1944)

Only the Church of Jesus Christ, Sobral wrote Archbishop Jayme Câmara in April, could save the human race. Unfortunately, he added, Catholics had failed to live in accordance with the Faith; and the world, largely on account of this failure, was in a deplorable situation. The rise of Communism, he told Dom Jayme, could be attributed mainly to "the lack of charity of all Christians."[1]

Convinced that Brazilian Catholicism needed to be shaken up, he painted an unflattering picture of Catholics, "who, in order to gain the trust of members of the ruling class, never fail to talk about the need to support the authorities and maintain order, forgetting those who live in extreme penury." "While the Communists face government threats and, with firm character, go to jail in support of the rights of the workers, we Catholics usually prefer to praise rulers who fear to face the complex social problem frankly."

These workers, Sobral told Dom Jayme, became desperate on account of "indescribable physical sufferings" and turned to Communism, "while we screamed about the need to back a government that uses its police and tribunals of exception to crush those who are pioneers in the redemption of the common man." Sobral described the government and the industrialists as appalled by the "ever more vigorous" demands of workers and as therefore seeking to transform Catholics into "mere instruments of the prevailing economic policy."

Sobral told Dom Jayme that the rule preventing Ação Católica directors from holding government posts should be extended to "all members of the Catholic social apostolate," making these lay Catholics subordinate to the Catholic hierarchy alone. "And so we would bring an end to our contradiction" of participating, on the one hand, in a systematic attack against everything in Russia, "as though only bandits and wicked rulings are to be found there," and, on the other hand, in a "systematic applause" of the social policy of the Brazilian government, "as though only saints and meritorious rulings can be found there." Sobral felt that the suggestion he was making for a "genuinely Catholic apostolate" would allow Catholics to attack

Communist atheism without condemning everything done by the Russian government and be also in a position to call attention to the "agnosticism of our rulers, without failing to recognize important steps occasionally taken by our government to improve the future of the workers."[2]

Writing Dom Jayme again in June, Sobral discussed his conflict with Cassiano Ricardo and predicted a rise in authoritarianism in the government. "Using the pretext of Communist infiltration, the government, made up of atheists or disdainers of the sacraments of the Church, is preparing, in the name of our people's Christian traditions, to carry out an oppression even more drastic than the present one." He argued that the people in power viewed the Church as an institution that preached obedience to the temporal authorities. Laws about religious education in schools and the indissolubility of marriage had the purpose, Sobral said, of persuading the Church hierarchy to side with the government and refrain from opposing laws that undermined "the most sacred individual rights."[3]

According to Sobral, the government maintained the country in a pagan condition and used immoral legislation to make illegitimate children a part of "the Brazilian family," to place private property rights at the mercy of arbitrary decree-laws, and to permit censorship of the word preached "in the sacred pulpits." The state, he wrote, had made it possible for the police to arrest a bishop, with no justification, and had made it impossible to free him because Constitutional Article 186 "suspended the rights and individual guarantees established by Article 122 of that same constitution."[4]

By this time Sobral had completed his draft of an organization for the Press Secretaryship of the Archdiocese. Among those who had received copies were Alceu Amoroso Lima and Dom Jayme, with the latter receiving also Sobral's admonition that an organization chart was of little importance compared with the selection of the right people—people who could develop the goodwill of writers, vicars, school directors, and leaders of congregations. "We shall need skill in our relations with the ABI [Brazilian Press Association] and the companies publishing newspapers."[5]

At the request of the president of the Sociedade Brasileira de Criminologia, Carlos Sussekind de Mendonça, Sobral addressed the society in May, speaking about the "legal right to punish, as understood by Catholic thinking." In a normal man, he told his audience, an excellent balance existed between what Catholics considered man's two sets of attributes: those associated with his animal nature, concerned with material needs and passions, and those associated with his angelic nature, whose spirit and intelligence exerted discipline over his animal nature. In criminals, he said, the balance between body and soul was sometimes imperfect, with the animal passions assuming a dominant role.[6]

This lack of balance, Sobral emphasized, was sometimes the result of factors beyond a person's control, such as illness, heredity, moral abandonment, and economic misery. Speaking of those who had been "morally and materially abandoned," he made two points: (1) they should be provided with adequate treatment in establishments that had the facilities and personnel for achieving "moral reeducation and social readaptation"; and (2) society had the obligation to organize its structure in a way that would do away with "the moral abandonment and economic misery" of the many who lacked adequate housing, clothing, food, primary education, and moral teaching.

Punishment, Sobral maintained, was proper in the case of a person who acted against society and who was "really free," that is, possessed of "will and a conscience" that allowed society rightfully to place blame on him. But he contended that it made no sense to attribute those characteristics to persons whose lack of balance was the result of factors beyond their control, making them irresponsible rather than responsible.[7]

Alceu Amoroso Lima, an officer of book publisher AGIR, asked Sobral to write a small book about lawyers for a collection about the professions. Sobral, expressing the hope of making his contribution, wrote Alceu in August that "lawyers should extol the natural law that limits abusive activities of the state . . . and that prevents the Executive from taking over the attributes of the Legislature and Judiciary; they should extol also a harmony between authority and liberty—a harmony that prevents the legalization of tyranny, and, at the same time, prevents the masses of citizens from implanting demagoguery." In Christian societies, he added, the lawyer played a role in temporal affairs akin to that of the priest in religious affairs.[8]

Sobral wrote that he could not understand some of Alceu's choices of authors for the other studies. He said that Francisco Campos, chosen to write about jurists, "does not believe in the Law as a moral force, able to erect barriers against the arbitrary ways of men in power. For Francisco Campos, the Law is a mere government technique, always at the service of politics, and anything that politics decrees is legal." Calling Campos a politician who believed only in force, "like Adolf Hitler, Benito Mussolini, General Franco, and Oliveira Salazar," Sobral wrote that a book about jurists should be written by "someone who accepts the juridical phenomenon as stemming from a metaphysical reality that transcends the limits of temporal interests, and not by a man who ridicules metaphysics and expels from his circle of collaborators all who believe sincerely in the reality of the spirit."

Sobral recognized that Campos possessed talent, education, and a brilliant, vigorous style, but said that he was not a jurist and never had been. In his place, Sobral recommended that Alceu choose from among José Sabóia Viriato de Medeiros, Alexandre Correia, Luiz Delgado, Andrade Bezerra, José Antônio Nogueira, and José Ferreira de Souza.

Nor could Sobral understand why Alceu, in planning a Catholic-oriented collection of books, had chosen the professions of medicine and science to be handled by Agenor Porto and Miguel Osório de Almeida, respectively. He pointed out that medical doctor José Fernando Carneiro and scientist Milton Fontes Magarão combined technical competence with devotion to the Faith. "You must be aware that Agenor Porto and Miguel Osório de Almeida are confessed materialists who consider the clinical and scientific spirits to be totally incompatible with the postulates of religious Faith."

Not surprisingly Sobral authorized Alceu to give Francisco Campos, Agenor Porto, and Miguel Osório copies of his letter. The letter, he told Alceu, could be used to justify the withdrawal of the invitations sent to them to contribute to the proposed collection of books.[9]

3. Dom Jayme Calls Sobral a Naughty Boy (December 1944)

Sobral accepted an invitation of Henrique Hargreaves to speak in Juiz de Fora on November 28 at an observance of the hundredth anniversary of the birth of Bishop Vital Gonçalves de Oliveira. He reminded Hargreaves of remarks made in 1922 by Jackson de Figueiredo and Sebastião Leme when those notable Catholics had sought to reverse what they had felt was a decline in social action by the members of the Church. Presently, Sobral wrote, Brazilian Catholicism needed to demonstrate a combative spirit lest inattention to social matters "cause us to waste away in a passivity that is a betrayal of the imperious duties of our faith."[1]

Writing to Father Ivo Calliari, secretary of Archbishop Jayme Câmara, Sobral said that what chiefly shocked him about his clash with Cassiano Ricardo and the DIP was the "inertia" shown in Catholic circles. "Priests and lay Catholics continue to be unable or unwilling to perceive that the blow against me . . . is against the activity of the Church, established on the principle of freedom of speech. . . . It seems to me that the most fundamental duty of the ecclesiastical hierarchy, in countries where governments systematically crush liberty of criticism, is to support and protect those who, unselfishly risking their own rights, keep struggling for freedom of speech. Unfortunately my warnings have not been heard." Sobral quoted passages written by French thinker Léon Bloy in the 1920s that expressed "amazement" at "the conformity of Catholics." He told Calliari: "I know that the Mother of God will give me courage to continue, even though alone, in my battle."[2]

"More than ever before," Sobral wrote in a letter to Augusto Frederico Schmidt, "I feel that my mission, painful and arduous, is to cry out, never weakening, against proudly triumphant injustice." He told the poet that his eagerness for "new and more terrible struggles" grew each day. "Loudly I make my views known" to the Archbishop of Rio, former minister Campos, and Vargas himself, "with no response except silence." Upon learning that Maurício Nabuco had been named Brazilian ambassador to the Vatican, Sobral wrote him about "the alarmingly timid mentality of our episcopacy, of which Dom Jayme de Barros Câmara seems to me to be the perfect example."[3]

When conversing in his office with Father José Távora early in December, Sobral was told that Dom Jayme was not annoyed by Sobral's positions because the archbishop considered Sobral to be merely "a naughty boy."[4]

In a letter to Távora, a close assistant of Dom Jayme, Sobral said: "I have not yet recovered from the dreadful shock caused by that surprising revelation. Those terrible words, deranging me, keep repeating themselves in my broken heart." They revealed, Sobral wrote, "the uselessness of all my effort in this struggle, a gigantic and savage one without quarter, that has been my life in this archdiocese."

Sobral wrote that distress, anguish, public humiliation, financial troubles—"all this drama that takes place daily in my restless soul because I have sought intrepidly to defend the truth"—had now been described by the priests of Christ in the Rio archdiocese as the mediocre and imbecilic manifestations of a naughty boy with no notion of reality.

Giving an emphatic "No" to Távora, Sobral asserted that it had not been frivolity that had characterized his positions, but, rather, "a sense of responsibility." He denied that his actions and words had been mischievous pranks. They had not, he said, been displays of naughtiness by a thoughtless child, but had been inspired by "the noble aspiration of bringing human beings to the path of liberating truth."

"Aware of the insurmountable chasm that separates my moral sufferings from the understanding of you and the archbishop, I contemplate with horror the future of the religious soul of Brazil." Noting that priests who ought to know him well were unable to appreciate the drama that raged in his religious conscience, Sobral asked Távora how he and the archbishop expected to understand the anguish of the common people who toiled long hours, abandoned to their misery. "If a man like me, esteemed by my peers, feared by adversaries, and respected even by the oppressors of the Nation, cannot manage to have the attention of the ecclesiastical authorities . . . , what must be the fate of the common man, who has no means of explaining to these same ecclesiastical authorities the agonies and terrible sufferings of his class, reduced to the sad condition of a pariah?"

Sobral wrote that all who had struggled at his side for thirty years knew that his only ambition was to save his soul. "Penitent of my past and present and fearful of the future, I implore Christ to free me from anything that might arouse my pride." He told of his belief that only by living humbly and in poverty could he serve his fellow men "instead of letting myself be served by them for my own glorification on earth. Is it possible that neither you nor the archbishop has appreciated that this is the permanent tragedy of my moral and religious life? Is it possible that all these anguishes, that make me a miserable creature, can be interpreted as the behavior of 'a naughty boy'?"[5]

Only on December 27, after recovering from an attack of neuralgic pains, did Sobral send Dom Jayme a copy of the letter to Távora together with a letter about the "depth of the wound" caused by the archbishop's "degrading judgment." While accepting Dom Jayme's "new humiliation" as a "just punishment for my many sins," he vowed, nevertheless, not to alter his positions. "I shall continue, humbly but sincerely, to raise my voice in your presence and in the presence of all the ecclesiastical authorities in order to open my heart without dissemblance and without bitterness."[6]

No dissemblance could be found in a second letter, written on the same day to Dom Jayme, this one to "protest vehemently" against the archbishopric's "disastrous" decision that TSN President Barros Barreto deliver greetings, on behalf of Brazilian Catholics, to Apostolic Nuncio Bento Aloisi Masella during a ceremony at the nuncio's residence. Sobral explained that illness had kept him from attending the jubilee but that, had he been present, he would have made his views known at the time.[7]

"What sort of insanity afflicted Brazilian Catholicism, persuading the ecclesiastical authorities to insult the religious conscience of the Nation by selecting a man who does not even participate in the observance of the Church sacraments and who presides over a tribunal that has sent prelates and priests of Christ to prison?"[8]

Sobral wrote that both Dom Jayme and the nuncio knew of the "haughty disrespect" shown by Barros Barreto for the clergy. "To give but one example," he discussed the case of Monsignor Manoel Kemer, prelate of the district of Iguaçu Falls, held "unjustly" for months in prison. Sobral, no longer handling TSN cases, had persuaded Mário Bulhões Pedreira to defend Kemer, whose hopes for freedom, according to Sobral's letter to Dom Jayme, were being blocked by Barros Barreto's determination to delay a review of the jail sentence. Sobral also reminded Dom Jayme of the case of greengrocer Augusto Pereira, imprisoned because he had dared to try to collect payments for fruit and vegetables delivered to the residence of the TSN president.

Observing that he was not protesting alone, Sobral told Dom Jayme that Alceu Amoroso Lima had been distressed to learn, on reaching the nuncio's residence, of the speech to be given by Barros Barreto, and, after receiving confirmation from Father José Távora, had heatedly expressed his indignation and departed from the ceremony.

Sobral noted that the Christmas message of Pope Pius XII, delivered just before the nuncio's jubilee, had encouraged Catholics to oppose dictatorships and to bear in mind that the war had occurred because of a lack of effective criticism of rulers by the people. The spirit of the message, Sobral said, had been violated by the choice of Barros Barreto "to speak on behalf of Brazil's religious conscience." He called Barros Barreto "one of the most formidable props of this dictatorial state" and a man "whose pagan and sybaritic life is the object of comments even in circles distant from Catholicism."

"It is not possible," Sobral told Dom Jayme, "to have any repetition of things like this, which have been going on day after day in our religious community. In the name of Christian truth, I urge you to put a stop to these capitulations that sully Christianity's good name."[9]

A copy of this protest to Dom Jayme was sent by Sobral to the nuncio, together with a letter that quoted from Sobral's column of December 27, 1941, about the TSN cases of several Catholic priests. He told the nuncio that the choice of Barros Barreto to honor him, in the name of lay Catholics, had produced "the worst sort of scandal" in the religious community of the Rio archdiocese.[10]

4. Orlando Leite Ribeiro, Prestes, and Vargas (May 1944)

One of the arguments that Sobral had used in getting permission to visit Prestes each week was that diplomat Orlando Leite Ribeiro, friend of Vargas and Prestes, had been given permission to do so and no reason existed for denying a similar right to Prestes' lawyer.[1]

In May 1944, when both diplomat and lawyer were making their separate weekly visits, Orlando told a mutual acquaintance that he had two complaints against the conduct of Sobral. In the first place, he accused Sobral of having revealed, to someone with police connections, the contents of a letter of February 1 from Prestes to Orlando about political matters, leading Police Chief Nelson de Mello to tell Orlando of his annoyance that Prestes' views had become widespread. In the second place, Orlando criticized Sobral for having spoken to friends about Orlando's work on behalf of an understanding between Vargas and Prestes to fortify a policy of National Union, deemed urgent for the war effort.[2]

Sobral, writing Orlando, pointed out that Prestes' letter about political matters had been delivered to Orlando on February 2 and that Orlando had criticized Sobral on February 23, all of this taking place while Sobral, most of the time absent from Rio, had not seen Prestes. He added that by the time of his return from vacationing in São Paulo and southern Minas, the contents of Prestes' letter had become well known, as Sobral had learned in Rio from his clients Antônio Rollenberg and Manoel Venancio Campos da Paz. Sobral had felt free, like others, to discuss the letter because neither client had called the matter confidential and both had said that a part of the letter had been shown by Orlando to Prestes' friend Trifino Corrêa.[3]

As for Orlando's second complaint, Sobral disclaimed having made the public aware of Orlando's visits to Prestes—visits that Rollenberg had brought to Sobral's attention in the period when Sobral was unable to see Prestes. Asked by acquaintances about Orlando's purpose in making them, Sobral had replied that the diplomat wished to mitigate the isolation of his imprisoned friend. Occasionally he had mentioned other possible reasons, which he had always described as suppositions on his part, and these he now explained in full to Orlando.[4]

Sobral wrote Orlando that the latter's visits to Prestes could have been made possible only by an authorization of Vargas, and he added that Orlando made them with the understanding that Vargas and Prestes shared a "revolutionary mentality," such as Orlando himself had displayed when he had helped organize the 1924 São Paulo uprising and had supported the 1930 movement.

Sobral told Orlando that while he did not agree with his view that Vargas was the embodiment of the 1930 revolution's ideals about reforming Brazil's political and social structure, Orlando's view was important, along with his equally unfounded belief that Vargas and Prestes shared a desire to organize Brazil as a popularly supported state, hostile to foreign imperialistic capital and the excessive profits made by Brazilian exploiters of their fellow citizens. Orlando was said by Sobral to feel that Brazil's two "revolutionary chiefs," Vargas and Prestes, differed only in their methods of achieving their ideal state, Prestes being "frank and positive" and Vargas being "reserved and devious."

According to this account, Orlando, in permanent contact with both friends, felt that he could, by using tact, develop harmony between them, leading them to make mutual concessions for achieving, together, the Brazilian revolutionary state. "This objective is seen by Orlando Leite Ribeiro as helped by the fact that neither

Prestes nor Vargas will let any 'juridical ordinance' stand in his way."[5]

Orlando, Sobral believed, regarded the war and the call for National Union as a splendid opportunity for achieving his objective. "Just as the Soviet Union, outspoken enemy of British imperialism, first joins up with England to resist Nazi Germany, while planning to destroy later the bourgeois social structure of Europe, so can Prestes, declared enemy of the Estado Novo, easily join up with Vargas to cooperate with him, first to resist South American Nazism and, later, to destroy the South American bourgeois social structure. . . . You think that Prestes, in cooperating with Vargas, will give mettle, decision, and explicit purpose to the administration," and, "with his executive ability, end the disorder, anarchy, and contradictions that presently characterize the government's administrative and social policy."[6]

Sobral told Orlando that his desire to bring Vargas and Prestes together could be considered "logical, praiseworthy, and noble" by those dedicated to the beliefs that were sincerely held by Orlando. But, Sobral also told him, his hope was based on illusions and could not become reality. Writing that no true National Union could be formed under Vargas, he argued that any combination in its name, established on account of the wartime and postwar situations, would have Vargas' backing only if all the final decisions were in Vargas' hands. Sobral reminded Orlando of the fate of many signers of the Manifesto of the Mineiros, men who had patriotically and unselfishly sought to deal with problems that were important for the future. "How is it possible to form the National Union in a setting of such intolerance?"

Sobral wrote about the "implacable and severe" TSN, the DIP's censorship of free expression, and the jails filled with "hundreds and hundreds" of political prisoners. He said that the men in power should do more than merely talk about the National Union; they should clearly reveal the conditions that were to prevail. In a reference to what Sobral described as Orlando's effort to exact concessions from each of his "now separated" friends, he wrote that the only one in a position to make concessions was the government.

In Sobral's opinion the situation was such that he did not see how Prestes could come to an understanding with Vargas, even if Prestes should be agreeable to accept the tactic of "compromise" described with warnings by Lenin in his *The Infantile Disease of "Leftism" in Communism.* To convince Orlando that Vargas was unwilling to part with personal power, Sobral dealt at length with what he called the coup d'état of August 31, 1942, when a decree was issued that, according to Sobral, voided the 1937 Constitution's provision to limit the presidential term to six years, and that, in doing so, left "the Head of State carrying out a mandate that has not yet begun."[7]

In conclusion, Sobral assured Orlando that in the future he would mention to no one the political ideas of Prestes that had not become public. But, as a Brazilian citizen, he claimed the right to discuss the position of Prestes as given in well-known documents, such as Prestes' message, written in March 1944, about a pronouncement issued late in 1943 by the Aliança Nacional Libertadora (ANL).[8] This message, which Prestes managed to get into Communists' hands, denounced the language and the "leftist and sectarian" views contained in the ANL's pronouncement and, instead, called for "open, frank, and decided support of the government war policy" in combination with a struggle for liberties and amnesty that would, in Prestes' opinion, strengthen national unity. "The struggle for liberties," Prestes also wrote, "does not mean, at this moment, a doctrinal combat against the Estado Novo and the present constitution, and much less, generalized insults" of government men facing complex problems.[9]

5. Police Chief Coriolano and the Fall of Aranha (August 1944)

In April Sobral was disturbed to discover that the Brazilian government, through its embassies, was providing the American republics with what he considered "revoltingly false information about crimes attributed to Prestes." He addressed Foreign Minister Oswaldo Aranha to point out that the false charge of Prestes' "guilt" of the "common crime" of ordering the murder of Elza Fernandes had already been made public by the Brazilian embassy in Mexico in 1942 when it had explained why Vargas had not acted on the request of Mexican General Lázaro Cárdenas that Prestes be allowed to go to Mexico for his mother's funeral and then return to prison.[1]

The renewed allegation about Prestes' guilt had appeared in an article in Chile's *El Siglo,* and from it Sobral learned that the allegation was being used to undermine a campaign to persuade the Emergency Commission for the Political Defense of the Continent, in Montevideo, to seek the liberation of anti-fascist political prisoners, including Prestes.

Sobral informed Aranha that the trial of Prestes, in the case of Elza Fernandes, had been handled by a political tribunal that had maintained that the crime had been a political one and not a common one. In 1940, Sobral wrote, the government had been convinced that if the case were handled by a jury trial in the regular justice system, his defense would demolish the "monstrous" denouncement, "a house of cards set up by the police." The police investigation, he told Aranha, had been carried out in secrecy in a setting of terror and without the proper use of witnesses. By calling the murder a political crime, he added, the prosecution had been able to use "laws of exception," such as Decree 474 of June 8, 1938, which held that denouncements at the TSN were to be regarded as proven unless disproved during the investigation.[2]

Aranha did not act on Sobral's request of April that he instruct Brazil's embassies to refrain from spreading untruths about Prestes, and so, a month later, Sobral repeated his request. But it remained unattended by Aranha, who was engaged at the time in a bitter struggle with War Minister Dutra, a political rival filled with apprehensions about the leftists and liberty-loving groups attracted to the foreign minister. The police and the generals of Dutra harried the Sociedade Amigos da América, which elected Aranha to be its vice president, and the DIP ordered the press not to mention the Sociedade. Thus in mid-August the press did not report that Rio policemen, directed by Coriolano de Góes, closed down the Sociedade, prior to the ceremony that was to install its vice president, and that on the next day they broke up a meeting attended by Aranha and Sociedade members at the Automobile Club. Aranha, failing to obtain Vargas' support after this setback, resigned as foreign minister.[3]

On August 26, three days after the resignation, Sobral wrote Aranha to praise him for leaving the government and to express gratitude for his position in October 1943 when the DIP had not allowed Sobral to respond to Cassiano Ricardo. "You and Colonel Nelson de Mello were the only members of the federal government who had the strength of character to voice your disapproval of that act of administrative despotism." Now Sobral urged Aranha to help restore civic life by joining the effort to have Brazil run by its citizens and not by the group of men who had taken over the governing machine.

Sobral told Aranha that if he would do this he would atone for many of his past errors, "which were fatal to our historic destinies." The Brazilian people, Sobral wrote, had never heard Aranha express a single vigorous criticism of the government's "juridical positivism, that confuses the issuance of laws with supporting the Rule of Law and that subjugates individual rights in order to uphold the single sovereign will of rulers who completely suppress the dignity of the human person and who abusively arrogate to themselves the right to think, speak, and act for all."[4]

Brazil, Sobral informed Aranha, was not the "desert of men and ideas" presented by Paul Frischauer in his recent biography of Vargas.[5] Sobral called it unjust of Frischauer to portray the Brazilian people as lacking in moral wisdom just because its rulers, in control of public statements, did not allow noble ideas to be expressed. "The book, lacking grandeur and generosity, is merely a picture of a cold politician, crafty and Messianic, who wishes to direct a country that is described as having no collective soul and as inhabited by people unaware of their country's destinies."

No episode in all of Brazil's political life, Sobral wrote, was as humiliating and grave as that of the writing of the Vargas biography by "a foreigner, a nomad totally unaware of our sufferings and completely indifferent to our real greatness. . . . I finished reading the book with my heart filled with somber apprehensions, especially because it closes for Brazil all perspectives of a lofty future." Readers abroad, Sobral said, would never understand how the supreme authority of the Nation could have allowed a foreigner, with allegiance to no country, to spend months and months on end at his side, carrying out the assignment of painting such a depreciating picture.[6]

In April, when Colonel Nelson de Mello prepared to leave his position as Rio police chief in order to join the Brazilian armed forces that were to fight Germans in Italy, Sobral thanked the colonel for having done everything in his power "to free the conscience of honest men."[7]

His successor, Coriolano de Góes, had a rather different reputation, especially after serving as state security secretary of São Paulo, where in November 1943 he had dispatched the police to engage in what became a bloody shooting of anti-Vargas students.[8] As the new chief of the Rio police, Coriolano received the title of head of the Federal Department of Public Security.

In mid-August Sobral turned to Coriolano in search of a reversal of a ruling, attributed to Coriolano by Sobral, that ended the weekly visits to Prestes by the prisoner's young first cousin, medical doctor Antônio Prestes de Menezes. Sobral reminded Coriolano of the days of the Bernardes administration when "I, you, and Pedro [de Oliveira Ribeiro Sobrinho] struggled for the establishment of a true order." "You and Pedro appreciated that the campaign against me was against a person of ideals in the *procuradoria criminal da república*. . . . When the most unjust of campaigns broke out against my poor person . . . , you firmly placed yourself at my side. . . . Never in the following sixteen years have you lacked my gratitude."[9]

Sobral wrote that Coriolano, during those sixteen years, had never failed to receive the backing of Sobral even though Sobral had frequently objected to positions assumed by Coriolano as a public figure—objections "clearly made known to you when I saw you in São Paulo in February of this year."

Turning to the case of Prestes' cousin, Sobral told Coriolano that only after the authorization of Orlando Leite Ribeiro's visits to Prestes was Sobral able to obtain permission for the young doctor to make the weekly visits that were his right as a relative of the prisoner. The recent news from prison director Caneppa about Coriolano's prohibition led Sobral to remind Coriolano that neither he nor Pedro had ever witnessed the approval of such a prohibition by Sobral "during the almost four years in which I held in my strong hands the orientation of the legal repression of the revolutionaries." Asking Coriolano to fulfill a promise made in July 1944 to work against violations of the law, Sobral called Coriolano's intervention in the prison regimen of Prestes a flagrant violation of regulations that placed the matter exclusively in the hands of the director of the penitentiary.[10]

In reply Sobral received a card on which Coriolano, in a few lines, denied having given the order against the visits by Prestes' cousin.[11] But Sobral by then had information that contradicted the denial. After writing Caneppa that Prestes' cousin would never cause any problem for the prison director,[12] he sent an unfriendly letter to Coriolano.

In it Sobral wrote that he was "filled with amazement" at the denial on Coriolano's card, "so reserved and formal." He explained that after discussing the matter with Prestes and his cousin and learning that "Caneppa was personally with you to consider the situation of Luiz Carlos Prestes, I can have no doubt about who was responsible for the prohibition. . . . According to the version that reached me from the two persons directly involved, it was you who told Lieutenant Caneppa that the only regular visits to be allowed to Luiz Carlos Prestes were to be mine, as his lawyer."[13] Sobral pointed out that the suspension of the visits by Prestes' cousin had coincided with Coriolano's becoming police chief in Rio, and added that Caneppa had no desire to see Prestes tormented. He wrote that if the political situation were to become less unsettled, Caneppa would be willing, although perhaps timidly, to relax the severity of the treatment of Prestes.

"You are, at this moment, a man of power, with indisputable prestige in the government, as became clear with the outcome of the recent political crisis. In fact, as police chief, you ordered the closure of the Sociedade Amigos da América."[14]

6. Dictatorial Pressures on the OAB, Dario, Adaucto, and Others (Late 1944)

On a Saturday night late in September, Francisco Campos and Augusto Frederico Schmidt discussed with Sobral, at his home, the situation in Brazil. Sobral described Brazil as having reached a deplorably low point, characterized by oppression, toadyism, incompetent administrators, and misery. Campos agreed that he and others had made mistakes. Perhaps, he remarked, some sort of public repentance, on a grand scale, was called for, such as a procession of "five thousand penitent personalities."[1]

Sobral took the suggestion of a procession seriously, more so perhaps than Campos, and he used it to make a point. Writing Campos, he said: "Only a spectacle like that can arouse our people from the skepticism into which the egoism of our ruling classes has thrown them. Only a clear display of public repentance for so many capitulations to evil can restore, to our abandoned population, the moral prestige of public men who . . . have been accomplices in the errors of the authorities in these last fifteen years."

Telling Campos to make it clear to the men in power that a demonstration of penitence was the only possible salvation for Brazil, he wrote: "It is up to you to take, with virile resolution, the path of redemption." Campos, he said, should advise Vargas, in a letter, of his resolve to call together the leading representatives of the professions to participate in a public demonstration of repentance of past errors. And he should, Sobral also insisted, address a document "of moral grandeur" to representatives of the Church, the government, the military, the professions, and the business world to start a movement that would perhaps even attract Vargas. "Thus you will elevate yourself in your own eyes."[2]

In November, a month after receiving the letter, Campos conversed with Vargas in the presidential workroom at Guanabara Palace. Vargas, a good listener, heard Campos explain that politics is the art of adapting and that Vargas would be lost unless he immediately espoused democracy and freedom of the press. Campos even told Vargas to assume the "leadership of the opposition against the government." But he did not expect Getúlio to follow his suggestion.[3]

It seemed to Sobral that Osório Borba, like Campos, was showing signs of understanding the true situation. Sobral wrote Borba to praise one of his articles because, he said, it did not "invoke the sectarian sentiments" that so often "made my heart bleed" and because it condemned eulogizers of the Estado Novo. Flattery of the men in power, Sobral told him, was "the great ulcer that corrodes the virile soul of the Nation."[4]

In the Ordem dos Advogados do Brasil (OAB), a considerable stir followed a denouncement by Sobral of the Minas government's activity prior to the December 1 election of members to that state's OAB Conselho. Sobral, a member of the OAB Conselho Federal, wrote Conselho Federal President Raul Fernandes on November 30 to say that men working for Minas Governor Benedicto Valladares had used the governor's influence and the state's wartime control of telegraph lines to tell all the Minas mayors, the principal state judges, and many bank directors to persuade the lawyers to vote against the slate that included Pedro Aleixo and Milton Campos and that opposed the arbitrary acts of the government and the absolute domination by the men in power. The state authorities, he added, had threatened economic reprisals against lawyers and their relatives if the lawyers ignored Valladares' wishes, and, in addition, had taken steps to make it difficult for the opponents of the Valladares slate to publicize their message about the need to return "juridical ordinance" to Brazil.[5]

Sobral's letter was read at the OAB Conselho Federal session of December 5, by which time Pedro Aleixo had also complained of state interference in the Minas OAB election. Alberto Venancio Filho, recording the Conselho session in his history of the OAB, writes: "The dictatorship was exerting intense pressure in an effort to deprive the OAB of its independence." Milton Campos, writing from Belo Horizonte on December 9, 1944, asserted that the charges made by Sobral and Pedro Aleixo were supported by reports from local OAB subsections.[6] At the Minas Conselho of the OAB, it was resolved not to accept the results of the December 1 OAB election in the state.[7]

In Rio in December 1944, shortly before Christmas, Coriolano's police arrested eighteen enemies of the regime who had been under surveillance. Thirteen of the eighteen were classified as Communists and their arrest did not cause nearly as much comment as the arrest of the other five: oppositionist politician Virgílio de Mello Franco, lawyers Adaucto Lucio Cardoso and Dario de Almeida Magalhães, and journalists Austregésilo de Athayde and Raphael Corrêa de Oliveira. Virgílio de Mello Franco had just returned to Rio from São Paulo, where he had obtained signatures on a pro-democracy manifesto which was to be used to launch the presidential candidacy of air force Brigadeiro Eduardo Gomes.[8]

The OAB Conselho Federal, learning of the arrests, declared itself in permanent session and drew up a habeas corpus petition on behalf of the five well-known prisoners.[9]

Sobral, in another of his long letters (this one nineteen pages), told Coriolano that his conduct could not be justified from any point of view and that, if he would recall their work together in the 1920s, he would appreciate that Sobral had never tolerated arbitrary acts and had intransigently upheld the law. He assured Coriolano that Dario and Adaucto, who had been close to him, did not have conspiracy or revolution in mind, but, on the contrary, hoped to prevent the outbreak of the civil war that would "inevitably" occur if Brazil failed to adopt their program favoring free and honest elections, free tribunals, a free press, an end to financial chaos, and the election of a Constituent Assembly. Sobral also told Coriolano that Adaucto, Dario, and others, feeling that the government would announce that elections were to be held without delay, had been preparing campaign topics, such as the unclear mandate of Vargas and the wartime cost-of-living increase that Sobral said was certainly in excess of 500 percent.[10]

Sobral described himself as having remained the "advance guard of a regime of Law," an expression Coriolano had used to praise him following his defense of Coriolano in 1931, and he reminded Coriolano that he had also defended him "in 1934 or 1935, when I testified to judges about your administration of the police during the presidency of the now glorious President Washington Luiz." In evoking such matters of the past, Sobral wrote, he was pleading that the five men, recently arrested, be released and allowed to "discuss freely, before their fellow citizens, problems that are vital to contemporary Brazil." In conclusion Sobral declared that all of the honest men he knew believed that the government served by Coriolano was inspired by the "same ideas that predominated in the Jacobin government of revolutionary France."[11]

The five oppositionists, defended in Sobral's letter and in the habeas corpus petition of the OAB, were set free after spending ten days in the barracks of the First Cavalry Regiment of the Rio police.[12]

7.   Doing Legal Work for Schmidt (1944–1945)

In August 1942, right after Brazil declared itself at war with Germany and Italy, the Rio police arrested some German citizens who they felt might be dangerous to the national security. A few were still in prison two years later, although no formal charges had been submitted to the judiciary against them.

The first of these late-1944 German clients of Sobral was Walter Zabel, engaged in commerce in Rio before his arrest. His wife, after two years of loneliness, sought Sobral's help and told him that the police had been wrong when they had said that her husband had possessed Nazi propaganda. Sobral, seeking Zabel's release, told the authorities that the police could make use of items from its large collection of seized pro-Nazi material to support unfounded charges against anyone.[1] His view prevailed, and in September he expressed his gratitude to Police Chief Coriolano de Góes for the liberation of Zabel. "As you see," he wrote, "I do not limit myself to criticizing improper acts by the public authorities."[2]

Following Zabel's release, Sobral was approached by friends of Germans who had been employees of the Banco Alemão Transatlântico, and he argued, again successfully, that the police were at fault for not having concluded investigations after more than two years.[3]

Sobral was less successful in the case of a young Brazilian woman, Maria Catharina Diniz, being made a scapegoat for fraudulent acts carried out by others at the Pension Institute of Workers in Commerce. Defending her without charging a fee, he ran into trouble because the head of the commission investigating her conduct became furious at the tone of the letters he received from Sobral and turned for help to former Police Chief Filinto Müller, who had become president of the National Labor Council. Müller, in the words of Sobral, took a position against Maria because he "has never lost hope of making me pay dearly for my intrepid defense of Luiz Carlos Prestes and has been seeking to persecute me."[4]

On October 16, 1944, Augusto Frederico Schmidt telephoned Sobral, telling him to be in Petrópolis on the 20th to handle the defense of the Werner Textile Company, in which Schmidt and his friend Peixoto de Castro had invested heavily. A German employee, Bosseljon, had returned to the textile company after spending time in prison on account of his nationality, but had been told that he had been dismissed. His position at the plant had been of some importance, and he was suing on the ground that his dismissal had been illegal and that, even if it could be justified, he ought to be paid a large indemnification.

Sobral, who had not known about the case, irritated Schmidt by saying he could not represent the company without learning more details. Schmidt told Sobral that he was to be the lawyer, "not the judge," and added: "We'll give you our arguments, which appear to be valid, and you can use them." But these remarks did not satisfy Sobral, and Schmidt broke off the phone conversation, apparently in a huff.[5]

Sobral, writing Schmidt on the 17th, said that "the most fundamental duty of a lawyer is to be the initial judge of the case; he must examine it carefully to see if it really has merit in accordance with the precepts of justice." This truth, he wrote, could not be altered by their friendship or by Schmidt's "noble idea" of assisting Sobral financially. "When we get together, I as a jurist and you as an industrialist, we do not always speak the same language. You are, above everything else, something I have never been able to be: a Poet, and therefore a herald of God, and so I cannot fail to see in you the eloquent voice that so frequently upholds the appeals of divine justice, asking for compassion and forgiveness of all errors, weaknesses, and betrayals. This is the Schmidt to whom I am deeply devoted."[6]

Although Sobral did not go to Petrópolis on October 20, Schmidt was able, a few days later, to persuade him to represent the textile firm. Sobral's first defense argument, that Bosseljon was guilty of having deserted the company, had to be withdrawn when he learned that Bosseljon had reported for work immediately after his release from prison. Placing the blame for this setback on Schmidt's failure to seek his help earlier, Sobral wrote: "Our difficulties have been caused by your turning to a competent lawyer only after your situation appeared to be desperate." He told Schmidt and his partner, Peixoto de Castro, to find evidence to show that Bosseljon, in his days with the company, had enjoyed their confidence and thus occupied two positions simultaneously: he had been a technician, the recipient of 2,500 cruzeiros monthly, and also a manager, the recipient of much more pay but without legal protection, such as tenure, applicable to less lofty posts. "When Bosseljon turned to you, after his release from prison, you did not wish to take him back as manager, and he, quite naturally, did not wish to return to being a mere 30,000-cruzeiro-a-year technician."[7]

The case did not appeal to Sobral. Further study led him to understand how Bosseljon had been able to obtain the services of a highly respected lawyer, Sobral's friend Pedro Baptista Martins. Even worse, Sobral told Schmidt, "the case fills my juridical conscience with worries, and I cannot get rid of them. . . . As I have told all my clients, the legal profession is not a passive instrument whereby lawyers can adjust the Law to the interests of their clients." Describing his "moral dilemma," Sobral wrote: "I feel that I cannot withdraw from the case because that would add enormously to your troubles."[8]

Sobral rejected Schmidt's suggestion that they turn to Vargas, asking him to overrule a decision of the labor minister that upheld Bosseljon's claim to the position he had held before his arrest. Sobral explained that legislation did not provide for such an appeal to the president, and suggested, instead, making use of Decree-Law 4,638, of August 31, 1942, which allowed the rescission of job contracts held by employees who were a threat to the production of material needed for the national security. The company, Sobral wrote, could show that it produced fabric used in the manufacture of parachutes and that Bosseljon had connections with Germans accused of spying. A letter was therefore obtained by Schmidt and Peixoto de Castro from the United States embassy requiring the dismissal of Bosseljon as a condition of the textile company's receipt of American raw materials.[9]

All of this, Sobral wrote, would have been useful if the company had not gone ahead and hired, as a replacement for Bosseljon, an Italian citizen. However, on the day after Sobral made this observation, he learned from the press that the Brazilian government had recognized the new government of Italy, a development that eliminated the problem.[10]

Still, there remained the question of how much indemnification to pay Bosseljon. Peixoto de Castro, making notes to be used to defend the textile company, claimed that Bosseljon's base pay had been 2,500 cruzeiros a month and that the remainder represented bonuses paid each year at no fixed rate. Sobral, citing Article 557 of the Consolidation of Labor Laws, wrote Schmidt that "this argument will not save you." He recommended turning instead to Article 499 of the Consolidation, which ruled that employees with managerial status did not enjoy tenure rights.[11]

At the time that Schmidt brought the case to Sobral's attention, Sobral's distressing financial situation had moved Plínio Barreto to write from São Paulo with an offer to put all his assets at Sobral's disposal. The offer, although not accepted, had brought Plínio a warm letter saying: "I felt like taking the first plane to São Paulo in order to go to your office and tell you: 'I have come to give you, with all my heart, this warm and sincere embrace.'"[12]

In December 1944 the neuralgic pains in Sobral's face kept him at home for two weeks. This absence from his law practice, he wrote Schmidt just before Christmas, had had such a "disastrous" effect on his income that he found himself forced to ask for an additional 3,000 cruzeiros on top of the 2,000 received as an advance for his work on the Bosseljon case.[13]

In April 1945, in response to a ruling of the labor court in favor of Bosseljon's indemnification claim, Peixoto de Castro drew up a bulky appeal, while Sobral was suffering from eczema that kept him in bed, once again, for two weeks. Although on April 15, when the illness began, Sobral had advised Schmidt and Peixoto that his health required that they find another lawyer, Schmidt sought Sobral's signature on Peixoto's appeal and therefore brought it to his home on the morning of April 23. The appeal, Schmidt said, had to be presented that very day to the labor court in Petrópolis, and he assured Sobral that it faithfully represented his views. Sobral, not given enough time to read the document, managed to sign it, although his fingers were covered with cold compresses.

Soon he regretted doing so, for the document was full of personal attacks against the opposing lawyer, his friend Pedro Baptista Martins. Martins telephoned Sobral on April 28 to say that he could not believe that such an appeal had been written by Sobral. Following Martins' phone call, which was received soon after the death of Sobral's beloved godmother and mother-in-law, Sobral sent Martins a letter to explain what had happened. And Sobral told Peixoto de Castro that the appeal he had signed upset him so much that he had serious doubts about continuing to be associated with the case. He also told Schmidt of his anger.[14]

8. Rebuking Coriolano and Pedro, São Paulo's Security Secretary (Early 1945)

The year 1945 opened with one of Sobral's friends offering a bank job to Idalina, the oldest of his seven children. But she preferred to continue teaching at the Jacobina School. It paid less than the bank but allowed her time to carry on with her education.[1]

From Mexico, Lygia Prestes sent Sobral a check to help take care of her brother's needs. Sobral, however, was receiving numerous donations for the same purpose, contributed by Brazilian admirers of the Cavalier of Hope, and therefore, at the suggestion of the prisoner, he returned the check.[2]

Lygia wrote that she had recovered from her illness and wanted news of her brother and the Brazilian situation. Sobral, with no lack of practice in painting a picture of Brazil's ills, did so for Lygia and described also the struggle on behalf of "justice and liberty" being carried out by himself and others, inspired by the virility of the early Christians, armed with the word of God and not with the usual weapons of battle.[3]

Sobral reminded Lygia of how different he was from her brother, believer in "the historic materialism of Marx," but promised to continue serving as Prestes' ex officio lawyer. "I am fifty-one years old and hope to live another ten years. And these years, I believe, will be more than enough for Brazilians to attain the serenity necessary for reaching a better judgment of my ex officio client."[4]

A recent client was Antônio Bayma, manager of the Anhanguera construction company, which was constructing the Majestic apartment building for George Blizniansky. At length, early in January,

Bayma and Blizniansky agreed to a rescission of the construction contract; and, as Bayma was demanding payment for having installed one-third of the building's reinforced concrete, it was agreed that the amount would be established by Sobral, acting as arbiter. When Sobral, after a careful but slow study, came up with a figure, Bayma refused to accept it. Sobral therefore resigned as arbiter and as lawyer for Bayma, who then turned for help to Police Chief Coriolano de Góes. Bayma revealed to Coriolano, a friend of his, that Blizniansky was defendant in a criminal case in France.[5]

Coriolano dispatched a police investigator to tell Blizniansky, at his Rio home, that he would not be allowed to leave Rio until he had settled his case with Bayma. This step brought Coriolano a scolding from Sobral. The criminal case in Europe, Sobral wrote, had nothing to do with the litigation in Brazil and neither did the Rio police department. "I cannot agree that Dr. Bayma, just because he is a friend of yours, should in this way be able to exert pressure on his adversary in a purely commercial matter, compelling Sr. Blizniansky to submit to the dictates of the police."[6]

An old case that resurfaced early in 1945 was that of Paulo Galvão Bueno of São Paulo. On Paulo's behalf, five years earlier, Paulista lawyer Thyrso Martins had asked Sobral to present a habeas corpus petition to the Supreme Court. Although the case had subsequently been resolved in the defendant's favor, the São Paulo police arrested him in February 1945. Thyrso had died in 1941, and so Sobral recommended to a friend of Paulo that the case be handled by Abelardo Cardoso. At the same time he wrote the new São Paulo state secretary of security, his longtime friend Pedro de Oliveira Ribeiro Sobrinho. "Your police," Sobral said, "have arrested Paulo, this former client of Thyrso, despite the invalidation of the sentence against him. . . . I know of your devotion to the duties of friendship, above all when this concerns the memory of our companion, taken from us by death."[7]

Already in January Sobral had reprimanded Pedro for becoming secretary of security of São Paulo state. When he had learned that Pedro was considering accepting the offer and that Coriolano was insisting that Pedro accept, Sobral had become worried, and when Pedro did assume the secretaryship, he wrote him that his decision brought him "one of the greatest sorrows of my already troubled and agonized life." "You know," he added, "that nothing is right in our country. It lacks laws, jurisprudence, justice, liberty, property rights, morality, administration, and respect for human dignity." He referred to the arrest by Coriolano of five citizens "who spoke of the need of free elections," and pointed out that Pedro, as secretary of security, would have to force "men who are like me" to appear before the TSN, and would have to silence students who were demanding "the liberation of their country." Pedro would, Sobral also warned, have to support the DEIP (São Paulo's DIP) in its silencing of "virile and independent writers who tell the truth, as happened to me in the shameful episode of Cassiano Ricardo."

"Just imagine Coriolano arresting me because I want Brazil liberated, and you, my *compadre* and beloved friend, upholding such an act of violence and iniquity. I am not just fantasizing: the last time you were here at my home, you said, after reading one of the most truthful documents I wrote about the situation, 'This time you are going to be jailed because nothing hurts worse than hearing the irrefutable truth.'

"You are not joining a government, but, rather, a despotism. . . . And so, my dear and fraternal friend, tears filled my eyes when I read the news that you are becoming part of this oppressive machine."[8]

PART IX

Emerging as a Hero with Brazil's Return to Liberties (Early 1945)

1. Contemplating a Popular Election for President (January–February 1945)

During January and February 1945, Brazilians interested in politics spoke of the possibility of Vargas bending, at least partially, before the winds of democracy that blew in from abroad, and therefore modifying the constitution to allow a popular election for president.

The belief that Vargas would run to succeed himself was strengthened by a newspaper article that made it clear that his candidacy was supported by a group of politicians who met on January 11 in the office of Federal District Mayor Henrique Dodsworth.[1] Sobral, reading in the press about this development, wrote Coriolano de Góes to reproach him for being unfair because he had allowed Dodsworth's visitors to discuss openly a future election and a candidacy but had arrested Dario, Adaucto, and their three friends for doing the same thing about two weeks earlier.[2]

More gratifying to Sobral was a verbal report that Francisco Campos, after hearing from Sobral in October, had met with Vargas and given him a scathing lecture on behalf of democracy. Writing Campos on January 22, Sobral expressed happy surprise to learn that "one of the men responsible for enslaving the Brazilian people" had become "the first to declare, late in 1944, that the regime of liberty must be restored." But Sobral was pained to have also heard that Campos planned to remedy the situation by writing another constitution "to be imposed on the Brazilian people."[3]

Asserting that Vargas had no right to promulgate constitutions, Sobral reminded Campos that on November 6, 1937, he had written him "with the soul of Don Quixote" to warn against what had happened four days later. Maintaining that Vargas had put Brazil in the war and signed treaties with other nations "without consulting the people," Sobral compared Vargas to Napoleon, whose downfall had been followed by a long peace in Europe. Choosing passages from the "lamentable" biography of Vargas by Frischauer, "an Israelite without a country," Sobral argued that Vargas believed Brazilians to be incapable of self-government and was determined to remain in office and in full command, even if he found himself forced temporarily "to wear the shirt of democracy."[4]

Sobral instructed Campos to persuade men in government that the 1937 Constitution was both "Nazi and fascist"—an instruction unlikely to be followed because Campos did not share this view and only felt that his creation had been misused. Sobral's other demand was that Campos use his talent to convince Vargas to leave office. Campos, acceding to neither of Sobral's demands, engaged in discussions with Justice Minister Marcondes Filho and the military about using a plebiscite to modify the 1937 Constitution and to authorize a direct election in which Vargas could be a presidential candidate.[5]

Not until January 22, 1945, did Sobral get around to responding to a letter that War Minister Dutra had sent him in December 1943, calling his quarrel with Cassiano Ricardo and the DIP a personal matter that had nothing to do with the ministry of war. Denying that the matter was a personal one, Sobral wrote that it concerned the "total suppression" of freedom to discuss the regime, criticize its leaders, and examine public administration, a right that was "essential for the progress and development of civilized nations." Denying that he had erred in having appealed to the war minister, he pointed out that the Estado Novo, creator of the DIP, had been installed by the military, whose officers, he added, were the ones "who can intervene with the President of the Republic to have him end unjust coercion against me as a citizen." Sobral accused the Vargas administration of encouraging vulgar flattery that portrayed government leaders as "illustrious geniuses" at a time when "almost all Brazilians criticize the regime ceaselessly."[6]

Dutra was reminded by Sobral that in November 1937 he, the war minister, had vouched for the truth of a claim by Vargas that the armed forces "will never act as instruments of oppression and tyranny" and "have invariably been the guardians of the law and the defenders of justice."[7] "The present regime," Sobral wrote Dutra, "is totally separated from the Christian ideal" of "a judiciary that can act independently. . . . It seems that a citizen, deprived of his rights of citizenship, has to have the soul of Don Quixote and plead with loyal and patriotic soldiers like yourself because it has become useless to turn to the judiciary."[8]

In February 1945, Sobral got around to reprimanding First Infantry Division Commander Renato Paquet for his much-applauded speech of November 10, 1944, eulogizing the Estado Novo and disparaging the Old Republic. The general, describing political decentralization before the Estado Novo, had said that the control of the interior had been divided among "small grotesque oligarchies," running "state kingdoms, associated with illiterate electoral bosses shielded by miniature armies that were used to threaten the central power and act against national unity." Speaking of the united Brazil created by the Estado Novo, he had exclaimed: "Today mighty Brazil exists, wants to live, work, and progress."[9]

Paquet learned from Sobral that he had ignored the true grandeur of Brazil, built during four centuries by the valor of its people and the vision of its public figures. Sobral spoke of "the aggrandizement of Brazilians," carried out by regimes that had had "political representation," and he disputed the general's assertion that the Brazilian people in 1937 had chosen to give the country an "ultra-democratic" government, the Estado Novo, which under Vargas had produced "wonderful fruits" while letting individuals take their problems directly to it, "bypassing those intermediaries" who in the past had stood in the way of solutions.[10]

In early February 1945, when Sobral wrote General Paquet, cautious references to the need of elections could be found in the press. The references could quote Vargas, who, in April 1944, had told the Brazilian Press Association (ABI) that "when we are again in possession of the benefits of peace" the people "will choose their leaders and representatives democratically, within order and the law." But his words to the military on December 31 served as a warning against premature agitations and demagogic disturbances and made it clear that the coming political reforms should be worked out by "processes of gradual evolution."[11]

Although the demand for liberty and elections made at the First Writers' Congress in São Paulo late in January 1945 could find no place in the press, on February 1 the *Folha Carioca* carried an interview in which General Góes Monteiro gave his blessing to elections, which he said had been promised by Vargas. Góes, after squabbling with Vargas in 1943, had taken a diplomatic post in Uruguay; he had returned late in 1944 for a conversation with Vargas in which he had argued that the time had come to end the Estado Novo.

Rio's *O Globo* had associated itself with those who were letting it be known that Brazil should return to democracy and who felt that Vargas' days were numbered.[12] Writing about elections in a manner calculated to avoid DIP penalties, it said on February 6 that Vargas, despite his power, did not fail to abide by the wishes of the people, one example of this "sensitivity" being his resolve in August 1942 to declare Brazil at war with Germany and Italy. This admirable trait of heeding the people, *O Globo* wrote, could be seen now in his noble response to "the irrepressible appeals of public opinion" in favor of the elections.[13]

This "monstrous article," Sobral wrote *O Globo*'s Roberto Marinho, "filled my eyes with tears" because it revealed "how lies and deception are infiltrating all the organs of publicity and communication." Explaining Vargas' "materialistic" response to the war, Sobral wrote that in June 1940 he had defied all national opinion and placed Brazil in a neutral position sympathetic to the Axis powers because events had indicated that they were about to dominate the world. By August 1942, Sobral added, "events were totally different": the United States had been forced to enter the war and needed the bases in Belém and Natal. "Every intelligent person knows that Brazil entered the war to make those parts of our national territory available to the United States."[14]

The false claim that Vargas had been influenced by public opinion in 1942 and 1945, Sobral told Marinho, was a part of the propaganda being used to strengthen the candidacy of Vargas in the coming presidential election. "You know, much better than I, that elections are coming, not on account of the pressure of public opinion on the powerful will of Getúlio Vargas," but because Vargas, after waiting for events to make a decision for him "in a way that assures the victory of his candidacy, has come to see that this is the best path to follow in order to legitimize his investiture in the presidency and consolidate, under the name of democracy, the authoritarian regime that he has been able to implant."[15]

2. The Exchange with Góes Monteiro (February–April 1945)

General Góes Monteiro had been recovering from illness at his apartment and was in his pajamas, smoking cigarettes, when he gave his interview of February 1 to the *Folha Carioca* backing the Vargas promise of direct elections. Surely, he said, Vargas would give Brazil an institutional structure appropriate for its democracy. Sobral, favoring the removal of Vargas from office, disliked what he called Góes' inference that the Brazilian people, lacking the ability to handle the matter well, should "accept, with tranquillity, directives from Vargas." Sobral objected to Góes' reservations about democracy in Brazil, apparent when the general told the *Folha Carioca* that the social climates in England, the United States, Switzerland, and Scandinavia were appropriate for democracy, whereas "the Brazilian situation is very different," characterized by "a mass immersed in misery" and a middle class "also living in poverty while the elite are unfortunately corrupt."[1]

In a seventy-one-page letter to Góes (Dutra had received only twenty-six pages), Sobral quoted from Góes' book about the 1930 revolution, which declared that "the representative system, using universal and direct suffrage as applied in Brazil, will always be ludicrous."[2] Góes, Sobral maintained, had agreed with Vargas that Brazil needed a long period of authoritarian rule, and had joined with him in 1930 to install a *castilhista* dictatorship, based on the positivist philosophy of Júlio de Castilhos and Borges de Medeiros that had dominated politics in Rio Grande do Sul for forty years. Sobral added that socialism, "the destroyer of individual rights," had been a vague ingredient of *castilhista* positivism but had had no opportunity to flourish until Vargas had taken over.[3]

Noting that Agamemnon Magalhães was about to replace Marcondes Filho as justice minister, Sobral reminded Góes that in July 1940 Agamemnon had praised Brazil for being the first country in America to appreciate that democracy was coming to an end in the world and had declared that "even rich countries can no longer give themselves the luxury of a liberty that permits everyone to offer opinions about the problems of state." "Clearly," Sobral wrote, "I cannot be so naïve as to think that you, Vargas, and Agamemnon Magalhães have been converted to the democratic ideals. . . . You all feel that you must bend momentarily before the winds of freedom in order to restore the authoritarian regime."[4]

Sobral told Góes that if, as he had told the *Folha Carioca*, the elite were corrupt and the masses miserable, the blame must fall on Brazil's "present rulers," who, unlike their predecessors, had been in full control. The proper thing for Góes, he wrote, was to ask those "present rulers" to resign patriotically.[5]

On February 22, the date of Sobral's letter to Góes, censorship of the press by the DIP came to an end. While the press rioted in freedom, filling its pages with the long-repressed views of the anti-Getulistas, Sobral's letter to Góes appeared in the *Jornal do Commercio.*

Góes was fond of expressing his opinions on subjects such as those handled in Sobral's letter, and he replied at length on April 7, blaming the delay on work and poor health. He rejected Sobral's thesis that he had sought to help Vargas set up the national government in accordance with the doctrine of *castilhismo borgista,* which, he said, was effective only in patriarchal "Lilliputian" republics and was a shirt much too small to be worn by Brazil, "an infantile giant, going through the crisis of growing." He had, he wrote, responded to a call of much broader import than "the *borgismo* that haunts you so much"—a call to defeat disaggregation and the "individualistic liberalism" that was inappropriate for Brazilian reality.[6]

Góes had good words for the selection of members of parliament by the elite during the Brazilian empire and observed that, since those days, the top administration had no longer been separated from the currents of the people but had been affected by a leveling, accompanied by the emergence of "people of the lowest stratum" and "universal clamor, the shouts of everyone."

Góes admitted that he had recommended, as Sobral charged, the use of "power, order, discipline, and zeal" for at least ten years in order to prepare "a new elite" and modify a situation notable for the ignorance and the misery of great masses. "It was," he wrote, "necessary to act with a strong hand on the nebulous nation and mold, with patriotic energy, the amorphous mass." "I have learned through suffering that my calculation of ten years was optimistic. A series of reprehensible ills in the national organism requires a labor of many decades."[7]

Without doubt, Góes asserted, the task of making Brazil orderly and providing health and education to her "millions of victims of diseases . . . , ignorance, and apathy" was no small one. Nor was it a simple matter to persuade the "ten million literates and semi-literates who make up our civic life" that they should not confuse words with deeds, should desist from living off the public coffers, should adopt religious, moral, and political principles in a conscientious manner, should be truthful and honest, and should make sure that the education of their children did not consist of attending the cinema and reading comic strips imported from abroad. "Fortunate are those who, like you, can kneel in the shadow of the right hand of God, and there at length find rest for your heart."

As for Sobral's assertion that blame for Brazil's misery and corruption should fall on the Vargas regime, Góes pointed out that some of the social legislation and administrative reforms enacted by Vargas were "irritating" what Góes called the "pachydermic skin of the monster." He concluded that posterity, with "a better historical perspective," would say whether the blame mentioned by Sobral "should be placed on the chief magistrate, or his political supporters, or the weaknesses of the nation."[8]

3.   Sobral Replies to Vargas' Interview of March 2, 1945

In February 1945 Vargas asked Marcondes Filho, who was still justice minister, to prepare a report about steps to be taken to give representative government to Brazil. The report, published in the pro-government *O Radical* on February 23, suggested that elections be held for executive and legislative positions on the state and national levels but advised against acceding to the opposition's demand for a Constituent Assembly.[1]

On February 28, Vargas and his cabinet signed Constitutional Law 9, known as the Ato Adicional, which amended the 1937 Constitution as suggested by the Marcondes Filho report and said that within ninety days a date would be set for the elections. The Ato Adicional, much attacked in most of the press, gave considerable power to the president of the republic, who was to serve for six years in what it said would be the "second presidential period" of the 1937 Constitution.[2]

Francisco Campos, in an interview given to the *Diário Carioca* on March 3, pleased the opposition by declaring that the 1937 Constitution had become extinct. He called attention to the failure to hold a plebiscite about its fate and said that Vargas' method of amending it and extending his mandate had been unconstitutional. He went on to explain that the article cited by the Vargas government as authorizing the issuance of the Ato Adicional was applicable only to ordinary legislation and that nothing in the 1937 Constitution gave the president the power to amend it.

Claiming that the crisis and decisions about a constitution could be handled only by the people, Campos told the *Diário Carioca* that it was time for Vargas to stop thinking so much about himself and start thinking about Brazil. He also maintained that the press censorship of recent years had contributed to the "civic, intellectual, and moral degradation" of Brazil.[3] For years Sobral had been saying things that Campos said now, but the words, coming from the author of the 1937 Constitution, made an impact that neither Sobral nor others could match.

Also on March 3 the press reported on Vargas' first collective press interview, given in Petrópolis on the previous day, to defend the Estado Novo and the Ato Adicional. Asked about a Constituent Assembly, he said it would be unnecessary because the Ato Adicional included provisions allowing the Congress to amend the constitution. In answer to other questions, Vargas said the DIP would limit itself to supplying information about Brazilian culture, and that Brazil could not continue without diplomatic relations with Russia, which he praised for having ended the Comintern.[4]

Vargas was asked about the National Security Tribunal (TSN) and replied that it had been created not by the 1937 regime but by the Congress chosen in accordance with the 1934 Constitution. Amnesty, he said in reply to another question, had always been viewed with sympathy by his government but had to be handled with care because of possible repercussions on the nation's life and on the armed forces, the group "most affected." He promised to study individual cases. When someone asked about a pardon for Prestes, Vargas said this was one of the cases he would be studying.

An inquiry about the forthcoming election campaign drew a response about the need to delay its start until after arrangements had been made for the organization of political parties. "Will you be a candidate?" someone asked. Vargas answered that his attention was focused not on candidates but on improving the 1932 election law. "Perhaps a national candidacy will emerge, one not yet considered, that will have a tranquilizing effect."[5]

Sobral's reactions to the Vargas interview and the appointment of Agamemnon Magalhães to be justice minister were negative, as he told the *Diário da Noite* in a headline-making pronouncement that was reprinted in other newspapers. He said Vargas' "sinister" statements had given the country "the most grave crisis in its history" because they made it clear that he had decided not to alter his program of imposing the positivism of a *castilhista* dictatorship on the Christian Brazilian people.

"Today," Sobral asserted, "Vargas is making exclusively practical concessions of a momentary nature. . . . He is dressing himself in the clothing of tolerance—a false clothing for hiding his weapons of aggression against the democratic institutions." Vargas was described as continuing to be Brazil's sole legislator and as failing to liberate the judicial power. The TSN, Sobral said, had been modified by the Estado Novo so that it had become unlike the creation of the 1934 democratic regime, which had made it a *tribuna da 1ª Instância* whose decisions were supposed to be examined and revised by the Supreme Military Tribunal.[6]

Asked for his opinion about Vargas' promise to consider a pardon for Prestes and amnesty for political prisoners, Sobral replied that Vargas, with Machiavellian skill, had portrayed his government as sympathetic to the release of political prisoners but impeded by the need to take into account the view of the armed forces. In truth, Sobral added, Vargas had no faith in anyone except himself, as had been revealed by that "shrewd scoundrel" Frischauer.

Frischauer, Sobral told the *Diário de Notícias*, had shown that Vargas was well aware of the practical value of pardoning adversaries to strengthen his position. But Sobral could not see how Prestes, if given his freedom, could benefit the presidential candidacy of Vargas, and therefore he told the newspaper that he doubted that Prestes would be released. "One must not forget that Luiz Carlos Prestes is a man faithful to the Communist Party of Brazil. Because Vargas, in accordance with his declarations to the press, opposes legality for the Communist Party on account of its antagonism to the present regime, I do not see how Prestes, a man of sterling character, can find a way to assist Vargas politically."

Asked for his own view about restrictions against legality for the Communist Party, Sobral said he radically opposed such restrictions. "It is incumbent on the parties that are to be formed, and on Ação Católica Brasileira, to confront Communism solely in the terrain of free debate and defeat it by reasoning."

In reply to a question about diplomatic relations with Soviet Russia, Sobral declared that "without any doubt" they should be established. He pointed out that the guarantee of religious freedom, contained in the Russian Constitution of 1936, had been a dead letter until the Soviet government had altered its attitude in response to the wartime situation. "Today religious freedom exists in Soviet Russia, at least with respect to religious services. And so it is urgent that Brazil renew relations with Russia." The Brazilian government, he said, should be eager to have postwar Russia consolidate this religious freedom, achieved during the period of Soviet hostilities with Germany.

In Sobral's opinion, the existence of diplomatic relations with Soviet Russia would "contribute decisively to the elimination of that fear of Communism that played so large a role in the installation of *caudilhismo castilhista* in the Brazilian federal government." He forecast that if the Communist Party of Brazil were to become legal, it would abandon its conspiratorial methods and turn to trying to persuade the public to accept its positions.

In discussing this struggle to win over the minds of the people, Sobral made a point that he would be stressing in the months ahead: he argued that Communism's opponents, "the political parties that defend the existence of private property," had to become "the vanguards of the proletariat" by entering into meaningful relationships with the masses. This "new mentality," he told the *Diário da Noite*, would give Brazil "civic and moral vitality truly adequate for the needs of our spiritual and material progress."[7]

4. Sobral, Honored for Past Battles, Fills Columns of the Press (March 1945)

In a letter written on March 2 to his sister, Natalina, Sobral said he had been "exceptionally busy." "As you must certainly have imagined, the whole world is seeking views and information from me about the regime of oppression that has been in effect in our unfortunate Nation these last eight years."[1]

Sobral's interviews with the press, reported under large headlines, commenced late in February with a detailed account of the "absurdities" of the rules governing the handling of TSN cases. The *Diário Carioca*, in publishing the analysis, called Sobral "one of our most illustrious lawyers, a brilliant cultural luminary and a man of great moral integrity."[2] A few days later Sobral gave the one-year-old *Folha Carioca* an interview favoring amnesty for political prisoners that was so badly mutilated that Sobral asked the Brazilian Press Association (ABI) to punish the newspaper for carrying out an "unforgivable fraud" in accordance with Vargas' wishes. A result of the incident was a headline, across a full page, in which the *Diário de Notícias* asked: "IS THE FALSIFICATION OF DOCU-MENTS BEING REVIVED?"[3]

Columnist Maurício de Medeiros, after reading the *Folha Carioca* version, wrote in the *Diário Carioca* that Sobral had best leave publicity about amnesty to people, like General Góes Monteiro, who could have no "suspect" reasons. Communists and their allies, Maurício de Medeiros warned, were falling into a trap set by the government, which had said that the signing of an amnesty decree would depend on a show of popular backing for it, but which planned to describe that backing as "Communist agitation" requiring a coup.[4]

As could be seen on March 2 in the *Diário de Notícias'* faithful version of Sobral's *Folha Carioca* interview, Sobral, like Maurício de Medeiros, had expressed the fear that Vargas would use the pro-amnesty movement to find a reason to crush "agitators." In this interview, Sobral had also discussed at great length the "crimes" of the Estado Novo and declared that the person most in need of amnesty was Vargas, whose government was responsible for physical and mental tortures suffered by Harry Berger and Prestes and whose administrators, with the exception of José Carlos de Macedo Soares and Vasco Leitão da Cunha, had ignored Sobral's protests.[5]

The busy days during the newfound freedom of the press and retreat of the dictatorship were exhilarating for Sobral. After he was praised in the press in February by Dario de Almeida Magalhães, Alceu Amoroso Lima, novelist Afrânio Peixoto, and others, the *Jornal do Commercio* published a letter of March 2 from Moura Carneiro, a former prisoner of the Estado Novo, that spoke of Sobral's "noble and beautiful character" and denounced Filinto Müller for having tossed Olga Benário Prestes, "like a bundle of meat, into the hands of the bloody Gestapo" when she was seven months' pregnant.[6] Sobral's reply, also published in the *Jornal do Commercio's* "Publicações a Pedido" section, affirmed that exclusive responsibility for the disgraceful episode belonged to Vargas, who had signed the expulsion decree and without whose decision "Filinto Müller could not have sent my client's wife to Hamburg on a German ship."[7]

Sobral accepted Elmano Cardim's invitation to renew his weekly column in the *Jornal do Commercio* and the invitation of Alceu Amoroso Lima to revive the monthly "Crônica Política" that he had written for *A Ordem* in the 1930s. In accepting Alceu's request, Sobral wrote him at the end of February: "Better than anyone, you know that, in my opinion, those most responsible for the moral, juridical, economic, and administrative catastrophe that has afflicted our abandoned Nation for many years are precisely the Catholics who, on account of halfhearted Faith and self-serving accommodation, left off being the light of the world and the salt of the earth. . . . I do believe that a section such as I maintained for three years in *A Ordem* will be a valuable contribution for improving the civic conscience of Catholics."[8]

The reappearance of Sobral's column in the *Jornal do Commercio* on March 10 brought him congratulations from faithful readers, such as former Senator Pedro da Cunha Pedrosa, father of his Trotskyite client, Mário Pedrosa.[9] And it coincided with the publication in the *Jornal do Commercio* of a tribute to Sobral by Dario de Almeida Magalhães that had been adopted by the OAB Conselho Federal in June 1944 and supported by leading jurists and lawyers' groups in São Paulo, Minas, Bahia, and elsewhere. Describing Sobral's eminent conduct, fearlessness, and exemplary fulfillment of the role of lawyer and jurist, it said:

> His professional office is not a commercial counter; his activity is not inspired by pecuniary interest. The causes he represents are not simply those that are submitted to him as a lawyer. Most of his time and extraordinary effort are expended on behalf of his fellow citizens, the law, morality, justice, and the noblest of ideals. He is constantly defending the destitute, the unprotected. . . . His voice is not intimidated by the powerful or by threats of the use of force or by tribunals that stray from their duties. In an era corroded by greed, indifference and egotism, he is a knight-errant. . . .
>
> Without concern for the risks and without fear of suffering, Sr. Sobral Pinto . . . struggles with the sole purpose of having his country enjoy a just and stable juridical order characterized by the prevalence of the rights and dignity of the human person. The fire that inflames his words comes from his unshakable faith in law and justice and from the revulsion he feels for iniquities, treacherousness, and cowardice, and for unjust, outrageous acts. Sr. Sobral Pinto is not among those responsible for what the Minister of War calls "accommodations, renunciations, and pusillanimous silences." . . . He knows that ignorance and the repression of

opinion are propitious for a climate in which extremisms prosper and attract converts. Sr. Sobral Pinto is a conscience; and this conscience—severe, indomitable, and virile—is reacting, crying out, and making demands when the brutality of force silences him.[10]

Sobral, writing Dario, called the "magnificent" testimonial "the greatest reward I have received from my compatriots during this campaign in which I am involved." In a reference to the rebirth of his weekly "Pelos Domínios do Direito" column, he called March 10 "a day of rejoicing for the liberation of the Brazilian intellect" and urged Dario to tell Adaucto Lucio Cardoso and Luiz Camillo de Oliveira Netto that they held, in his thankful heart, a place equal to that of Dario.[11]

As Sobral had promised in October 1943, he devoted the first of his new series of *Jornal do Commercio* columns, that of March 10, to the reply to Cassiano Ricardo that the DIP had forbidden him to publish. In it he denied what he called Cassiano's charge that he was "a poor ignoramus" because of his insistence on the existence of "absolute truth." After describing Cassiano as seeking to serve Vargas by proclaiming the regime of November 1937 a "social democracy," Sobral pointed out that Vargas' brother Viriato had said, in a speech in 1943, that "no intellectually responsible" person could call the Estado Novo anything but a dictatorship. As Sobral revealed, Colonel Viriato Vargas' speech, published in a scholarly journal under the title of "Combating Insincerity," had made it known that Getúlio, unable to do anything in a democratic regime of "parliamentary blabbermouths," had established "our glorious Republican Dictatorship to make it possible for him to accomplish all that he has done for the good of the Nation." Noting that Viriato had urged his fellow citizens to use proper terms, calling the dictatorship a dictatorship, Sobral said that this was what he had been doing.[12]

Supplementing his weekly columns which appeared on Saturdays, Sobral published articles on Sundays in the *Jornal do Commercio*'s "Publicações a Pedido." Starting on March 4 and continuing throughout the month, these Sunday articles consisted of sections of his booklet *As Forças Armadas em face do Momento Político*, which was about to be published and which contained his recent letters to Generals Góes Monteiro, Renato Paquet, and Eurico Gaspar Dutra, together with commentaries and a conclusion. The conclusion, published in the *Jornal do Commercio* on March 25, condemned Vargas and the armed forces for overturning the 1934 Constitution. Sobral argued that the nine "constitutional laws" promulgated during the Estado Novo had violated the 1937 Constitution and added that it was the duty of the armed forces to proclaim that Vargas had ceased to be president upon completion of his six-year term on November 10, 1943. He argued, as he had when writing the generals, that the responsibility of the military officers to act was especially great because Article 187 of the 1937 Constitution made them the only voters in Brazil—a point of view based on a clause of that article that gave military officers the right to vote in the plebiscite mentioned in the constitution.

As for himself, Sobral wrote in his booklet's conclusion that he was modest and disinterested and wished nothing more than to remain in Ação Católica Brasileira, seeking to fulfill his ideal of liberating Brazil from the situation brought about by Vargas and the armed forces. "In the name of that ideal, I find myself obliged to affirm that what exists in Brazil is the reign of Bolshevism."

Bolshevism, Sobral explained, was a state of spirit that had invaded most countries—"a mentality of violence, force, passion, and rage," determined to dominate without any consideration of morals, justice, and juridical limitations. This mentality, he said, had given a nontraditional meaning to the word "Order." "Never before has so much been said about Order and the need for it to be the chief concern of all Brazilians and principally those in the Armed Forces." Scarcely anyone, he concluded, had raised a voice to point out that Brazil, in truth, was submerged in disorder, the result of Vargas' domination. "No longer do we have a constitution or hierarchy of powers; no longer do we know the meanings of law, justice, liberty, or property. This is the hallucinating chaos that is called 'Order' by the National Episcopate, the Armed Forces, administrators, and a large part of the daily press."[13]

Sobral's boldly expressed ideas were cited late in March by Alceu Amoroso Lima, writing in *O Jornal*, as a reason why Sobral was one of the most important men of contemporary Brazil and was needed to guide the country. Recalling that in 1925 Jackson de Figueiredo had said of the little-known Sobral, "There is a man," Alceu wrote: "Today who does not know him! Who, even among his most intransigent adversaries, does not consider him one of the greatest moral forces of our Nation!"

Discussing Sobral's political ideas, Alceu said that Sobral, unlike others, did not opportunistically modify them in accordance with events. "His discernment takes precedence over expediency or con-summated facts. . . . If I see in Sobral Pinto the leading figure of our generation and the best one to guide us in the difficult tran-sition we are experiencing, it is precisely because his moral forti-tude and juridical and democratic convictions are not based on hap-penings or caprice, but on the immovable rock of Faith, Hope, and Charity, the supreme virtues that take us to God." His fearless com-bativity, Alceu declared, had never been weakened by "the general atmosphere of conformity" and had made him, to a greater extent than the prisoners or exiles, the chief of the Moral Resistance.

Alceu, who was writing articles about Brazil's foremost literary figures, explained his inclusion of Sobral because of what he called his enormous importance for the social and cultural history of Bra-zil. Mentioning the articles that Sobral had written, Alceu called attention, "above all else, to the LETTERS" that had made Sobral the "epistolary chief of the Resistance against the illegality of the last fifteen years" and had brought him the appellation of the "Mar-quise de Sévigné of the regime." Alceu preferred, as he made clear in closing his article, that Sobral should be known by the tribute given to Seigneur de Bayard: "The good knight without fear and without reproach."[14]

Sobral, after reading the article aloud to his wife and children, wrote Alceu that he had gone too far in comparing him to Bayard. "Many times I have told you and other friends that these exagger-ated encomiums about my modest activities fill me with discom-fort." They made him feel, he explained, that he had the responsi-bility of carrying out his work with far more discernment, energy, and persuasiveness than he possessed.[15]

5. Better Days for Prestes (March–April 1945)

While Sobral was preparing his booklet for publication, Vargas was informed by advisers that the opposition was gaining much strength and that only a Dutra presidential candidacy could prevent much of the military from supporting air force Brigadeiro Eduardo Gomes, favorite of the opposition. Vargas, after telling the military that he would not run for president, authorized Minas Governor Valladares to sound out the possibilities of a Dutra candidacy, and in mid-March it was reported that this candidacy was acceptable to Vargas.

While political observers wondered whether Vargas' step was a maneuver to gain time over forces intent on his overthrow, Sobral wrote, in the introduction to his booklet, that the Dutra candidacy, "launched by Benedicto Valladares," was a disturbance to "everything that is good and patriotic" and was viewed by "all shades of public opinion" as a "mere game" of Vargas to divide the armed forces and, in that way, initiate a moral and civic setback of the military institutions.[1]

Vargas, in choosing João Alberto Lins de Barros on March 9 to succeed Coriolano de Góes as head of the Rio police, was reportedly taking another step to appease the military.[2] But the replacement of the repressive Coriolano, who was given an important Bank of Brazil position, was also a blessing for Communists and Prestes. Communists, whose labor leaders were now finding no government objections to their penetration of the unions, could only be pleased at João Alberto's call for amnesty "without restrictions." Furthermore, João Alberto, revolutionary companion and close friend of the Cavalier of Hope in the 1920s, allowed Prestes to receive all the visitors he wanted. Often filled with emotion, old companions and more recent admirers came to the prison in droves to hear Prestes advocate a capitalist republic for Brazil and Communist support for the Vargas administration in its struggle against foreign fascism and in its effort to bring democracy to Brazil. Prestes' message was carried in *O Globo* on March 15.[3]

Harry Berger, an incurable mental case, was in Rio's Judiciary Insane Asylum. News of the death of Berger's wife Elise, victim of pneumonia in a German prison in 1939, was given to Prestes in March 1945 by novelist Jorge Amado, one of his visitors.[4] But it was not until two months later that Prestes learned of the death of Olga in a German concentration camp in 1942.[5]

Prestes, while worrying about Olga in March 1945, received news from Mexico about the renewed illness of his sister Lygia that made it difficult for her to care for his eight-year-old daughter, Anita Leocádia. The press reported on March 1 that Itamaraty (the Foreign Office) was cooperating with plans to have Lygia and Anita Leocádia flown to Brazil. But Sobral, informal treasurer to handle donations made for the plane fare, was not receiving from government offices as much cooperation as he felt he needed for arranging the trip.[6]

Around mid-March, Prestes and Sobral decided to try to persuade the prisoner's sister Eloiza, or one of the other sisters who were with her in Russia, to go to Mexico and care for Lygia and the girl. Sobral, writing Eloiza to explain the wish, said her brother was in good health and spirits. He added: "We view his future with great optimism because the political situation is changing day by day. . . . The press in the principal cities was able to free itself from government oppression. People are beginning to learn about the persecutions and tortures inflicted on the political adversaries of the men who continue in power. Already a large part of public opinion is openly demanding amnesty. Therefore I have well-founded hopes that the sufferings of your brother will end soon. Maybe even the present year will see him set free."[7]

Sobral told Eloiza that, although he was guided by ideas directly opposed to those of her brother, he was at the forefront of the people who fought for his freedom. "The sentences handed down against him have not the slightest legitimacy. Their purpose was to serve a persecution and not the imperatives of the serene and impartial will of judges inspired by the noble ideal of justice."[8]

So radically had the situation of Prestes changed since early March that the press informed the public of the prisoner's telegram sent early in April to congratulate Vargas on the "renewal" of diplomatic relations with the "heroic Soviet people." Prestes' telegram also called on Vargas to "reestablish popular confidence in Your Excellency's democratic inclinations by immediately declaring amnesty, excluding, if necessary, my own case," and by arranging for the prompt organization of parties so that their representatives could participate in writing an election law that would assure "the free and honest elections demanded by the nation."[9]

For his years of work on behalf of Prestes, Sobral received expressions of praise from groups whose declarations were reported in the press. Law students in Bahia called him the perfect example for his profession on account of his fearless work to help the prisoner, "condemned by the notorious TSN, hangman used by the despotism of the dictator Vargas." A somewhat similar motion was adopted by the Instituto dos Advogados Brasileiros (IAB) of the state of Paraíba, which expressed its admiration for the "dedication and sacrifice" shown by Sobral in defending Prestes and others. That sacrifice, according to Alceu's article comparing Sobral to Bayard, had cost Sobral "at least half" of his former legal clients.[10]

Continuing to defend Prestes in the press, Sobral denounced João Batista Luzardo, ambassador to Uruguay, for asserting that political amnesty might not be enough to gain the freedom of Prestes because "he was condemned also for a common crime." Using the *Jornal do Commercio*, Sobral called the ambassador's statement "absolutely false" and pointed out that Prestes had been condemned by the TSN, in two cases, only for political crimes.[11]

While Prestes was quoted in the press on April 8 as attributing "democratic inclinations" to Vargas, Sobral, writing on the same day in the *Jornal do Commercio*'s "Publicações a Pedido," told his readers not to fool themselves on that score. Expressing regret that Arthur Bernardes, Antônio Carlos, and Raul Fernandes had not read Frischauer's biography of Vargas, Sobral again described Vargas as convinced that the Brazilian people were unfit to vote and needed a dictatorship. Therefore, according to Sobral, Vargas' chief preoccupation was "to destroy the candidacy of Dutra along with that of Eduardo Gomes." Strikes by workers and violent acts of disorder, which Sobral said were breaking out all over Brazil, would, he predicted, furnish Vargas with a pretext to put the blame on electioneering and come forward as the only man capable of providing the order needed in Brazil for progress.[12]

During the next few days Sobral dealt with the confusion about the publication of Góes' long letter of April 7 in reply to Sobral's longer letter of February 22. Both Góes and his assistant, Antenor Novaes, told Sobral they had no knowledge about an article in *A Noite*, published before Sobral received Góes' letter, saying that the general awaited Sobral's authorization before publishing it.[13] Novaes, coming to Sobral's office on April 9, delivered the letter and said Góes was leaving it up to Sobral to decide what newspaper should publish it. Góes, he said, only wished that Sobral would delete a remark in it criticizing Vargas for acting on reforms with insufficient dynamism and daring. Sobral removed the remark, the only unfavorable comment about Vargas in Góes' letter.[14]

On the next morning Sobral was visited at his residence by a reporter who said she had come to arrange for copies of the Góes letter to be supplied, with the deletion, to the *Correio da Noite* and *A Noite*. She maintained that Sobral had made a promise to another reporter, a Sr. Luna, that these two newspapers would be the ones to publish the letter. Sobral, who had never heard of Luna, learned that he was a friend of Góes and had told the director of the *Correio da Noite* that Góes wanted his letter published in it. Sobral gave the letter to *O Globo* for publication.[15]

The incident, Sobral wrote Góes on the 10th, was of no great importance but was nevertheless significant, revealing behavior that was "deplorable and pernicious" when carried out in politics. "Those who want to implant order and discipline should act clearly and properly and speak with absolute frankness. . . . The illness of Brazil does not lie with the common people, miserable but noble; it lies with the pride of those who govern and who believe themselves made of a clay that differs from that of their humble fellow citizens." Sobral wrote that men like Góes, Vargas, Agamemnon Magalhães, and João Alberto, who had done so poorly in running the "irresponsible dictatorship," should analyze their own defects instead of those of the abandoned members of the masses.[16]

Commenting on the long Góes letter, Sobral told Góes that his "powerful boss" failed to understand that to govern well required having unlimited confidence in the "anonymous mass" and therefore he was determined that the common people spend many decades, even centuries, condemned to a "degraded and totally debased" existence.[17]

6. Attributing Egalitarianism to Vargas (April 1945)

In his weekly column on March 24, Sobral wrote that it was beyond comprehension that Christian jurists, and above all, the Catholic National Episcopate, remained silent in the face of dangers that threatened to destroy completely the structure of Brazilian society. "In a moment like the present one, when we are faced with choosing either the positivist republican dictatorship or the liberties of democracy, the Brazilian people await guidance from their spiritual leaders."[1]

Gionísio Curvello de Mendonça, prominent defender of positivism, wrote in the *Jornal do Commercio* of the "ignorance" of Sobral, who, he said, should become acquainted with the history of positivism and thus appreciate that the founders of the Brazilian Positive Church had been advocates of democratic liberties. Writing also of the "forgetfulness" of Sobral, Curvello de Mendonça reminded him that Vargas, defender of the Christian civilization, had always surrounded himself with Catholics and had taken steps helpful to the Catholic clergy, which, in turn, had "explicitly acclaimed the policy of the Estado Novo."[2]

Sobral, in reply, wrote in his weekly column that the words of

Vargas and the men around him in defense of Catholicism were at variance with their practices. He made use of a statement by Auguste Comte to demonstrate that positivism required that citizens accept principles proclaimed by a dictator. If, he added, some Brazilian positivist leaders had supported democratic liberties, they had done so not on account of positivism but on account of religious principles, based on the existence of the supernatural, developed in the Brazilian community over many years. These principles, he warned, would be wiped out "if Catholic cultural thought continues to ignore" the corrosive work of *castilhista* positivism.[3]

On the following Saturday, April 14, Sobral used his column to accuse the Vargas government of having always been guided by the philosophy of the naturalists, whose ideal, Sobral wrote, was to have people organized on the principle of egalitarianism, an ideal that required a dictatorship. He said that the naturalists "believe we are made of material and shall become a part of the same material when we die," whereas "the spiritualists say we came from the realm of Omnipotent God, are a part of the divine essence, and will return to the realm of Eternity." Contemporary materialistic governments, he pointed out, were working to establish societies in which everything was distributed according to egalitarian principles and therefore lacked respect for human beings and differences in their earthly aspirations and intellectual capacities.

Looking for Brazilian governments that most nobly rejected the materialists' views and therefore best protected the existence of differences among individuals, Sobral mentioned that of the empire, "except for the stain of slavery and the regalism of Pedro II," and that of the republic under the 1891 Constitution, "except for its positivist agnosticism."[4]

7. Resistência Democrática (April 1945)

Following the publication of his article on April 14, Sobral was incapacitated by the eczema that wracked his whole body. Unable to attend a meeting of the OAB Conselho Federal on April 18 and vote there for making Adaucto Lucio Cardoso a Conselho member, Sobral asked Jorge Dyott Fontenelle to advise the Conselho of his wish,[1] which, as it turned out, was the wish of the majority.

Sobral was able to sign the manifesto of Resistência Democrática, which was published in the *Diário de Notícias* on April 21. The wording was largely the work of Luiz Camillo de Oliveira Netto and Adaucto Lucio Cardoso, who, according to Sobral's recollection in later years, had been meeting in Luiz Camillo's home with Dario de Almeida Magalhães, former congressman José Barreto Filho, physician José Fernando Carneiro, hygienist Gustavo de Sá Lessa, and banker Tancredo Ribas Carneiro. So many adhered to the idea of organizing this anti-dictatorship "society," favoring a Constituent Assembly and the presidential candidacy of Brigadeiro Eduardo Gomes, that its headquarters (Sobral also recalled) were moved from Luiz Camillo's home to a downtown office made available by some lawyers.[2]

Among the manifesto's 125 signers were the men mentioned by Sobral as having attended the organizing meetings and also poet Murilo Mendes; Catholic writer Gustavo Corção; lawyers Haryberto de Miranda Jordão, Luís Gonzaga do Nascimento Silva, José Tocqueville de Carvalho Filho, and Gabriel Costa Carvalho; and professor José Arthur Rios. Literary critic Otto Lara Rezende was among the 19 from Belo Horizonte who signed.[3]

The manifesto described the signers as belonging to a generation that had lacked influence in public life. In view of the "national crisis, without precedent in all our political history," they believed that "men of our age" should "save" the next generation, a majority of whose members "do not have the preparation" needed to handle the problems of Brazil "within the principles of democracy." The younger men were described as having been prevented by the dictatorship from developing public responsibilities and as having missed the good fortune of "knowing the better existence" that pre-dated the dictatorship.[4]

The new generation was warned against the administrative technicians who had taken over from men of vision. According to the manifesto, technical solutions, lacking appreciation of human beings, had been forced on the collectivity by a totalitarian government that had no interest in morality, allowed no dissenting opinions, and considered the law a mere vehicle for carrying out its wishes. Bent on installing uniformity, such governments "establish monopolies of production, distribution, publicity, teaching, and unionism." High administrative posts "go to inelegant flatterers," and thus "the government ends up in the hands of the least qualified."[5]

Brazil's "personalistic dictatorship," although "stigmatized by all responsible voices, cultural institutions, and the people in the street," was said to be "determined not to die," for which reason Resistência Democrática was being formed to engage in the urgent work of completing its extinction along with preparing for "true democracy." To help achieve these goals, the manifesto provided a "Declaration of Principles" and a set of rules for political behavior.[6]

According to the "Principles," thirty-nine in number, government action should not encroach on the rights of human beings, the church, the family, unions, or professional groups. The state, refraining from any takeover of private initiative, "must guarantee conditions for the full development of that initiative." It was also to promote "distributive justice," freedom to make contracts, and a progressive increase in "the acquisitive power of wages."

"Ahead of positive law, decreed by the State, there exist other superior juridical principles to which positive law must conform: those of the natural law, or the unwritten law," the foundation for the basic rights of individuals. These rights, according to Principle 12, required the existence of an international organization that would assure, for all the world, freedom of expression, of worshipping God, of having material needs satisfied, and of living without fear.

Other principles opposed "the management of public opinion" by the state, and demanded "universal and secret suffrage" and a Constituent Assembly, made up of authentic representatives of the people.[7]

Turning to "rules for political behavior," the Resistência Democrática manifesto submitted a list of ten. Political activity was to abide by moral standards and not make the government "the privilege of a single group or party." Public men were to use their power only for the common good.[8]

The signing of the manifesto was followed at once by the issuance of Resistência Democrática's "Initial Program of Political Action" in two sections: one for the period before the meeting of the Constituent Assembly and the other for the days when that assembly would be at work. The objectives during the earlier period were the removal of the dictatorship, support for the presidential candidacy of Eduardo Gomes, the organization of a provisional government that would preside over elections for a president of Brazil and a Constituent Assembly, elimination of all government propaganda, abolition of the special justice system and its rulings, and amnesty for those found guilty by the TSN of political crimes. The military justice system was to review cases of violations of military rules, and the regular justice system was to review cases involving the popular economy.

Turning to objectives to be sought while the constitution was being written, Resistência Democrática called for "an accounting covering the period of the dictatorship" and an end of government tutelage of associations of employees, employers, and professional men. The pension institutes were to be placed in the hands of the associations whose members they were supposed to benefit, and workers in agriculture were to receive the benefits of social justice and be given access to the ownership of land.[9]

Resistência Democrática's "Initial Program of Political Action" was expanded before it was approved at a meeting on April 30, held at the headquarters of the National Union of Students (UNE) at Rio's Praia do Flamengo.[10] The expanded version, listing eighteen economic matters that required "immediate attention," was considerate of workers and consumers. It called for re-establishment of the right to strike, participation of workers in the management and profits of companies, and assistance to people in agriculture by having the government loan them agricultural machinery and reduce their taxes and freight rates.

To combat inflation, work was to be suspended on all public construction projects that did not foster production, and the official banks were to withhold credit to "inflationary sectors." Cash held by pension institutes, savings banks, and government-controlled companies was to be remitted to the Bank of Brazil in return for treasury bonds. In the case of goods essential for public consumption, investigations were to be made so that the authorities could do away with "exorbitant profits and unjustifiable price increases." To make sure that basic industries and all manufacturers of articles in general use carried on their operations at the lowest possible cost and did not provide "inequitable" remuneration to capital, these enterprises were to be carefully inspected and the findings given publicity.

The writers of the expanded program admitted disliking the totalitarian "interference in economic activities," and said that its arbitrary, inept, and demagogic solutions had proved disastrous. But, they explained, their program called for prudence on the part of the democratic state, which, they argued, could not have a role in the economy that was the negative one of abstention, especially during the "emergency" that made it necessary to improve "the conditions of life of the Brazilian people, whose situation is really extremely alarming." Furthermore, the program was not to be viewed as the final word. Democrats, described as lacking the conceit of totalitarians, would rely on public discussions to modify programs, and these discussions, Resistência Democrática promised, would be promptly organized.[11]

PART X

Participant in Preparations for Elections (June–October 1945)

1. Renewing His Campaign, Sobral Attacks the "Malaysian Law" (June 1945)

On April 18, Vargas signed a decree that granted amnesty to political prisoners, including Luiz Carlos Prestes. The crowd that gathered that day on Frei Caneca Street, hoping to see the Cavalier of Hope emerge from prison, was disappointed because Prestes, escorted by Trifino Corrêa and Orlando Leite Ribeiro, used an exit far from the main gate.[1] He was taken to the Lagoa district house of Leoncio Basbaum, a leader of Communist Youth in the 1920s, and there he resided for months, a polite and serious guest who neither drank nor smoked and who received a stream of visitors.[2]

During his imprisonment, the strongest wing of the Partido Comunista do Brasil (PCB) had named Prestes secretary-general (the top post) of the party. Able now to run the PCB, he frequently met with associates in an office that architect Oscar Niemeyer put at their disposal at his home. Sobral had no address for Prestes, and when, somewhat later, he read in the press that his former client was ill, he sent wishes for a rapid recovery in a telegram addressed to him at the *Tribuna Popular*, the first-rate popular daily that Communists established in May 1945.[3]

A few days after his release from prison, Prestes went to the residence of Brigadeiro Eduardo Gomes, and there, in the presence of colonels Juarez Távora and Tasso Tinoco, he told the oppositionist presidential aspirant that the proletariat disliked military candidates. Speaking to the press on April 26, he said that it would be difficult to find two candidates as similar as Gomes and Dutra, and that the replacement of Vargas by another de facto chief executive would be undemocratic and pleasing to the fascists. Vargas, he said, was a man of good intentions who had demonstrated his desire to heed the people when he had put Brazil into the war in 1942 and when he had, more recently, decreed amnesty.

Asked by one of the reporters about the Integralista movement, Prestes asserted that it included many good people who recognized past errors, just as Communists recognized now the error of their uprising in 1935. It was necessary, he said, for the Brazilian proletariat to extend its hand to the bourgeoisie and march with it to democracy. He pointed out that the proletariat was handicapped by the backwardness of industrial development in Brazil and should cooperate with industrialists to further that development.[4]

Sobral, before leaving for a vacation in Minas in May and June, gave his wife, Maria José, an envelope containing three thousand cruzeiros that belonged to Prestes. It was not picked up and so Sobral, returning after mid-June, gave it, for delivery to Prestes, to Manoel Venancio Campos da Paz, an ANL founder who had been jailed following the 1935 Communist uprising. In an accompanying letter for Prestes, Sobral said he had returned from Minas reinvigorated and ready to renew "my campaign to revive the honor of Brazilians, threatened today, as never before in our history, by those who hold the reins of the government."[5] By this time Prestes had made it clear that he did not agree with Sobral and that the PCB favored a Constituent Assembly with Vargas remaining in office. Prestes' position alienated some of his former followers but convinced others that they had erred in joining the coalition that supported Eduardo Gomes.[6]

Sobral, writing friends he had visited in Poços de Caldas, described Prestes as "organizing his legions" to implant a Marxist style of government and Vargas as using his "steamroller" on behalf of a castilhista style of government. This "extremely grave" situation, he wrote, made it necessary for sincere democrats to support "a program for the juridical organization of the state, based on the nation's moral traditions. This will be the objective of my campaign."[7]

Sobral's return to his campaign coincided with the issuance, on June 22, of the Vargas administration's Decree-Law 7,666 for abolishing economic trusts. Businessmen and others, frightened by its numerous clauses, named it the "Malaysian Law" because its author, Justice Minister Agamemnon Magalhães, had been nicknamed "The Malaysian" on account of his Asian facial features.[8]

Octavio Mangabeira, fiery UDN orator, said the decree was a

"new monster," and Arthur Bernardes called it a Nazi-fascist weapon that threatened the Brazilian economy. Sobral, in his letter thanking Lindolpho Pio da Silva Dias for his recent hospitality, said the decree was the first step in the socialization of property in Brazil: "The press and radio, and companies engaged in the pharmaceutical, iron, and aluminum industries, along with *fazendas* and cold storage plants, will suddenly pass into the hands of the Federal Union."[9]

The Lei Malaia was discussed by Sobral in a press interview published on June 24. The *Diário Carioca*, introducing Sobral's remarks, explained that he had recovered from illness and from the exhaustion of his long struggle "to alleviate the cruel treatment imposed on political prisoners by the dictator who claims to have 'democratic inclinations.'" The *Diário Carioca* explained also that the release of Prestes from prison allowed his lawyer to express publicly his divergences with his client.[10]

"The so-called antitrust decree," Sobral told the press, "does not surprise me. It coincides with the logic of the *castilhista-socialista* thinking of Getúlio Vargas. It is the initial step to transform contemporary Brazil from a land of private property into one of public property." He warned that Vargas had the ambition of becoming known as "a sort of Brazilian Lenin," a desire whose fulfillment required no new coups but simply a continuation of the Estado Novo. "Unless Vargas' adversaries unite around a program of 'national salvation,' other decrees will surely be promulgated to complete the Bolshevization of Brazil now being carried out . . . with incredible indifference and even occasional applause from the 'clergy,' 'the nobility,' and 'the common people.'"[11]

Historian Edgard Carone writes that all political groups "except the Communists and Socialists" condemned the Vargas antitrust decree.[12] The politically active Socialists were enrolling in the Esquerda Democrática (Democratic Left) and favored the gradual socialization of the means of production; but they did not find the new decree a reason for altering their position in support of Eduardo Gomes, which had been made public on June 12.[13]

On June 28 the public learned of a new pro-Gomes manifesto—this one signed by over a thousand lawyers, among them Sobral. The wording of the manifesto and the gathering of signatures had been carried out by a commission headed by Adaucto Lucio Cardoso and made up of Evandro Lins e Silva, Jorge Dyott Fontenelle, Targino

Ribeiro, Dario de Almeida Magalhães, Justo Mendes de Moraes, and others. They maintained, as they wrote in the manifesto, that the government apparatus had "disorganized" public opinion, depriving the masses of the ability to make proper judgments about social and political matters, but that an elite group, blessed with democratic roots and a liberal tradition, had been able to resist this "corrupt and destructive" activity.

These intellectual elites, the manifesto said, had the immense task of restoring democracy—a task that fell most heavily on the jurists and lawyers, a class that included men who had an "exact notion of the fundamental political problems." Understanding the importance of having the presidency of the republic in the hands of a person whose life revealed the correct sort of convictions, the authors of the manifesto pointed out that Eduardo Gomes' devotion "to our republican institutions in the last quarter of a century" showed him to be unselfish, honest, brave, enlightened, prudent, and a crusader for justice and liberty.[14]

Sobral, at this time, studied a set of principles that he had received from Alceu Amoroso Lima for adoption by a Catholic movement to be called the Coluna do Centro. Informing Alceu that he was about to renew his journalistic campaign, interrupted by his April illness and subsequent vacation, he told him to wait until it was under way and to await also the formation of "a stable nucleus of collaborators" before presenting "precise definitions" in the set of principles. "In order that your suggestion succeed and not be rebuffed by José Fernando Carneiro and José Barreto Filho, always very jealous of their own autonomy, it is imperative that you send them the basic items simply in the guise of an effort to unify the doctrinal thinking of the Coluna do Centro, while stressing the need to build up a solid bloc, at least in this anarchical phase of the Nation's public life."

"It is urgent" Sobral told Alceu, "that I and you display much tact in our understandings with our brothers in the Catholic Faith. Lacking serenity and a comprehension of the gravity of the hour, many of them forget they are Catholics and unwittingly think of themselves as Getulistas or anti-Getulistas, proletarians or members of the bourgeoisie, liberals or reactionaries." Only with patience and charity, Sobral wrote, would it be possible to convince these Catholics that faith in Jesus Christ and obedience to His precepts should take first place.[15]

2. Warning the Christian Democratic Party against Vargas' Communism (July 9, 1945)

Sobral, while preparing a speech to be given in São Paulo on July 9 at the organizing meeting of the Partido Democrata Cristão, was shocked to be told by one of the bishops that Frischauer's book had convinced him to support Vargas. Sobral wrote the bishop that the DIP, after paying Frischauer 6,000 cruzeiros a month for writing the biography, had taken the entire edition and distributed many copies to government offices and to Rio newspapers, with orders that the latter give it publicity. He revealed also that Vargas had issued a decree making Frischauer a Brazilian citizen. "When I realize that the ecclesiastical hierarchy in Brazil and the majority of men in public life in the Nation's interior share your false idea about the man who can issue, whenever he wants, the most sinister laws, I appreciate how disarmed the Nation is and how seriously its social structure and religious destiny are threatened."[1]

Presiding on July 9 at the Partido Democrata Cristão (PDC) meeting at São Paulo's Municipal Theater, Sobral announced the names of the party's provisional officers, headed by São Paulo Law School Professor Antônio Ferreira Cesarino Júnior.[2] Sobral's heartily applauded closing address, "Law and Politics," assailed Vargas for stimulating the Brazilian Communist movement.

All soldiers of Christ, Sobral told his audience, had to assume resolutely their posts in the crusade that the gravity of the moment required of those who believed in the reality of the spirit. No part of the crusade, he said, was more important than the one that opposed materialists who sought to separate politics from "rational Law," defender of the dignity of persons.[3]

The PDC directors, Sobral said, had correctly decided to initiate their civic activities by affirming that politics must be the servant of the Law, respectful of persons, and had therefore turned to him, a principal advocate of that truth and, for ten years, a defender of clients victimized by a policy of brutality. The invitation, he said, had moved him deeply, especially when he recalled that on another July 9, thirteen years earlier, the people of São Paulo had initiated a virile march that had resulted in the constitutionalization of the nation in 1934.

In a Communist civilization, Sobral pointed out, man was viewed as a mere individual whose destiny "is lost in the destiny of society."

"Law, according to that philosophy, is nothing more than an expression of the imperatives of society and becomes a simple technique of government. . . . In Soviet Russia, everything is legal if the government so decides, no matter how much harm is done to the dignity of the human person." On the other hand, he said, human dignity was practiced in Christian civilizations, like those in England, the United States, and Ireland, where juridical principles served as barriers to the exercise of governmental authority.

Sobral drew the attention of the PDC to the clash of the two opposing civilizations in Brazil, where, he said, Communism "has made gigantic efforts to organize in recent months." At the time that Sobral spoke, this effort in Brazil was being assisted by the Communists' moderate, democratic stance, the prospect of legality for the party, esteem felt for Prestes, admiration for the struggle of the Russians against the Nazis, and the Vargas administration's assistance to Communist penetration of labor unions.

Sobral, concerned with the maneuvers of Vargas, alluded to the last of these factors and told the PDC to recognize the entry of the common people into political life, "a modern phenomenon." The vigorous call of the Communist Party, he said, was being heard by the masses, suffering in misery. He pictured the Communists as presenting themselves as able to introduce a new Godless civilization that would end that misery; and therefore he pleaded that spiritual-minded citizens recognize the injustices of capitalism and devote themselves to forming, at the side of the people, a new social order that would put God in the place of atheism, universal education in the place of generalized ignorance, the practice of virtue in the place of the rule of vice, and the well-being of everybody in the place of comfort only for the upper classes. Declaring that these objectives must form the "political mission of the PDC," he told the party to defeat Communism by being convincing about the truth of its message. It would, he said, be a great error to favor the use of brute force against Communists and their propaganda, or to criticize Communists for denouncing the capitalist regime installed in industrialized countries.

Explaining that the advocates of human dignity should base their arguments on the need to prevent Brazil from becoming socialized in the manner of Russia, Sobral warned that their mission would be opposed by Vargas, who "prefers a Communist civilization to a Christian civilization"—a preference that he said could be deduced from reading Frischauer's "official biography" and the pro-positivism statements by Vargas to be found in it. Sobral quoted Auguste Comte to show that the founder of positivism had advised those members of the proletariat who had not adhered to positivism that they should adopt atheistic Communism instead of what Comte had called "retrograde Catholicism."

"Vargas," Sobral said, "does not see Communism as destructive of our cultural progress, but, on the contrary, sees it as a step forward for our country." He told the PDC that the very government that had butchered Communists and called them bandits was now "scandalously" expressing its solidarity with them and was encouraging them to mobilize the workers. A quote from Frischauer was used to show that Vargas had been reading captured Communist literature and had found in it helpful suggestions about what path to follow. "With his usual cunning, the Head of State is carrying out a grandiose political maneuver . . . to give his government a popular base."

In addition to this impediment to the mission of the PDC, Sobral mentioned another: the annihilation, during the Estado Novo, of "any notion of rational Law as superior to governmental activities," leaving the nation without knowledge about "the hierarchy of morals."

Faced with these difficulties, which Sobral said he understood "better than anyone," the PDC was urged to "restore the spiritual juridical order" in accordance with the teachings of Christian philosophy. It was urged to become the "authorized vanguard of the Brazilian worker" by establishing a stable social order in which "governmental politics are completely submissive to rational Law."[4]

In its lead editorial of July 10, the *Diário Carioca* wrote that Sobral's speech in São Paulo "deserves the attention of all Brazilians who are disturbed by the political and social panorama of the country." It said that the "illustrious advocate," using his authority as an orthodox Catholic and valorous defender of the law, had correctly asserted that the battle against Communism should be carried out in the realm of ideas and should not consist of appeals to the authorities to use force to crush individuals and deny the expression of their opinions, such as had occurred during "the bestial repression" by the Vargas police.[5]

A less prominent Rio newspaper, *Reação Brasileira*, responded to Sobral's speech by publishing an article bearing the headline "Sobral

Pinto, in the name of Christian juridical order, defends Bolshevik propaganda in the universities." Sobral, citing a law of July 14, 1934, forced the newspaper to publish a rectification, and he sent a telegram to Recife law professor Francisco Barreto Rodrigues Campello, whose views about Sobral's speech, published earlier in a prominent Recife daily, formed the basis of the *Reação Brasileira* article. Sobral told the professor, a Centro Dom Vital member and former congressman, that his remarks had been absurd.[6]

Heartened by the generally enthusiastic response to his speech, Sobral arranged to have it published in the *Jornal do Commercio* and sent copies of the publication to friends. The speech, he told one of them, "is the beginning of my attack against the atheistic politics of the Communists."[7] To another he wrote: "I categorically refused the offer of the presidency of the Partido Democrata Cristão. However, I believe that, in the cultural sector, I must play a very positive role in helping to create such a political organization." He declared that the PDC would be "the remedy to be used against Communist propaganda," and added that he was telling PDC members to favor the candidacy of Eduardo Gomes.[8]

Writing Lindolpho Pio da Silva Dias about the speech, Sobral said: "At the side of the campaign of Eduardo Gomes, we must try to form a political current based on positive Christian ideas that can serve to support tomorrow's rulers, desirous of orienting the Nation within the moral principles appropriate for Christian civilization. I do not know what direction my life will take, but I consider it my duty to give my fellow-citizens the impressions made on my soul by political life. That is what I did in my speech."[9]

3.   Sobral, LEC Counselor, Discusses the Social Problem (July–August 1945)

Soon after Sobral's speech of July 9, the Liga Eleitoral Católica (LEC), which had hibernated during the Estado Novo, declared itself reconstituted, again as a section of Ação Católica Brasileira. The revival, it announced, resulted from a decision of the Catholic episcopate, made with the support of "almost all its venerable prelates," and was to be followed by LEC encouragement of the registration of voters favoring its program and the indication of which candidates and parties accepted the program. The program, the LEC said, would be made known later.[1]

Hildebrando Acioly, former ambassador to the Vatican, was named LEC president, and Alceu Amoroso Lima, who had declined the presidency, became secretary general. Hamilton Nogueira became president of the Federal District board (and later national treasurer). Sobral, along with five others, was chosen to be an LEC counselor.[2]

The announcement in July of the return of the LEC to activity coincided with a rally in Belo Horizonte by the União Democrática Nacional (UDN), the chief party supporting Eduardo Gomes in his contest against Eurico Gaspar Dutra, presidential candidate of the Partido Social Democrático (PSD). Gomes, speaking for an hour from a text of forty typewritten pages, was joined at the rally by a battery of more experienced orators: Arthur Bernardes, Pedro Aleixo, Daniel de Carvalho, Octavio Mangabeira, Juracy Magalhães, and João Carlos Machado.[3] From a fellow Mineiro, Sobral learned that Gomes had displayed resolution and an ability to arouse "an elucidated enthusiasm." Lindolpho Pio da Silva Dias, busy selling coffee, was told by Sobral: "We are thinking of holding a rally in your Poços de Caldas, with Eduardo Gomes participating."[4]

Sobral, in his speech to the PDC, had stressed the need to attract the workers. It was no easy task because vast numbers of them felt that past benefits decreed by Vargas might be lost without his continuance in office,[5] and thus they were attracted to the Communist Party (PCB) and the Partido Trabalhista Brasileiro (PTB, Brazilian Labor Party), founded in May 1945 by Labor Minister Marcondes Filho and others close to Vargas. Sobral's "Warnings to the Working Class," drawn up in July, described conditions in Soviet Russia to show that it was erroneous to suppose that, under Communism, the Brazilian workers would possess the factories and wealth of the rich or that class distinctions would disappear. Soviet workers, he wrote, lacked ample liberties and were forced to toil in a regime that was tough and rigorous, while bureaucrats, their oppressors, ate better than they.[6]

The need for Catholics to assist the working class was given emphasis in Sobral's speech delivered in mid-August in a church in Rio's Urca district. The speech, critical of Catholics for inactivity, reminded the gathering that Pope Pius XI, founder of Ação Católica, had called for "direct and effective" action by the Catholic laity. Ação Católica, Sobral said, should behave in accordance with Church doctrine about a just distribution of wealth or else "Christian civilization will disappear from our land."[7]

Many Catholics, Sobral said, simply blamed Communism, and not themselves, for humanity's ills and believed, incorrectly, that the cardinal sin of Communists was to want to transfer the property of capitalism to the proletariat. In Sobral's view, the sin of Communism lay in its wish to build a society on the basis of the inexistence of God, its insistence on the class struggle, to be carried out by force, and its advocacy of a dictatorial state for completely doing away with legitimately acquired private property. He said that the Communists should not be jailed as common criminals for wanting to abolish private property because their purpose was not to enrich themselves personally. "The venom lies not with them but with their cruel, implacable, and inhuman doctrine."

Calling attention to the strides made by Communism in Brazil in four months, Sobral placed the blame on the "immense majority" of Brazilian Catholics who "insist on refusing to understand the sinister reality of the social question" and who had remained deaf to warnings against the Estado Novo's systematic destruction of the nation's traditional spiritual, moral, and juridical forces. He quoted Lenin as calling the idea of God a tool used by the bourgeoisie "to defend its exploitation" and as having asserted that "what is moral is what supports the class struggle." Contemporary Brazilian Communism, Sobral explained, considered this Communist "morality" as best served by the *positivista-castilhista* government, and for that reason no one should be surprised that the Communists, their eyes on their "final victory," were supporting a government that "has given them so much help in these recent months."

The response of Catholics, Sobral said, should be to reorganize their ranks, within Ação Católica, in order to reveal to the unfortunate common man that it was the social doctrine of the Church that could bring about a new social order, "one without misery and poverty and without any lack of the essential things of life, such as a home, sustenance, and education." Sobral called for "the entire national ecclesiastical hierarchy" and laity to mobilize the Brazilian spiritual forces, "presently asleep," in a way that would produce cultural, economic, and social institutions able to resolve "all the problems" brought about by the unjust distribution of wealth. "The common man is at our disposal if only we . . . concern ourselves with his misery and ignorance and work fraternally to give him a companionship in keeping with his dignity. . . .

"Just as the Apostles at the beginning of the Christian era, blessed with far fewer resources than we possess, conquered the pagan world, . . . let us conquer the pagan world of the present tragic and bloody era. Have courage and spirit. Victory will be ours."[8]

Practicing what he had been preaching, Sobral in August became one of the two founders of the Movimento Operário Social Cristão (Christian Social Labor Movement), an organization of Ação Católica Brasileira for letting workers know that the Catholic Church was their friend and protector and for bringing them together in Christianity.[9] The other founder was Francisco Mangabeira, who had been arrested in 1936 for his work with the ANL (Aliança Nacional Libertadora). He was the son of João Mangabeira, leader of the Esquerda Democrática (the Democratic Left), and nephew of Octavio Mangabeira, recently named president of the UDN.

Diário Carioca columnist Joaquim de Sales wrote on August 17 that the new Movimento Operário Social Cristão was bound to succeed thanks to the zeal of Brazil's Christian workers and the virtues of its two founders. Above all, he praised Sobral.

"Heráclito Sobral Pinto," he wrote, "is respected, liked, and admired by all of Brazil. He is one of the country's most noble moral possessions. He is one of those rare heroic figures out of Plutarch, with a heart devoted to the highest ideals of Christian charity and human understanding. He is the perfect example of the knight without blemish or fear. One could say that he is untouched by any impurity that might tarnish the splendor of his faith or impair the firmness of his Christian character."

Joaquim de Sales wrote that Sobral, Brazil's most fearless fighter for Christian truth and most courageous Christian legionnaire, was a flamethrower, who, in his inflexible defense of the doctrine of Christ, pursued enemies "in their most recondite burrows and hideouts. He faces dangers and, when necessary, resorts to severe rebukes and objurgations to send enemies scurrying." Thus, in the opinion of Joaquim de Sales, Sobral was like Saint Paul, whereas Alceu Amoroso Lima, "a saint" to whom the columnist was "especially devoted," was like Saint John, "the beloved disciple" who "learned from Jesus to be gentle and humble of heart."

According to Joaquim de Sales, Sobral had made a convincing argument to Francisco Mangabeira, "one of the most authoritative, ardent, and able lay apostles of the Church," and so the pair was establishing the new labor movement in preparation for the coming of "the new Order," which was to remove from the world the "inadmissible inequalities and iniquitous injustices" that had led to "the abyss of an infamous, hideous war." Within the Alceu-directed Ação Católica Brasileira, Joaquim de Sales wrote, Sobral and Francisco Mangabeira would act like shock troop commanders for the achievement of the material, moral, and spiritual improvement that the Christian proletariat was demanding in order that the world might have "the evangelic spirit of the equality of men, all of them being sons of the Heavenly Father."[10]

Sobral, after reading Joaquim de Sales' article, wrote him to tell of the "humility, confusion, and unease" he felt on reading about his "supposed merits." The great value of Joaquim's article, he wrote, lay not in its praise of Sobral but in the disclosure to the *Diário Carioca*'s readers of information about "our movement." "You revealed to the Brazilian workforce that, among its real friends, none can come anywhere near equaling Our Lord Jesus Christ, because He also was a modest and poor worker."[11]

4. The LEC Denies Suffering a Schism (September 1945)

In August, after Eduardo Gomes accepted the support of the Socialists of the Esquerda Democrática (Democratic Left), many Catholics raised their voices in alarm. Sobral, not sharing the alarm, promised to have the LEC (Liga Eleitoral Católica) issue a circular replying to what he called the "unjust and irrelevant fallacies" in a "wretched pamphlet" that had condemned the alliance of Gomes and the Esquerda Democrática. In a letter to Miguel, son of Lindolpho Pio da Silva Dias, Sobral wrote that Catholics should not object to the alliance, but should understand, from their own experience, why the Esquerda Democrática preferred Gomes, proponent of "a regime of liberty," to Dutra, favorable to "a mitigated authoritarian regime."[1]

So busy was Sobral with political matters that he had to tell Lindolpho of his difficulty in finding time to send him regularly the amusing anti-Vargas articles published by humorist Aparício Torelli, or to draw up papers for a company that Lindolpho wished to form. The political situation in Rio, Sobral wrote him, "is mired in confusion, the result of an atmosphere full of contradictory and sinister rumors."[2] Vargas had withdrawn his support of Dutra and was said to be considering replacing him with another candidate, possibly General Góes Monteiro; but, instead, he chose Góes to take over the war ministry from the PSD candidate, who left his office to plod on with his campaign. So dismal was the outlook for a Dutra victory that Police Chief João Alberto Lins de Barros, a PSD director, let it be known that Dutra should withdraw. Influential Colonel Juarez Távora, arguing that the Dutra candidacy was causing a split in the military, asked Dutra to step aside, and then, when Dutra rejected the suggestion, came out in favor of Gomes.[3]

The position of the hierarchy of the Brazilian Catholic Church, according to writer Luís Werneck Viana, was one of avoiding involvement in any reform movement that might jeopardize its "pact with sectors of the dominant class" or put it "in a position critical of the state apparatus." Viana gives this as a reason for the failure of the Church to back the PDC (Partido Democrata Cristão), even though that party, like the Church, refused to come out in favor of either Gomes or Dutra.[4]

The LEC (Liga Eleitoral Católica), sponsored by the Church, proclaimed itself above parties and interested in getting people to register in order to vote for candidates who accepted its program. The program, presented in September in the form of a decalogue, called for the promulgation of a constitution in the name of God, recognition of the fundamental rights of man, the indissolubility of marriage, the right to have religious education in schools, a rejection of any monopoly of education, a policy of political party plurality (with the exclusion of antidemocratic organizations), labor legislation inspired by social justice, the preservation of individual liberties, a plurality of unions *(pluralidade sindical)*, combat against legislation that opposed natural law or Christian doctrine, and the provision of church services in the armed forces.[5]

In contrast to the position "above parties" of the LEC and Ação Católica, Sobral was clearly pro-Gomes, and other LEC leaders were known also to favor the *brigadeiro*. For this reason the *Diário Carioca* ran an article on September 9 under a headline proclaiming "A schism in the LEC." The article said that Alceu, Sobral, and biology professor Hamilton Nogueira had left their LEC positions because they disagreed with "the orientation of top ecclesiastic circles."[6] (In the case of Alceu, his divergences with Dom Jayme Câmara could hardly have escaped the knowledge of the *Diário Carioca*.)[7]

For publication in the *Diário Carioca*, Sobral sent a letter to Horácio de Carvalho Júnior denying the existence of an LEC schism or the departure of himself, Alceu, and Hamilton from the LEC positions conferred on them because of "Archbishop Jayme de Barros Câmara's confidence" in them. Insisting on limiting his observations to his own case, Sobral wrote that his eight-year combat against the government of usurpation and oppression had been carried out under his "personal responsibility" as a Christian jurist and Catholic citizen, and never as part of his responsibility as an officer of Ação Católica and the LEC.[8]

But Sobral admitted in his letter that he had found himself recently with a problem. Learning that "a large number of Catholics" disliked his view and believed it incompatible with his "functions in the two Church organizations," he had decided to resign from his positions in Ação Católica and the LEC in order to avoid "further embarrassment" for Alceu and especially for the archbishop, "whose kindness and affection for me in recent times have exceeded simple generosity."

Sobral explained further that he had delayed acting on his decision at the request of Alceu, who had been about to leave for São Paulo and wished to discuss the matter upon his return. In conclusion, Sobral admitted having mentioned his decision in private to a few friends, "never imagining that they would alter the facts in a way that would lead to the erroneous publication about a schism in the LEC."[9]

In publishing Sobral's letter, the *Diário Carioca* wrote an introduction saying that its news story of September 9 had been substantially correct, "although perhaps the headline was excessive, mentioning a schism when all that had been verified were the decisions of the three LEC leaders, the most important ones, to leave their posts." The newspaper added that it was pleased to announce that the decisions were not carried out, signifying the preservation of the unity of the Liga Eleitoral Católica, "which constitutes, without doubt, one of the most powerful forces for the defense of the foremost principles of Christianity in the realm of politics."[10]

Other Rio dailies carried a notice, submitted by the LEC, to deny any basis for the *Diário Carioca*'s story of September 9 and to refute its suggestion that the national episcopate and the LEC leaders had had a disagreement. The LEC, it pointed out, was acting rigorously within a spirit that transcended political parties, as had been made known in its recent telegrams to its local boards.[11]

Meanwhile in São Paulo, the LEC announced its organization of 196 voter registration posts within the state and the distribution of millions of leaflets. In Rio, Father Tapajóz told an LEC gathering that it would be a sin for Catholics to refrain from voting while Communists, hiding their true intentions, materialistic and anti-religious, "threaten to intervene in the country's legislation."[12]

Later in September, the role of the LEC was among the matters discussed at a three-day meeting held in Rio by Archbishops Jayme Câmara of Rio, Carlos Carmello de Vasconcellos Motta of São Paulo, Antônio dos Santos Cabral of Belo Horizonte, and Augusto Álvaro da Silva of Bahia, with the bishop of Niterói in attendance and with Canon José Távora, archdiocesan director of social action, serving as secretary. The purpose of the meeting was to examine Ação Católica Brasileira, and it resulted in proposals to the Vatican for altering the organization's statutes, along with a statement making it very clear that Ação Católica and the LEC were to be run by the archbishops and bishops. The LEC, the archbishops declared, would remain above political parties in order to orient the electoral conscience of Catholics for the defense of "postulates such as the permanence of optional religious education in schools, the indissolubility of marriage, and religious services in the armed forces and hospitals."[13]

The LEC, in the months that followed, let it be known that its decisions about the parties and candidates it favored would be based on their acceptance of these three points and agreement that labor legislation should be inspired by social justice and Christian principles. Thus a "minimum program" took the place of the full decalogue in the LEC's discussions with the electoral contestants.[14]

5. Resistência Democrática and the OAB Oppose the Queremistas (September–October 1945)

Vargas, by remaining in office after September 2, became ineligible to run for the presidency. After that, the Queremistas ("Queremos Getúlio"—We Want Getúlio), associated with the Communist and Labor Parties (PCB and PTB), insisted at their rallies that the December 2 election should be for a Constituent Assembly and that Vargas should continue in the presidency. They were joined by São Paulo cotton speculator Hugo Borghi, who had recently received money from Finance Minister Artur de Sousa Costa for the purchase of radio stations.[1]

The Queremistas' demand for the cancellation of the scheduled presidential election worried military figures such as Góes, Dutra, and Gomes, not to mention the supporters of the two presidential candidates. Rio Police Chief João Alberto issued rulings against Queremista rallies, but they were frequently defied.[2]

The Queremista movement did not owe its inception to Vargas,[3] and on September 7 he delivered a speech which was hardly encouraging to its objectives. He promised that he had no intention other than to preside over the elections already scheduled by him for choosing Brazil's new rulers and for giving the country a new political framework. "The currents of public opinion," he said, "are organizing themselves in political parties."[4]

In a "Warning to the Nation," Resistência Democrática wrote that Vargas had described "currents of public opinion, organized in parties," as being able to "alter the election arrangements" and had "insinuated that a pronouncement by the parties can reduce what the future election is all about . . . in order to allow the dictatorship to continue."[5]

Resistência Democrática, which now had its office in the Rio building that housed the UDN, was headed by lawyers Adaucto Lucio Cardoso, its president, and Haryberto de Miranda Jordão, who served as secretary general until he was replaced, late in October, by the movement's active vice president, erudite medical doctor José Fernando Carneiro. Others notable for participating in Resistência Democrática work were lawyer José Barreto Filho and banker Tancredo Ribas Carneiro, who became vice president when José Fernando Carneiro was promoted.[6]

Resistência Democrática's "Warning to the Nation" denounced the Queremistas' "abundant" *matéria paga* (paid-for press articles) and inscriptions on walls and sidewalks calling for "A Constituent Assembly with Getúlio." It attributed this "gigantic propaganda effort" to financing by the dictatorship and to the efficiency of the Communist organization. To acquaint or remind the people of Queremismo's Communist ties, Resistência Democrática devised a slogan, "The Communist Constitutional Assembly is a Queremista coup."[7]

Late in September, Resistência Democrática published a document in reply to War Minister Góes, who had given a melancholy speech informing army officers, back from Italy, that they would find Brazil a "vast and appalling political insane asylum," beset with "sterile, factious struggles," inspired by extremist preconceptions and greedy appetites. Fearing that a dreadful civil war would be the result of "bad faith, hypocrisy, the war of nerves, intransigent positions, and other factors of a moral and political nature," Góes had offered to lead the returning army officers against those whose whims were creating anarchy and threatening Brazil's unity.[8]

Resistência Democrática, describing a different Brazil, wrote that Góes should have told the army officers that they were returning to a country involved in a decisive phase of political renovation, with an electoral campaign destined to revive the democratic institutions. The Brazilian scene, in the opinion of Resistência Democrática, would no doubt fill the officers with joy because it represented a march toward the principles for which they had fought overseas. Their new mission was described as one that would assure the peaceful conclusion of the election campaign, including the contest for the presidency, promised by the government.[9]

Like Resistência Democrática, the OAB (Ordem dos Advogados do Brasil) was distressed by Queremismo. More than in any other organization, Sobral distinguished himself in its Conselho Federal at this time, and when the Conselho met on September 18, to decide how to react to Queremismo, Sobral participated in the lengthy discussion.[10]

Augusto Pinto Lima ("dean of the Federal District lawyers")[11] presented a draft of a resolution in which the Conselho Federal declared that it had the duty to warn the public against "tendentious propaganda" which was incompatible with democracy and which sought to "subvert electoral legislation now in effect." This electoral legislation, the draft said, should be defended "with inflexible firmness" by organs representing all social classes in order to preserve peace and bring about a return to the rule of law, as had been guaranteed by the armed forces "in a formal declaration of the war minister." After the draft was applauded and approved, Raul Fernandes, the presiding officer, named a commission, composed of Augusto Pinto Lima, Sobral Pinto, and Dario de Almeida Magalhães, to write the final version.[12]

Sobral argued that the resolution should be presented to the military leaders, clergy, teachers, and representatives of the conservative and working classes. However, a majority agreed with Nelson Carneiro that it would suffice to publish it in the press, "addressed to all social classes and especially the armed forces, responsible for the execution of the laws." The final version, known as the Conselho

Federal's "motion of September 18," was approved by the Conselho of the OAB's Federal District section on September 20.[13]

On September 21, *O Globo* gave publicity, on two pages of its morning and afternoon editions, to Queremista propaganda that attacked the OAB Conselho Federal and its position. Sobral therefore wrote *O Globo*'s Roberto Marinho about the desolation that had filled him on reading these "revolting" Queremista columns. Declaring that a more brazen attack against the nation's moral hierarchy had never occurred, he pointed out that one of the pages was full of "sinister hatred" that sought "to destroy, in the mind of the people," the moral force of an institution that, "in these tragic days, . . . has been battling, ardently and almost without hope, against a willfulness which is taking the Brazilian people to the greatest social convulsion in its history." Telling Marinho that a newspaper was not "a mere sales counter," Sobral wrote that *O Globo* should follow the example of Orlando Ribeiro Dantas, owner of the *Diário de Notícias*, who had rejected *matéria-paga* submitted by the Queremistas, calling it deplorable.[14]

The OAB's Conselho Federal, at its meeting on September 25, approved the motion of Sobral to have his letter to Marinho transcribed in the press.[15]

The Conselho of the Federal District of the OAB asked the Tribunal Superior Eleitoral (TSE) for its decision on whether the Congress to be elected on December 2 would have the authority to give Brazil a new constitution. Sobral, a member of the Federal District section who believed the decision to be of utmost importance for a prompt restoration of a just juridical order, followed the TSE debates closely and was pleased when a majority of the Tribunal (Antônio de Sampaio Dória, Lafayette de Andrada, and Waldemar Falcão) ruled, on October 2, that the Congress would have the right, if it so decided, to act as a Constituent Assembly. This decision, Sobral told the *Diário de Notícias*, meant "the definitive demise of this stubborn agitation that has been made with purely revolutionary objectives and with calls for a Constituent Assembly. Only those who wish the country to endure confusion, disorder, and unrest, with the purpose of achieving or conserving their own power, will continue clamoring for a Constituent Assembly."[16]

When the Conselho of the Federal District section of the OAB met on October 3, Sobral persuaded it to include in its minutes a defense he had recently made of the September 18 motion of the

Conselho Federal. In this defense, Sobral said that he had read in the Communists' *Tribuna Popular* a protest signed by lawyers who opposed the motion. He spoke of his long struggle to defend the right of the people to offer dissenting opinions but asserted that they ought not to violate the principle of sticking to the truth. "It is not licit for anyone, especially lawyers, to falsify facts in order to misrepresent the decisions of the Conselhos of the OAB and the intentions of Conselho members." Lawyers signing in the *Tribuna Popular*, he said, had attributed an improper "political party character" to the OAB's September 18 motion and had used this "false" accusation in an effort to show that the OAB had departed from the principles on which it had been founded. In reply to this charge, Sobral said that he, like the vast majority of his fellow Conselho members, had never been a party politician or at the service of any political faction; he added that the lawyers who were at the service of political ideas were the ones who had used the *Tribuna Popular* to attack the Conselho Federal.[17]

Heitor Rocha Faria, one of the lawyers to whom Sobral was referring, wrote several letters to Sobral. He argued that Sobral, despite his words, had been acting like a party politician, and he again accused the OAB's Conselho Federal of trying to influence public opinion in a political party manner. Sobral, in his answer, accused Rocha Faria of failing to distinguish between a voter and a politician—a failure that was "inadmissible in a lawyer." In the course of trying to enlighten the "confused" Rocha Faria about the difference, Sobral described "a voter" as avoiding party discipline and making his choice of candidates in accordance with his personal criteria. He pointed out that the Liga Eleitoral Católica, "possessor of the country's largest electorate," was acting "beyond and above parties."

Rocha Faria, in one of his letters to Sobral, revealed that the signers of the protest against the OAB motion had been limited to using the *Tribuna Popular*, the *Folha Carioca*, and *O Radical* because no other Rio newspaper would publish their protest. Sobral, no doubt pleased to note the absence of *O Globo* from the list, called Rocha Faria's disclosure a "confession." He said that the *Tribuna Popular*, being Communist, and the other two dailies, being Queremista, were firmly opposed to "traditional juridical order in Brazil."[18] These words were written at a time when the Queremistas were receiving encouragement from statements by Vargas.[19]

The LEC, especially busy registering voters while this could still be done, began to seek the responses of political parties to its program.[20] After Hildebrando Acioly and Alceu Amoroso Lima consulted the Partido Democrata Cristão on October 22, they learned from its Federal District leader, Osório Lopes, that the party had adopted, at its convention on October 14, a program similar to the LEC decalogue.[21] In São Paulo on October 16, Archbishop Vasconcellos Motta told an LEC meeting that Catholic principles were having a decisive influence on party programs and that, from what he had so far learned, only the Communist Party (PCB) was unworthy of the votes of Catholics. The LEC, active in denouncing the PCB, distributed a study of conditions in Russia to try to destroy, as Sobral had tried, the "myth" about Communism being advantageous to workers.[22]

An editorial in the *Diário Carioca* in mid-October argued against far leftists who called the LEC an antidemocratic "oppressor of consciences." It pointed out that the LEC, "the major electoral force in the country," could not stop voters from supporting candidates who opposed its principles.[23]

PART XI

Declining to Run for Congress and Explaining Vargas' Fall (October 1945)

1. Condemning the Alteration of State Election Procedures (Mid-October 1945)

On October 10 Vargas dismayed the opposition by issuing Decree-Law 8,063. It favored his state *interventores* by establishing that elections for state legislatures and governors would take place on December 2 (simultaneously with the national elections) instead of on May 6, 1946, as had been decreed on May 28, 1945. It also made the *interventores* eligible for the gubernatorial elections and instructed them to promulgate state constitutions within twenty days of the new decree.[1]

The UDN, the Partido Republicano (headed by Arthur Bernardes), and the Partido Libertador issued a joint manifesto that called Decree-Law 8,063 an "act of insanity" devised to bring about chaos and prevent the "inevitable" election of Eduardo Gomes.[2]

Like the joint manifesto, the manifesto of the Esquerda Democrática cited laws already issued and attributed the purpose of Decree-Law 8,063 to a desire to create bedlam. It maintained that the dictatorship, acting while the opposition had been devoting its attention to the presidential election, was "arming twenty of its puppets with the power to promulgate twenty constitutions in twenty states so that all of them can perpetuate themselves in the positions they already occupy"; and it contended that elections of governors and state legislators should be carried out in accordance with a national constitution, yet to be written.[3]

Resistência Democrática, also quick to protest, declared that Vargas had violated his solemn pledge, given in an electoral law that had been endorsed by the armed forces, and was creating something unheard of in Brazil, a "monstrosity" that allowed "twenty manipulators" to promulgate state constitutions. Like Sobral, Resistência Democrática pictured Vargas as fostering confusion in order to allege that Brazil was unable to act in a democratic manner. The situation, it wrote, was so full of danger that the only solution was the overthrow of the man who had done nothing but prevent democratization.[4]

The *Diário Carioca* was able to join other dailies in giving exposure to the protest of Resistência Democrática following a week of suspended publication brought about because the Departamento Nacional de Informações, successor of the DIP, had made it impossible for the violently anti-Vargas newspaper to continue importing newsprint. Adaucto Lucio Cardoso, representing the *Diário Carioca*, had obtained a favorable court ruling on October 8.[5]

When the OAB's Conselho Federal met on October 16 to discuss Decree-Law 8,063, the session was even more lively than that of September 18. After Augusto Pinto Lima proposed a motion denouncing "this transgression" against government promises, two lawyers (the representatives from Santa Catarina and Mato Grosso) questioned whether it was proper for the Conselho to issue an opinion about the new decree. The ensuing debate ended with Sobral asking for a vote, and the question was laid to rest as the two hesitant lawyers at length decided to go along with the majority and make Pinto Lima's motion unanimous.[6]

Nelson Carneiro said the lawyers should take to the streets and hold public meetings to acquaint the people with the nation's "humiliating and legally destitute situation." Pinto Lima acknowledged the need to remove the dictator but told Carneiro that the lawyers' message would be read during the forthcoming pro-Gomes rally in Rio's Teatro Municipal, being organized by lawyers. Carneiro then explained that what he wanted was a movement apart from party politics. Targino Ribeiro supported Carneiro, leading to a vote that produced a unanimous resolution to have the Conselho direct the OAB state organizations to ask lawyers to initiate a "great campaign to enlighten the people about the need to restore juridical order, eliminated by the dictatorship."

The Conselho next listened to a lengthy opinion that Sobral had prepared about Decree 8,063. He reviewed recent electoral legislation in detail but added that no sensible jurist could approach the subject from the viewpoint of legal science as long as Vargas had at his side Justice Minister Agamemnon Magalhães, who had declared in 1940 that democracy was ineffective, and War Minister Góes Monteiro, advocate in the 1930s of the use of force by governments.

Sobral asserted that he could hold his head high because he had never asked for anything from people in government and owed them nothing.

My life as a jurist, obscured almost to anonymity, is a rosary of sacrifices, consciously embraced, to defend rights that have been defiled, to give prestige to lawyers, who have been disparaged, to give dignity to a Brazilian judiciary that has been disrespected, to improve juridical institutions that have been attacked, and to safeguard a Brazilian juridical order that has been permanently neglected.

I have been a fighter, vibrant but serene, unequivocal but doctrinary, frank but gentlemanly, struggling against the disorder that seized power in Brazil and that is taking us, gradually but fatally, to total ruin. . . . It is this profound affection for my country that leads me to say now, with the irrepressible strength of an unshakable conviction, that we must defend the Nation's brazenly violated juridical order by declaring that Decree-Law 8,063 is the most insulting act ever carried out in Brazil against its sovereignty. Nowhere in the annals of our history can there be found so criminal an assault.

Citing Articles 175 and 80 of the 1937 Constitution, Sobral argued that the six-year "provisional mandate" given Vargas in Article 175 (and extended by Vargas in 1942) did not have "the slightest legitimacy" because no plebiscite favorable to the constitution was held. Discussing the governors, Sobral pointed out that Constitutional Article 176 had given Vargas thirty days in which to confirm their mandates, and he noted that only Benedicto Valladares of Minas Gerais had received such a confirmation; therefore, he said, only Valladares could carry out Constitutional Article 181 authorizing the promulgation of state constitutions by "their respective governors." He described the remaining states as existing without governments, "only mere administrations directed by *interventores*," and as requiring, if they were to receive valid constitutions, the ratification of the 1937 federal Constitution by the plebiscite mentioned in it but never held. Vargas, he said, was simply imposing, illegally, his personal rule in authorizing the promulgation of state constitutions before October 30, 1945.

In his closing remarks, Sobral said: "My conscience as a jurist and patriot makes it my duty to proclaim, in this Conselho, that if our national leaders, civilian and military, permit the unhindered use of Decree 8,063, with its affront to the most sacred rights of the Brazilian people, Brazil will cease to be a nation and will become a barren territory, stripped of Citizenship, Constitution, Justice, Law, and Liberty—a territory from which any semblance of juridical and stable order will have been swept away by a chief of state backed by the armed forces."[7]

After all the members of the Conselho applauded Sobral, Oscar Stevenson proposed that Sobral's final ringing words be incorporated in the Conselho's motion as reflecting its view. The proposal was adopted unanimously, as was a proposal of Raul Fernandes that Sobral's full opinion be considered a supplement to the motion.

Raul Fernandes also received approval of his suggestion that Sobral be chosen to deliver the Conselho's motion to the Tribunal Superior Eleitoral (TSE), "the only competent unarmed power that is able to erect barriers against the illegality in progress." The motion that Sobral took to the TSE, much shorter than his study, was a defense of "the restoration of juridical order" that pointed out that Decree-Law 8,063 had not been the initiative of the TSE, "the organ with the task of supervising the Nation's political reconstruction."[8]

Along with the Conselho's motion, the long opinion that had been read by Sobral was published in much of the Rio press. O Globo, writing about the Conselho's meeting, said that the lawyers, "approving the vibrant, informative, and well-founded opinion of Sobral Pinto, declared that Vargas violated promises made to the people."[9]

A different view was expressed by the Gazeta de Notícias, which had supported the Estado Novo and now favored the candidacy of Dutra. The OAB's Conselho Federal, it wrote, had become a branch of the UDN and was itself breaking the law by flagrantly betraying the regulations that governed the OAB. Members of the Conselho were described by the Gazeta de Notícias as motivated by "political appetites." The Diário de Notícias, coming to the defense of the Conselho Federal, wrote that masses of lawyers, by their presence at their pro-Gomes rally, would ratify the Conselho's stand and would thus provide a reply to those who were calling that stand a mere consequence of "infiltration by oppositionists in the Conselho."[10]

2.   The Lawyers' Pro-Gomes Rally (October 19, 1945)

Adaucto Lucio Cardoso headed the commission to arrange for the rally at which Eduardo Gomes was to be presented with the manifesto in his favor signed by over one thousand lawyers. Sobral, with the task of obtaining the use of Rio's Teatro Municipal, found Mayor Henrique Dodsworth cooperative despite the reschedulings of the date occasioned by two postponements.[1] The rally was held on the evening of October 19, by which time Gomes supporters were describing the manifesto as signed by "over two thousand lawyers, jurists, and judges in Rio alone."[2]

To observe the occasion, *Diário de Notícias* columnist Raphael Corrêa de Oliveira published an article, "Lawyers of Brazil," in which he wrote that defense attorneys, in the years following "the treason of 1937," had struggled at "tribunals of exception," facing odious terror and defying the rage and retaliatory acts of men in power.

Except for Ruy Barbosa, "faultless defender of all legitimate human liberties," the only Brazilian named in the article was Sobral Pinto. Raphael Corrêa de Oliveira recalled the glorious but tragic age of defense lawyers during and after the French Revolution but said that even Antoine Berryer, famous for defending Marshal Ney and French monarchs, did not demonstrate a better fulfillment of duty than was "achieved in Latin America a century later by Sobral Pinto." He described Sobral as "the Catholic who, for eight years, gave Communist Luiz Carlos Prestes uninterrupted moral and legal support, without remuneration of any sort and exposing himself to the excesses and caprices of the dictatorship's despotism. Deeds like these honor the profession and dignify the political culture of a people."

Raphael Corrêa de Oliveira warned against being fooled by "individuals who disparage legal formulas. . . . Those individuals are full of violent passions and are induced by ambition, egoism, and envy to carry out criminal acts. . . . They are dangerous because they do not understand or accept the limitations of the law. . . . What we are going to witness this evening is a splendid and dauntless manifestation of resistance against the tide of brute force."[3]

The crowd that filled the Teatro Municipal applauded prominent oppositionists such as Arthur Bernardes, Virgílio de Mello Franco, Octavio Mangabeira, Sobral Pinto, and Raul Fernandes. Speeches by

Plínio Barreto, representing São Paulo lawyers, and Milton Campos, representing Minas lawyers, were read by Targino Ribeiro and José Monteiro de Castro. Then Adaucto Lucio Cardoso presented the lawyers' manifesto to Eduardo Gomes and gave a speech calling the *brigadeiro* a candidate with a civilian spirit who "is the embodiment of our aspirations to have the law prevail." The Brazilian lawyers, he said, were struggling as lovers of justice and liberty and not as political party members. "We have done everything possible during these tragic years with the purpose of abolishing tyranny from the soil of the Nation and implanting juridical order."[4]

Eduardo Gomes, who was assisted in speech writing by José Eduardo Prado Kelly (son of Judge Octavio Kelly), delivered a lofty address befitting an audience of lawyers devoted to justice and liberty. Declaring that "the Law, so often violated by people with power, will be reborn in the splendor of its majesty," he was enthusiastically applauded by his listeners, waving their white handkerchiefs.[5] Following the singing of the national anthem, the meeting was brought to a close by the presiding officer, veteran lawyer Moitinho Dória, and then much of the audience joined a crowd in the neighboring Praça Marechal Floriano that was calling on UDN President Octavio Mangabeira to speak. Mangabeira declared that it had become clearer than ever that Eduardo Gomes was the voice of the nation, "a nation that can no longer breathe under the dictatorship and is demanding juridical order, that is, democratic legality."[6]

On the next day, the UDN announced a series of public debates in order to keep itself in constant touch with the people. Sobral was chosen to preside at the first debate, where the speakers were to include Luiz Camillo de Oliveira Netto and socialist professor Hermes Lima, a founder of Esquerda Democrática.[7]

3. Maciel Filho Recalls Sobral's 1928 Scandal (October 1945)

José Soares Maciel Filho, journalist and Vargas speechwriter, attacked Sobral Pinto, Adaucto Lucio Cardoso, and Raul Fernandes in articles in *A Noite*, the Rio daily that had been taken over by the government in 1940 and was in the hands of Colonel Luiz Carlos da Costa Netto, a former TSN judge, and André Carrazzoni, pro-Vargas president of the Rio de Janeiro Union of Professional Journalists.[1]

Referring to Sobral on October 17, Maciel Filho wrote about the lawyer who had told the OAB's Conselho Federal that the presence of Agamemnon Magalhães and Góes Monteiro at Vargas' side made it meaningless to consider legal aspects when debating constitutional matters. It might seem, Maciel Filho wrote, that the author of this opinion was a jurist inspired by his love of the law and a gentleman highly regarded on account of an exemplary life.[2]

Not so, Maciel Filho added. "For the good of public service, he was dismissed from his position of *procurador geral* of the Federal District because he was whipped in the face in a street in broad daylight. The one who whipped him was an upright person of good character who had placed his trust in the friendship and loyalty of that man and who became obliged to act as he did for personal reasons that fully justified the whipping."[3]

Maciel Filho called Raul Fernandes "the leader of big business deals of foreigners in Brazil" and the head of a group of "political lawyers" whose purpose was the encouragement of a military coup against the wishes of the people. Adaucto Lucio Cardoso was described by Maciel Filho on October 22 as unhappy with the Vargas regime because of his dismissal from the position of juridical consultant of one of the ministries.[4]

Sobral, replying in the *Jornal do Commercio*, called the "distortion of facts" about himself by the "perverse slanderer" another bitter expiation imposed by God, and said he was accepting it just as he had accepted, in 1928, "the torrent of infamies, vileness, and lies" heaped upon him by political hatred, exacerbated by his "inflexible performance in defense of legality" when he had been *procurador criminal* of the republic.[5] This, he wrote, was not the first time, nor would it be the last, that the scandal, which had cost him "tears of blood," would be invoked by gratuitous, haughty foes: men who envied his public reputation, men at the service of evil interests that he had uncovered and denounced, and men whom he had defeated in doctrinal polemics, "during which I never pried into private lives."

His past public confessions, Sobral wrote, had never been able to prevent "furious, impotent, and miserable opponents," filled with "the bile of spite, jealousy, and defamation," from turning to the single degrading episode to disfigure his private and public behavior, thus piercing the heart of one who "never looked after his personal interests but dedicated himself to the constant service of his fellow beings and, above all, of his unfortunate Nation." As an example of a public confession, Sobral transcribed passages from his talk, given in appreciation of Sebastião Leme at the Centro Dom Vital in 1942 and later printed in his weekly column, that described his visit to the archbishop in 1928 following his neglect of his "sacred duties as a Christian husband."[6]

Sobral accused Maciel Filho of giving publicity to the false version of 1928 that had transformed a brief exchange of blows into a debasing whipping, never carried out. And he explained that it was deceitful to write about "a dismissal for the good of public order" because a truthful account would have spoken of a resignation granted at Sobral's request, made in a letter to Washington Luiz that revealed Sobral's only concern: protection of the dignity of his office "in the face of a badly informed public opinion." "I placed in the President's hands the government post, given me without any solicitation on my part by His Excellency, who was not a personal friend of mine but who always showed me the highest esteem on account of my public spirit and loyalty." His letter to Washington Luiz, Sobral informed Maciel Filho, should be in the possession of Vargas, who had "abusively" made off with private files of "that man of Plutarch."

Sobral wrote that his departure from his post in 1928, made without a word of recrimination, complaint, or disrespect, had been followed by his bitter struggle to support himself and his large family and to restore, by work, honesty, and loyalty, his spotless reputation. He told of his "isolated, withdrawn" lifestyle, devoid of diversions and social pleasures.

No reputable journalist, Sobral wrote, would make use of slanders and rehash a long-forgotten scandal to "unjustly disparage me in the eyes of new generations" or make it possible for "my children, some still young, to receive the demoralizing report of their father's past sins, heretofore not known to them." Sobral promised Maciel Filho never to descend to the quagmire that "is so much to your liking" and that "provides the morass that envelops your soul." As a Catholic, Sobral also promised to remain without hate for the person who "on account of mere servility" had attacked him despicably and brutally "although I never hurt you." "May God forgive you, J. S. Maciel Filho, because I have already done so."[7]

Sobral wrote later that his published message to Maciel Filho "found an echo in the spirit of noble people and in the hearts of worthy men." One of the "comforting compliments" he received was a letter from TSN President Frederico de Barros Barreto, who had been accused sensationally by Sobral in 1942, in the courtroom, the press, and a book, of using his high office to crush a poor green-grocer. Noting that Barros Barreto called the reply to Maciel Filho "noble and moving," Sobral praised the judge's "serene and ennobling attitude" and said it would allow the judge to understand the past position of "your old friend, who, on account of the exigencies of Justice, had to protect the trampled rights of a fellow being," and who therefore had placed the "imperatives of his juridical conscience" ahead of "the sentimental inclinations of his heart." He asked Barros Barreto to accept his friendship.[8]

Maciel Filho's article of October 17 about Sobral was mentioned by Adaucto Lucio Cardoso as a reason for a letter he sent to the *Diário de Notícias* in reply to the journalist's article of October 22 in *A Noite*. Adaucto remarked that he might have dismissed misstatements about himself as unintentional but for the fact that a few days earlier "Maciel Filho sought so repugnantly to besmirch Sr. Sobral Pinto, who, for the Brazilian lawyers, is a standard of moral integrity."[9]

Adaucto appeared to be not much worried about Maciel's misstatements because, he wrote, no one believed anything written in *A Noite*; but he nevertheless undertook to set the record straight by telling the *Diário de Notícias* that he had not been dismissed from the post of juridical consultant of the transport ministry but had resigned in 1942, as the minister, João de Mendonça Lima, could confirm to the "deceitful journalist." His resignation, he explained, was the result of his decision to have nothing to do with the Vargas administration, whose wrongdoings included a decree to protect the gambling casinos from legal steps to close them, taken by Adaucto, Dario de Almeida Magalhães, and Antônio Vianna de Souza. Adaucto added that in 1943 his signature on the Manifesto of the Mineiros had brought about his dismissal from the Lloyd Brasileiro steamship company, which he had served for twenty-one years.[10]

Adaucto's letter to the *Diário de Notícias* was written at a time when Maciel Filho, in *A Noite*, was examining "how Dr. Sobral Pinto acts without hate, as a Catholic forgiver." He filled a paragraph with all the degrading epithets used by Sobral to describe him and added: "Just imagine what he would write if he harbored hatred, were not a Catholic, and had not forgiven me."

Maciel Filho pointed out that the very newspapers that "give so much publicity today" to Sobral's "violent denunciations" of Vargas had spread "the torrent" in 1928 against the *procurador*, and that the very men whom "he now calls the saviors of the country," *tenentes* like Eduardo Gomes, were the ones accused by Sobral in the 1920s of having been criminals guilty of contributing to the "political hatred" against Sobral's so-called "inflexible performance in the defense of legality." "Today he incites them to carry out what he once said were crimes."

Maciel Filho called himself a man of serenity defending Vargas, "a friend who has been betrayed, slandered, and vilified by the greatest accumulation of ingratitude and lack of understanding I have ever witnessed." He said that Sobral, whose "exhibitionist frenzy even causes him to make use of a sin," was a leader of violence in the name of piety and a slanderer in the name of religion; he behaved, Maciel added, with meanness and cruelty in the name of kindness and made use of hatred in the name of forgiveness.[11]

Like Maciel Filho, Cassiano Ricardo left no doubt that he remained loyal to Vargas. He had departed from the financially troubled *A Manhã* but found an opportunity to defend the head of state at the Brazilian Academy of Letters' discussions about whether Vargas should remain one of Brazil's forty living "immortals."

The case against Vargas' membership was presented by Academy member Hélio Lobo, who attributed his dismissal as Brazil's representative at the International Labor Bureau to his opposition, expressed in Canada in 1941, to the admittance of Vargas into the Academy.[12] Now he asserted that the admittance of Vargas had been a "death blow" to liberty of thought and accused the Academy of having behaved as submissively in 1941 as the French Academy had behaved during the Nazi occupation of France.[13]

In the course of disputing these and other charges of Hélio Lobo, Cassiano Ricardo reminded his peers that Vargas had given the Academy the land on which its building stood and had not initiated the idea of his becoming an Academy member. After his near-unanimous election, Cassiano said, Vargas had always acted cordially and insisted that decisions reached by the majority be implemented even when he had voted the other way.

O Estado de S. Paulo, still dominated by pro-Vargas interests that had forcibly taken it over in 1940, reported on October 28 that Cassiano Ricardo's position received the unanimous support of the Academy members who were present.[14]

4. Sobral Rejects Appeals That He Run for Congress (October 27–29, 1945)

Before the UDN's Federal District section announced its slate of candidates for parliament, Eduardo Gomes sought to have Alceu Amoroso Lima become the party's candidate for a Senate seat, but Alceu chose not to run, thus abiding by the rules of Ação Católica Brasileira and the Liga Eleitoral Católica forbidding such activities by its officers.[1]

The list of candidates, given in the press on October 17 as coming from the UDN, presented Hamilton Nogueira as a candidate for the Senate. Both he and veteran *tenente* Juarez Távora, listed as one of the fifteen UDN local candidates for the Chamber of Deputies, were shown in the press to have been selected by the Liga Eleitoral Católica. The UDN therefore advised the press that the LEC had not selected any candidates and that Hamilton Nogueira, in order to run for the Senate, had resigned from his positions in Ação Católica and the LEC. It also pointed out that Juarez Távora had written UDN President Octavio Mangabeira to say he would not run for any elective position.[2]

The list that the Federal District UDN released on the 17th included, as candidates for the Chamber of Deputies, Euclydes Figueiredo, whom Sobral had defended at the TSN, João Baptista de Azevedo Lima, whom Sobral had accused of subversion in the mid-1920s, and Maurício de Lacerda, who had been jailed for subversion by the Bernardes government. It was a provisional list not only because Távora refused to run and Azevedo Lima became a senatorial candidate but also because the selections of the UDN–Esquerda Democrática alliance had yet to be made.

"A while back," the *Diário de Notícias* wrote on October 27, "one of the great democratic parties, now engaged in the political struggle, invited lawyer Heráclito Sobral Pinto to be on its slate of congressional candidates from the Federal District. But he refused, alleging that he had no wish to carry out activities that are directly related to political parties."

This refusal, the *Diário de Notícias* informed its readers, had been followed by "a strong movement" to persuade Sobral to change his mind. An appeal was described as having already been signed by about a hundred people, "of various ideological currents," among them Alceu Amoroso Lima, Padre José Sobreira, and Francisco Mangabeira.[3]

On October 26 Sobral spoke to the secretary of the *Jornal do Commercio*, Antônio Cícero, in order to prevent the news of the appeal from appearing in what Sobral called the "senior member of the Carioca press." After the news appeared in the *Diário de Notícias*, he wrote its owner, Orlando Ribeiro Dantas, to say that the movement in his favor was contrary to his wishes and had to be ended, and he asked for the publication of a statement he enclosed.[4]

The statement, which appeared in the *Diário de Notícias* on October 28, referred to the appeal of fellow citizens and friends that he revoke his resolution against allowing his name to be considered in the coming elections. He reaffirmed, categorically, that he would never be a politician and added that he was determined not to carry out any public function, elective or appointive. "My position, the result of long and careful consideration, has been expressed privately and publicly for over ten years." If he were to break his word, he wrote, he would "feel inferior to a person who has lost his self-respect." He reviewed his "bitter and savage" struggle, made simply with the weapon of words, to bring about the restoration of juridical order—a struggle carried out in accordance with his religious conscience and the demands of his role as a jurist, "dedicated entirely to the well-being of the Nation and the best interests of my fellow citizens."

He would, he made known in his statement, be willing to serve as a legislator only in case the National Episcopate authorized the formation of a Catholic Party with the task of carrying out and defending the policy of the Church.

"I cherish the hope that, in view of the above, the initiators of the appeal will immediately end their activities, sparing me the bitter and painful need to give them, serenely but firmly, the always terrible word which is NO."[5]

Sobral found it necessary on October 29 to send Horácio de Carvalho Júnior a statement for publication in the *Diário Carioca*. He told Horácio: "I have read in the *Diário Carioca* about the start of a movement of electors to force me to be a candidate." He added that his resolve not to become involved in "militant politics" remained inalterable.[6]

5. Legality for the PCB and a Family Life for Its Leader (October 1945)

The Communist Party of Brazil (PCB), in making its case for registration as a legal party, told the Tribunal Superior Eleitoral that it was devoted to democracy, progress, and better conditions for the workers. It stressed the need to strengthen national capitalism "because the proletariat suffers more from the weakness of capitalism than from capitalism itself." It was, it said, a foe of dictatorships, including the dictatorship of the proletariat; and it denied the inclusion of Marxist-Leninist principles in its program.[1]

The question of legality for the PCB was being debated when Sobral published his views in his weekly column on October 27. Eduardo Gomes, he wrote, deserved applause for opposing Communism and for pointing out that Communist theory, banishing true concepts about good and evil, maintained that anything was moral and licit if it contributed to the success of the Communist Party. But, Sobral said, those who were seeking to inaugurate a truly democratic regime had the duty to recognize that the Communists possessed the right to organize as a political party. With their party legal, he explained, they would exhaust their revolutionary impetus, as had been the case with the European socialist parties in the nineteenth century.[2]

"In our moment of confusion and unrest," Sobral wrote, the Communist danger lay not in its doctrine nor in the large numbers adhering to the PCB, but in the support the Communists received from Vargas and some of his principal collaborators. With this support, he said, the Communists hoped to use the weakness of morality and juridical principles in government to prevent the restoration of the old republican organs of public authority, knowing that such a restoration would mean "the strengthening of the bourgeois government state machine, opponent of Communist agitation." The Communist objective, Sobral warned, was to add to the existing confusion and instability in the hope of destroying the regime of Christian Brazil, already deeply shaken by Vargas, and replacing it with a new regime of proletarian power.

Repeating that a legal Communist Party would lose its revolutionary impetus, Sobral wrote that it would be faced with the necessities of political life and practical action, together with a doctrinal debate, unlikely to be favorable to Marxist theories about social life.

He attributed the strength of the revolutionary impetus to a not uncommon attraction to what was prohibited and to the revulsion felt by all honest men for the violent, implacable persecution against all new political ideals, even if they were erroneous.[3]

On October 27 the Tribunal Superior Eleitoral (TSE) ordered the provisional registration of the Communist Party of Brazil (PCB)—leading to a definite registration two weeks later. In the ruling of October 27, the TSE pointed out that the party had solemnly declared in writing that it was "a liberal, capitalist, democratic party," committed to democratic principles, and had rejected Marxism, Leninism, the dictatorship of the proletariat, and ideology considered Communist. TSE judges, such as Waldemar Falcão, made it clear that if the PCB should ever demonstrate that its assurances were insincere, its registration would be canceled.[4]

By this time the press had reported "official confirmation" of the "slaughter" of Olga Benário Prestes in a Nazi concentration camp. The *Diário Carioca*, disclosing the news in September, wrote that moral sensitivity made it impossible for the head of the Brazilian Communist movement ever to have good relations with "the chief of a government that authorized the monstrosity of delivering a defenseless creature to her certain death in the hands of implacable enemies." Nevertheless, it added, the public was aware that Captain Prestes, while still in prison, had extended greetings to the dictator, and, after his release, had continued "his incredible love affair with the 'professional president of the Republic.'"

The *Diário Carioca* quoted Filinto Müller as saying that the decision to deport Olga, made by the police, had been sent to the justice minister, who had passed it on for final approval to the president of the republic. The *Diário Carioca* concluded that Müller and Vargas were responsible for Olga's death. "Perhaps," it added, "Luiz Carlos Prestes thinks differently."[5]

On October 28, one day after the TSE declared that the PCB deserved legality, Prestes' sister Lygia and daughter Anita Leocádia arrived in Rio by plane from Mexico. The Cavalier of Hope, accompanied by a crowd, was at the airport, and when he kissed and hugged his eight-year-old daughter a warm applause broke out.[6]

Sobral, writing Lygia on the 29th, explained that he had not been at the airport because his religious conscience required him to attend the procession of the Sacred Heart of Jesus.

"I have," he wrote Lygia, "always been worried about Luiz Carlos Prestes' isolation from affection. Now, when he is in the midst of so many impassioned admirers, so many self-seeking fools, so many fanatical adversaries, and so many implacable enemies, you will, I am sure, be the word of equilibrium, of moderation, of prudence, which, guided by sisterly affection, will know how to correct and rectify, with noble good sense, biased manifestations and thus prevent that Luiz Carlos Prestes stray, on account of credulity or prejudice, from the serene course that he ought to follow."

Sobral added that in a home and a setting of tranquillity, where Prestes could find daily repose from the difficult and hectic work of directing the PCB, "you will, without doubt, be the visible guardian angel of Luiz Carlos Prestes. In this simple family setting, with your solicitous affection and the caresses of his daughter, Luiz Carlos Prestes will find, in the midst of the inevitable irritations, disappointments, and pains of public life, the comfort and inner peace that are indispensable for the reinvigoration of his fighting spirit."[7]

Sobral also sent letters to Anita Leocádia and her father. He told the girl that he expected she would find a joyful life "in this immense and generous Brazil," thanks to God, "whose commandments have guided my life." He sent Anita Leocádia kisses from his eight-year-old daughter Gilda, the youngest of his seven children. "She is a girl like you; and, like you, she is innocent."[8]

In his letter to Prestes, Sobral expressed the belief that the presence of Lygia and Anita Leocádia would act as a "soothing balm," mitigating the tragic loss of Prestes' mother and wife. "Having for years on end been close to your sufferings, I bring the assurance of my friendship at this moment when, at last, a bitter separation ends—one that tormented you and tormented also your ex officio lawyer, who was unable, on account of the inexistence of juridical order, to hold back the evil of men who governed for so long in accordance with their own wills."[9]

In Brazil, Anita Leocádia was told of the death of her mother. Prestes spoke to her often about Olga, sometimes with emotion. The girl learned that Olga had been a sweet and happy person, fond of art, music, and nature, who liked to sing and draw pictures.[10]

6. The Overthrow of Vargas (October 29, 1945)

Late in October, War Minister Góes Monteiro was full of apprehensions about the situation. He decided that conspiracies were being hatched not only by Queremistas and others who wished to have

Vargas continue in office but also by the UDN, which he accused of planning to act "unconstitutionally" to depose the president.[1] He was in agreement with the opening sentence of a letter sent to him on October 24 by Sobral Pinto: "Neither I nor you nor any honest citizen, serene and impartial, can have the slightest doubt about the gravity of the days ahead."[2]

Sobral, in the letter, said that the steps that had been required of the wartime allies, starting with the expulsion of the Germans from North Africa, could be compared with the steps needed in Brazil, starting with "the removal of Getúlio Vargas from power." Observing that after the military victory over Germany at least five years would be needed to reconstruct nations long occupied by the Nazis, Sobral wrote that similarly in Brazil "the political, moral, economic, and social reconstruction" would require, on the part of conscientious citizens, "a daily effort that must reach almost heroic levels, especially because it cannot last less than five years."[3]

Vargas, before receiving Góes Monteiro on October 25 for their routine weekly meeting, had made arrangements that seemed likely to satisfy the Queremistas, who were unhappy with the police. He had named Mayor Dodsworth ambassador to Portugal, promoted Police Chief João Alberto to the mayorship, and appointed, as the new police chief, his brother Benjamim Vargas, sympathetic to the Queremista movement.[4]

General Góes Monteiro, unaware of these plans, found the president unfriendly. He attributed this to his having told Vargas earlier that Gomes was likely to win the election and that Vargas ought to come out in favor of one of the two presidential candidates. Now, on October 25, Góes interrupted Vargas' lecture to him on "the power of the masses" by saying that the recent political changes in Argentina had been brought about principally by the military and not the masses.[5]

Early on October 29, Góes became furious when he learned from João Alberto about the new appointments being made by Vargas, especially the one putting Benjamim Vargas in charge of the police. João Alberto had been working closely with Góes in opposition to Queremista rallies, and when Góes asked him why he had delayed so long before informing him that he would leave the police post, João Alberto explained that Vargas had ordered the delay in notifying Góes. Góes retorted that Vargas, whose government he had been upholding by "superhuman efforts," had made use of a brutal blow to betray his war minister. He would, he said, leave the ministry and "let Vargas suffer his fate."[6]

Upon reaching the war ministry, Góes dictated a letter of resignation. He also sent coded messages to troop commanders to carry out "Directive 1," a plan to defend the government in case of serious subversive activities. Determined to place troops on the alert, he called generals to his office. General Gustavo Cordeiro de Farias said that Góes should assume command of all the military, and, as the other generals agreed, Góes accepted the idea although he was in poor health. Góes called his friend Dutra to his office and brought him up to date.[7]

Dutra received confirmation of Vargas' new appointments from Justice Minister Agamemnon Magalhães and then placed himself at the orders of Góes, who sent him and General Canrobert Pereira da Costa to alert officers at the São Cristóvão barracks. Later in the day, after navy and air force leaders pledged support to Góes, Góes ordered the marines to occupy strategic points at the docks and the mail and telegraph offices. Maintaining that Vargas had lost the right to remain in the presidency, Góes rejected suggestions of Agamemnon Magalhães and Benjamim Vargas that he negotiate with the president. Góes continued opposed to negotiation when Dutra, after speaking with Vargas, brought a report that Vargas would let the army choose a new police chief[8]—a report denied later by Vargas, who reportedly told Dutra, "If I am not free even to choose a police chief whom I can trust, I am no longer president."[9]

At the war ministry, Góes, who was approaching complete exhaustion, appreciated that the question of a temporary occupant of the presidency was ticklish considering the rival candidates for that office; he decided that the problem should be solved by the rivals, Dutra and Gomes, who were both present because the latter, interrupting his campaign in the south of Brazil, had reached Rio late in the day. Dutra felt that Góes, wanting to be chosen, might become dictatorial in office and call off the election. He therefore suggested that José Linhares, head of the Supreme Court, take over, and the idea was accepted by Gomes, whose party, the UDN, had for some time been preaching "all power to the judiciary."[10]

Góes had named Oswaldo Cordeiro de Farias (Gustavo's brother) his chief of staff, and now he ordered him to go to Guanabara Palace and get Vargas to resign in return for full guarantees for himself, his family, and his friends. Oswaldo, citing his warm relations with

Getúlio, demurred, but Góes insisted, and so Oswaldo left for the palace, accompanied by Agamemnon Magalhães. Góes issued a "proclamation to the army" to announce that he was again becoming war minister in order to help prevent anarchy from taking over. "My physical strength," the manifesto said, "is at its end and I do not know how much longer I can continue. . . . I only know that I must be worthy of the support given me by my comrades."[11]

At Guanabara Palace, Vargas admitted to Oswaldo Cordeiro de Farias that he lacked military backing. After expressing interest in dying in a fight against an "unconstitutional coup d'état," he said: "I would prefer that you all attack me and that my death remain as a protest against this violence. However, as this is a bloodless coup, I shall not be a cause of disturbance." He spoke of his wish to retire in Rio Grande do Sul and emphasized how important it was that "public order" be maintained.[12]

Before Vargas agreed with Oswaldo Cordeiro de Farias to accept the situation, Orlando Leite Ribeiro brought him a message from Luiz Carlos Prestes, offering to stir up the public to act on his behalf. Although Vargas rejected the offer, Prestes stayed close to the palace ready to be available in case Vargas decided to resist.[13] Press reports told of the arrest of Prestes, but they were untrue. As his daughter has remarked, he went into hiding on the day after she first saw him.[14] Developments did not require that he hide for long.

At the war ministry at about 3:00 A.M. on October 30, José Linhares took over the presidency, with Góes reading a "proclamation to the people" telling of the end of the Vargas regime. Invitations to the ceremony were extended only to the other Supreme Court justices and, according to Sobral, to the members of the OAB's Conselho Federal, "in recognition of the struggle of the OAB against the Estado Novo." The ceremony was attended by numerous members of the military.[15]

7. Sobral Explains the Fall of Vargas (November 1945)

The OAB's Conselho Federal met on October 30 and heard Raul Fernandes read a statement declaring that the OAB was profoundly moved by the step that placed the nation's executive power in the hands of the head of the Supreme Court. This first step to bring legality to Brazil had been taken, Fernandes said, under the inspiration of a pure and disinterested devotion to the nation's interests, and with so much firmness and decorum that it seemed certain that Brazil would be returned "to its true form, grossly distorted by the accursed regime under which we have lived, oppressed and humiliated ever since the funereal coup of November 10, 1937." Raul Fernandes' statement also said that the OAB, in honoring the armed forces and in joining the country's jubilation, was conscious of never having failed in its duties "during the tormenting years of the dictatorial regime." The Conselho members approved a motion of Alcino Salazar that Fernandes' statement be signed by all of them and delivered to the new president of the republic.[1]

After Augusto Pinto Lima advised the Conselho that the staff of the Federal District Court of Appeals had sent it a message to congratulate it for its pro-legality stance, Sobral Pinto told the Conselho of his pleasure at the victory of the views of Brazil's lawyers.[2]

In his *Jornal do Commercio* column on November 10, Sobral explained the overthrow of Vargas. He recalled the brave voices in pulpits, lawyers' meetings, courtrooms, universities, and clandestine publications that after November 1937, in the face of great risks, reminded Brazil that the moral forces of the nation had not capitulated. The movement, Sobral wrote, reached a peak with the glorious defiance of the dictatorship by the Instituto dos Advogados Brasileiros (IAB) at its one hundredth anniversary congress in August 1943. He praised the banquet that followed, where Pedro Aleixo was honored by a gathering of "many of the most expressive representatives of the nation's cultural ideas," and he noted that, "a few weeks later," illustrious Mineiros had issued a call for the orderly restoration of justice, liberty, and representative government.

The armed forces, Sobral wrote, were attentive to public opinion and began to show that they were no longer willing to uphold "the illegitimate power that oppressed the nation." In February 1945, he said, both Dutra and Góes defended the right of the *Diário Carioca* to criticize the government. "At that point, Luiz Camillo de Oliveira Netto felt that the moral situation in Brazil had matured enough to allow complete freedom of the press, and he obtained, in collaboration with intrepid journalists Carlos Lacerda and Raphael Corrêa de Oliveira, the famous interview" that José Américo de Almeida gave to Lacerda. According to Sobral's account, the decision of the *Correio da Manhã*, a morning newspaper, to publish the anti-Vargas interview on February 22 was made after *O Globo*, an afternoon newspaper, had planned to publish it the same day; and, because the appearance of the interview in the morning left *O Globo* behind, José Américo, on the 22nd, gave *O Globo* another interview "which was no less important" and which mentioned the candidacy of Eduardo Gomes.[3]

"From that moment on, the authoritarian state saw all its foundations crumble; nothing could hold back the victorious march of the moral forces of the country. These forces became stronger each day until on October 29 they attained the splendid, definitive victory awaited with so much eagerness by the Brazilian people: the removal from the national organism of the dictatorial regime that had so deeply humiliated and weakened it. The Armed Forces, identifying themselves with the national spirit, brought an end to a government of usurpation and replaced it immediately with a government of unimpeachable legitimacy. Spurning any unworthy ambition, the Armed Forces resolved to set up a civilian government, eminently symbolized by the head of the Supreme Court, thus carrying out the most notable political accomplishment in our history, allowing the country to pass, without disorder or anarchy, from a regime of usurpation to one of legitimacy."[4]

Writing to one of his Catholic friends abroad, Sobral said that he had been unable to keep up his correspondence with him after returning from the United States in 1942 because he had been involved in a "tremendous struggle against the Vargas regime. . . . To prevent the police and the political Tribunal from organizing against me, using laws of oppression . . . , I based my campaign on the need to restore juridical order. The movement grew and finally, on October 29 of this year, the Brazilian people, without firing a shot and without a single act of revenge, deposed Getúlio Vargas." He added that the conduct of the armed forces was exemplary and that the unselfishness of its leaders made it possible to place the government in the hands of "serene and impartial judges" who would preside over the elections on December 2.[5]

Sobral got around to replying to letters of support and praise received before Vargas was overthrown. In his replies, he spoke of his "immense ten-year effort" to liberate Brazil from those who had "enslaved" it, and from the *"borgismo-castilhista"* or *"caudilhismo positivista"* of Vargas. "I sacrificed everything," he wrote one admirer, "to prevent my fellow citizens from abandoning the movement against the dictatorship." He told another that his financial situation had been "totally ruined" by his ten-year struggle, but that he could now return peacefully to his law practice in order to earn what he needed to support his large family and his office companions.[6]

Learning on November 20 that General Góes Monteiro had suffered a heart attack, Sobral planned to visit him at the hospital on November 22. But before Sobral could make the visit, the patient returned home, and there he received a telegram from Sobral wishing him a speedy recovery.[7]

PART XII

Shocked by the Electorate's Message (December 1945)

1. Finding Fault with President Linhares (November 1945)

It did not take long for Sobral Pinto to use the press and letters to submit recommendations for correcting what he considered to be errors of the new administration. He sent fourteen typewritten pages to President José Linhares on November 1 after he read "with the most excruciating apprehension" a published note from the new administration that suggested that political groups and parties ought to demonstrate the same sort of cohesion as that shown by the armed forces.[1]

The purpose of the note, Sobral told Linhares, was to urge political groups "to congregate behind a single candidate for president and a single slate of candidates for parliament." "Such a proposal is based on the supposition that, in the absence of the above-mentioned cohesion by the parties, the government will be forced to adopt the solution of backing one of the presidential candidates, on whose behalf all of the administration's political machinery will be used." "You think," Sobral wrote, "that if the central and state governments assume a neutral position in regard to Dutra and Gomes, the December 2 elections will produce anarchy and disorder. Allow me to disagree radically." Contributing to Sobral's fear about the electoral ideas of the Linhares administration was what Sobral considered to be the alarming failure of the government note to include a single word about revoking Vargas' Decree-Law 8,063, which had placed his *interventores* in commanding positions.[2]

Measures adopted by Linhares on the day that Sobral wrote his letter eliminated the prospect of local and central government machines working for a PSD victory. But Sobral's continuing concern was evident in the title of his article published on November 3 in the "A Pedido" section of the *Jornal do Commercio:* "The Contamination of the Present by the Errors of the Dictatorship." Brazilians, he wrote, should shake off the evil ways of thinking instilled, over many years, by Vargas, and should not allow themselves to be deluded by "the multiple and successive errors of the government of President José Linhares."

Sobral, in the article, listed some of the initial acts of the Linhares administration, placing them in three categories: (1) those that should be applauded; (2) those that contradicted the government's principles but had to be tolerated as compromises in the name of social peace; and (3) those that, being "the consequences of the personal errors of the present rulers," had to be "rigorously and vehemently" condemned.[3]

In the first category Sobral placed the revocation by Linhares, on November 1, of Decree-Law 8,063, and the appointments of judges to be *interventores,* thus replacing the Vargas men and satisfying what Sobral called the "moralizing" and "democratically honest" principle of "all power to the judiciary."

Turning to the second category, Sobral noted the appointment of some *interventores* who were "not members of the judiciary" and were "even connected with the PSD," a party that Sobral accused of having been created on the assumption that the government could intervene in the electoral struggle. According to Sobral, Linhares had found it necessary in a few states to reach "defective solutions" because of "abusive" demands of some military chiefs and because, for political reasons, it seemed necessary to avoid the extinction of the PSD.[4]

Among the acts deserving of vehement condemnation, Sobral listed the appointment by Linhares of José de Castro Nunes to be vice president and interim president of the Supreme Court (STF). Sobral wrote that Linhares, of all people, had no right to "attack the autonomy and independence" of the STF, thus continuing the Vargas practice of belittling the judicial power. Another Linhares step condemned by Sobral was the promulgation of Constitutional Law 11, limiting the functions that judges of any court could assume outside their roles as judges. It seemed preposterous to Sobral that Linhares and his justice minister, São Paulo law professor Antônio de Sampaio Dória, should follow Vargas' practice of issuing constitutional laws based on the authority given in the 1937 Constitution

and numbered in accordance with the series started by Vargas, especially as Sampaio Dória, when a member of the Tribunal Superior
Eleitoral, had "constantly declared" the 1937 Constitution illegitimate. "All this is incomprehensible and pernicious to the restoration
of the true juridical order of the nation."[5]

In his "Pelos Domínios do Direito" article of November 10, Sobral expressed dismay that his "A Pedido" article of November 3—
"our cry of alarm"—had resulted in "no echo or reply" and that
the Linhares administration had, instead, promulgated still another
constitutional law, Number 12 (revoking the government's ability
to dismiss public employees). "Obviously the present government is
perverting the noble objectives of the peaceful movement of October 29." Sobral maintained that the selection of the head of the
Supreme Court to be the nation's president had ignored the 1937
Constitution's provision about the presidential succession and thus
had recognized, as did all Brazilians, that the 1937 Constitution did
not exist.[6]

The first act of Linhares, Sobral wrote, should have been the promulgation of an Institutional Law, defining and limiting the governmental powers and listing the rights of Brazilian citizens. Sobral admitted that the Institutional Law, in order to avoid juridical chaos,
might retain some stipulations of the 1937 Constitution, but the
latter, he said, should have the status of a mere ordinary law, subject
to modifications.

"The present government," Sobral wrote, "must not act indiffer-
ently to, or belittle, our suggestion, which owes its existence to the
most splendid aspects of our patriotism." The immediate promulgation of an Institutional Law by Linhares, he said, was the "only way
known to juridical science for legitimizing his government and the
laws it needs to issue." He also maintained that without an Institutional Law, the Linhares government could not proceed on moral
and juridical bases substantially different from those of the Estado
Novo. "This is a truth that the government inaugurated on October 29 cannot dismiss, or it will be fatally deserting its noble and
lofty mission."[7]

The Linhares administration, ignoring Sobral's warnings of No-
vember 3 and 10, issued Constitutional Law 13 on November 12, this
one giving the new Congress the power to enact a constitution. Also
Linhares revoked the Vargas antitrust law (the Lei Malaia) and, by
Constitutional Law 14, extinguished the National Security Tribunal
(TSN).

Sobral did not agree that the TSN should be closed down. Shortly before that measure was taken he gave his reasons in a letter to Justice Minister Sampaio Dória, which opened by saying, "I am well aware that the appeals I send to public men are almost always made in vain." He also admitted that "the defects in the composition of the TSN, the iniquities of its court procedures, and its absolute submission to the arbitrary acts of the unscrupulous police" had caused injustices and discredited it in public opinion. However, he told Sampaio Dória, the TSN could provide useful, even necessary, services if its judges were men of experience, knowledge, and unsullied reputation, if defense lawyers were allowed their full rights, if the prosecuting attorneys were decent and competent, and if this system of special justice were to control the police working for it.[8]

The overburdened common justice system, Sobral explained, had not been set up in a way to guarantee the defense of the political power of the state against its enemies, or the defense of the people, whose need for articles of prime necessity was exploited by greedy profiteers. He mentioned specialized courts, such as those of the military and labor justice systems, and said he saw no reason not to have a *justiça especial* to handle crimes against the state and against a "true *economia popular*." "All these *justiças* should be linked to the Supreme Court, which should be able to curb their abuses."[9]

Linhares named so many judges to be *interventores*, irritating the PSD,[10] that Sobral, in his column on November 17, expressed praise for the "neutrality" of Linhares and his justice minister. And Sobral praised a decree of November 16 that ordered local judges to act as both mayors and judges in situations where the *interventores* had been unable to find worthy replacements for mayors who had departed or been dismissed. This decree conformed to a clause of Constitutional Law 11 allowing judges to add to their normal duties if asked to do so by the *interventores* or the president, and was described by Sobral as protecting the "freedom of voters."[11]

PSD President Benedicto Valladares, who had been replaced as governor of Minas by a judge, regarded these developments as unfavorable to the party he headed. He has written that none of the mayors or police *delegados* who had served in his state during his governorship remained in office.[12]

2. Leaders of the LEC Defend Gomes (November 1945)

As the representative of the OAB at the investiture of a new president of the Federal District Court of Appeals, Sobral delivered an address on November 20 praising the transformation of Brazil, brought about by "the civic movement of October 29."[1]

To contribute to the transformation, on November 22 the Instituto dos Advogados Brasileiros (IAB) approved the proposal of Themistocles Cavalcanti that it receive suggestions for the elaboration of a draft of a constitution to be presented to the forthcoming Congress (National Constituent Assembly). Sobral was appointed to the commission that would write the draft, along with Themistocles Cavalcanti, Raul Fernandes, Targino Ribeiro, Affonso Penna Júnior, Haroldo Valladão, Otto Gil, Arnoldo Medeiros, Pedro Calmon, Haryberto de Miranda Jordão, and Levy Carneiro.[2]

During the following days, the IAB met to hear talks by its members about the new constitution, among them a talk by Sobral entitled "Public Liberties and the Future Constitution." When the IAB met on November 29 under the presidency of Professor Haroldo Valladão, Raul Fernandes was named *relator geral* to supervise the work on the draft. Each of the other ten members of the commission was named *relator parcial* to handle a specific part of the project. Sobral was assigned "The Legislative Power."[3]

At about the same time, the Liga Eleitoral Católica (LEC) undertook to provide "political education" to the public by its series of talks, with Sobral discussing "Democracy and Totalitarianism" at a meeting in the Santa Teresa district on November 19.[4]

Shortly before Gustavo Corção gave the second LEC talk for the Santa Teresa residents on November 23, the LEC listed eight political parties that had accepted its "minimum points," the notable exception being the Partido Comunista do Brasil (PCB). The list of São Paulo senatorial candidates said to have accepted the minimum points included Labor Party (PTB) members Alexandre Marcondes Filho and Getúlio Vargas.[5] The PTB had named Vargas a senatorial candidate in São Paulo and a congressional candidate in the Federal District and in most of the seven states where it presented candidates. It hoped that his name would garner a large vote and thus many seats for the PTB, in accordance with the proportional representation principle that distributed seats on the basis of votes obtained by parties rather than individuals. For the same reason the PCB put up the name of Prestes in a number of states.

The LEC's "minimum points" were not accepted by engineer Yeddo Fiuza, a non-Communist, whose candidacy for the presidency was launched in November by the PCB. The PCB, opposed to the two military candidates, hoped that Vargas, also unhappy with the men who had helped depose him, would favor his friend Fiuza.[6]

Following the first Fiuza rally, held in Rio on November 17, the *Diário Carioca* called Fiuza's "Nipponese-Nazi-fascist" candidacy a maneuver to take "leftist" votes from Eduardo Gomes. Journalist Carlos Lacerda, who shared that fear, published a series of sensational front-page articles, "Fiuza, the Rat," in the *Diário Carioca* to show that the PCB presidential candidate had become wealthy through corruption while heading the road building program during the Estado Novo.[7]

Although Fiuza and the PCB did not accept the LEC's program, many far leftists did so according to *O Estado de S. Paulo*, which was still in the hands of the state government and favored the PSD and Dutra. Roberto Sabóia de Medeiros, a Jesuit, wrote in *O Estado de S. Paulo* that the immense number of candidates accepting the LEC program represented no victory for the Catholics because so many candidates were insincere. The LEC, he wrote, had expressed approval of parties whose candidates included Stalinists, Trotskyites, atheists, and Masons.[8] *O Estado de S. Paulo*, observing that Trotskyites, "more Marxist than Prestes," were running for Congress on the UDN ticket, accused the UDN of participating in the betrayal of Brazil's Christian traditions.[9]

The LEC and Catholic leaders came to the support of Eduardo Gomes after his response to the LEC questionnaire was belittled by his opponents—opponents described by the UDN as "pro-Dutra Integralistas allied with Communists of the absurd Yeddo Fiuza candidacy and with the so-called working-class people of cotton speculator Hugo Borghi." A published declaration by Sobral said that the accusations against Gomes had been made "in bad faith" and that if the candidate had accepted only four of the LEC's ten points, it was because the others had not been presented to him; and, Sobral added, Dutra, presented with the ten points, had also accepted only four.[10]

LEC President Hildebrando Acioly announced that although press releases had spoken of Gomes' acceptance of the main points, in his "personal response" he had agreed to "all the principles of our program." Catholic leader Hamilton Nogueira, UDN candidate for the Senate from the Federal District, observed that the "intrigues" against Gomes "make it clear that the victory of the *brigadeiro* is assured."[11]

The "intrigues" included the charge that Eduardo Gomes, "candidate of the wealthy," was unfriendly to blacks and was not interested in receiving the votes of the workers and the unemployed. The charge, given publicity by the Queremistas' Hugo Borghi, followed a remark by Gomes about not needing the votes of "that mob of unemployed who support the dictator."[12]

While the pro-Gomes press published statements by "authentic workers" who rejected the "miserable" anti-Gomes "lies," the Christian Democratic Party (PDC) offered to help the workers with a program, "drawn up by the great intellectual, Alceu Amoroso Lima," that promised to banish unemployment and make poor people less poor and the wealthy less rich. The PDC attacked Communism but otherwise remained "neutral" in the presidential race, and it asked voters to eliminate poverty in Brazil by voting for its congressional candidates.[13]

General Dutra, a sincere Catholic, gave a lengthy interview about his good relations with the LEC and the Catholic Church. He praised the four "minimum points" and said that, as war minister, he had made arrangements so that Brazilian soldiers in the war could attend religious services. He had, he added, helped establish a church at the Vila Militar barracks near Rio and had named military chaplains at the barracks in Natal and on Fernando de Noronha Island.[14]

On the eve of the elections, Hildebrando Acioly issued an LEC announcement taking the Dutra supporters to task for having pointed out that Pope Pius XII had conferred on Dutra the Grand Cross of the Order of Gregory the Great. The decoration, Acioly said, ranked below three other papal decorations and had no political significance, having been given to Brazil's war minister during the war to show appreciation for work by Brazilian Catholics to help starving Italians.[15] Alceu Amoroso Lima and Hildebrando Acioly sent telegrams telling the state branches of the LEC to continue neutral in the electoral contest and ignore "political insinuations" stemming from the decoration. On election day, the *Diário Carioca* published headlines about the "telegram of the LEC against General Dutra" and about Archbishop Jayme Câmara's "contradiction of the campaign of Dutra." The article beneath the "contradiction" headline contained the archbishop's statement that no connection existed between the decoration and Brazil's "present political situation."[16]

3. Sobral, Recommending Candidates, Distresses the PDC (November 29, 1945)

On November 24 Sobral told his readers that in October the Tribunal Superior Eleitoral (TSE) and Sampaio Dória (a TSE judge before becoming Linhares' justice minister) had granted legality to the Communist Party of Brazil (PCB) for the wrong reasons. They had claimed, he said, to have been guided by Vargas' election law of May 28, 1945, which denied legality to any party opposed to "democratic principles or the fundamental rights of man defined in the constitution." Therefore, he added, the TSE could find the PCB legal only by acting dishonestly and pretending to believe the party's false assurances that it had abandoned its principles, including Marxism-Leninism. Sampaio Dória, in his vote, had said that the PCB now favored "none of the things for which Communism is known in the world." "In this very serious episode," Sobral wrote, "not a single serene and lofty voice" had been raised "to defend juridical and sociological truths."

Sobral declared that the time had come to acknowledge that the PCB had been insincere in its declarations to the TSE and to acknowledge that the PCB should nevertheless be able to function like other parties in a setting of tolerance and mutual respect, in which debates would take place about how best to achieve the necessary alleviation of the ever increasing misery of a large and neglected part of the human family. Sobral expressed the hope that these debates, "bloodless encounters," would be carried out without defamation or lies and with chivalry.[1]

Sobral has written that, on the eve of the elections, his opinion about how to vote was sought daily at his office and home, in phone calls and in person, by many fellow-citizens, some of them unknown to him.[2] Deciding to reveal his preference for the candidates of the Partido Republicano (PR), a minor pro-Gomes party headed by Arthur Bernardes, he published his views in an article that appeared in the *Jornal do Commercio* on November 29. It was reprinted in the same newspaper on November 30 and December 1, and on Novem-

ber 30 the *Diário Carioca* published it with an introduction that
told of Sobral's fame for having denounced abuses and called him
splendidly authorized to guide the Federal District voters.[3]

Before listing names, Sobral wrote that he had, "without a single
minute of rest in these last ten years," engaged in a bitter struggle
against oppression, always taking the positions that his conscience
told him were the best for the national welfare even though the
positions had exposed him to risks and painful personal setbacks.
He forecast "distressing, difficult, and dangerous" days ahead and
contemplated sorrowfully "the generalized failure to recognize the
threatening dangers brought on by inordinately ambitious people"
along with revolutionary-minded Communists and supporters of
Vargas' policies.

"It is astounding," he wrote, that so many Catholics, instead of
setting good examples, failed to practice "renunciation and discipline" and failed to show any understanding of "the exceptional
gravity of the situation that engulfs the Nation." He promised to discuss, after the elections, "the confusion and anarchy that unfortunately reign among our comrades" and in that way "do what I can to
prevent the Nation from ceasing to be Christian." He called the moment inopportune for his explanation. "Debating so delicate a problem would increase the dire disorder that has already infiltrated the
electorate of this Capital."[4]

Sobral wrote that voters wishing to protect Christian traditions
had their choices limited to Gomes and Dutra in the presidential
race and should choose congressmen and senators "ONLY AND EX-
CLUSIVELY" from the UDN, PR, and PSD. Then, after reminding
his readers that "the whole Nation knows I seek no posts, advantages, or glories," he said that the Federal District voters would be
carrying out their electoral duty "in the most perfect manner" if
they cast their ballots as follows:

> For President: Eduardo Gomes;
> For Senators: Hamilton Nogueira and Augusto Pinto Lima;
> For Congressmen: Partido Republicano, José Barreto Filho.[5]

Immediately after publication of the article, Sobral received a
telegram from Osório Lopes, head of the Federal District directorship of the PDC (Partido Democrata Cristão). The telegram, published in the *Jornal do Commercio* on November 30, said:

I deplore your article, "How to Fulfill Your Electoral Duty," according to which "the elector who wishes to protect the Christian traditions of Brazilian society" must limit his choice to the slates of the UDN, PR, and PSD. Your article is devoid of impartiality. You are aware that the candidates of the PDC truly defend the "Christian traditions" in contrast to the slates of your preference, such as the UDN, which presents candidates who do not even accept the so-called "minimum points" of the LEC. I await with interest your new argumentations defending a point of view that is factious and extremely unjust, and I tell you right now that the PDC will survive the tempest of this hour of erroneous concessions.[6]

Sobral's reply, a letter written to Osório Lopes on November 30, expressed surprise at the "entirely unjust" statements in the telegram. Explaining that he had never doubted that the PDC candidates, if elected, would defend the Christian traditions, he said that the problem was one of preventing the scattering of the votes of Catholics among many parties. He told Osório Lopes that the PDC was in no position to contest seats in parliament because it had been in existence only briefly and lacked a program that had long been given publicity; it also lacked, Sobral wrote, a directorship made up of popular leaders, worthy of public confidence, and the organization of cadres of solidly disciplined voters.

In this reply, Sobral called himself a simple lawyer whose talents were limited to "argumentation." For this reason, he wrote, he had categorically opposed the "vehement appeals" of "at least two parties" that he accept nomination for a seat in Congress and had prevented the original supporters of his candidacy from obtaining thousands of signatures on petitions pleading that he retreat from his original position. As for his party preference, he wrote that his choice was not the UDN. "Contrary to what you affirm, I prefer, without a moment's hesitation, the ticket of the PR."[7]

Osório Lopes' response to this letter from his "inflexible" friend was published in the *Jornal do Commercio* on election day, December 2. Convinced that the defense of Christian traditions should not be limited to the three parties named by Sobral, he pointed out that all parties except the "ideologically inconsistent" PSD and UDN had been in existence but briefly. The PR, he said, had been formed much later than the PDC, and he quoted its president, Arthur Ber-

nardes, as having admitted that it might not elect a single congressman because it had not had time to enroll voters. As for the organization of "cadres of solidly disciplined electors," Osório Lopes said
that only two parties had achieved this: the PCB of the Communists
and the PRP (Partido de Representação Popular), headed by former
Integralista Plínio Salgado. Between the slates of the PDC, on the
one hand, and those of the UDN, PR, and PSD, on the other, Osório
Lopes said that a truly Catholic conscience could have no difficulty
in making a choice. "Imagine pure and saintly Catholics coming
from convents and holding in their hands ballots that allow the
election of Professor Hermes Lima, Nicanor Nascimento, Raphael
Corrêa de Oliveira, Vítor do Espírito Santo, and Araújo Jorge (of *your*
party)!"[8]

Another who quarreled with Sobral's preferences was Paulo Seabra, who understood that some LEC leaders felt him qualified to
head the local PR congressional slate. Sobral told him that 120 of
the 180 candidates for the seventeen seats from the Federal District
had agreed to defend the fundamental points of the LEC program,
and he explained that he had chosen José Barreto Filho to head the
PR slate of constitution writers because of his political experience,
past legislative work, and fighting spirit, together with his spiritual
and moral virtues. Barreto Filho, Sobral pointed out, had been the
principal author of the draft that became the constitution of the
state of Sergipe, and, after serving as a magnificent leader in the Sergipe legislature, had displayed great talent in the federal legislature.
Deeply religious, and a writer of strong anti-dictatorship articles,
Barreto Filho, in Sobral's opinion, deserved the place at the head of
the PR congressional candidates.[9]

4. The Election Results Surprise and Disappoint
    Sobral (December 1945)

José Linhares, in selecting his cabinet, had consulted Eduardo
Gomes (but not Dutra), and all the cabinet ministers, with one exception, favored the election of Gomes. The exception was War Minister Góes Monteiro, whose preference for Dutra was shared by General Canrobert Pereira da Costa, who ran the ministry when Góes
was ill.[1]

The new *interventores* of the states were pro-Gomes in all but a few cases, most notably that of São Paulo, where Dutra backer Carlos de Macedo Soares took over. The Brazilian press overwhelmingly favored the *brigadeiro* and condemned Vargas. *New York Times* correspondent William S. White called Vargas "a South American Caesar who understood everything but the passage of time." On November 23, the PRP, dominated by Plínio Salgado, issued a proclamation in favor of Gomes.[2]

Oswaldo Aranha, backer of the UDN campaign for Gomes, hoped to see the Labor Party (PTB) turn to the *brigadeiro*. But PTB support was also sought by the PSD. João Neves da Fontoura and other PSD leaders, faced by the threat of a Gomes landslide, tried to convince Vargas that he should urge his PTB followers to vote for Dutra; and Dutra, on November 21, informed the PTB of his willingness to give it a voice in his administration if he won the presidency. Finally on November 27, at the concluding Dutra rally in Rio, Hugo Borghi announced the recommendation of Vargas in favor of votes for Dutra.[3]

Those who had been certain of a Gomes victory and the unpopularity of the former dictator were shocked by the results of the elections of December 2. The PSD presidential victory, which Dutra attributed to Vargas' recommendation,[4] was impressive: Dutra received about 3,250,000 votes, in contrast to about 2,040,000 for Gomes and 570,000 for Fiuza. Even more startling was the strength of non-campaigner Vargas in the races where his name had been placed on ballots, usually by the PTB. As historian Carlos E. Cortés has written, "Dutra won the presidency, but Vargas won the election."[5]

In Rio Grande do Sul, Dutra crushed Gomes, 447,462 votes to 110,444. Vargas, a PSD candidate for the Senate from that state, won first place with 461,913 votes, and was elected to the lower house on the PTB ticket. In São Paulo state the PTB won the two Senate seats, electing Vargas (in first place with 414,942 votes) and Alexandre Marcondes Filho. In São Paulo city each major party presented about thirty-three contestants for the lower house, and there Vargas (PTB) received 75,793 votes, far ahead of second-place José Maria Crispim of the PCB (32,668) and third-place Mário Masagão of the UDN (21,573 votes). The votes throughout São Paulo state for the Chamber of Deputies showed Vargas to be the state's most popular congressional candidate.[6]

In the Federal District, where Vargas was not a candidate for the Senate, the seats in the upper house were won by the PCB's Prestes and the UDN's Hamilton Nogueira. In the crowded Federal District congressional race, Vargas received by far the most votes, 117,884. He was followed by Prestes (in second place with 26,631 votes) and three other Communists. In sixth place was socialist Hermes Lima, of the Esquerda Democrática–UDN combination; his 13,453 votes made him the most successful UDN Federal District congressional candidate. Sobral's favorite, José Barreto Filho (PR), did very poorly.[7]

The PR's strength was in Minas, where it elected six of its seven representatives to the 286-member Chamber of Deputies. The PDC was able to elect only two (one from São Paulo and one from Pernambuco). Of the 328 members of the Constituent Assembly, which included senators, the PSD had 55 percent, the UDN 27 percent, the PTB 8 percent, and the PCB 5 percent. The PTB, which presented candidates only in the Federal District and seven states, could attribute its showing to Vargas, who received 318,000 of the 603,000 PTB votes for Chamber of Deputies candidates. Besides his congressional victories in Rio Grande do Sul, São Paulo, and the Federal District, he was in second place in Rio de Janeiro state and in Minas, and was also elected in Bahia and Paraná.[8]

A Noite, commenting on the candidates favored by the LEC, found the LEC votes well scattered among all parties except the PCB. The *Dicionário Histórico-Biográfico Brasileiro,* analyzing the campaign of 1945, concluded that the LEC was less important than it had been in the 1930s.[9]

Sobral, examining "the surprising election" and the "bad choice that Brazilian citizens have just made for their president," called attention, in his weekly columns, to the "disorder that has prevailed since 1930 in the education ministry," the small number of school-age children who attended schools, and the lack of training of workers. "The middle class and the poor, having little or no education, are unable to participate in the great debates . . . about the fundamental problems that affect their true happiness. . . . In a setting characterized by this mental and moral poverty, aggravated by years of an absolutist regime, the national parliament will meet to write a new constitution."

Making matters worse, Sobral continued, was the "colossal" vote received by Dutra. "He is a Brazilian whose entire career has been in the army. . . . He never concerned himself with public policy and administration. . . . He never wrote an article or gave a talk or speech about political or administrative culture. . . . Upon accept-

ing his candidacy, he failed to bring to his side a single one of the
many great figures who participated in our public life in positions of
important responsibility. The people who supported him were precisely the collaborators of Getúlio Vargas, in the nefarious work of
the dictatorship, whose governmental incapacity and lack of moral
sense devastated and ruined the civic, cultural, and spiritual patrimony of the Nation. Without exaggerating, we can assert that, except for one or two individuals, the supporters of Dutra were the
most hackneyed and incompetent in our public life."[10]

Sobral also wrote that the election demonstrated that "from now
on" the workers' role would be "unopposable and legitimate." He
condemned the upper classes, who, he said, had ignored the Christian principle of human fraternity and had organized society on the
bases of privilege and social injustice. He found it understandable
that, in the recent elections, Brazilian workers had turned to political organizations that they felt would best satisfy their aspirations.
"This accounts for the surprising victory, in some parts of Brazil,
of the PTB and PCB. Those who voted for the PTB and PCB did so
because—to our humiliation—they saw, in those political organizations, instruments able to build Brazilian society in new ways, more
appropriate to the needs of the worker."

"It is not a matter, right now, of asking whether the leaders of
those organizations are correct in their theories, were honest in the
ways they presented their propaganda, and are really eager to serve
the true interests of their followers." Sobral said that such doubts,
even if based on the truth, could not and should not "hide the fact
of the unquestionable eloquence of those who knew how to stimu-
late the hopes of the workers, speaking to them in a manner they
understood and found to their liking."[11]

"What we must do," Sobral wrote, "is not rail against the common people who no longer believe in us; nor should we seek to destroy, using subjective standards, the intentions, good or bad, of the
leaders they decided to support." It was, he asserted, the duty of sincere democratic Christian jurists to recognize, "in this grave hour,"
that the time had come for the intervention of the worker in public life, and to give him help. "We must proclaim, and loudly, the
need to create, at once, juridical institutions able to develop fully
the personal dignity of the worker."[12]

Another conclusion reached by Sobral was that the forthcoming
"governmental period," with serious political, social, economic, and

cultural problems to solve, would be "the most difficult since the Nation proclaimed its independence" and would require that jurists not retreat into despondency merely because of "the massive vote" for a presidential candidate "with so few credentials." Sobral saw in the very fact that Brazilians had made a "bad choice" in electing Dutra an excellent reason for jurists to play a particularly active and vigilant role. They could help Dutra by warning him "against the risks of his imprudence." "Keeping apart from purely destructive criticism," jurists were to speak to Dutra "with respectful but vehement frankness" whenever he might deviate, or think of deviating, from "the moral and juridical principles of true democracy."[13]

5.   Sobral Pinto, the Conscience of Brazil

The year 1945 saw the emergence, into the view of the public, of Sobral Pinto—a powerful voice on morals and politics, a leader in legal and Catholic organizations, and the recipient of praise for his virtues and past struggles. Like others featured prominently and just as suddenly in the press after the long censorship, he was called on to give interviews and speeches and to draw up pronouncements.

Goals that Sobral had espoused with vigor, sometimes with little or no support, were achieved in 1945. They were, he felt, firmly linked to the principles he held about religion and morals. These principles, however, were not always foremost in the minds of others who at length adopted the same goals and contributed to their achievement.

Sobral was seen by the public as having long battled, in a uniquely strident and courageous way, for much that unfolded in 1945: freedom of the press, the release of Prestes and other political prisoners, the overthrow of Vargas, the repudiation of some of the Estado Novo decrees, and the holding of democratic elections for a new president and a Congress that would write a constitution. In the opinion of Sobral, the cause of these developments was a wave of moral sentiment in their favor ("the victorious march of the moral forces of the country").[1] As a dauntless contributor to that sentiment, Sobral had never wavered even when he had found members of the Catholic hierarchy seeking to be in the good graces of the dictator.

In the face of his newfound fame, Sobral remained as he had been for so long, practicing self-denial and making it clear, in what he said and wrote, that he worked hard and without self-interest. After rejecting pleas that he run for Congress, he continued to deny himself legal fees that he regarded as undeserved. Writing Adroaldo Mesquita da Costa about a fee of 40,000 cruzeiros deposited in his bank account in January 1946 by a client grateful for his work in obtaining the cancellation of a 1940 Vargas decree, he said he would not accept the fee. He explained that he had always opposed the kind of "legal work that takes the form of procuring decree-laws" and "does not require submitting arguments to judges." President Linhares and Justice Minister Sampaio Dória, he wrote, had such confidence in him that they had accepted his recommendation for rescuing his client from a grievous wrong, knowing very well that he was not using his personal relations with them in order to receive financial benefits. "I worked simply on behalf of juridical order, violated by the decree of 1940." In the same way, he pointed out, he had been working without a fee in order to persuade the new administration to overturn another illegal Vargas ruling and thus allow Luiz Camillo de Oliveira Netto to be reinstated in his foreign ministry position and receive 100,000 cruzeiros in accumulated salary payments.[2]

As many had been hoping, a new era began in Brazil in 1945. Vargas, hardly blind to "the passage of time," had taken steps to be in tune with what he had called, in speaking to Góes Monteiro, "the power of the masses." He had been in a good position to do so, having issued, after 1930, numerous decrees to favor urban workers —part of a reshaping of Brazil that he had believed could not be achieved without forcibly abolishing the prevailing legislative and political practices.

The dictatorship, dependent on the goodwill of military officers, had allowed the efficient enactment of reforms, many of them beneficial. But dictatorship was abhorrent to Sobral and was accompanied by evils that he denounced and fought against. It must be kept in mind, however, that his fight was not against vast reforms for Brazil. As he revealed in a letter of April 1944 to Archbishop Jayme Câmara, he did not let his complaints against Vargas blind him to the benefits that he said could be found in reforms enacted by the dictatorship to "improve the future of our working class."[3] He was a harsh critic of the country's social structure, which he repeatedly described as un-Christian and unfair to the downtrodden majority.

In 1945, Sobral had the satisfaction of seeing many of his long-held views about reforms proclaimed in the election programs of anti-Vargas political groups. But these groups were at a disadvantage. Manifestoes and promises had to compete with decrees already issued by the "Father of the Poor," long extolled by the controlled media. They had to compete also with arguments made in the workplaces themselves by the indefatigable team headed by the Cavalier of Hope—a team made up, in large part, of authentic workers, some formerly jailed for their beliefs. The "Communist penetration of the unions" was a fruit of the "Vargas-Prestes alliance."

Vargas and Prestes appeared to be able to alter important positions radically for political reasons, something that Sobral could not do. While he might adjust his views about men and events, the adjustments had nothing to do with political expediency and were made in conformity with his inalterable positions. This inflexibility, however, did not mean that the start of a political career was out of his reach in 1945. Unlike Hamilton Nogueira, who initiated a career that took him to the congressional leadership of the UDN in the 1960s, Sobral refused to run for office. In adhering to the word he had given about rejecting a role for himself in politics, he remained true to opinions he had expressed about the proper conduct for officers of Ação Católica Brasileira. The path that he did follow led admirers to call him the conscience of Brazil.

In 1955 he founded (with Victor Nunes Leal and Evandro Lins e Silva) the League for Defending Legality, which demanded that the military not veto the presidential candidacy of Juscelino Kubitschek and subsequently demanded that the election results of that year not be overturned but be upheld in favor of Kubitschek, the victorious candidate, who, incidentally, was not the candidate preferred by Sobral. After the League's purpose was achieved, Sobral rejected the offer of a Supreme Court judgeship, feeling that it could be construed as a reward for his work with the League. He stuck to his tasks of defending clients, advising and condemning political leaders, writing newspaper articles, and teaching law students at the Catholic University and the University of Brazil.

Fellow lawyers chose him in 1963 to head the Instituto dos Advogados Brasileiros (IAB), and other organizations awarded him medals, prizes, honorary degrees, and honorary citizenships of cities. The Catholic University of Minas established a medal to be awarded annually in his name, and in Rio a school was named after him. The Ordem dos Advogados do Brasil nominated him for the Nobel Peace

Prize in 1983, and the municipal council of Campinas did the same in 1986. In 1979 he was chosen "the Intellectual of the Year" (Juca Pato Prize) by the Brazilian Writers' Association, and in 1986 he received the annual "Man of Vision" award of *Visão* magazine. Twice he became president of the Centro Dom Vital, and in 1981 Pope John Paul II honored him with the title of Knight of the Order of Gregory the Great.

Dressed in the black clothing he always wore after the death in 1956 of his beloved daughter Maria do Carmo, he defended the victims of the post-1964 military rule, including Prestes. Some of the cases, involving top administrative and political figures of the pre-1964 era as well as nine members of a Chinese Communist mission to Brazil, were sensational. For his activities he spent three days in prison late in 1968.[4]

His views continued to appear until his death in 1991, and one cannot help being fascinated by the logic and phrasing in letters he addressed to the directors of Brazil's destinies—letters no less virile than those written during the Estado Novo, when he bore down on men like Francisco Campos and Góes Monteiro. The letters, always dictated, contained passages that others might have found it difficult to match even with studied preparation. Somehow he found time to do a great deal of reading, and he liked to include, in letters and articles, quotations from books, old and new.

Unlike Sobral, Evandro Lins e Silva was not averse to holding government posts, and he went on to have considerable influence as *procurador geral da república* in 1961 and as head of the presidential *gabinete civil* in 1963, before becoming foreign minister and then a Supreme Court justice. Evandro, in an article to observe Sobral's death in 1991, recalled that Rubem Braga, in the 1930s, had described Sobral as "the monster." Evandro wrote:

With the firmness of his convictions and his religious faith . . . , the lawyer revealed himself to be an extraordinary example of humanity, a fighter, a fearless swordsman, an altruistic defender of the rights of citizens, . . . receiving no remuneration and crying out against the cruel, infamous prison conditions, the violations of laws, the incommunicability of prisoners, and the tortures. When the censorship would not let his protests be printed, he availed himself of his famous letters, writing them to the authorities, denouncing the brutality of jailers, facing the arrogance

and threats of policemen and their superiors, risking reprisals. . . .
Nothing quieted this intrepid Don Quixote, this symbol of the
legal profession. . . . He fought against an avalanche of stupidity,
of incomprehension, and of prejudices instilled in society against
those who stood accused. His fame spread and Sobral Pinto became a universal lawyer, equal or superior to all his predecessors in the history of the profession. With a solitary voice he took
upon himself the defense of individual rights against the tide of
accommodations, halfheartedness, and cowardice.[5]

In the opinion of Evandro, Sobral provided lessons in the love of
persons and showed a rare understanding of the duty of giving moral
and personal support to defendants.

In the acute hours of political repression, intolerance is unlimited and blind and the acts of the hangman are brutal. Sobral
Pinto, in such praetorian catastrophes, experienced the greatest
moments of his career. As a victorious lawyer, acclaimed and applauded by his colleagues all over the country, he died in the most
Franciscan poverty. He left a legend of altruism, abnegation, and
honorability.
    Yes, Sobral Pinto was different from others; he was an anomaly;
he was a marvel; he was enormous. Rubem Braga was right: he
was a monster.[6]

No less enthusiastic articles appeared during his lifetime. As we
have shown, in 1945 the *Diário Carioca* columnist Joaquim de Sales
called Sobral one of the country's "most noble possessions . . . ,
one of those rare heroic figures out of Plutarch who still exist . . . ,
a spirit of incomparable purity, with a heart devoted to the highest ideals of Christian charity." Joaquim de Sales, comparing Alceu
Amoroso Lima to John the Beloved Disciple, found that Sobral, more
like Saint Paul, acted in a way to send his enemies scurrying when
he felt it necessary to deal with the dangers he faced.[7]
Sobral never hesitated to make his positions known. A good example of this was his response in January 1946 to his former client,
Roberto Sisson, who invited him to become a member of the Anti-
fascist Lawyers Commission. Sisson, bent on saving "anti-fascists"
who were being tried in the courts of Franco's Spain, had joined
Prestes in the Communist Party of Brazil.[8]

"I am not a fascist or anti-fascist lawyer," Sobral told Sisson. "I am, and have always tried to be, a Catholic lawyer. Acting in accordance with my views, I participate in litigation that involves the honor, liberty, and dignity of defendants, guided only by the principles of enduring and sovereign justice. In this way, each legal case appears in my eyes as an individual drama and problem of justice. . . . The fact that the accused is a fascist or anti-fascist is of no importance to me because justice for the person has nothing to do with his political ideas or his views about life."[9]

Sobral told Sisson that the labeling of men as fascist and anti-fascist had been, in the twentieth century, a cause of fatal dissensions, and was similar to "that other sinister labeling" of Communist and anti-Communist "that prevailed in Brazil from 1935 to 1945." During that period, Sobral pointed out, most of Brazil's population had equated Communism with bandits and attributed every sort of virtue to anti-Communists. "Today the situation is the reverse: to be fascist is to be the bandit and to be anti-fascist is to be virtuous."

Sobral described himself as an intransigent adversary of the regime of Franco, who, he said, deprived the Spanish people of the practice of legitimate liberty. "For the same reason I was opposed to Vargas in Brazil, Hitler in Germany, and Mussolini in Italy, and continue to oppose Salazar in Portugal and Stalin in Russia."

"It is," Sobral told Sisson, "perfectly natural that you, using the principles of pure dialectical materialism, wish to stir up Brazil in favor of the two Spanish citizens simply because they are being tried by the fascist government of Franco. The fact that they are anti-fascists is, for you, reason enough to side entirely with them. For me, however, the problem is more serious."

Sobral went on to say that he had concluded that Franco, although a Catholic, had established a Vargas-like "system of organized injustice," but that this conclusion did not allow him to find Franco's adversaries beyond criticism. "Many of them wish to overthrow Franco not because they want a government based on the principle of Justice but because they favor the principle of the class struggle. Obviously, under no circumstances can I join with these people against Franco." Sobral said that these adversaries of Franco, seeking to replace one dictatorship with another, were guided, like Franco, by principles that contradicted Sobral's own principles.

"No one knows better than you the frankness I express. In the hour when the Vargas government, doing away with the principle of liberty, failed to respect your personal dignity, I resolved, without vacillation, to give you my support, mediocre but absolutely sincere—a support that was not easy for defendants to find in those days and that called for resisting the evil and grim regime of force that debased our unfortunate Nation."[10]

NOTES

Preface

1. Tristão de Athayde (Alceu Amoroso Lima), "Nosso Bayard," *O Jornal,* March 25, 1945.
2. Ibid.
3. Alceu Amoroso Lima, letter to HSP, May 2, 1951 (see HSP, letter to Carlos Pontes, May 12, 1951, in *A Ordem,* June 1951, pp. 47–48).
4. Evandro Lins e Silva, "Sobral Pinto, o Monstro," *Jornal do Brasil,* December 8, 1991.
5. Clemente Hungria, letter to JWFD, Rio de Janeiro, October 29, 1998.
6. Conselho Federal da Ordem dos Advogados do Brasil (resolution of June 22, 1944, by Dario de Almeida Magalhães), *Jornal do Commercio,* March 10, 1945.
7. HSP, letter to (Arthur) Bernardes, November 4, 1930. HSP, "Chronica Política," *A Ordem,* nos. 13, 15, 18, 19, 29 (March, May, August, September 1931, July 1932). HSP, letter to Jaime de Barros Câmara, April 27, 1944.
8. Joaquim de Sales in *Diário Carioca,* August 17, 1945. Rafael Corrêa de Oliveira in *Diário de Notícias,* October 19, 1945.
9. See resolution of Conselho Federal da Ordem dos Advogados do Brasil, March 10, 1945.
10. Silva, "Sobral Pinto, o Monstro."
11. Tristão de Athayde (Alceu Amoroso Lima), "Nosso Bayard."

I. Advocate of Order during the Old Republic (pre-1930)

1. CATHOLIC UPBRINGING (1893–1912)

1. Heráclito Fontoura Sobral Pinto (henceforth shown as HSP), letter to José César Borba, Rio de Janeiro (henceforth not shown for HSP's letters if Rio de Janeiro), December 30, 1941. All letters are in HSP files in Rio de Janeiro unless otherwise indicated.
2. HSP and Ary Quintella in HSP, *Lições de Liberdade* (Belo Horizonte: Editora Comunicação, 1977), introductory pages, not numbered.
3. Ibid.
4. HSP, letter to Natalina (Sobral Pinto), n.d. HSP, in "Publicações a Pedido," *Jornal do Commercio,* February 10, 1955.

5. HSP in introductory pages of HSP, *Lições de Liberdade.*

6. Ibid. HSP, letter to Alceu (Amoroso Lima), November 22, 1935.

7. João Eduardo Magalhães, interview, Rio de Janeiro, January 8, 1996. Margarida Parreiras Horta and Paula Laclette, interview, Rio de Janeiro, January 10, 1996. HSP, letter to Nair, Ruth, and Edith, April 30, 1969.

8. Ibid. Alfredo Carlos de Andrade Palmer, "Rato de Arquivo: Memória Fotográfica e Histórico-Genealógica," typescript, Petrópolis, 1989 (in possession of Palmer), vol. 2, p. 226.

9. HSP, letter to José César Borba, December 30, 1941.

10. HSP, letter to Luiz Corrêa de Brito, August 19, 1941. Roberto Sobral Pinto Ribeiro, interview, Rio de Janeiro, January 4, 1995. HSP, letter to Octavinho (a Colégio Anchieta classmate), June 28, 1972.

11. Roberto Sobral Pinto Ribeiro, interview, Rio de Janeiro, August 20, 1994.

12. Ibid.

13. HSP, "Mensagem de Gratidão e de Esperança," attached to HSP, letter to Padre Pedro Canísio Melchert (Reitor do Colégio Anchieta), April 13, 1986.

2. LAW SCHOOL AND LATER (1912–1924)

1. HSP, *Lições de Liberdade* (Belo Horizonte: Editora Comunicação, 1977), introductory pages.

2. Ibid. HSP, diary entries, June 8, 9, 1915.

3. Roberto Sobral Pinto Ribeiro, interview, Rio de Janeiro, August 13, 1994.

4. HSP, *Lições de Liberdade,* introductory pages, quoting HSP, in *A Ordem,* August 18–September 17, 1931.

5. HSP, letter to Benjamin (Antunes de Oliveira Filho), March 27, 1944. HSP, letter to (Francisco) Campos, January 13, 1936.

6. HSP, letter to (João Martins de) Carvalho Mourão, November 10, 1941.

7. Idalina Sobral Pinto Ribeiro and Amaury Ribeiro, interviews, Rio de Janeiro, August 25, 1994, January 8, 1995.

8. Ibid. Roberto Sobral Pinto Ribeiro, interviews, Rio de Janeiro, August 8, 9, 14, 1994.

9. Idalina Sobral Pinto Ribeiro and Amaury Ribeiro, interviews, Rio de Janeiro, August 25, 1994, January 8, 1995. HSP, letter to (Francisco) Campos, January 13, 1936.

10. HSP, letter to João Saldanha, July 22, 1974.

11. HSP, letter to M. Paulo Filho, August 19, 1942.

12. HSP, *Lições de Liberdade,* introductory pages.

3. PROCURADOR CRIMINAL INTERINO (1924–1926)

1. "O caso das estampilhas falsas," in "Justiça Federal," *Correio da Manhã,* March 21, 22, 25, 1924.

2. Roberto Sobral Pinto Ribeiro, interview, Rio de Janeiro, August 14,

1994. A salary of 3.6 contos is mentioned in the *Correio da Manhã*, June 22, 1928.

3. HSP, letter to (Francisco) Campos, October 23, 1939. Domingos Meirelles, *As Noites das Grandes Fogueiras* (Rio de Janeiro: Editora Record, 1995), p. 437.

4. Meirelles, *As Noites das Grandes Fogueiras*, p. 717. Paulo Sérgio Pinheiro, *Estratégias da Ilusão: A Revolução Mundial e o Brasil* (São Paulo: Companhia de Letras, 1991), p. 110.

5. Meirelles, *As Noites das Grandes Fogueiras*, p. 293. HSP, *Lições de Liberdade* (Belo Horizonte: Editora Comunicação, 1977), introductory pages. Adolpho Bergamini, in *Correio da Manhã* and *O Jornal*, September 6, 1928.

6. "O processo Protógenes," *Correio da Manhã*, March 9, 1926. HSP, *A Conspiração Protógenes Pereira Guimarães: A Atuação da Procuradoria Criminal da República* (Rio de Janeiro: Imprensa Nacional, 1926), pp. 41–42, 64–67. Bergamini, in *Correio da Manhã* and *O Jornal*, September 6, 1928, and *O Globo*, September 5, 1928.

7. Augusto do Amaral Peixoto, interview, Rio de Janeiro, August 17, 1963.

8. HSP, *A Insurreição do Encouraçado S. Paulo* (Rio de Janeiro: Imprensa Nacional, 1926), pp. 15, 49.

9. *O Jornal*, March 13, 1926, *Correio da Manhã*, March 9, 23, 26, May 22, 1926.

10. *Correio da Manhã*, March 26, April 4, 1926.

11. *O Jornal*, March 13, 1926, *Correio da Manhã*, April 4, 1926.

12. HSP, letter to Olympio de Sá e Albuquerque, April 5, 1926, in HSP, *A Conspiração Protógenes Guimarães*, pp. 299–307.

13. *O Jornal*, March 13, 1926, *Correio da Manhã*, May 22, 1926.

14. HSP, *Lições de Liberdade*, introductory pages.

15. Everardo Dias, *Bastilhas Modernas, 1924–1926* (São Paulo: Emprensa Editora de Obras Sociaes e Literarias, 1926), pp. 144–152.

16. HSP, letter to Alceu (Amoroso Lima), December 1, 1937.

17. HSP, *Lições de Liberdade*, introductory pages. *O Jornal*, January 3, 8, February 4, 1927. *A Plebe*, February 12, 26, 1927. Dias, *Bastilhas Modernas*, pp. 237–254.

18. *Correio da Manhã*, June 13, 1926.

19. Meirelles, *As Noites das Grandes Fogueiras*, p. 604. HSP, letter to Francisco Negrão de Lima, February 19, 1938. HSP, *Lições de Liberdade*, introductory pages.

20. HSP, letter to (Francisco) Negrão de Lima, February 19, 1938.

21. Ibid. HSP, letter to (Francisco) Campos, October 23, 1939. Roberto Sobral Pinto Ribeiro, interview, Rio de Janeiro, January 10, 1996.

22. *O Paiz*, November 21, 1926. *Correio da Manhã* entry in Fundação Getúlio Vargas, Centro de Pesquisa e Documentação de História Contemporânea do Brasil (CPDOC), *Dicionário Histórico-Biográfico Brasileiro, 1930–1983* (Rio de Janeiro: Editora Forense-Universitária, 1984).

23. *Correio da Manhã*, November 18, 1926. *O Paiz*, November 21, 1926. *O Jornal*, June 28, 1925.

24. *O Jornal*, June 28, 30, 1925. HSP entry in CPDOC, *Dicionário Histó-rico-Biográfico Brasileiro, 1930–1983*.

25. HSP, letter to (Augusto Frederico) Schmidt, October 31, 1935.

4. ROUGH DAYS FOR THE PROCURADOR CRIMINAL (1927–1928)

1. "Conspiração Protógenes (1925)," in Edgard Costa, *Os Grandes Julga-mentos do Supremo Tribunal Federal* (Rio de Janeiro: Editôra Civilização Brasileira, 1964), vol. 1, pp. 494–516. *O Jornal*, January 6, February 20, 1927.

2. HSP, *A Conspiração Protógenes Pereira Guimarães* (Rio de Janeiro: Imprensa Nacional, 1926), p. 122. *O Jornal*, February 20, March 30, April 13, 22, 27, 29, 1927.

3. *O Jornal*, March 26, 30, April 28, 29, 1927. *Jornal do Commercio*, May 5, 1927.

4. *O Jornal*, May 3, 1927. *Jornal do Commercio*, May 5, 1927.

5. Levy Carneiro, in *O Jornal*, May 8, 1927.

6. *O Jornal*, May 21, 1927. Costa, *Os Grandes Julgamentos*, vol. 1, p. 508.

7. HSP, *Por Libello-Crime Accusatorio* (Rio de Janeiro: Imprensa Nacio-nal, 1927), pp. 1–2. *Correio da Manhã*, September 27, 1927. Costa, *Os Grandes Julgamentos*, vol. 1, pp. 440–442.

8. Neill Macaulay, *The Prestes Column: Revolution in Brazil* (New York: New Viewpoints, 1974), pp. 205–210, 98.

9. HSP, in *O Paiz*, May 17, 1928.

10. *O Jornal*, May 22, 1928. *Correio da Manhã*, May 29, 1928.

11. *Correio da Manhã*, May 29, 1928.

12. *O Jornal*, June 9, 10, 1928. "Um observador judiciário," in *O Jornal*, June 7, 1928 (reprinted September 8, 1928). *Correio da Manhã*, June 22, Sep-tember 9, 1928.

5. JACKSON DE FIGUEIREDO (1891–1928)

1. Cléa Alves Figueiredo Fernandes, *Jackson de Figueiredo: Uma Traje-tória Apaixonada* (Rio de Janeiro: Editora Forense Universitária, 1989), pp. 360, 161, 416, 459, 480.

2. Ibid., p. 416. HSP, "O Realista Político," *A Ordem*, March 1929 (in vol. 8), pp. 306–317 (see p. 306).

3. João Etienne Filho, compiler, *Alceu Amoroso Lima, Jackson de Fi-gueiredo, Correspondência, 1919–1928: Harmonia dos Contrastes* (Rio de Janeiro: Coleção Afrânio Peixoto da Academia de Letras, 1991), vol. 1, p. 11. José Arthur Rios, "Jackson de Figueiredo," *Carta Mensal*, Rio de Janeiro, De-cember 1991, p. 26. Francisco Iglésias, "Estudo sôbre o pensamento reacio-nário: Jackson de Figueiredo," *Revista Brasileira de Ciências Sociais da Fa-culdade de Ciências Economicas da U.M.G.*, Belo Horizonte, vol. 2, no. 2 (July 1962), p. 26. Fernandes, *Jackson de Figueiredo*, pp. 251–265, 271.

4. Fernandes, *Jackson de Figueiredo*, pp. 300–305, 313–315. HSP, "Dur-val de Moraes e o Centro Dom Vital," *A Ordem*, vol. 77, nos. 1–4 (January–December 1982), p. 12.

5. Fernandes, *Jackson de Figueiredo*, pp. 304, 308, 313, 367.

6. Ibid., pp. 319, 336. Iglésias, "Estudo sôbre o pensamento reacionário," pp. 37, 41, 42, 47.

7. Fernandes, *Jackson de Figueiredo*, pp. 329, 354–355. Centro Dom Vital entry in Robert M. Levine, *Historical Dictionary of Brazil* (Metuchen, N.J., and London: Scarecrow Press, 1979). HSP, "Durval de Moraes e o Centro Dom Vital," pp. 12–15.

8. Fernandes, *Jackson de Figueiredo*, pp. 457–458, 466–469. Ariosvaldo Figueiredo, *História Política de Sergipe* (Aracaju: Sociedade Editorial de Sergipe, 1989), pp. 95, 113. J. Pires Wynne, *História de Sergipe, 1930–1972*, vol. 1 (Rio de Janeiro: Editôra Pongetti, 1970), pp. 449, 451.

9. Fernandes, *Jackson de Figueiredo*, pp. 271, 315, 360–361, 406, 409, 448, 452–453, 459, 499, 539.

10. Ibid., pp. 449, 518, 523, 526, 548, 553. Iglésias, "Estudo sôbre o pensamento reacionário," pp. 31, 34. Alceu Amoroso Lima entry in CPDOC, *Dicionário Histórico-Biográfico Brasileiro, 1930–1983* (Rio de Janeiro: Editora Forense-Universitária, 1984).

11. Zildo José Jorge, quoted in Fernandes, *Jackson de Figueiredo*, pp. 602–603. José Arthur Rios, "Jackson de Figueiredo," p. 32, and letter to JWFD, Rio de Janeiro, September 27, 1996.

12. Jackson de Figueiredo, letter to Alceu Amoroso Lima, March 12–13, 1928, in *Alceu Amoroso Lima, Jackson de Figueiredo, Correspondência,* vol. 1, p. 355, and Alceu Amoroso Lima, letter to Jackson de Figueiredo, Rio de Janeiro, September 18–20, 1928, in vol. 2, pp. 259–260.

13. HSP, letter to Mena (Philomena Farias Brito Pontes de Miranda), September 10, 1930. Fernandes, *Jackson de Figueiredo*, pp. 564, 565. José Barreto Filho entry in *Dicionário Histórico-Biográfico Brasileiro, 1930–1983*.

14. Fernandes, *Jackson de Figueiredo*, pp. 571–577.

15. HSP, "Jackson de Figueiredo," *A Ordem*, vol. 49 (June 1953), pp. 366–372. See p. 370.

6. THE DOWNFALL OF THE PROCURADOR CRIMINAL (JUNE 1928)

1. HSP, letter to (Dom) Xavier, February 9, 1940. HSP, letter to (Francisco) Campos, October 23, 1939.

2. Ibid.

3. HSP, *Destruição da Mentira pela Confissão da Verdade* (Rio de Janeiro: Jornal do Commercio, Rodrigues & Cia., 1955), pp. 19, 25.

4. *Correio da Manhã*, June 22, 1928.

5. Assis Chateaubriand, "O Gesto do Procurador Criminal," *O Jornal*, June 22, 1928.

6. *A Noite*, June 26, 1928 (reprinted in *O Jornal*, July 28, 1928).

7. HSP, letter to (Augusto Frederico) Schmidt, October 31, 1935.

8. HSP, *Destruição da Mentira pela Confissão da Verdade*, p. 24. Roberto Sobral Pinto Ribeiro, interview, Rio de Janeiro, January 13, 1995.

9. HSP, letter to Schmidt, October 31, 1935. HSP, letter to Cláudio, September 10, 1938. HSP included Cláudio's name on the list.

10. HSP, *Destruição da Mentira pela Confissão da Verdade*, pp. 17–18.
11. HSP, letter to (Dom) Xavier, February 9, 1940.

7. A STREET BRAWL LEADS TO MORE WOES FOR SOBRAL
(SEPTEMBER 1928)

1. *O Jornal*, September 5, 6, 7, 12, 1928. *Correio da Manhã*, September 9, 12, 1928. *O Paiz*, September 7, 16, 1928.
2. Assis Chateaubriand, "O innocente," *O Jornal*, September 6, 1928. "Procurador Desidioso," *Correio da Manhã*, September 9, 1928. *O Globo*, September 24, 1928.
3. Congressional speech of Adolpho Bergamini in *Correio da Manhã*, September 6, 1928, and *O Globo*, September 5, 1928.
4. HSP, in *O Paiz*, September 9, 1928. *O Paiz*, September 8, 1928.
5. HSP, letter to (Augusto Frederico) Schmidt, October 31, 1935.
6. *O Jornal*, September 23, 25, 1928. *Correio da Manhã*, September 23, 26, 1928.
7. HSP, letter to Schmidt, October 31, 1935.
8. *O Globo*, September 24, 1928. *Correio da Manhã*, September 26, 1928.
9. *O Jornal*, September 25, 1928.
10. Ibid.
11. HSP, letter to Schmidt, October 31, 1935.

8. A POLEMIC DURING THE OLD REPUBLIC'S COLLAPSE
(OCTOBER 1930)

1. Roberto Sobral Pinto Ribeiro, letter to JWFD, December 1, 1997.
2. HSP, letter to Benjamin (Antunes de Oliveira Filho), April 18, 1939. Roberto Sobral Pinto Ribeiro, interview, Rio de Janeiro, January 13, 1995.
3. HSP, letter to Targino (Ribeiro), August 28, 1929. HSP, correspondence with companies, January 30, March 31, July 5, 1930.
4. HSP, letter to (Joaquim de Magalhães) Barata, September 30, 1930.
5. HSP, letter to Lauro, September 11, 1930.
6. HSP, letter to Coriolano (de Góes), September 10, 1930. HSP, letter to Pedro (de Oliveira Ribeiro Sobrinho), September 27, 1930.
7. HSP, letters to Alceu (Amoroso Lima), October 9, 14, 1930. Alceu Amoroso Lima, letter to HSP, n.p., October 13, 1930.
8. Alceu Amoroso Lima, letter to HSP, n.p., October 14, 1930. HSP, letters to Alceu (Amoroso Lima), October 13, 14, 15, 1930.
9. Alceu Amoroso Lima, letter to HSP, October 14, 1930. Tristão de Athayde (Alceu Amoroso Lima), "Palavras aos companheiros," *A Ordem*, no. 9 (October 1930).
10. HSP, letter to Hamilton (Nogueira), October 18, 1930, and letter to Alceu (Amoroso Lima), October 21, 1930.
11. HSP, letter to (Augusto Frederico) Schmidt, October 19, 1930, and letter to Perilo Gomes, October 17, 1930.

12. HSP, letters to Hamilton (Nogueira), October 18, 22, 1930. HSP, letter to Alceu (Amoroso Lima), October 21, 1930. Hamilton Nogueira, letter to HSP, n.p., October 21, 1930.

13. Jarbas Medeiros, *Ideologia Autoritária no Brasil, 1930–1945* (Rio de Janeiro: Instituto de Documentação, Editora da Fundação Getúlio Vargas, 1978), p. 226.

II. Critic of Post-1930 Confusion (1931–1935)

1. COMBATING LIBERALISM AND *TENENTISMO* (1931)

1. HSP, letter to Sylvio Motta, April 27, 1931. HSP and R. Lopes Machado, *O caso da "Narrativa do motim a bordo do ENCOURAÇADO SÃO PAULO exarada no livro da Torre 3": Allegações de Defesa* (Rio de Janeiro: Justiça Militar, 1932), pp. 3, 4, 12.

2. HSP, letter to Rodrigo, October 29, 1930. HSP, letters to Pedro (de Oliveira Ribeiro Sobrinho), July 30, September 29, 1931.

3. HSP, letter to (Arthur) Bernardes, November 4, 1930.

4. HSP, letter to Hamilton (de Paula), March 21, 1931. HSP, letter to Pedro, May 29, 1931.

5. HSP, "Como?," *A Razão*, June 30, 1931. See also Virgílio de Mello Franco, letter to HSP, n.p., July 1, 1931, and HSP, letter to Virgílio de Mello Franco, July 2, 1931.

6. HSP, "Vício de Mentalidade," *A Razão*, July 15, 1931.

7. HSP, letter to Francisco (de) Assis Barbosa, April 8, 1942. "Posição," *A Ordem*, no. 11 (January 1931).

8. Joaquim de Magalhães Barata, quoted in HSP, "Chronica Política," *A Ordem*, no. 18 (August 1931).

9. HSP, "Chronica Política," *A Ordem*, no. 13 (March 1931), no. 15 (May 1931), no. 18 (August 1931), no. 19 (September 1931).

10. Severino Sombra entry in CPDOC, *Dicionário Histórico-Biográfico Brasileiro, 1930–1983* (Rio de Janeiro: Editora Forense-Universitária, 1984). Severino Sombra, letter to Alceu Amoroso Lima, n.p., n.d. (October 1931), in HSP papers. HSP, letter to (Severino) Sombra, October 27, 1931. HSP, "confidential" letter to (Arthur) Bernardes, April 28, 1931.

2. SUPPORTING BERNARDES AGAINST FRANCISCO CAMPOS (1931)

1. HSP, letters to Arthur Bernardes, April 28 ("confidential"), May 6 ("confidential"), June 2, 8, 1931.

2. HSP, letter to Bernardes, April 28, 1931. HSP, letters to Alceu Amoroso Lima, April 15, 29, 1931. HSP, "Chronica Política," *A Ordem*, no. 15 (May 1931), no. 16 (June 1931). Sobral, in his letter of April 15 to Alceu, listed Professors Azevedo do Amaral and Fernando de Azevedo as sharing Campos' erroneous idea about morality being the equivalent of rationalism.

3. Alceu Amoroso Lima, letter to HSP, n.p., April 29, 1931.

4. HSP, "Chronica Política," *A Ordem*, no. 16 (June 1931).

5. HSP, letter to Hamilton de Paula, June 13, 1931. HSP, "Chronica Política," *A Ordem,* no. 18 (August 1931).

6. HSP, letter to Hamilton de Paula, June 13, 1931.

7. HSP, "Chronica Política," *A Ordem,* no. 19 (September 1931).

8. Carolina Nabuco, *A Vida de Virgílio de Melo Franco* (Rio de Janeiro: Livraria José Olympio, 1962), p. 76.

9. Ibid., pp. 76–78. HSP, "Chronica Política," *A Ordem,* no. 20 (October 1931).

3. CRITIC OF THE REGIME AND OF ITS PAULISTA OPPONENTS (1932)

1. HSP, letter to Nonóta (a cousin), September 1, 1932. HSP, letters to Affonso Penna Júnior, October 6, 7, 1932. HSP, letter to Basilio Bica, October 8, 1932. HSP, letter to Alceu (Amoroso Lima), November 12, 1934. Cândido Motta Filho, letter to HSP, São Paulo, October 26, 1932. HSP, letter to Cândido Motta Filho, November 1, 1932.

2. Oscar Mendes, letter to HSP, Bonfim, Minas Gerais, March 9, 1932, with clipping of Mendes' *Estado de Minas* review of Sobral's booklet, March 2, 1932.

3. HSP, letter to Plínio Salgado, February 11, 1932.

4. HSP, letter to Plínio Salgado, May 10, 1932.

5. Ibid. Pedro de Oliveira Ribeiro Sobrinho, letter to HSP, São Paulo, May 26, 1932. HSP, letters to Pedro, May 29, 1931, November 22, 1932.

6. HSP, "Chronica Política," *A Ordem,* no. 22 (December 1931), pp. 366–367.

7. Antônio Fernandes, letter to Alceu Amoroso Lima, Recife, March 3, 1932.

8. HSP, letter to Antônio Fernandes, March 16, 1932.

9. Ibid. HSP, "Chronica Política," *A Ordem,* no. 24 (February 1932), p. 142. HSP, "Chronica Política," *A Ordem,* no. 27 (May 1932), p. 366, and no. 30 (August 1932), p. 145.

10. HSP, "Chronica Política," *A Ordem,* no. 29 (July 1932), pp. 55–56.

11. Pedro de Toledo, message, *A Ordem,* no. 31 (September 1932), pp. 161–165.

12. HSP, "Chronica Política," *A Ordem,* no. 30 (August 1932), p. 145; no. 32 (October 1932), pp. 273–274; no. 34 (December 1932), pp. 454–456.

13. HSP, letter to Antônio de Queiroz Filho, December 17, 1932.

14. HSP, "Chronica Política," *A Ordem,* no. 33 (November 1932), pp. 372–380, quoting Vargas and replying to him; no. 34 (December 1932), p. 456.

15. HSP, letter to Alceu (Amoroso Lima), April 4, 1932.

16. HSP, letter to Alceu, November 11, 1932.

4. SOBRAL'S DEPARTURE FROM *A ORDEM* AND *A UNIÃO* (1933–1934)

1. HSP, letter to Alceu (Amoroso Lima), December 29, 1932, May 29, June 1, 3, 1933. HSP, letter to (Henrique) Hargreaves, May 17, 1933.

2. Evandro Lins e Silva, letter to Sérgio Lacerda, Rio de Janeiro, May 5,

1980 (copy in possession of JWFD). Carlos Lacerda, "As confissões de Lacerda," *Jornal da Tarde*, May 27, 1977.

3. *A Nação* entry in CPDOC, *Dicionário Histórico-Biográfico Brasileiro, 1930–1983* (Rio de Janeiro: Editora Forense-Universitária, 1984). Fernando Morais, *Chatô: O Rei do Brasil* (São Paulo: Companhia de Letras, 1994), pp. 302–329. HSP, letters to Leonel Franca and Alceu (Amoroso Lima), January 10, 1933. Nelson Werneck Sodré, *História da Imprensa no Brasil* (Rio de Janeiro: Editôra Civilização Brasileira, 1966), p. 435.

4. List (December 1932) in HSP files. See also Liga Eleitoral Católica entry in *Dicionário Histórico-Biográfico Brasileiro, 1930–1983*.

5. HSP, letters to Padres Luiz Lecoulieux, Carlos Lanso, and Manoel Barbosa, January 11, 1933.

6. HSP, "Chronica Política," *A Ordem*, nos. 37–38 (March–April 1933), pp. 288–290.

7. Irmã Maria Regina do Santo Rosário, o.c.d. (Laurita Pessôa Raja Gabaglia), *O Cardeal Leme* (Rio de Janeiro: Livraria José Olympio Editôra, 1962), p. 316.

8. Ibid., p. 317. Tristão de Athayde (Alceu Amoroso Lima) in *A Ordem*, no. 53 (July 1934), p. 3. HSP, "Chronica Política," *A Ordem*, nos. 37–38, p. 289.

9. Santo Rosário, *O Cardeal Leme*, pp. 317–318.

10. HSP, letter to José Burnier Pessoa de Mello, January 25, 1933. HSP, letter to Monsenhor João Lauriano, December 23, 1932.

11. Roberto Sobral Pinto Ribeiro, interview, Rio de Janeiro, August 23, 1994.

12. Alceu Amoroso Lima, letter to HSP, Rio de Janeiro, February 17, 1933.

13. HSP, letter to Alceu, June 30, 1933. HSP, letter to (Elmano) Cardim, October 29, 1943, p. 3.

14. Osório Lopes, letter to HSP, Rio de Janeiro, July 24, 1937. HSP, letter to Alceu, November 12, 1934.

15. HSP, letter to Alceu, November 12, 1934.

5. "INCURSIONS" INTO CEARÁ AND SERGIPE POLITICS (1934–1935)

1. Tristão de Athayde (Alceu Amoroso Lima), "O Sentido da Nossa Victoria," *A Ordem*, no. 52 (June 1934), pp. 417–423.

2. HSP, letter to Plínio (Correia de Oliveira), April 13, 1934. HSP, letters to Alceu (Amoroso Lima), May 8, October 29, 1934.

3. HSP, letter to Alceu, September 21, 1934.

4. HSP, letter to (Luiz Cavalcanti) Sucupira, September 14, 1934.

5. Ibid. HSP, letter to Alceu, September 21, 1934.

6. HSP, letter to (Francisco de) Assis Chateaubriand, October 4, 1934, and note at end: "O Alceu não consentiu na remessa desta carta." Fernando Morais, *Chatô: O Rei do Brasil* (São Paulo: Companhia de Letras, 1994), p. 329.

7. Simone Souza, "As Interventorias no Ceará (1930–1945)," in *História de Ceará*, ed. Simone Souza, p. 329 (Fortaleza: Fundação Demócrito Rocha,

1989). Aroldo Mota, *História de Ceará, 1930-1945* (Fortaleza: Stylus Comunicações, 1989), pp. 116, 117.

8. HSP, letter to Sucupira, September 14, 1934. HSP, letter to Alceu, September 21, 1934. Souza, "As Interventorias no Ceará (1930-1945)," p. 330.

9. HSP, letters to Edgar de Arruda, November 30, December 24, 1934. Edgar de Arruda, letter to HSP, n.p., December 12, 1934. Souza, "As Interventorias no Ceará (1930-1945)," p. 329. Mota, *História de Ceará, 1930-1945*, pp. 116, 125, 137, 141. Meneses Pimentel entry in CPDOC, *Dicionário Histórico-Biográfico Brasileiro, 1930-1983* (Rio de Janeiro: Editora Forense-Universitária, 1984).

10. HSP, letter to Augusto (César Leite), May 21, 1935.

11. Information given here and in paragraphs that follow may be found in Ibarê Dantas, *Os Partidos Políticos em Sergipe (1889-1964)* (Rio de Janeiro: Tempo Brasileiro, 1989), pp. 109-112, 129; Ariosvaldo Figueiredo, *História Política de Sergipe* (Aracaju: Sociedade Editorial de Sergipe, 1989), pp. 300-305; J. Pires Wynne, *Históra de Sergipe, 1930-1972*, vol. 2 (Rio de Janeiro: Editora Pongetti, 1973), pp. 53-57.

12. Figueiredo, *História Política de Sergipe*, p. 344. Dantas, *Os Partidos Políticos em Sergipe (1889-1964)*, pp. 116-120.

13. HSP, letter to Amando Fontes, May 16, 1935.

14. Amando Fontes and José Barreto Filho entries in *Dicionário Histórico-Biográfico Brasileiro, 1930-1983*. Cléa Alves Figueiredo Fernandes, *Jackson de Figueiredo: Uma Trajetória Apaixonada* (Rio de Janeiro: Editora Forense Universitária, 1989), pp. 602-603.

15. HSP, letter to Augusto (César Leite), May 21, 1935. HSP, letters to Amando (Fontes), June 11, July 13, September 17, 1935.

16. HSP, letters to Erônides (de Carvalho), June 13, September 6, 1935. HSP, letter to (José) Vicente (de Souza), September 17, 1935.

17. HSP, letter to Garcia Rosa, July 5, 1935.

18. HSP, letters to (Augusto Frederico) Schmidt, July 20, 23, 1935.

19. HSP, letter to Rubens (Figueiredo Martins), July 12, 1935. HSP, letter to Pedro (de Oliveira Ribeiro Sobrinho), July 29, 1935. HSP, letter to (José) Vicente (de Souza), September 18, 1935. Rubens Figueiredo Martins, letter to HSP, Carmo, August 21, 1935.

20. HSP, letter to Erônides (de Carvalho), September 9, 1935.

21. HSP, letter to Erônides (de Carvalho), September 21, 1935.

22. HSP, letters to (José) Vicente (de Souza), September 17, 18, 1935. José Vicente de Souza, letter to HSP, n.p., September 18, 1935.

23. HSP, letter to Vicente, September 18, 1935.

24. HSP, letter to (José) Barreto (Filho), October 23, 1935.

6. FAMILY, FRIENDS, AND WORK (1934-1935)

1. HSP, letters to Virginia (Fassehber), June 23, 1934, October 10, 1935, and to Carlos (Fassehber Banho), October 9, 1935. HSP, letter to Alceu, May 4, 1934.

2. Roberto Sobral Pinto Ribeiro, interviews, Rio de Janeiro, August 8, 9,

1994. HSP, letter to Natalina (Sobral Pinto), March 26, 1935. HSP, letter to Benjamin (Antunes de Oliveira Filho), April 18, 1939. Idalina and Amaury Ribeiro, interview, Rio de Janeiro, August 25, 1994.

3. HSP, letters to Pedro (de Oliveira Ribeiro Sobrinho), October 3, 1935, and Waldemar (de Moraes), October 3, 1935.

4. HSP, letters to Milton (Magarão), February 24, May 14, 1934. HSP, letter to Octavio (de Faria), March 8, 1934. HSP, letter to Carneiro, March 6, 1934. HSP, letters to Mena (Philomena Farias Brito Pontes de Miranda), March 17, April 6, August 1, 1934. HSP, letter to Mário, July 12, 1934. Statements of account of Philomena, Pensão-Sanatorio São Geraldo, as of October 10, November 30, 1934.

5. HSP, letter to Dom Keller, March 21, 1938. HSP, letter to Leocádia Prestes, August 14, 1937. HSP, letter to Miguel Dias, November 24, 1938. HSP, letter to Natalina (Sobral Pinto), March 7, 1936. Roberto Sobral Pinto Ribeiro, interview, Rio de Janeiro, August 13, 1994.

6. Instituto da Ordem dos Advogados Brasileiros, letter to HSP, December 11, 1934.

7. Alberto Venancio Filho, *Notícia Histórica da Ordem dos Advogados do Brasil (1930–1980)* (Rio de Janeiro: n.p., 1982), pp. 22–25, 30, 34, 58. Clemente Hungria, letter to JWFD, Rio de Janeiro, January 31, 1997.

8. HSP, letters to (Álvaro) Goulart (de Oliveira), October 12, 16, 1935.

9. Colligação Catholica Brasileira, notice (signed by Alceu Amoroso Lima), Rio de Janeiro, July 5, 1934. HSP, letters to (Alfredo de) Arruda (Câmara), May 10, June 19, 1935.

10. José Vicente de Souza, letter to HSP, Rio de Janeiro, November 5, 1935.

11. Regina Figueiredo, letter to HSP, Rio de Janeiro, November 5, 1935.

12. HSP, letter to Regina Figueiredo, November 8, 1935.

13. HSP, letter to Alceu, November 9, 1935.

14. HSP, letter to Waldemar (de Moraes), November 12, 1935.

15. HSP, letter to Alceu, December 19, 1935. Alceu, letter to HSP, n.p., December 20, 1935.

16. HSP, letter to Pedro, April 1, 1936. HSP, letter to Alceu, July 9, 1936.

7. OPPOSING THE ALIANÇA NACIONAL LIBERTADORA (1935)

1. Tristão de Athayde (Alceu Amoroso Lima), "Catholicismo e Integralismo," *A Ordem,* no. 58 (December 1934), pp. 405–413. Jarbas Medeiros, *Ideologia Autoritário no Brasil, 1930–1945* (Rio de Janeiro: Instituto de Documentação, Editora da Fundação Getúlio Vargas, 1978), p. 269.

2. HSP, letters to Alceu (Amoroso Lima), July 30, 1935, November 3, 1934.

3. HSP, letter to Alceu, November 22, 1935.

4. HSP, letter to Alceu, July 10, 1935.

5. Ibid.

6. Ibid. HSP, letter to Eminência (Sebastião Leme), March 7, 1935.

7. HSP, letter to Alceu, July 10, 1935.

III. Opponent of the Post-1935 Repression (1936–1938)

1. EFFECTS OF THE NOVEMBER 1935 UPRISINGS (1935–1936)

1. HSP, letter to Affonso Penna Júnior, December 2, 1935, and attached "Exposição."
2. HSP, letters to Alceu (Amoroso Lima) and Wagner (Dutra), December 10, 1935.
3. HSP, letters to (Francisco) Campos, January 13, 17, February 1, 1936. HSP, letters to Eminência (Cardinal Leme), March 14, 20, 1936.
4. HSP, letter to (Francisco) Campos, June 18, 1936. HSP, letter to Padre Olympio (de Mello), February 3, 1937.
5. HSP, letters to Alceu, February 28, May 27, 1936.
6. HSP, letters to José Corrêa Lopes & Cia., June 16, 23, August 19, 1936.
7. HSP, letter to Lélia F. Vieira Lima, January 3, 1936.
8. HSP, letters to Leontina Figner Sisson, January 7, March 5, October 5, 1936. HSP, letter to Capitão Chefe de Policia, January 25, 1936. HSP, letter to Sr. Ministro da Justiça, October 2, 1936. HSP, letter to Capitão Miranda Corrêa, November 6, 1936.
9. HSP, letter to Sr. Presidente do Tribunal de Segurança Nacional (henceforth sometimes shown as TSN), October 3, 1936. HSP, letter to Roberto Henrique Faller Sisson, January 29, 1937. Ordem dos Advogados do Brasil, Secção do Distrito Federal, letter to HSP, Rio de Janeiro, January 18, 1937. Targino Ribeiro, letter to Luiz Carlos da Costa Netto, Rio de Janeiro, January 18, 1937. Luiz Carlos da Costa Netto, letter to HSP, Rio de Janeiro, January 22, 1937.
10. HSP, letter to Osório Lopes, July 20, 1937. HSP, letter to Almirante Presidente do Supremo Tribunal Militar, September 11, 1937. HSP, letter to Presidente do TSN, May 24, 1937.
11. HSP, letter to Hermenegildo de Barros, March 7, 1936. HSP, letters to Targino Ribeiro, March 7, 10, 1936.
12. Sebastião Paz Pereira da Hora, letter to HSP, n.p., n.d. HSP, "Em Defesa de Dr. Sebastião da Hora," December 14, 1936. HSP, letter to Agamemnon (Magalhães), February 13, 1937.
13. HSP, letter to Leovigildo Franca, November 12, 1936. HSP, letter to José Maria, November 23, 1938.
14. Adalberto Correia entry in CPDOC, *Dicionário Histórico-Biográfico Brasileiro, 1930–1983* (Rio de Janeiro: Editora Forense-Universitária, 1984). HSP, letter to Edmundo, November 5, 1936.
15. HSP, letter to (Francisco) Campos, September 1, 1936.
16. Antônio Carlos entry in *Dicionário Histórico-Biográfico Brasileiro, 1930–1983.*

2. EX OFFICIO LAWYER OF HARRY BERGER (1935–1937)

1. Euzébio de Queiroz Filho, interview, Rio de Janeiro, June 26, 1963.
2. Robert M. Levine, *The Vargas Regime* (New York and London: Co-

lumbia University Press, 1970), p. 127. *O Estado de S. Paulo*, March 10, 11, 1936.

3. Targino Ribeiro, letter to Raul Machado, Rio de Janeiro, January 7, 1937; Targino Ribeiro, letter to HSP, Rio de Janeiro, January 8, 1937 (in HSP papers).

4. HSP, letter to Targino Ribeiro, January 12, 1937.

5. HSP, *Por que defendo os Comunistas* (Belo Horizonte: Universidade Católica de Minas Gerais, 1979), p. 23. HSP, letter to Raul Machado, January 15, 1937.

6. HSP, letter to Raul Machado, January 15, 1937 (a second letter). Evandro Lins e Silva, *O Salão dos Passos Perdidos* (Rio de Janeiro: Editora Nova Fronteira, 1997), p. 157.

7. HSP, letter to Natalina (Sobral Pinto), January 11, 1937, in HSP, *Por que defendo os Comunistas*, pp. 37–39. HSP, letters to Affonso Penna Júnior, Eminência, and Alceu Amoroso Lima, January 14, 1937.

8. HSP, letter to Alceu, August 24, 1936.

9. Alceu Amoroso Lima, letter to HSP, n.p., January 15, 1937 (in HSP papers).

10. HSP, "Defesa Prévia de Harry Berger," to Raul Machado, March 29, 1937.

11. David Levinson, letter to Edmundo Miranda Jordão, Rio de Janeiro, February 6, 1937 (in HSP papers). Minna Ewert, letter to HSP, London, June 1, 1937 (in HSP papers).

12. Levinson, letter to Miranda Jordão, February 6, 1937. HSP, letter to Raul Machado, February 11, 1937.

13. HSP, letter to Raul Machado, February 11, 1937.

14. *O Estado de S. Paulo*, February 14, 1937.

15. HSP, letter to Agamemnon (Magalhães), February 13, 1937, in HSP, *Por que defendo os Comunistas*, pp. 70–72. HSP, letter to Raul Machado, February 17, 1937. *O Estado de S. Paulo*, March 17, 1937.

16. HSP, letter to Raul Machado, March 2, 1937, in HSP, *Por que defendo os Comunistas*, pp. 73–81.

17. HSP, letter to Leocádia (Prestes), April 10, 1937. HSP, letters to Raul Machado, March 2, 5, 1937. Minna Ewert, letter to Arthur Ewert (Harry Berger), London, March 24, 1937. HSP, letter to Minna (Ewert), April 27, 1937.

18. P. R. Kimber, letter to HSP, London, n.d. (in HSP papers). HSP, letter to Kimber, April 24, 1937.

19. *O Estado de S. Paulo*, May 8, 1937. HSP, cable to Minna Ewert, May 7, 1937, and letter to her, May 12, 1937.

20. HSP, letter to Philadelpho de Azevedo, May 14, 17, 18, 1937. Philadelpho de Azevedo, letter to Minister of Justice, Rio de Janeiro, May 17, 1937, and F. de Barros Barreto, letter to president of OAB, Rio de Janeiro, May 15, 1937 (copies in HSP papers).

3. BERGER BECOMES DERANGED (JUNE–NOVEMBER 1937)

1. HSP, letter to Minna (Ewert), June 11, 1937. See also HSP, letter to Leocádia (Prestes), June 12, 1937.
2. HSP, letters to Leocádia (Prestes), June 19, July 3, 1937.
3. Leocádia Prestes, letter to HSP, Paris, March 3, 1937. Minna Ewert, letters to HSP and Arthur Ewert, London, June 29, 1937. The Howard League for Penal Reform, letter to HSP, London, May 25, 1937.
4. Minna Ewert, letters to HSP, London, June 1, 29, 1937. J. C. de Macedo Soares, letter to HSP, Rio de Janeiro, June 28, 1937. HSP, letter to Leocádia, July 3, 1937.
5. HSP, letter to Eminência (Cardinal Leme), July 3, 1937. HSP, letter to Presidente da República, July 8, 1937.
6. HSP, letter to Osório (Lopes), July 20, 1937.
7. HSP, letter to Bruno Behrandt (Salvation Army), July 12, 1937. HSP, letter to Minna (Ewert), August 6, 1937.
8. HSP, letter to Minna, August 6, 1937. HSP, letter to Alceu (Amoroso Lima), August 26, 1937.
9. O Estado de S. Paulo, September 9, 1937. Jorge Amado, O Cavaleiro da Esperança, 10th ed. (Rio de Janeiro: Editorial Vitória, 1956), pp. 307–308.
10. HSP, letter to Presidente do Conselho da Ordem, Seção do Distrito Federal, September 11, 1937. O Estado de S. Paulo, September 9, 10, 1937. Hélio Silva, 1937: Todos os Golpes se Parecem (Rio de Janeiro: Editôra Civilização Brasileira, 1970), pp. 213–215.
11. HSP, letter to Almirante Presidente do Supremo Tribunal Militar, September 9, 1937. HSP, "Pelo Appellado Arthur Ernst Ewert ou Harry Berger," May 24, 1937.
12. O Estado de S. Paulo, September 10, 12, 15, 30, 1937. HSP, letter to Mário (Bulhões Pedreira), September 14, 1937.
13. Rubem Braga, "Sobral Pinto, o monstro," O Popular, September 10, 1937.
14. HSP, letters to Leocádia (Prestes) and Elise Ewert, October 11, 1937. Sabo (Elise Ewert), letter to Arthur Ewert, Berlin, August 31, 1937.
15. HSP, letter to Carlos Lassance, October 19, 1937.
16. HSP, letter to (Francisco) Campos, January 4, 1938. Jorge Amado, O Cavaleiro da Esperança, p. 329. "Da Prisão," A Luta de Classe, no. 35 (December 25, 1937). HSP, letter to Leocádia (Prestes), December 4, 1937.
17. Luiz Carlos Prestes, Depoimento perante a Comissão de Inquérito sobre atos delituosos da ditadura (Rio de Janeiro: Editorial Vitória, 1948), pp. 21, 23.

4. THE DEVELOPMENT OF AFFECTION BETWEEN PRESTES AND SOBRAL (MARCH–MAY 1937)

1. O Estado de S. Paulo, March 6, 11, 1936.
2. HSP, "Pelo Appellado Luiz Carlos Prestes" (appeal to the Supremo Tribunal Militar), May 24, 1937, p. 3. HSP, letters to Raul Machado, January 15, 29, 1937.

3. *O Estado de S. Paulo*, February 27, 1937. Luiz Carlos Prestes, *Depoimento perante a Comissão de Inquérito sobre atos delituosos da ditadura* (Rio de Janeiro: Editorial Vitória, 1948), p. 5.

4. Olga Benário Prestes, letter to Leocádia (Prestes), Berlin, February 24, 1937. Leocádia Prestes, letters to HSP, Paris, March 3, 6, 1937. (Letters are in HSP papers.)

5. HSP, letters to Raul Machado, March 11, 12, April 28, 1937. HSP, letters to Leocádia (Prestes), March 12, April 10, 1937.

6. Leocádia Prestes, letter to HSP, Paris, March 20, 1937. Lygia Prestes, letter to Luiz Carlos Prestes, Paris, April 7, 1937. HSP, letters to Leocádia (Prestes), May 7, 12, 28, 1937. HSP, letter to Raul Machado, May 5, 1937.

7. HSP, letter to Raul Machado, April 13, 1937.

8. Luiz Carlos Prestes, thirty-one handwritten pages to HSP, Rio de Janeiro, n.d. (after Macedo Soares became justice minister), repeating thoughts Prestes tried to express on May 4, 1937.

9. HSP, letter to Raul Machado, May 5, 1937. HSP, "Pelo Appellado Luiz Carlos Prestes," May 24, 1937.

10. HSP, letter to Leocádia (Prestes), May 8, 1937.

11. HSP, letter to Leocádia (Prestes), May 28, 1937.

12. Leocádia Prestes, letter to HSP, Paris, June 5, 1937.

5. THE INDEFATIGABLE LEOCÁDIA PRESTES
(JUNE–NOVEMBER 1937)

1. HSP, "Pelo Appellado Luiz Carlos Prestes," May 24, 1937.

2. Leocádia Prestes, letters to HSP, Paris, May 19, July 10, 1937. Leocádia Prestes, letter to Juizes do Supremo Tribunal Militar, Paris, May 14, 1937. HSP, letter to Ministro de Appellação, n.d.

3. HSP, letter to Leocádia (Prestes), July 3, 1937. Leocádia, letter to HSP, Paris, July 10, 1937.

4. Olga Prestes, letter to Luiz Carlos Prestes, Berlin, May 15, 1937. Leocádia Prestes, letter to HSP, Paris, May 29, 1937. HSP, letter to Leocádia, July 17, 1937.

5. Leocádia Prestes, letter to HSP, Paris, April 30, 1937. Eugênio Carvalho do Nascimento, letter to Leocádia Prestes, May 10, 1937, and her letter to him, Paris, July 31, 1937.

6. Leocádia Prestes, letters to HSP, Paris, July 31, August 4, 28, 1937, and letter to José Carlos de Macedo Soares, Paris, August 11, 1937. HSP, letters to Macedo Soares, August 19, September 15, 1937.

7. HSP, letters to Leocádia (Prestes), September 18, 22, 28, 1937.

8. Euzébio de Queiroz Filho, interview, Rio de Janeiro, June 26, 1963.

9. Luiz Carlos Prestes, *Depoimento perante a Comissão de Inquérito sobre atos delituosos da ditadura* (Rio de Janeiro: Editorial Vitória, 1948), p. 19.

10. Ibid., p. 18. *O Estado de S. Paulo*, September 9, 10, 1937. Hélio Silva, *1937: Todos os Golpes se Parecem* (Rio de Janeiro: Editôra Civilização Brasileira, 1970), pp. 213–215. Jorge Amado, *O Cavaleiro da Esperança*, 10th ed. (Rio de Janeiro: Editorial Vitória, 1956), pp. 309–316.

11. HSP, letters to Leocádia (Prestes), September 18, 22, 25, 1937. Leocádia, letter to HSP, Paris, October 20, 1937.

12. HSP, letters (two) to Leocádia (Prestes), December 4, 1937.

6. DEFENDING BARRETO LEITE, GRACILIANO RAMOS, AND OTHERS (1936–1937)

1. HSP, letter to (Luiz Carlos da) Costa Netto, March 8, 1937.

2. HSP, Allegações Finaes (case of Azôr Galvão de Souza), October 2, 1937. See also Eurico Bellens Porto, A Insurreição de 27 de Novembro (Rio de Janeiro: Imprensa Nacional, 1936), p. 222. Azôr Galvão de Souza, letters to Antônio Pereira Braga, n.p., August 9, October 11, 1937. Azôr Galvão de Souza, communications to Presidente do TSN, n.p., November 5, 17, 1937. HSP, letters to Antônio Pereira Braga, August 26, October 1, 2, 1937. HSP, communications to Presidente do STM, August 9, September 8, 23, 27, October 1, 1937. HSP, Razões de Appellação de Azôr Galvão de Souza, November 23, 1937.

3. HSP, communications to TSN (November 17, 1937) and to Justiça Militar (June 22, 1939), appealing the condemnation of Azôr Galvão de Souza.

4. HSP, letter to Eminência (Cardinal Leme), November 26, 1937, and letter to Alceu (Amoroso Lima), November 29, 1937. HSP, communication to Ministro Relator da Appellação 5.203, June 22, 1939, and to Justiça Militar, June 22, 1939. HSP, letter to Azôr Galvão de Souza, February 3, 1940.

5. Bellens Porto, A Insurreição de 27 de Novembro, pp. 104–105. O Estado de S. Paulo, January 7, April 16, 1937.

6. José Gutman, communications to Ministro Relator da Appellação 4.899, August 27, September 4, 1937. HSP, letter to Samuel Gutman, October 26, 1938.

7. "Expulsões," A Classe Operária, Rio de Janeiro, II, no. 196 (December 25, 1935). João Batista Barreto Leite Filho, notes for JWFD, Rio de Janeiro, August 1981, and interview, August 21, 1981. Bellens Porto, A Insurreição de 27 de Novembro, p. 150.

8. HSP, letters to (Luiz Carlos da) Costa Rego, April 5, June 17, 1937.

9. Ibid.

10. O Estado de S. Paulo, June 24, 26, July 1, 1937. Filinto Müller, report to Vargas, Rio de Janeiro, June 18, 1937, in Hélio Silva, 1937: Todos os Golpes se Parecem (Rio de Janeiro: Editôra Civilização Brasileira, 1970), pp. 577–582. HSP, letter to Pedro Bona, June 26, 1937. Pedro Bona, letter to HSP, São Luís, July 19, 1937.

11. Graciliano Ramos' daughter Clara, quoted in Marilene Felinto, "Caminhos de Graciliano," Folha de S. Paulo, October 18, 1992. HSP, letter to TSN, November 4, 1936. Graciliano Ramos, Memórias do Cárcere, 4th ed. (São Paulo: Livraria Martins Editôra, 1960), Part IV (in vol. 2).

12. Ramos, Memórias do Cárcere, vol. 2, pp. 288–291.

13. Ibid. See also HSP, letter to R. Magalhães Júnior, November 3, 1953,

about the role of Graciliano's friend, Rodrigo de Mello Franco Andrade, in persuading Sobral to visit the imprisoned Graciliano, and about Sobral's visits.

14. HSP, letter to TSN, November 4, 1936. HSP, letter to Capitão Chefe de Policia, January 2, 1937.

15. Felinto, "Caminhos de Graciliano." René P. Garay, in *Dictionary of Brazilian Literature*, ed. Irwin Stone, pp. 269–271 (New York, Westport, Conn., and London: Greenwood Press, 1988).

7. CONDEMNING CHURCH SUPPORT OF THE ESTADO NOVO (LATE 1937)

1. HSP, letter to Alceu (Amoroso Lima), December 1, 1937.
2. Ibid.
3. HSP, letter to (Francisco) Campos, November 6, 1937.
4. HSP, letter to (Augusto Frederico) Schmidt, November 19, 1937.
5. HSP, letters to Eminência (Cardinal Leme), November 20, 26, 1937.
6. HSP, letter to Alceu, November 29, 1937.
7. Alceu Amoroso Lima, letter to HSP, n.p., November 29, 1937 (his letters are in HSP papers).
8. HSP, letter to Alceu, December 1, 1937.
9. Alceu Amoroso Lima, letter to HSP, Rio de Janeiro, December 3, 1937.
10. Ibid. HSP, letters to Eminência and Alceu, December 6, 1937.
11. HSP, letter to Eminência, December 9, 1937.
12. HSP, letter to Campos, December 18, 1937.
13. Alceu Amoroso Lima, letter ("confidential") to HSP, December 9, 1937.
14. HSP, letter to Alceu, December 15, 1937.
15. HSP, letter to Alceu, December 31, 1937.

8. DEFENDING CAPTAIN CORTEZ AND MARY AND MÁRIO PEDROSA (1938)

1. HSP, Razões Finaes de Alcebiades Nunes Almeida et al., February 21, 1938. HSP, Pelos Appellantes, March 31, 1938.
2. Eurico Bellens Porto, *A Insurreição de 27 de Novembro* (Rio de Janeiro: Imprensa Nacional, 1936), pp. 184–185. HSP, Defesa Prévia de Amarilio Vieira Cortez, December 23, 1937.
3. HSP, Razões Finaes de Amarilio Vieira Cortez, January 17, 1938.
4. HSP, letter to Alberto de Lemos Basto, January 27, 1938. A. de Lemos Basto, note for HSP, Rio de Janeiro, January 29, 1938 (in HSP papers).
5. Amarilio Vieira Cortez, letter to Alberto de Lemos Basto, Rio de Janeiro, February 9, 1938 (in HSP papers). HSP, Pelo Appellante Amarilio Vieira Cortez, letter to Pedro Borges, March 14, 1938 (in HSP papers).
6. HSP, letter to Pedro Borges, March 11, 1938.
7. Pedro Borges, note for HSP, March 14, 1938 (in HSP papers).

8. HSP, letters to Pedro Borges and Philadelpho de Azevedo, April 7, 1938.

9. *A Situação Nacional: Theses approvadas pelo Comité Central Provisório do Partido Operário Leninista, em Junho de 1937* (loaned to JWFD by Hermínio Sacchetta, São Paulo, 1979). Mário Pedrosa, interviews, Rio de Janeiro, December 4, 1967, June 24, 1979. HSP, Allegações Finaes de Mário Pedrosa, December 23, 1937. HSP, letter to Alberto de Lemos Basto, n.d. Mário Pedrosa entry in CPDOC, *Dicionário Histórico-Biográfico Brasileiro, 1930-1983* (Rio de Janeiro: Editora Forense-Universitária, 1984).

10. HSP, Allegações Finaes de Mário Pedrosa, December 23, 1937.

11. Mary Houston Pedrosa, interview, Rio de Janeiro, June 24, 1979. Arinda Galdo Houston, declaration to the police, January 19, 1938 (Processo 495, Appellação 128, Brazilian National Archives).

12. *Diário da Noite* and *O Estado de S. Paulo*, January 1, 1938. Declarations of Investigator João Gonçalves Guimarães Machado, February 10, 1938. Prontidão 9.942 of January 17, 1938, about Elias Mariano da Silva Lobo. (The last two items are in Processo 495, Brazilian National Archives.)

13. HSP, letter to Francisco Campos, January 10, 1938, in HSP, *Por que defendo os Comunistas* (Belo Horizonte: Universidade Católica de Minas Gerais, 1979), pp. 191-193.

14. HSP, "Mary Houston Pedrosa," February 19, 1938. HSP, letter to Francisco Negrão de Lima, March 14, 1938.

15. Pedro da Cunha Pedrosa, letter to HSP, Rio de Janeiro, June 17, 1938 (in HSP papers).

16. Conclusions of Judge Alberto de Lemos Basto following declarations of Investigator Antônio Alves Filho, February 10, 1938 (Processo 495, Appellação 128, Brazilian National Archives). *O Estado de S. Paulo*, June 28, 1938. Álvaro Paes Leme, interview, São Paulo, July 15, 1979. Mary Houston Pedrosa said of her imprisonment, "It wasn't bad" (interview, June 24, 1979).

17. HSP, letter to (José) Barreto (Filho), March 4, 1941. Mário Pedrosa, interviews, Rio de Janeiro, December 4, 1967, June 24, 1979.

18. HSP, letter to Pasquale Petracconi, October 18, 1938.

IV. In the Aftermath of the 1938 Uprisings (1938-1941)

1. DEFENDING RAYMUNDO PADILHA AND LANARI JÚNIOR (1938)

1. Hélio Silva, *1938: Terrorismo em Campo Verde* (Rio de Janeiro: Editôra Civilização Brasileira, 1971), pp. 46, 135-136, 149-153, with quotations from Jatir de Carvalho Serejo, *Meu Depoimento* (Rio de Janeiro, 1959).

2. Ibid. HSP, Memorial [to the TSN], June 1, 1938.

3. Silva, *1938*, pp. 257-259.

4. HSP, letter to Mário (Bulhões Pedreira), November 19, 1938. Raimundo Padilha entry in CPDOC, *Dicionário Histórico-Biográfico Brasileiro, 1930-1983* (Rio de Janeiro: Editora Forense-Universitária, 1984). Raymundo Padilha, letter to the president of the TSN, August 29, 1938 (in HSP papers).

5. Ibid. HSP, petition to the president of the TSN, July 28, 1938. Silva, *1938*, pp. 53–54.

6. Amaro Lanari Júnior, letter to Judge Costa Netto, August 2, 1938. Amaro Lanari Júnior, petition to the president of the TSN, September 5, 1938. (Both in HSP papers.)

7. Clemente Hungria, letter to JWFD, Rio de Janeiro, December 12, 1997, quoting explanation of *sursis*, or Suspensão Condicional da Pena, in Vicente Cernicchiaro, *Dicionário de Direito Penal*. Evandro Lins e Silva, *O Salão dos Passos Perdidos* (Rio de Janeiro: Editora Nova Fronteira, 1997), pp. 166–167. Amaro Lanari Júnior, petition to the president of the TSN, September 10, 1938 (in HSP papers). HSP, letter to Evandro (Lins e Silva), September 10, 1938. HSP, two letters to Amaro Lanari, September 10, 1938.

8. HSP, letter to Amaro Lanari, October 12, 1938. HSP, letter to Mário (Bulhões Pedreira), November 19, 1938.

2. COLONEL FIGUEIREDO, GENERAL CASTRO, AND YOUTHFUL INTEGRALISTAS (1938)

1. HSP, letters to Raul Machado, September 25, 29, 1938.

2. Hélio Silva, *1938: Terrorismo em Campo Verde* (Rio de Janeiro: Editôra Civilização Brasileira, 1971), pp. 189–191. Alcebiades Delmare, letter to HSP, Rio de Janeiro, July 6, 1938 (in HSP papers). HSP, letter to Raul Machado, October 4, 1938.

3. HSP, document about the case of Renato Rosati, n.d. (January 1939). HSP, letters to Raul Machado, September 29, October 1, 1938.

4. HSP, letter to Raul Machado, September 29, 1938. HSP, letter to TSN, n.d.

5. HSP, letter to Raul Machado, October 4, 1938.

6. HSP, letter to Judge Costa Netto, October 8, 1938.

7. Euclides Figueiredo entry in CPDOC, *Dicionário Histórico-Biográfico Brasileiro, 1930–1983* (Rio de Janeiro: Editora Forense-Universitária, 1984). Silva, *1938*, pp. 163–164, 192–193 (based on interview with Octavio Mangabeira). Israel Souto, declaration (in Brazilian National Archives), quoted in Silva, *1938*, p. 249.

8. Guilherme Figueiredo, interview, Rio de Janeiro, January 11, 1995. Euclydes Figueiredo and others, letters to Judge Antônio Pereira Braga, August 19, September 14, 1938 (in HSP papers).

9. Guilherme Figueiredo, interview, January 11, 1995. Guilherme Figueiredo, "Defesa perante o Tribunal de Segurança Nacional em 1938," in Câmara dos Deputados, *Perfis Parlamentares 23: Euclides Figueiredo, Discursos Parlamentares* (Brasília: Câmara dos Deputados, Centro de Documentação e Informação, 1982), pp. 75–102. Euclydes de Oliveira Figueiredo, petition to president of the TSN, n.d., and Memorial, August 24, 1940 (in HSP papers).

10. Silva, *1938*, p. 246. João Candido Pereira de Castro Júnior entry in *Dicionário Histórico-Biográfico Brasileiro, 1930–1983*.

11. HSP, letter to Costa Netto, October 8, 1938.

12. Castro Júnior entry in *Dicionário Histórico-Biográfico Brasileiro, 1930–1983*. HSP, letter to José Menezes, October 11, 1938.
13. HSP, letter to Annibal Freire, October 12, 1938.

3. GOOD-BYE, ROMANO, OLD FRIEND (JUNE–DECEMBER 1938)

1. *O Estado de S. Paulo* and *Jornal do Brasil*, June 28, 1938.
2. *O Globo*, March 18, 1938. Hélio Silva, *1938: Terrorismo em Campo Verde* (Rio de Janeiro: Editôra Civilização Brasileira, 1971), pp. 90–93.
3. HSP, letter to (Antônio Emílio) Romano, December 1, 1938.
4. *Jornal do Brasil*, August 20, 25, 1938. *O Estado de S. Paulo*, August 23, 25, 26, 1938.
5. Carlos Marighella, *O Estudante Marighella nas Prisões do Estado Novo* (Rio de Janeiro: Editorial Vitória, 1948), pp. 8–12. Casa de Detenção prisoners, letter to Vargas, June 29, 1936 (papers of Hermínio Sacchetta). Silva, *1938*, p. 261.
6. Ananias Serpa, denouncement, *Jornal do Brasil*, August 25, 1938.
7. *O Estado de S. Paulo*, June 28, 1938.
8. *O Estado de S. Paulo*, August 23, 1938. HSP, letter to Romano, December 1, 1938.
9. *O Estado de S. Paulo*, August 24, 26, 1938.
10. HSP, letter to Desembargador Carneiro da Cunha, September 9, 1938.
11. Silva, *1938*, p. 54. HSP, letter to (Francisco) Campos, September 12, 1938.
12. HSP, letter to Mário (Bulhões Pedreira), May 10, 1939. *Correio da Manhã*, November 30, 1938, quoted in HSP, letter to Antônio Baptista Bittencourt, December 7, 1938.
13. HSP, letter to Romano, December 1, 1938.
14. HSP, letter to Antônio Baptista Bittencourt, December 7, 1938. HSP, letter to Fernando, January 5, 1939.

4. DISAGREEING AGAIN WITH ALCEU (1938–1939)

1. "Uma encantadora festa de confraternização nipo-brasileira," *Jornal do Brasil*, July 16, 1938. (Admiral Shinjiro Yamamoto not to be confused with Admiral Isoroku Yamamoto, commander of attack on Pearl Harbor, 1941.)
2. HSP, letter to Alceu Amoroso Lima, July 16, 1938.
3. Ibid.
4. HSP, letter to Exmo. Sr. Embaixador do Japão, July 18, 1938.
5. HSP, letters to Alceu (Amoroso Lima), July 19, 22, 1938.
6. HSP, letter to Alceu, July 22, 1938.
7. Ibid., quoting Alceu.
8. Alceu Amoroso Lima, letter to HSP, Rio de Janeiro, August 28, [1939] (in HSP papers).
9. HSP, letters to Alceu, October 21, 24, 1939.
10. HSP, letter to Alceu, October 24, 1939.

11. HSP, letter to Alceu, October 21, 1939.

12. HSP, letter to Alceu, October 24, 1939.

13. Alceu Amoroso Lima, letter to HSP, n.p., April 12, 1940 (in HSP papers).

5. RETURNING TO TSN CASES (1939–1940)

1. HSP, letter to (Francisco) Campos, November 11, 1938.

2. Evandro Lins e Silva, interview, Rio de Janeiro, January 11, 1995.

3. Decreto-Lei 869 de 18 Novembro de 1938.

4. HSP, letters to Campos and the president of the Conselho of the OAB, December 7, 1938.

5. HSP, letter to Miguel Dias, November 24, 1938.

6. Ibid. HSP, Argumento em favor da absolução do Dr. Gil Guatemozim e do Sr. Cassio Umberto Lanari, February 9, 1939. HSP, O Caso da "Pequena Cruzada," February 6, 1939.

7. HSP, letter to Gabriel (Costa Carvalho), July 11, 1938. Gabriel Costa Carvalho, letter to HSP, São Paulo, November 5, 1940 (in HSP papers). HSP, letters to Lindolpho (Pio da Silva Dias) and (José) Tocqueville (Costa Carvalho), March 3, 1939.

8. HSP, letter to Benjamin (Antunes de Oliveira Filho), April 18, 1939. HSP, letter to Waldemar (de Moraes) and (Augusto Frederico) Schmidt, March 18, 1941.

9. HSP, letter to Alberto, January 24, 1939.

10. HSP, letters to João Pinto do Carmo, August 9, 1939, and to Joaquim Pinto do Carmo, September 9, December 14, 23, 1939, January 8, 19, 1940. HSP, Memorial about Samuel (Teixeira) de Siqueira Magalhães, September 2, 1939.

11. HSP, letter to Samuel Teixeira de Siqueira Magalhães, February 16, 1940.

12. HSP, letters to Luiz (Corrêa de Brito), April 30, May 7, 14, 1940. HSP, letter to Souza Netto, September 10, 1940.

13. Pola Rezende, letter to HSP, n.p., July 31, 1940 (in HSP papers). HSP, letters to Luiz, May 7, June 1, August 7, 1940.

14. Ibid. HSP, letter to Souza Netto, September 10, 1940.

15. HSP, letters to Luiz, August 3, 6, 1940.

16. HSP, letters to Luiz and to (José Joaquim) Cardoso de Mello Netto, August 10, 1940.

17. HSP, letters to Luiz, August 6, 26, 1940.

18. HSP, letters to Luiz and to Souza Netto, September 10, 1940.

6. A PHYSICAL SCUFFLE WITH "HORSE TRAINER" CANEPPA (1938)

1. "O verdugo do povo alemão esta assassinando a filhinha de Prestes!," translation of handbill released in Montevideo (in Hermínio Sacchetta papers). Octavio Brandão, interview, Rio de Janeiro, July 1, 1979. Leocádia Prestes, letter to HSP, Paris, April 27, 1938 (in HSP papers).

2. HSP, letter to Leocádia (Prestes), May 7, 1938. HSP, "Declarações no 14° Distrito Policial," June 1, 1938.

3. Luiz Carlos Prestes, letter to HSP, Casa de Correção, Rio de Janeiro, May 27, 1938 (in HSP papers).

4. HSP, "Declarações," June 1, 1938. HSP, letter to Antônio Baptista Bittencourt (of OAB), June 2, 1938.

5. Ibid.

6. Ibid.

7. HSP, letter to Eminência (Cardinal Leme), June 9, 1938.

8. HSP, letter to Antônio Baptista Bittencourt, June 2, 1938.

9. Ibid.

10. Ibid.

11. HSP, letter to Benjamin (Antunes de Oliveira Filho), June 4, 1938.

12. HSP, letter to Antônio Baptista Bittencourt, June 2, 1938.

13. Card to HSP from Pedro da Cunha Pedrosa, June 7, 1938, and other communications in HSP papers.

14. Carlos da Silva Costa, letters to HSP and Vitório Caneppa, Rio de Janeiro, June 3, 1938 (in HSP papers).

15. HSP, letter to Eminência, June 9, 1938.

16. HSP, letter to Justice Minister, August 5, 1938. HSP, letter to Leocádia, September 16, 1939.

17. HSP, letter to Geraldo (Rocha), June 4, 1938.

18. HSP, letter to (Francisco) Campos, June 17, 1938.

19. HSP, request to the STM president, June 13, 1938. HSP, letters to Justice Minister, July 6, August 5, 1938. HSP, letter to (Francisco) Negrão de Lima, August 5, 1938.

20. HSP, letter to Negrão de Lima and two letters to Justice Minister Campos, August 5, 1938.

21. HSP, letter to Antônio Baptista Bittencourt, August 12, 1938. HSP, letter to Leocádia (Prestes), August 13, 1938.

22. Eduardo Ribeiro Xavier, declaration to the Civil Police of the Federal District, April 10, 1940 (Brazilian National Archives).

23. Luiz Carlos Prestes, 5 Cartas da Prisão (Rio de Janeiro: Edições Horizonte, n.d.).

24. Leocádia Prestes, cable to HSP, Mexico City, November 8, 1938. Minna Ewert, letter to HSP, Mexico City, June 9, 1938. Sabo (Elise Ewert), letter to Arthur Ewert, n.p., March 21, 1938. (All in HSP papers.)

25. HSP, letter to the STM president, September 28, 1938. HSP, letter to Leocádia, December 9, 1938.

26. HSP, letter and document to Ministro Relator, Appellação 4.899, October 3, 1938. HSP, "Pelos Embargantes," addressed to Ministros da STM, November 28, 1938.

27. HSP, letters to Leocádia, December 9, 1938, January 27, 1939. Leocádia Prestes, letter to HSP, Mexico City, August 31, 1939 (in HSP papers).

7. BERGER AND PRESTES (1939–1941)

1. HSP, letters (two) to Ministro da Justiça, January 26, 1939.
2. HSP, letter to (Francisco) Campos, September 14, 1939.
3. HSP, letter to Campos, October 23, 1939.
4. HSP, letter to (Francisco) Negrão (de Lima), March 4, 1941.
5. José Joffily, *Harry Berger* (Rio de Janeiro and Curitiba: Editora Paz e Terra and Universidade Federal do Paraná, 1987), p. 116. Leoncio Basbaum, interview, São Paulo, November 9, 1967. João Batista Barreto Leite Filho, interview, Rio de Janeiro, June 28, 1981.
6. HSP, letters to Campos, January 26, March 13, May 3, 11, 1939.
7. HSP, letters to Leocádia (Prestes), May 3, June 24, 1939. HSP, letter to Luiz Carlos Prestes, June 19, 1939.
8. HSP, letter to Leocádia, June 24, 1939. Luiz Carlos Prestes, letter to Auditor da 3ª Auditoria da 1ª Região Militar, Rio de Janeiro, June 29, 1939 (in HSP papers).
9. Leocádia Prestes, letter to HSP, México, D.F., August 31, 1939 (in HSP papers).
10. HSP, letter to Leocádia, September 16, 1939.
11. HSP, letter to 3ª Auditoria da Justiça Militar, April 2, May 17, 1940. *Jornal do Brasil* and *O Estado de S. Paulo*, April 18, 1940.
12. Eurico Gaspar Dutra, letter to Auditor da 3ª Auditoria da 1ª Região Militar, June 9, 1941 (in HSP papers).
13. HSP, Razões do Appellado, Luiz Carlos Prestes, July 19, 1941.

8. THE CASE OF THE ELZA FERNANDES MURDER (1940–1941)

1. *Jornal do Brasil*, April 14, 16, 1940. Sebastião Francisco, declaration to Civil Police of the Federal District, May 13, 1940 (in Brazilian National Archives). Sebastião Francisco, interview, São Paulo, August 26, 1981. Davino Francisco dos Santos, interview, São Paulo, November 9, 1968.
2. Declarations of Manuel Severiano Cavalcante, Eduardo Ribeiro Xavier, Francisco Natividade Lima, and Honório de Freitas Guimarães to Civil Police of the Federal District, April 1940 (in Brazilian National Archives). *Jornal do Brasil*, April 25, 27, 28, 1940.
3. Honório de Freitas Guimarães, letter to Luiz Carlos Prestes, n.p., February 14, 1936. Prestes, letter to "Caro Amigo" (Freitas Guimarães), n.p., February 16, 1936. (Both letters in Brazilian National Archives.)
4. B. (Lauro Reginaldo da Rocha), letter to G. (Prestes), n.p., February 20, 1936 (in Brazilian National Archives).
5. G. (Prestes), letter to Compos. do S.N. (Companions of the National Secretaryship of the PCB), n.p., February 19, 1936 (in Brazilian National Archives). João Batista Barreto Leite Filho wrote in 1981 to JWFD about these "letters of Prestes, etc.": "I identified the handwriting of the author and advised my companions . . . on the *Pedro I* that the letters were authentic." Communists involved in the Elza Fernandes case verified the correspondence after their arrest in 1940.

6. *Jornal do Brasil,* April 14, 16, 1940.

7. *Jornal do Brasil* and *O Estado de S. Paulo,* May 15, 1940.

8. Luiz Carlos Prestes, document for Raul Campello Machado, November 25, 1940 (in HSP papers). Luiz Carlos Prestes, letter to Augusto Maynard Gomes, October 10, 1940 (in HSP papers). HSP, letter to Augusto Maynard Gomes, October 22, 1940.

9. Luiz Carlos Prestes, document for Augusto Maynard Gomes, November 5, 1940.

10. Geraldo Mello Mourão, interview, Rio de Janeiro, August 13, 1979. Heron P. Pinto, *Nos Subterraneos do Estado Novo* (Rio de Janeiro: n.p., 1950), pp. 85-89, quoting from *O Globo,* March 14, 1945. Hermínio Sacchetta, interviews, São Paulo, August 19, December 24, 1979. *Jornal do Brasil,* April 14, 16, 1940. *O Estado de S. Paulo,* April 23, 24, 26, 1940. Sebastião Francisco, interview, São Paulo, August 26, 1981.

11. Pinto, *Nos Subterraneos do Estado Novo,* pp. 88-89. Jorge Amado, *O Cavaleiro da Esperança,* 10th ed. (Rio de Janeiro: Editorial Vitória, 1956), p. 333.

12. HSP, interview, August 6, 1979. Dênis de Moraes and Francisco Viana, *Prestes: Lutas e Autocríticas* (Petrópolis: Editora Vozes, 1982), p. 88.

13. *O Estado de S. Paulo,* November 8, 1940. Amado, *O Cavaleiro da Esperança,* p. 346.

14. Luiz Carlos Prestes, document for Raul Campello Machado, November 25, 1940.

15. HSP, letter to (Francisco) Negrão (de Lima), March 4, 1941.

16. HSP, letter to Edmundo (Luz Pinto), February 20, 1941. HSP, letter to (José Eduardo de) Macedo Soares, February 18, 1941.

17. HSP, letter to Edmundo, February 20, 1941. HSP, letter to Leocádia (Prestes), January 13, 1941.

18. HSP, letter to (José Eduardo de) Macedo Soares, February 18, 1941. HSP, letter to Edmundo, February 20, 1941.

19. HSP, letter to Leocádia, January 13, 1941.

V. Dealing with the Economia Popular and Matarazzo (1940–1944)

I. EARLY POLEMICS IN "PELOS DOMÍNIOS DO DIREITO" (1940–1941)

1. HSP, "Pelos Domínios do Direito," *Jornal do Commercio,* May 31, 1941.

2. HSP, letter to Plínio Casado, July 29, 1940. HSP, letter to Francisco (de) Assis Barbosa, April 8, 1942.

3. HSP, "O crime de possuir ou guardar armas de guerra," in "Pelos Domínios do Direito," *Jornal do Commercio,* August 31, 1940.

4. "Pelos Domínios do Direito," *Jornal do Commercio,* September 21, October 5, 12, 19, 1940.

5. Antônio Pereira Braga, quoted in HSP, "Pelos Domínios do Direito," September 21, October 12, 1940.

6. HSP, letter to Raul (Machado), October 29, 1940.

7. HSP, letters to Raul (Machado), October 26, 29, 1940.

8. HSP, letter to Raul (Machado), October 29, 1940.

9. HSP, letter to Souza Netto, September 10, 1940.

10. Plínio Barreto entry in CPDOC, *Dicionário Histórico-Biográfico Brasileiro, 1930–1983* (Rio de Janeiro: Editora Forense-Universitária, 1984). HSP, letter to José Maria (MacDowell da Costa), March 25, 1939. HSP, "O estilo forense," in "Pelos Domínios do Direito," *Jornal do Commercio*, July 4, 1941.

11. Plínio Barreto, "Vida Forense," *O Jornal*, April 5, 1941, quoted in HSP, "Das injúrias irrogadas em juizo," in "Pelos Domínios do Direito," *Jornal do Commercio*, July 5, 1941.

12. HSP, "Pelos Domínios do Direito," July 5, 26, 1941. Plínio Barreto, "Vida Forense," *Diário de S. Paulo*, July 12, 1941, quoted in HSP, "Pelos Domínios do Direito," July 26, 1941.

13. HSP, letter to Plínio Barreto, August 5, 1941.

14. HSP, letter to Luiz (Corrêa de Brito), October 5, 1940.

15. HSP, letter to Alceu (Amoroso Lima), August 24, 1938.

16. San Tiago Dantas entry in *Dicionário Histórico-Biográfico Brasileiro, 1930–1983*.

17. HSP, "O Direito em face da política," in "Pelos Domínios do Direito," *Jornal do Commercio*, November 8, 1941, quoting San Tiago Dantas.

18. HSP, "O Direito em face da política," in "Pelos Domínios do Direito."

19. HSP, letter to Leonel (Franca), November 10, 1941.

2. OBSERVATIONS ABOUT THE EARLY YEARS OF THE WAR (1939–1941)

1. HSP, letter to (Francisco) Campos, December 22, 1939.

2. Ibid.

3. HSP, letters to Luiz (Corrêa de Brito), July 30, December 9, 1940.

4. HSP, "A confraternisação juridica dos povos," in "Pelos Domínios do Direito," *Jornal do Commercio*, December 28, 1940.

5. HSP, letter to (José) Barreto (Filho), February 4, 1941.

6. HSP, letter to Narcélio (de Queiroz), April 15, 1941.

7. HSP, "Os povos christãos, e o imperialismo japonês," in "Pelos Domínios do Direito," *Jornal do Commercio*, December 20, 1941.

3. IMMIGRANTS AND MISSIONARIES (1939–1943)

1. HSP, letters to (Francisco) Campos, May 26, June 27, July 14, 1939.

2. HSP, letter to Monteiro, July 31, 1941.

3. HSP, letter to Presidente da República, August 4, 1942. HSP, letter to Ministro da Justiça, n.d. HSP, letter to Faustino E. Jorge (of Buenos Aires), August 13, 1942.

4. HSP, "O sacerdócio e a legislação sobre estrangeiros," in "Pelos Domínios do Direito," *Jornal do Commercio*, September 27, 1941.

5. Ibid.

6. HSP, letter to Arcebispo de Bello-Horizonte Antônio dos Santos Cabral, February 11, 1942.

7. HSP, letter to Afrânio Peixoto, September 25, 1941.

8. Alceu Amoroso Lima, confidential letter to HSP, Rio de Janeiro, August 7, 1941 (in HSP papers).

9. HSP, letter to Wilson (Salazar), January 24, 1942. HSP, letter to (Henrique) Hargreaves, February 10, 1942.

10. HSP, letter to Motta and Edith, and letter to Abel, both dated January 14, 1942. HSP, letter to Nair and Castello, January 5, 1942. HSP, letter to Motta, August 1, 1942.

11. HSP, letter to João Franzen, March 3, 1942. HSP, letter to Sr. Arcebispo D. Antônio (dos Santos Cabral), February 25, 1942. HSP, letter to Lara Rezende, February 24, 1942. HSP, letter to Tancredo Martins, February 24, 1942. HSP, letter to Caio, February 25, 1942. HSP, letter to (Francisco) Campos, February 25, 1942.

12. HSP, letter to Joel Silveira, January 16, 1943. (The interview with the bishop was in *Diretrizes*, October 1, 1942.)

13. Osório Borba, "Como um alemão ensina história nas escolas brasileiras," *Diário de Notícias*, January 17, 1943.

14. HSP, letter to Osório Borba, January 18, 1943.

15. HSP, "Missionário Católico e a segurança nacional," in "Pelos Domínios do Direito," *Jornal do Commercio*, February 27, 1943.

16. HSP, letter to (Emílio) Ippolito, July 8, 1943. HSP, letter to Raphael de Barros Monteiro, June 15, 1943. HSP, letter to J. C. de Azevedo Marques, June 23, 1943.

17. Ibid. HSP, letters to Noé Azevedo, June 23, 26, 1943.

18. HSP, letter to Desembargador Presidente Manuel Carlos de Figueiredo Ferraz, June 26, 1943. HSP, letter to (Emílio) Ippolito, June 29, 1943. HSP, letter to Pedro (de Oliveira Ribeiro Sobrinho), July 7, 1943.

19. HSP, letters to (Emílio) Ippolito, June 29, July 8, 1943.

4. ECONOMIA POPULAR CASES (1940–1942)

1. HSP, "O sindicato em face da lei da economia popular," in "Pelos Domínios do Direito," *Jornal do Commercio*, July 19, 1941.

2. HSP, letter to Ribas, September 21, 1940.

3. Francisco Giannattasio, Onofre Grasiano, and Paulo Uras, document for Raul Campello Machado, August 17, 1940 (in HSP papers). HSP, letter to Souza Netto, October 2, 1940.

4. HSP, letter to Souza Netto, August 19, 1940. Paulo Uras, letter to a sister, Presídio Especial, São Paulo, October 1940 (in HSP papers).

5. HSP, letter to Souza Netto, September 2, 1940.

6. Souza Netto, letter to HSP, São Paulo, September 4, 1940 (in HSP papers). Paulo Uras, letter to a sister, October 1940.

7. HSP, correspondence with Paulo Uras and Souza Netto, October and November 1940 (in HSP papers). HSP, letters to (Barros) Barreto, Raul (Machado), and Pedro Borges, November 9, 1940.

8. HSP, letter to Theodoro Pereira Raymundo, May 13, 1941.

9. HSP, letters to (Alfredo) Miranda Rodrigues and Barros Barreto, December 2, 1940. HSP, letters to José de Castro Nunes, Annibal Freire, and Laudo de Camargo, January 22, 1941.

10. HSP, letter to Cardoso, July 26, 1941.
11. HSP, letter to Antônio de Almeida, December 14, 1940.
12. Evandro Lins e Silva, *O Salão dos Passos Perdidos* (Rio de Janeiro: Editora Nova Fronteira, 1997), pp. 130–132. Evandro Lins e Silva, interview, Rio de Janeiro, January 11, 1995. Roberto Sobral Pinto Ribeiro, interview, Rio de Janeiro, January 12, 1995.
13. Ibid.
14. HSP, letters to José de Sampaio Moreira and Mário (Bulhões Pedreira), December 31, 1941.
15. Lins e Silva, *O Salão dos Passos Perdidos*, p. 132.
16. HSP, "Memorial" (about Appellação 572), September 6, 1940. HSP, correspondence with Nasr Fayad, Alfredo Fayad, Jair Negrão de Lima, Antônio J. Azzi, and Michael Gabriel, 1940–1941. Alfredo Fayad, document for Antônio Pereira Braga, December 12, 1940 (in HSP papers).
17. HSP, letters to Annibal Freire, Laudo de Camargo, Castro Nunes, José Linhares, Orozimbo Nonato, Bento de Faria, and Waldemar Falcão, January 6, 1942. HSP, letter to STF President Eduardo Espínola, January 20, 1942, in "Os deveres árduos do jurista," in "Pelos Domínios do Direito," *Jornal do Commercio*, January 24, 1942.
18. HSP, letter to Jair Negrão de Lima, February 2, 1942.

5. JUDGE MIRANDA RODRIGUES BREAKS RELATIONS WITH SOBRAL (DECEMBER 1941)

1. HSP, "A Igreja perante o Tribunal de Segurança Nacional," in "Pelos Domínios do Direito," *Jornal do Commercio*, December 27, 1941.
2. Ibid.
3. HSP, letter to (Augusto Frederico) Schmidt, January 2, 1942, containing note of HSP to Comandante Miranda Rodrigues dated December 27, 1941. Alfredo Miranda Rodrigues, letter to HSP, Rio de Janeiro, December 29, 1941, in "Pelos Domínios do Direito," *Jornal do Commercio*, January 24, 1942.
4. See HSP, letter to Schmidt, January 2, 1942, and "Pelos Domínios do Direito," January 24, 1942, both containing HSP, letter to Alfredo Miranda Rodrigues, December 31, 1941.
5. HSP, letter to Schmidt, January 2, 1942.
6. HSP, letter to Eduardo Espínola, January 20, 1942, in "Os árduos deveres do jurista," in "Pelos Domínios do Direito," *Jornal do Commercio*, January 24, 1942. *A Noite*, January 15, 1942.
7. Ibid.
8. HSP, letter to (José de) Castro Nunes, January 15, 1942. HSP, letter to Eduardo Espínola, January 15, 1942, including quotation from Pedro da Cunha Pedrosa, letter to HSP, December 27, 1941, and quotations from other letters.
9. HSP, letters to (Francisco Tavares da) Cunha Mello, January 16, 1942, Natalina (Sobral Pinto), January 17, 1942, and Tarquino Ribeiro, January 27, 1942. Tarquino Ribeiro's refusal to handle TSN cases is mentioned in HSP's legal document (about Christophoro Ozorio de Miranda), May 28, 1938.

10. HSP, "Pelos Domínios do Direito," January 24, 1942, including citation of Decree 1,393 preventing the TSN president from participating in STF cases "judged or to be judged by the TSN."

11. HSP, "Pelos Domínios do Direito," January 24, 1942.

12. Ibid. HSP, letter to Plínio Barreto, February 2, 1942.

6. SOBRAL BREAKS RELATIONS WITH ALL THE TSN JUDGES
(JULY 1942)

1. HSP, letters to Erônides de Carvalho, June 3, 6, 1942. (All documents about the case are shown in HSP, *Autópsia de uma calúnia* [Rio de Janeiro: Jornal do Commercio, Rodrigues & Cia., 1942].)

2. HSP, letter to Paulo Filho, June 16, 1942. HSP, *Autópsia de uma calúnia*, pp. 95–99.

3. Ibid.

4. HSP, letter to Augusto Pereira, July 18, 1942. HSP, *Autópsia de uma calúnia*, pp. 135–140.

5. HSP, letter to Erônides (de Carvalho), June 8, 1942. HSP, letter to Paulo Filho, June 16, 1942.

6. HSP, letter to Paulo Filho, June 16, 1942.

7. HSP, letters to Erônides (de Carvalho) and Raul (Machado), June 8, 1942.

8. HSP, letter to Erônides, June 9, 1942.

9. HSP, letter to Paulo Filho, June 16, 1942.

10. HSP, letter to (Antônio Pereira) Braga, June 26, 1942. HSP, letter to Augusto Pereira, July 18, 1942.

11. HSP, letters to Raul Campello Machado, July 21, 1942, and to Antônio Pereira Braga, July 22, 1942. HSP, defense argument, in HSP, *Autópsia de uma calúnia*, pp. 117–131 (see also p. 103). HSP, letter to Augusto Pereira, July 18, 1942.

12. HSP, letter to Augusto Pereira, July 18, 1942. Augusto Pereira, letter to Heronides de Carvalho, Federal District Prison, July 13, 1942, in HSP, *Autópsia de uma calúnia*, pp. 133–135.

13. HSP, letter to Augusto Pereira, July 18, 1942.

14. HSP, letter to Raul Campello Machado, July 21, 1942.

15. HSP, letters to Antônio Pereira Braga, July 22, 1942, and to Pedro Borges da Silva, July 23, 1942.

16. HSP, letters to Adroaldo (Mesquita da Costa), January 16, February 11, 1943.

17. Miguel Álvaro Osório de Almeida entry in CPDOC, *Dicionário Histórico-Biográfico Brasileiro, 1930–1983* (Rio de Janeiro: Editora Forense-Universitária, 1984).

18. HSP, letter to Miguel Álvaro Osório de Almeida, January 28, 1943. HSP, "Resposta a Questionário formulado pelo Consul Miguel Álvaro Osório de Almeida."

19. HSP, "Resposta a Questionário formulado pelo Consul Miguel Álvaro Osório de Almeida."

7. SOBRAL VERSUS MATARAZZO (1936–1944)

1. HSP, Memorial, March 31, 1937. Max Naegeli Júnior, letters to JWFD, Cabo Frio, May 11, 29, July 7, 1998.

2. HSP, letter to Narcélio (de Queiroz), April 9, 1941. HSP, letter to Max (Naegeli Júnior), July 8, 1939.

3. HSP, Memorial, March 31, 1937. HSP, letter to Pedro (de Oliveira Ribeiro Sobrinho), December 16, 1939. HSP, Nulidade do Processo, May 5, 1944.

4. Ibid.

5. HSP, Nulidade do Processo, May 5, 1944.

6. HSP, letter to Narcélio (de Queiroz), April 9, 1941. HSP, Memorial, March 31, 1937.

7. HSP, letter to Narcélio, April 9, 1941.

8. HSP, confidential letter to (Horácio) Lafer, November 18, 1938. Max Naegeli Júnior, letter to JWFD, May 11, 1998.

9. HSP, letters to Pedro (de Oliveira Ribeiro Sobrinho), October 21, 1941, December 15, 1939. HSP, letter to Narcélio, April 9, 1941. HSP, letter to João Neves (da Fontoura), October 21, 1941. HSP, letter to Gabriel Passos, April 30, 1941. Max Naegeli Júnior, letter to JWFD, May 11, 1998.

10. HSP, letter to (Horácio) Lafer, November 22, 1938. HSP, letter to Max (Naegeli Júnior), May 9, 1939.

11. HSP, letters to Max (Naegeli Júnior), May 4, 9, July 8, 14, 1939.

12. Ibid. HSP, letter to Pedro (de Oliveira Ribeiro Sobrinho), December 15, 1939.

13. HSP, letter to Pedro, December 28, 1939.

14. Ibid. HSP, letter to Mário (Bulhões Pedreira), December 29, 1939.

15. HSP, letter to Orozimbo Nonato, July 15, 1941. HSP, letters to Pedro, February 3, March 15, 1940. HSP, letter to Souza Netto, March 15, 1940.

16. HSP, letter to Narcélio, April 9, 1941. HSP, letter to Pedro, April 3, 1941.

17. HSP, letter to Pedro, April 19, 1941. HSP, letter to (Luiz) Gallotti, April 28, 1941. HSP, letter to Gabriel Passos, April 30, 1941.

18. HSP, letters to Orozimbo Nonato, Castro Nunes, and Laudo de Camargo, May 31, 1941. HSP, letters to Barros Barreto, José Linhares, Annibal Freire, and (Octavio) Kelly, June 2, 1941.

19. HSP, letters to João Neves (da Fontoura) and Pedro, October 21, 1941.

20. Ibid. HSP, letter to Affonso Penna Júnior, October 7, 1941.

21. Ibid. HSP, letter to Waldemar Falcão, November 13, 1941. HSP, letter to José Linhares, November 21, 1941.

22. HSP, letter to Supreme Court justices, October and November 1941. HSP, letter to Afrânio (Antonio da Costa), February 3, 1942.

23. HSP, letter to Afrânio (Antonio da Costa), February 3, 1942.

24. HSP, letters to *desembargadores*, February 3, 10, 1942.

25. HSP, letter to Pedro (de Oliveira Ribeiro Sobrinho), March 25, 1942. HSP, letter to Waldemar Falcão, June 27, 1942.

26. HSP, letters to Orozimbo Nonato, Waldemar Falcão, and José Linhares, June 27, 1942. HSP, letter to Bahouth, July 1, 1942.

27. HSP, letters to Hugo Carneiro and Alfredo Cavalcanti, August 7, 1943.
28. HSP, letters to Angelo, March 23, 29, 1944. HSP, letter to Abelardo (Cardoso), March 24, 1944.
29. HSP, letter to (Jorge Dyott) Fontenelle, August 20, 1951. Roberto Sobral Pinto Ribeiro, interviews, Rio de Janeiro, December 28, 30, 1995, January 2, 1996. HSP, letter to Cecy, August 29, 1951.

VI. Giving Attention to International Matters (1942–1943)

1. BRAZIL BREAKS RELATIONS WITH THE AXIS (JANUARY 1942)

1. HSP, letter to Itiberê de Moura, January 24, 1942.
2. HSP, letter to Itiberê de Moura, January 28, 1942. HSP, letter to (José) Vicente (de Souza), January 29, 1942.
3. HSP, "Consciência jurídica e decisão política," in "Pelos Domínios do Direito," Jornal do Commercio, April 11, 1942.
4. Ibid. HSP, "O instituto da não intervenção no direito internacional," in "Pelos Domínios do Direito," Jornal do Commercio, April 25, 1942.
5. HSP, letters to Francisco (de) Assis Barbosa, March 28, April 8, 1942.
6. HSP, letters to Francisco (de) Assis Barbosa, April 8, 11, 1942.
7. "Declaração dos Princípios," typed, showing 120 typed signatures, including that of HSP, though not authorized by him (in HSP papers). See also Diretrizes, June 11, 1942.
8. Eurico Gaspar Dutra, letter to Getúlio Vargas, Rio de Janeiro, June 15, 1942, in the Vargas papers at the Centro de Pesquisa e Documentação de História Contemporânea do Brasil (CPDOC) at the Fundação Getúlio Vargas, Rio de Janeiro.
9. "No sentido da guerra atual para os juristas," in "Pelos Domínios do Direito," Jornal do Commercio, May 9, 1942.
10. Ibid.
11. Vasco Leitão da Cunha, interview, Washington, D.C., June 24, 1966. Alzira Vargas do Amaral Peixoto, Chapter 8 of "A Vida de Getúlio Contada por Sua Filha, Alzira Vargas, ao Jornalista Raul Giudicelli," Fatos & Fotos, August 3, 1963. Cable, Jefferson Caffery to U.S. Secretary of State, Rio de Janeiro, July 20, 1942 (National Archives, Washington, D.C.).
12. HSP, letter to Francisco Campos, August 12, 1942.
13. Ibid.
14. HSP, letter to Atilio Denys, July 30, 1942. Davino Francisco dos Santos, A Marcha Vermelha (São Paulo: Saraiva, S.A., 1948), pp. 487–488. Edmundo Moniz, interview, Rio de Janeiro, December 8, 1967.
15. HSP, letter to Atilio Denys, July 30, 1942.

2. PREPARING TO ATTEND THE AMERICAN CATHOLIC SEMINAR (JULY–AUGUST 1942)

1. HSP, letter to Eminência, July 25, 1942.
2. Edward Mooney, letter (and program) to HSP, quoted in "O problema

da civilização em face do Christianismo," in "Pelos Domínios do Direito," *Jornal do Commercio,* July 18, 1942.

3. HSP, "O problema da civilização em face do Christianismo."

4. HSP, letter to Eminência, July 25, 1942.

5. Sebastião Leme, telegram to HSP, quoted in HSP, letter to Antônio dos Santos Cabral, July 30, 1942. HSP, letter to Eminência, July 30, 1942.

6. HSP, letter to Antônio dos Santos Cabral, July 30, 1942. HSP, letter to José Caspar d'Affonseca, n.d. HSP, letter to Pedro (de Oliveira Ribeiro Sobrinho), August 8, 1942.

7. HSP, letter to Edward Mooney, August 5, 1942.

8. "'O Congresso Católico de Washington Não Será Uma Romaria,' a posição dos Católicos . . . ," interview of HSP, *Diretrizes* 5, no. III, August 13, 1942.

9. Ibid.

10. Ibid.

11. HSP, letters to R. A. McGowan, August 8, 15, 1942.

12. HSP, "Pelos Domínios do Direito," *Jornal do Commercio,* August 8, 1942.

13. Ibid., August 15, 1942.

14. HSP, letter to Paulo Filho, August 19, 1942.

3. THE AMERICAN SEMINAR AND THE DEATH OF CARDINAL LEME (1942–1943)

1. HSP, "Os católicos do continente americano em face da crise da civilização," in "Pelos Domínios do Direito," *Jornal do Commercio,* September 26, 1942. HSP, letter to Pedro Sinzig, November 19, 1942.

2. HSP, "A nova ordem mundial," in "Pelos Domínios do Direito," *Jornal do Commercio,* October 31, 1942. HSP, letter to (Richard) Pattee, October 31, 1942.

3. HSP, letter to Pattee, October 31, 1942. HSP, "Os católicos do continente americano em face da crise da civilização." HSP, letter to Hildebrando (Leal), October 6, 1942.

4. HSP, "Os católicos do continente americano em face da crise da civilização."

5. Ibid.

6. HSP, "A nova ordem mundial."

7. HSP, "A organização internacional futura," in "Pelos Domínios do Direito," *Jornal do Commercio,* November 7, 1942.

8. HSP, "A nova ordem mundial."

9. HSP, letter to R. A. McGowan, September 26, 1942. HSP, letter to Pattee, October 31, 1942. HSP, letter to (Armando) Câmara, November 12, 1942.

10. HSP, "A organização internacional futura."

11. HSP in "Pelos Domínios do Direito," *Jornal do Commercio,* August 21, 1942.

12. HSP, "O apostolado do bispo," in "Pelos Domínios do Direito," *Jornal do Commercio,* October 24, 1942.

13. HSP, telegrams to Jayme Câmara, July 12, 1943. Jaime Câmara entry in CPDOC, *Dicionário Histórico-Biográfico Brasileiro, 1930–1983* (Rio de Janeiro: Editora Forense-Universitária, 1984).

14. Roberto Sobral Pinto Ribeiro, e-mail message to JWFD, Rio de Janeiro, August 14, 2000. HSP, letter to Richard Pattee, July 5, 1948.

15. Ação Católica Brasileira entry in *Dicionário Histórico-Biográfico Brasileiro, 1930–1983.* Emanuel de Kadt, *Catholic Radicals in Brazil* (London and New York: Oxford University Press, 1970), p. 59.

16. HSP, letter to Alceu (Amoroso Lima), November 12, 1943.

17. Ibid.

4. QUESTIONS RAISED AFTER BRAZIL'S DECLARATION OF WAR (1942–1943)

1. HSP, letter to Jorge Amado, November 3, 1942.

2. HSP, "O Direito e a guerra," in "Pelos Domínios do Direito," *Jornal do Commercio,* October 10, 1942. HSP, letter to (João Batista) Barreto Leite Filho, September 28, 1942.

3. HSP, letter to Barreto Leite Filho, September 28, 1942.

4. HSP, letter to Barreto Leite Filho, October 1, 1942.

5. Ibid.

6. HSP, letter to Alceu (Amoroso Lima), October 10, 1942.

7. HSP, letter to Jorge Amado, September 29, 1942.

8. Ibid.

9. HSP, letter to Jorge Amado, November 3, 1942. HSP, letter to Alceu, November 23, 1942. Alceu Amoroso Lima, letter to Jorge Amado, Rio de Janeiro, November 27, 1942, in *Folha da Manhã,* September 25, 1949.

10. HSP, letter to Jorge Amado, November 3, 1942.

11. Ibid.

12. HSP, letters to Arthur Bernardes, November 23, 1942, Tarquinio, November 25, 1942, Lucia Miguel Pereira, November 25, 1942, Murillo Miranda, November 30, 1942, and Hamilton Nogueira, December 2, 1942. HSP, letter to Álvaro Lins, November 30, 1942. HSP, letters to (Augusto Frederico) Schmidt and Leonel Franca, November 24, 1942.

13. HSP, letter to Alceu (Amoroso Lima), November 23, 1942.

14. Alceu Amoroso Lima, letter to Jorge Amado, Rio de Janeiro, November 27, 1942, in *Folha da Manhã,* September 25, 1949.

15. HSP, letter to Leocádia Prestes, November 14, 1942. "I Talk to Prestes" (based on a letter from Blas Roca), *World News and Views* 22, no. 30 (July 25, 1942).

16. HSP, letter to Leocádia Prestes, November 14, 1942.

17. "Coordenação administrativa e autonomia judiciária," in "Pelos Domínios do Direito," *Jornal do Commercio,* November 28, 1942.

18. HSP, letter to Sr. Embaixador do Governo de Sua Majestade Britânica, July 26, 1943. HSP, letter to Nuncio Apostólico, July 31, 1943.

19. HSP, letter to (Augusto Frederico) Schmidt, July 26, 1943.

20. HSP, letter to Afrânio Peixoto, July 28, 1943.

5. THE LAW OFFICE: AN "AFFECTIONATE FAMILY" LOSES
RAYMUNDO (1943)

1. HSP, letter to (Maurício) Graccho Cardoso, January 30, 1943. HSP, notes to Oswaldo (Murgel de Rezende), Mário (Bulhões Pedreira), and Evandro (Lins e Silva), January 30, 1943. Before Oswaldo Rezende was replaced as Holck's lawyer, Sobral declined the Holck case in deference to Rezende.

2. Manuel Rabello entry in CPDOC, *Dicionário Histórico-Biográfico Brasileiro, 1930–1983* (Rio de Janeiro: Editora Forense-Universitária, 1984).

3. HSP, letter to Manoel Rabello, July 13, 1943.

4. Ibid.

5. HSP, letter to Aulette (Albuquerque Silva do Valle), September 29, 1943.

6. Ibid.

7. Ibid.

8. Roberto Sobral Pinto Ribeiro, interview, Rio de Janeiro, January 13, 1995.

9. HSP, letter to Raymundo (Lopes Machado), January 25, 1943.

10. HSP, letter to Gabriel (Costa Carvalho), February 8, 1943. HSP, letter to (Francisco) Monteiro (Filho), February 10, 1943.

11. HSP, letters to Gabriel, Wilson (Salazar), and Henrique, February 9, 1943. HSP, letter to Monteiro (Filho), February 10, 1943. HSP, letter to José (Tocqueville Costa Carvalho Filho), July 31, 1943.

12. Nélson de Melo entry in *Dicionário Histórico-Biográfico Brasileiro, 1930–1983*.

13. HSP, letters to Max Hamers, November 5, 9, 1943. Receipt for Max Hamers, November 5, 1943.

14. HSP, letter to Max Hamers, November 5, 1943.

6. PRESTES' SITUATION AT THE TIME OF LEOCÁDIA'S DEATH (1943)

1. HSP, letters to Leocádia Prestes, February 20, 1943, and Tenente Caneppa, December 26, 1942, February 22, March 2, 6, 1943.

2. Ibid. HSP, letter to Tenente Caneppa, May 4, 1943.

3. HSP, letter to Lygia Prestes, April 20, 1943.

4. Ibid.

5. Ibid. HSP, letter to Tenente Caneppa, May 4, 1943.

6. HSP, letter to Tenente Caneppa, May 4, 1943.

7. HSP, letters to Tenente Caneppa, May 4, 8, 1943.

8. HSP, letter to Tenente Caneppa, June 3, 1943.

9. Pedro Motta Lima, "Março de 1945," in Antonio J. Osorio et al., *Prestes: Estudos E Depoimentos* (n.p.: Comissão Central do Cinquentenário de Luiz Carlos Prestes, ca. 1948), p. 74. Carlos de Lima Cavalcanti, interview, Rio de Janeiro, August 1, 1963.

10. Luiz Carlos Prestes, speech in Congress, in *Tribuna Popular*, March 28, 1946. Luiz Carlos Prestes, *Problemas Atuais da Democracia* (Rio de Janeiro: Editorial Vitória, n.d.), p. 292.

11. HSP, letters to Tenente Caneppa, July 21, 22, 29, 1943.

12. HSP, cable to Anibal Escalanti, *Diario Hoy*, Habana, Cuba, September 28, 1943. HSP, letter to A. Marcondes Filho, November 27, 1943.

13. HSP, letter to Alceu (Amoroso Lima), January 3, 1944.

7. THE MANIFESTO OF THE MINEIROS (OCTOBER 1943)

1. Carolina Nabuco, *A Vida de Virgílio de Melo Franco* (Rio de Janeiro: Livraria José Olympio Editora, 1962), pp. 132–153. Manifesto dos Mineiros entry in CPDOC, *Dicionário Histórico-Biográfico Brasileiro, 1930–1983* (Rio de Janeiro: Editora Forense-Universitária, 1984).

2. Nabuco, *A Vida de Virgílio de Melo Franco*, pp. 148–152.

3. Ibid.

4. HSP, letter to Affonso Arinos (de Mello Franco), December 4, 1943.

5. Ibid.

6. Afonso Arinos entry in *Dicionário Histórico-Biográfico Brasileiro, 1930–1983*.

7. Luiz Felippe de Oliveira Penna, interviews, Rio de Janeiro, August 11, 16, 1983.

8. HSP, letter to Luiz Camillo (de Oliveira Netto), December 7, 1943.

9. Adauto Lúcio Cardoso entry in *Dicionário Histórico-Biográfico Brasileiro, 1930–1983*.

10. HSP, letter to Adaucto (Lucio Cardoso), December 11, 1943.

VII. Battling Cassiano Ricardo and the DIP (1943–1944)

1. THE POLEMIC WITH CASSIANO RICARDO (SEPTEMBER–OCTOBER 1943)

1. HSP, *Do Primato do Espírito nas Polemicas Doutrinárias (As iras do Sr. Cassiano)* (Rio de Janeiro: Jornal do Commercio, Rodrigues & Cia., 1943), pp. 13–14. HSP, "Pelos Domínios do Direito," *Jornal do Commercio*, November 10, 1945.

2. HSP, *Do Primato do Espírito nas Polemicas Doutrinárias*, pp. 15–24.

3. Ibid., pp. 25–26.

4. Cassiano Ricardo, "O homem que vestiu o couro da onça," *A Manhã*, October 24, 1943.

5. Cassiano Ricardo, "O saudosismo e o combate ao fascismo," *A Manhã*, September 5, 1943.

6. Ibid.

7. HSP, *Do Primato do Espírito nas Polemicas Doutrinárias*, p. 25.

8. HSP, "A verdade jurídica fator de convivência social," in "Pelos Domínios do Direito," *Jornal do Commercio*, October 9, 1943, quoting from HSP's article of September 18, 1943.

9. Cassiano Ricardo, "O apostolo e seus equivocos," *A Manhã*, September 29, 1943, pp. 4, 6; see p. 4, column 2.

10. Cassiano Ricardo, "O apostolo e seus equivocos."

11. HSP, "O exemplo do jurista como fator de significação do Direito," in "Pelos Domínios do Direito," *Jornal do Commercio,* October 2, 1943.

12. Ibid.

13. HSP, "A verdade jurídica fator de convivência social."

14. Cassiano Ricardo, "Intrepidez & Larousse," *A Manhã,* October 10, 1943.

15. Ibid.

2. THE DIP INTERVENES AGAINST SOBRAL (OCTOBER 19, 1943)

1. HSP, *Do Primato do Espírito nas Polemicas Doutrinárias (As iras do Sr. Cassiano)* (Rio de Janeiro: Jornal do Commercio, Rodrigues & Cia., 1943), p. 25.

2. Ibid., p. 26.

3. HSP, "Reintegração da ordenação," in "Pelos Domínios do Direito," *Jornal do Commercio,* October 16, 1943, reproduced in HSP, *Do Primato do Espírito,* pp. 27–37 (see pp. 29, 31).

4. HSP, *Do Primato do Espírito,* pp. 27–37.

5. Ibid., p. 38.

6. Ibid., pp. 38–39.

7. HSP, letter to Capitão Amilcar Dutra de Menezes, October 20, 1943, in ibid., pp. 39–48.

8. Ibid.

9. HSP, *Do Primato do Espírito,* p. 47.

10. Cassiano Ricardo, "O homem que vestiu o couro da onça," *A Manhã,* October 24, 1943.

11. Ibid.

3. INEFFECTIVE APPEALS BY THE SILENCED COLUMNIST (OCTOBER–NOVEMBER 1943)

1. HSP, *Do Primato do Espírito nas Polemicas Doutrinárias (As iras do Sr. Cassiano)* (Rio de Janeiro: Jornal do Commercio, Rodrigues & Cia., 1943), pp. 48, 51.

2. Ibid., pp. 51–52, 55.

3. Ibid., pp. 52–54.

4. Ibid., pp. 57–62.

5. Ibid.

6. Ibid., p. 65.

7. Ibid., pp. 67–73.

8. Ibid., pp. 74–75.

9. Ibid., pp. 83–85.

10. Ibid., p. 91.

11. Ibid., p. 88.

12. Ibid., pp. 77–79, 89–90.

13. Ibid., p. 92.

14. Ibid., pp. 93–104.

15. Ibid.
16. Ibid.

4. RESPONSES TO BOOKLETS ABOUT CASSIANO AND THE DIP
(LATE 1943–EARLY 1944)

1. HSP, letters to Alceu (Amoroso Lima) and Affonso Arinos (de Mello Franco), November 17, 1943.
2. HSP, *Do Primato do Espírito nas Polemicas Doutrinárias (As iras do Sr. Cassiano)* (Rio de Janeiro: Jornal do Commercio, Rodrigues & Cia., 1943).
3. HSP, *Recurso ao Exmo. Sr. Presidente da República: Interpelação ao Sr. Cassiano Ricardo* (Rio de Janeiro: Jornal do Commercio, Rodrigues & Cia., 1943), nine pages.
4. HSP, letter to Affonso Arinos, December 9, 1943. HSP, letter to Oswaldo, December 20, 1943.
5. HSP, letter to Monsenhor Benedicto Marinho, December 4, 1943.
6. HSP, letter to Affonso Arinos, December 9, 1943.
7. HSP, letter to Affonso Arinos, December 11, 1943.
8. Ibid.
9. HSP, letter to J. C. de Azevedo Marques, December 30, 1943.
10. HSP, letter to José Pimentel, January 15, 1944. John W. F. Dulles, *The São Paulo Law School and the Anti-Vargas Resistance, 1938-1945* (Austin: University of Texas Press, 1986), p. 124, quoting José Bento Monteiro Lobato.
11. HSP, letter to Clementino Fraga, January 11, 1944.
12. HSP, letter to Cláudio de (Mello e) Souza, December 18, 1943.
13. HSP, letters to Natalina (Sobral Pinto), Plínio Barreto, and Lindolpho (Pio da Silva Dias), February 24, 1944.

5. COMMENTS ON AGAMEMNON MAGALHÃES AND CASSIANO'S
NEW POST (MARCH 1944)

1. HSP, letter to Agamemnon Magalhães, March 2, 1944.
2. Agamemnon Magalhães, "Contra o peor dos trusts" and "Um mundo que desbala," in *Diário de Notícias*, March 1, 2, 1944.
3. HSP, letter to Agamemnon Magalhães, March 2, 1944.
4. Ibid.
5. HSP, letters to (Francisco de Assis) Chateaubriand, March 2, 9, 1944. HSP, letter to Adroaldo (Mesquita da Costa), March 8, 1944.
6. HSP, letter to Cassiano Ricardo, March 6, 1944.
7. HSP, letter to Mário Moreira da Silva, March 6, 1944.
8. Ibid.

6. REJECTING THE CHARGE OF PERSECUTING CASSIANO
(MAY–JULY 1944)

1. Cassiano Ricardo, statement in *O Globo*, April 29, 1944, quoted in HSP, letter to Cassiano Ricardo, May 2, 1944.

2. HSP, letter to Cassiano Ricardo, May 2, 1944.
3. HSP, letter to J. E. de Macedo Soares, May 4, 1944.
4. HSP, letter to Cassiano Ricardo, June 9, 1944.
5. Ibid.
6. HSP, letters to Acadêmico Getúlio Vargas, Acadêmico Aloysio de Castro, and Cassiano Ricardo, July 30, 1944.
7. HSP, letter to Acadêmico Getúlio Vargas, July 30, 1944.
8. Ibid. HSP, letter to Acadêmico Aloysio de Castro, July 30, 1944.
9. HSP, letter to Cassiano Ricardo, July 30, 1944.

7. JACYRA, THE INDIAN GIRL FROM AMAZÔNIA
(MARCH–APRIL 1944)

1. Maurício de Medeiros, "Uma Recusa Insultuosa," *Diário Carioca*, March 7, 1944. HSP, "Uma Injustiça a Reparar," letter to Maurício de Medeiros, March 11, 1944, in *Jornal do Commercio*, March 12, 1944, and letter to Maurício de Medeiros, March 18, 1944.
2. Medeiros, "Uma Recusa Insultuosa."
3. Rubem Braga, "Ordem do Dia" column in *Diário Carioca*, March 7, 1944.
4. Doraci de Souza, quoted in HSP, letter to Maurício de Medeiros, March 18, 1944, and cited in Maurício de Medeiros, "Colégios Estrangeiros," *Diário Carioca*, March 11, 1944.
5. Medeiros, "Colégios Estrangeiros."
6. HSP, "Uma Injustiça a Reparar," *Jornal do Commercio*, March 12, 1944.
7. HSP, letter to Jayme de Barros Câmara, March 13, 1944.
8. Maurício de Medeiros, letter to HSP, in *Diário Carioca*, March 15, 1944. Osório Borba, "Ainda o livro do Pe. Schneller," *Diário de Notícias*, March 18, 1944.
9. Rubem Braga, "Ordem do Dia" column in *Diário Carioca*, March 18, 1944.
10. Ibid.
11. HSP, letter to Maurício de Medeiros, March 18, 1944.
12. Ibid.

8. THE DIP ENDS THE DEBATE ABOUT JACYRA (MARCH–APRIL 1944)

1. HSP, letter to Amilcar Dutra de Menezes, March 20, 1944.
2. Ibid.
3. Ibid.
4. HSP, letter to Gustavo Capanema, March 20, 1944.
5. HSP, letters to Jayme de Barros Câmara, March 20, 27, 1944.
6. HSP, letter to Alceu (Amoroso Lima), March 22, 1944.
7. Ibid.
8. Ibid. HSP, letters to (Elmano) Cardim and Herbert Moses, March 23, 1944.

9. Gustavo Capanema, telegram to HSP, Rio de Janeiro, March 25, 1944, quoted in HSP, letter to Jayme de Barros Câmara, March 27, 1944.

10. HSP, letter to Jayme de Barros Câmara, March 27, 1944.

11. HSP, letters to Gustavo Capanema and Amilcar Dutra de Menezes, March 27, 1944.

12. HSP, letters to Amilcar Dutra de Menezes, Gustavo Capanema, and Jayme de Barros Câmara, April 4, 1944.

13. HSP, letter to Alceu (Amoroso Lima), April 17, 1944.

9. "THE EVICTION OF DR. SOBRAL PINTO" (MAY–OCTOBER 1944)

1. HSP, letter to Conselho da Ordem dos Advogados da Secção do Districto Federal, June 14, 1944.

2. Ibid.

3. Ibid. HSP, letter in *Jornal do Commercio*, October 8, 1944.

4. HSP, letter to Conselho da Ordem dos Advogados, June 14, 1944. Roberto Sobral Pinto Ribeiro, interview, Rio de Janeiro, January 13, 1995.

5. HSP, letter in *Jornal do Commercio*, October 8, 1944.

6. Ibid. HSP, letter to Conselho da Ordem dos Advogados, June 14, 1944. HSP, letter to José Linhares, June 16, 1944. "Justiça Local, Varas Civeis," *Jornal do Commercio*, September 17, 1944 (p. 11).

7. HSP, letter to José Linhares, June 16, 1944. HSP, letter to Conselho da Ordem dos Advogados, June 14, 1944.

8. HSP, letter to Evandro (Lins e Silva), July 7, 1944.

9. HSP, letter to José Linhares, August 30, 1944.

10. HSP, letters to Humberto (Duarte), June 21, 30, 1944.

11. "Justiça Local, Varas Civeis," *Jornal do Commercio*, September 17, 1944. HSP, letter in *Jornal do Commercio*, October 8, 1944.

12. HSP, letter to Emmanuel Sodré, September 18, 1944.

13. "O Despejo do Dr. Sobral Pinto . . . (Razões de Apelação, pró Apelante), Egrégio Tribunal," *Correia da Manhã*, October 1, 1944.

14. HSP, letter to (Augusto) Pinto Lima, October 3, 1944.

15. HSP, letter in *Jornal do Commercio*, October 8, 1944.

VIII. Reacting to Catholic Conformity and Coriolano's Repression (1944–1945)

1. "THE BRAZILIAN NAZI BOY" (MARCH–APRIL 1944)

1. Osório Borba, "O Brasileirinho 'Nazista,'" *Diário de Notícias*, April 19, 1944. Osório Borba, "Incrível mas Autêntico," *Diário de Notícias*, March 12, 1944, cited in HSP, letter to Osório Borba, April 15, 1944 (in *Jornal do Commercio*, April 16, 1944) and in Vicente Álvaro de Oliveira Ribeiro, letter to Osório Borba, Rio de Janeiro, April 21, 1944 (in *Diário de Notícias*, April 27, 1944).

2. Borba, "Incrível mas Autêntico."

3. HSP, letter to Osório Borba, *Jornal do Commercio*, April 16, 1944.

4. Ibid.

5. Borba, "O Brasileirinho 'Nazista.'"
6. Ibid.
7. Vicente Álvaro de Oliveira Ribeiro, OSB, letter to Osório Borba, Internato de São Bento do Alto de Boa Vista, Rio de Janeiro, April 21, 1944, in *Diário de Notícias*, April 27, 1944.
8. Ibid.
9. Osório Borba, "Ainda o livro do Pe. Schneller," *Diário de Notícias*, March 17, 1944. Osório Borba, "Ponto Final," *Diário de Notícias*, March 29, 1944. Osório Borba, "Arianismo e 'Linha de Cor,'" *Diário de Notícias*, April 5, 1944.
10. HSP, "Luta pela verdade histórica," letter to Osório Borba in *Jornal do Commercio*, March 26, 1944. HSP, "O espírito de seita no anti-clericalismo," letter to Osório Borba in *Jornal do Commercio*, April 2, 1944. HSP, "A ingratidão dos anti-clericais para com os monges de São Bento," letter to Osório Borba, in *Jornal do Commercio*, April 16, 1944.

2. THE CHURCH AND THE LAW (APRIL–AUGUST 1944)

1. HSP, letter to Jaime de Barros Câmara, April 27, 1944.
2. Ibid.
3. HSP, letter to Jaime de Barros Câmara, June 30, 1944.
4. Ibid.
5. HSP, letters to Jaime de Barros Câmara, Alceu (Amoroso Lima), and Jonathas Serrano, April 28, 1944.
6. HSP, "O direito de punir em face do pensamento católico," address given to Sociedade Brasileira de Criminologia, May 12, 1944, in HSP papers.
7. Ibid.
8. HSP, letter to Alceu Amoroso Lima, August 19, 1944.
9. Ibid.

3. DOM JAYME CALLS SOBRAL A NAUGHTY BOY (DECEMBER 1944)

1. HSP, letter to (Henrique) Hargreaves, September 20, 1944.
2. HSP, letter to Ivo Calliari, October 2, 1944.
3. HSP, letters to (Augusto Frederico) Schmidt and Maurício Nabuco, October 4, 1944.
4. HSP, letter to José Távora, December 13, 1944.
5. Ibid.
6. HSP, letter to Jaime de Barros Câmara, December 27, 1944.
7. HSP, letter to Jaime de Barros Câmara, December 27, 1944 (second letter of the same date). HSP, letter to Núncio D. Aloisi Masella, December 28, 1944. See "O jubileu Episcopal de S. Exa. Revma. Dom Bento Aloisi Masella," *Jornal do Commercio*, December 25, 26, 27, 1944.
8. HSP, letter to Jaime de Barros Câmara, December 27, 1944 (second letter of the same date).
9. Ibid.
10. HSP, letter to Aloisi Masella, December 28, 1944.

4. ORLANDO LEITE RIBEIRO, PRESTES, AND VARGAS (MAY 1944)

1. HSP, letter to Coriolano (de Góes), August 15, 1944.
2. HSP, letter to Orlando Leite Ribeiro, May 15, 1944.
3. Ibid.
4. Ibid.
5. Ibid.
6. Ibid.
7. Ibid.
8. Ibid.
9. Luiz Carlos Prestes, "Comentários a um documento aliancista aparecido nos últimos meses de 1943," Rio de Janeiro, March 14, 1944, in Luiz Carlos Prestes, *Problemas Atuais da Democracia* (Rio de Janeiro: Editorial Vitória, n.d.), pp. 45–49.

5. POLICE CHIEF CORIOLANO AND THE FALL OF ARANHA (AUGUST 1944)

1. HSP, letter to Oswaldo Aranha, April 20 (and repeated on May 24), 1944.
2. Ibid.
3. Coriolano de Góes and Osvaldo Aranha entries in CPDOC, *Dicionário Histórico-Biográfico Brasileiro, 1930–1983* (Rio de Janeiro: Editora Forense-Universitária, 1984).
4. HSP, letter to Oswaldo Aranha, August 26, 1944.
5. Paul Frischauer, *Presidente Vargas: Biografia* (São Paulo, Rio de Janeiro, Recife, and Porto Alegre: Companhia Editôra Nacional, 1943).
6. HSP, letter to Oswaldo Aranha, August 26, 1944.
7. HSP, letter to Nelson de Mello, April 11, 1944.
8. John W. F. Dulles, *The São Paulo Law School and the Anti-Vargas Resistance, 1938–1945* (Austin: University of Texas Press, 1986), pp. 129–145.
9. HSP, letter to Coriolano (de Góes), August 15, 1944.
10. Ibid.
11. Coriolano de Góes, message to HSP, Rio de Janeiro, August 22, 1944, reproduced in HSP, letter to Coriolano, August 26, 1944.
12. HSP, letter to (Vitório) Caneppa, August 24, 1944.
13. HSP, letter to Coriolano (de Góes), August 28, 1944.
14. Ibid.

6. DICTATORIAL PRESSURES ON THE OAB, DARIO, ADAUCTO, AND OTHERS (LATE 1944)

1. HSP, letter to (Francisco) Campos, October 2, 1944.
2. Ibid.
3. Francisco Campos, interview, Rio de Janeiro, September 3, 1963.
4. HSP, letter to Osório Borba, November 18, 1944.
5. HSP, letter to Raul Fernandes, November 30, 1944.

6. Alberto Venancio Filho, *Notícia Histórica da Ordem dos Advogados do Brasil (1930-1980)* (Rio de Janeiro: n.p., 1982), p. 67, and letter from Milton Soares Campos to Dario de Almeida Magalhães and others, Belo Horizonte, December 9, 1944, quoted by Venancio Filho, pp. 67-69.

7. Venancio Filho, *Notícia Histórica da Ordem*, p. 69.

8. Joseph Newman, "5 Vargas Foes Reported Held by Brazilian Army," *New York Herald Tribune*, December 29, 1944. War Ministry, 2nd Military Region, Estado Maior Regional, 2nd Section, Boletim Secreto de Informações 14, December 22, 1944 (Vargas papers, CPDOC). Carolina Nabuco, *A Vida de Virgílio de Melo Franco* (Rio de Janeiro: Livraria José Olympio Editora, 1962), pp. 159-160.

9. Venancio Filho, *Notícia Histórica da Ordem*, p. 69.

10. HSP, letter to Coriolano (de Góes), December 29, 1944.

11. Ibid.

12. Nabuco, *A Vida de Virgílio de Melo Franco*, pp. 159-160.

7. DOING LEGAL WORK FOR SCHMIDT (1944-1945)

1. Sra. Zabel, letter to Ranulpho Cunha, Rio de Janeiro, August 31, 1944, copy in HSP papers.

2. HSP, letter to Coriolano (de Góes), September 14, 1944. HSP, letter to Ranulpho Cunha, September 14, 1944.

3. HSP, letter to Frederico Mindello (DOPS director), October 26, 1944.

4. HSP, letter to Samuel Silveira Lobo, August 31, 1944. HSP, letters to Moacyr, August 31, October 19, 1944.

5. HSP, letters to (Augusto Frederico) Schmidt, October 17, 23, 1944.

6. HSP, letter to Schmidt, October 17, 1944.

7. HSP, letters to Schmidt, October 17, 23, 25, 1944.

8. HSP, letters to Schmidt, October 23, 25, 1944.

9. HSP, letter to Schmidt, October 25, 1944.

10. HSP, letters to Schmidt, October 25, 26, 1944.

11. HSP, letter to Schmidt, October 26, 1944.

12. HSP, letter to Plínio Barreto, October 21, 1944.

13. HSP, letter to Schmidt, December 22, 1944.

14. HSP, letters to Pedro (Baptista Martins), Schmidt, and Peixoto (de Castro), April 30, 1945.

8. REBUKING CORIOLANO AND PEDRO, SÃO PAULO'S SECURITY SECRETARY (EARLY 1945)

1. HSP, letter to Paulo, February 2, 1945.

2. HSP, letter to Lygia Prestes, January 24, 1945.

3. HSP, letter to Lygia Prestes, January 16, 1945.

4. Ibid.

5. HSP, letter to Antônio Bayma, February 1, 1945. HSP, letter to Coriolano (de Góes), February 5, 1945.

6. HSP, letter to Coriolano, February 5, 1945.

7. HSP, letter to Pedro (de Oliveira Ribeiro Sobrinho), February 21, 1945.
8. HSP, letter to Pedro (de Oliveira Ribeiro Sobrinho), January 11, 1945.

IX. Emerging as a Hero with Brazil's Return to Liberties (Early 1945)

1. CONTEMPLATING A POPULAR ELECTION FOR PRESIDENT (JANUARY–FEBRUARY 1945)

1. *Diário de Notícias,* January 12, 1945, quoted in HSP, letter to Coriolano (de Góes), January 12, 1945.
2. HSP, letter to Coriolano, January 12, 1945.
3. HSP, letter to (Francisco) Campos, January 22, 1945.
4. Ibid.
5. Ibid. Francisco Campos entry in CPDOC, *Dicionário Histórico-Biográfico Brasileiro, 1930–1983* (Rio de Janeiro: Editora Forense-Universitária, 1984).
6. HSP, letter to Eurico Gaspar Dutra, January 22, 1945.
7. Getúlio Vargas, *A Nova Política do Brasil,* vol. 1 (Rio de Janeiro: Livraria José Olympio Editora, 1938), p. 32.
8. HSP, letter to Eurico Gaspar Dutra, January 22, 1945.
9. Renato Paquet, speech of November 10, 1944, in *Jornal do Commercio,* November 11, 1944.
10. HSP, letter to Renato Paquet, February 7, 1945.
11. Getúlio Vargas, *A Nova Política do Brasil,* vol. 10 (Rio de Janeiro: Livraria José Olympio Editora, 1944), p. 282.
12. *O Globo* entry in *Dicionário Histórico-Biográfico Brasileiro, 1930–1983.*
13. *O Globo* editorial, February 6, 1945, quoted in HSP, letter to Roberto Marinho, February 7, 1945.
14. HSP, letter to Roberto Marinho, February 7, 1945.
15. Ibid.

2. THE EXCHANGE WITH GÓES MONTEIRO (FEBRUARY–APRIL 1945)

1. Pedro Aurélio de Góes Monteiro, "O Momento Mundial e a Atual Política Brasileira," *Folha Carioca,* February 1, 1945, transcribed in *Diário Carioca,* February 2, 1945. HSP, letter to General (Pedro Aurélio de) Góes Monteiro, February 22, 1945, p. 66.
2. Pedro Aurélio de Góes Monteiro, *A Revolução de 30 e a Finalidade do Exército* (Rio de Janeiro: Adersen, n.d.), p. 181.
3. HSP, letter to General (Pedro Aurélio de) Góes Monteiro, February 22, 1945. The letter is reproduced on pp. 11–40 of HSP, *As Forças Armadas em face do Momento Político* (Rio de Janeiro: Jornal do Commercio, Rodrigues & Cia., 1945). See pp. 15, 30–34 of the letter in HSP papers.
4. HSP, letter to General Góes Monteiro, February 22, 1945, p. 68 of the letter in HSP papers.

5. Ibid., p. 71.

6. P. Góes (Monteiro), letter to HSP, Rio de Janeiro, April 7, 1945, in *O Globo*, April 11, 1945.

7. Ibid.

8. Ibid.

3. SOBRAL REPLIES TO VARGAS' INTERVIEW OF MARCH 2, 1945

1. Alexandre Marcondes Filho entry in CPDOC, *Dicionário Histórico-Biográfico Brasileiro, 1930–1983* (Rio de Janeiro: Editora Forense-Universitária, 1984).

2. Lei Constitucional No. 9, de 28 de fevereiro de 1945.

3. Francisco Campos, interview, *Diário Carioca*, March 3, 1945.

4. "Entrevista concedida aos jornalistas em Petrópolis a 2 de março de 1945," in Getúlio Vargas, *A Nova Política do Brasil*, vol. 11 (Rio de Janeiro: Livraria José Olympio Editora, 1947), pp. 89–116.

5. Ibid.

6. HSP, interview, *Diário da Noite*, in response to Vargas' interview of March 2, 1945.

7. Ibid.

4. SOBRAL, HONORED FOR PAST BATTLES, FILLS COLUMNS OF THE PRESS (MARCH 1945)

1. HSP, letter to Natalina (Sobral Pinto), March 2, 1945.

2. "Fala ao *Diário Carioca* o advogado Sobral Pinto," *Diário Carioca*, February 25, 1945.

3. HSP, telegram to Adherbal Novaes, March 1, 1945. HSP, letter to Herbert Moses, March 2, 1945.

4. Maurício de Medeiros, "Gato Escaldado," *Diário Carioca*, March 4, 1945.

5. "O *Diário de Notícias* publica a íntegra da entrevista dada a *Folha Carioca*," March 2, 1945.

6. Moura Carneiro, "Olga Benário Prestes e Strübing Müller," letter to HSP, March 2, 1945, published in *Jornal do Commercio*, March 2, 13, 1945.

7. HSP, letter to Moura Carneiro, *Jornal do Commercio*, March 13, 1945.

8. HSP, letter to Alceu (Amoroso Lima), February 28, 1945.

9. HSP, letter to (Pedro da) Cunha Pedrosa, March 13, 1945.

10. Conselho Federal da Ordem dos Advogados do Brasil (resolution of June 22, 1944, by Dario de Almeida Magalhães), *Jornal do Commercio*, March 10, 1945.

11. HSP, letter to Dario (de Almeida Magalhães), March 10, 1945.

12. HSP, "A sentença de morte do homem que se fantasiou de urso," in "Pelos Domínios do Direito," *Jornal do Commercio*, March 10, 1945. HSP quotes from Viriato Vargas, "Combate à insinceridade," *Ciência Política*, vol. 6, pp. 16–17.

13. HSP in "Publicações a Pedido," *Jornal do Commercio*, on Sundays

throughout March 1945. See "As Forças Armadas e o Dever Cívico: Conclusão," March 25, 1945. See also part of HSP letter to Dutra, on p. 55 of HSP, *As Forças Armadas em face do Momento Político* (Rio de Janeiro: Jornal do Commercio, Rodrigues & Cia., 1945).

14. Tristão de Athayde (Alceu Amoroso Lima), "Nosso Bayard," *O Jornal,* March 25, 1945.

15. HSP, letter to Alceu (Amoroso Lima), March 27, 1945.

5. BETTER DAYS FOR PRESTES (MARCH–APRIL 1945)

1. HSP, *As Forças Armadas em face do Momento Político* (Rio de Janeiro: Jornal do Commercio, Rodrigues & Cia., 1945), pp. 8–9.

2. João Alberto entry in CPDOC, *Dicionário Histórico-Biográfico Brasileiro, 1930–1983* (Rio de Janeiro: Editora Forense-Universitária, 1984).

3. Luiz Carlos Prestes, *A Situação no Brasil e no Mundo* (booklet transcribed from *O Globo,* March 15, 1945). See also Prestes, *Problemas Atuais da Democracia* (Rio de Janeiro: Editorial Vitória, n.d.), pp. 69–74.

4. Pedro Motta Lima, "Março de 1945," in Antonio J. Osorio et al., *Prestes: Estudos E Depoimentos,* (n.p.: Comissão Central do Cinquentenário de Luiz Carlos Prestes, ca. 1948), pp. 68–77; see p. 76.

5. Emygdio da Costa Miranda, interview, Rio de Janeiro, October 5, 1966. The date and circumstances of Olga's death are given in Dênis de Moraes and Francisco Viana, *Prestes: Lutas e Autocríticas* (Petrópolis: Editora Vozes, 1982), p. 85, and Fernando Morais, *Olga* (São Paulo: Editora Alfa-Omega, 1985), pp. 281–283.

6. HSP, letter to Eloísa Prestes, March 14, 1945. *Diário Carioca,* March 1, 1945. "Lista de donativos para aquisição de passagens aéreas para duas brasileiras exiladas . . . , Entregue ao Dr. Sobral Pinto" (in HSP papers).

7. HSP, letter to Eloísa Prestes, March 14, 1945.

8. Ibid.

9. "Telegrama do Sr. Luiz Carlos Prestes ao Presidente Getúlio Vargas," *O Estado de S. Paulo,* April 8, 1945.

10. *Jornal do Commercio,* April 2–3, March 28, 1945. Tristão de Athayde, "Nosso Bayard," *O Jornal,* March 25, 1945.

11. HSP in "Publicações a Pedido," *Jornal do Commercio,* April 11, 1945.

12. HSP in "Publicações a Pedido," *Jornal do Commercio,* April 8, 1945.

13. HSP, telegram to Góes Monteiro, April 8, 1945. Góes Monteiro, telegram to HSP, Rio de Janeiro, April 9, 1945, in HSP, letter to Góes Monteiro, April 10, 1945.

14. HSP, letter to Góes Monteiro, April 10, 1945.

15. Ibid.

16. Ibid.

17. Ibid.

6. ATTRIBUTING EGALITARIANISM TO VARGAS (APRIL 1945)

1. HSP, "O positivismo jurídico em face do direito cristão," in "Pelos Domínios do Direito," *Jornal do Commercio,* March 24, 1945.

2. Gionísio Curvello de Mendoça, "O positivismo jurídico em face do direito cristão," *Jornal do Commercio*, March 29, 1945. See Ivan Lins, *História do Positivismo no Brasil* (São Paulo: Companhia Editora Nacional, 1967), including pp. 175, 417.

3. HSP, "As consequências funestas do positivismo jurídico," in "Pelos Domínios do Direito," *Jornal do Commercio*, April 7, 1945.

4. HSP, "O Naturalismo no Governo dos Povos Modernos," in "Pelos Domínios do Direito," *Jornal do Commercio*, April 14, 1945.

7. RESISTÊNCIA DEMOCRÁTICA (APRIL 1945)

1. HSP, letter to (Jorge Dyott) Fontenelle, April 18, 1945.

2. HSP, letter to Hélio (Silva), September 19, 1975.

3. *Manifesto da Resistência Democrática aos Brasileiros* (Rio de Janeiro: Resistência Democrática, 1945). See pp. 18–20.

4. Ibid., pp. 3–4, 6.

5. Ibid., pp. 4–10.

6. Ibid., pp. 10–12.

7. Ibid., pp. 12–16.

8. Ibid., pp. 17–18.

9. Ibid., pp. 21–22.

10. "Programa de ação imediata da 'Resistência Democrática,' em face da atual situação do país, Aprovado em assembléia de 30 de abril de 1945," *Diário de Notícias*, June 16, 1945.

11. Ibid.

X. Participant in Preparations for Elections (June–October 1945)

1. RENEWING HIS CAMPAIGN, SOBRAL ATTACKS THE "MALAYSIAN LAW" (JUNE 1945)

1. *O Estado de S. Paulo*, April 19, 1945.

2. Leoncio Basbaum, *Uma Vida em Seis Tempos* (São Paulo: Editora Alfa-Omega, 1976), pp. 183–187.

3. Ibid., p. 180. "Arquiteto cedeu casa a tenentes," *Jornal do Brasil*, December 15, 1996. HSP, telegram to Luiz Carlos Prestes, July 14, 1945.

4. *O Estado de S. Paulo*, April 26, 27, 1945.

5. HSP, letter to Luiz Carlos Prestes, June 22, 1945.

6. Antonio Franca, *Modernismo Brasileiro* (Recife: Região, 1948), p. 132 and, on pp. 173–179, letter, Silo Meireles to Prestes, Uberlândia, November 21, 1945. Astrojildo Pereira, "Uma advertência aos intelectuais honestos," *Tribuna Popular*, July 4, 1945.

7. HSP, letters to Lindolpho (Pio da Silva Dias), June 23, 30, 1945. HSP, letter to Fabrinio, June 30, 1945.

8. "A 'Lei Malaia,'" in Virgílio A. de Mello Franco, *A Campanha da U.D.N. (1944–1945)* (Rio de Janeiro: Livraria Editora Zelio Valverde, 1946), pp. 288–295. Agamemnon Magalhães entry in CPDOC, *Dicionário Histó-*

rico-Biográfico Brasileiro, 1930–1983 (Rio de Janeiro: Editora Forense-Universitária, 1984).

9. Mello Franco, *A Campanha da U.D.N.*, pp. 296–297. HSP, letter to Lindolpho, June 23, 1945.

10. "Fala o Sr. Sobral Pinto: Impressionante Depoimento de um Líder do Pensamento Católico," *Diário Carioca*, June 24, 1945.

11. Ibid.

12. Edgard Carone, *O Estado Novo (1937–1945)* (Rio de Janeiro and São Paulo: Difel, 1977), p. 328.

13. "O Manifesto da Esquerda Democrática," *Diário de Notícias*, August 25, 1945.

14. "Apoio dos Advogados a Eduardo Gomes," *Diário Carioca*, June 28, 1945.

15. HSP, letter to Alceu (Amoroso Lima), June 30, 1945.

2. WARNING THE CHRISTIAN DEMOCRATIC PARTY AGAINST VARGAS' COMMUNISM (JULY 9, 1945)

1. HSP, letter to Eliseu van de Weyer, July 2, 1945.

2. *O Estado de S. Paulo*, July 3, 10, 1945.

3. Speech of HSP at the São Paulo Municipal Theater, July 9, 1945, as published in the *Jornal do Commercio*, July 15, 1945.

4. Ibid.

5. "A nossa opinião," *Diário Carioca*, July 10, 1945.

6. HSP, telegram to (Francisco) Barreto Campello, August 27, 1945. HSP, letter to Pedro Lafayette (director of *Reação Brasileira*), September 14, 1945.

7. HSP, letter to Lindolpho (Pio da Silva Dias), July 13, 1945. HSP, letter to José Bento, July 14, 1945.

8. HSP, letter to Miguel (de Carvalho Dias), July 16, 1945. See also HSP letters to (Emílio) Ippolito and Dr. Oscavio, of the same date.

9. HSP, letter to Lindolpho, July 16, 1945.

3. SOBRAL, LEC COUNSELOR, DISCUSSES THE SOCIAL PROBLEM (JULY–AUGUST 1945)

1. *Jornal do Commercio*, July 14, 28, 1945. *Diário de Notícias*, July 15, 1945. Hélio Silva, *1945: Porque depuseram Vargas* (Rio de Janeiro: Editora Civilização Brasileira, 1976), p. 183. Liga Eleitoral Católica entry in CPDOC, *Dicionário Histórico-Biográfico Brasileiro, 1930–1983* (Rio de Janeiro: Editora Forense-Universitária, 1984).

2. Ibid.

3. *Diário de Notícias*, July 15, 1945.

4. HSP, letter to Caio, July 21, 1945. HSP, letter to Lindolpho (Pio da Silva Dias), July 28, 1945.

5. Mauro Renault Leite and Luiz Gonzaga Novelli Júnior, *Marechal Eurico Gaspar Dutra: O dever da verdade* (Rio de Janeiro: Editora Nova Fronteira, 1983), p. 699.

6. HSP, "Advertências ao Operário Brasileiro," July 1945.

7. HSP, "Os Católicas e os Comunistas (Conferência feita na Matriz da Urca, em 15 de Agosto de 1945)," *Jornal do Commercio*, August 19, 1945.

8. Ibid.

9. Joaquim de Sales, "Movimento Operário Social Cristão," *Diário Carioca*, August 17, 1945.

10. Ibid.

11. HSP, letter to Joaquim (de Sales), August 18, 1945.

4. THE LEC DENIES SUFFERING A SCHISM (SEPTEMBER 1945)

1. HSP, letter to Miguel (de Carvalho Dias), August 11, 1945.

2. HSP, letter to Lindolpho (Pio da Silva Dias), August 18, 1945.

3. Lourival Coutinho, *O General Góes Depõe* (Rio de Janeiro: Livraria Editôra Coelho Branco, 1956), pp. 417–418. Mauro Renault Leite and Luiz Gonzaga Novelli Júnior, *Marechal Eurico Gaspar Dutra: O dever da verdade* (Rio de Janeiro: Editora Nova Fronteira, 1983), p. 676. Juarez Távora entry in CPDOC, *Dicionário Histórico-Biográfico Brasileiro, 1930–1983* (Rio de Janeiro: Editora Forense-Universitária, 1984).

4. Partido Democrata Cristão entry in *Dicionário Histórico-Biográfico Brasileiro, 1930–1983*, including observation of Luís Werneck Viana.

5. *O Estado de S. Paulo*, September 9, 1945. *Jornal do Commercio*, September 10, 1945.

6. *Diário Carioca*, September 9, 1945.

7. Alceu Amoroso Lima entry in *Dicionário Histórico-Biográfico Brasileiro, 1930–1983*.

8. HSP in *Diário Carioca*, September 11, 1945.

9. Ibid.

10. *Diário Carioca*, September 11, 1945.

11. *Jornal do Commercio*, September 10–11, 1945. *Diário de Notícias*, September 11, 1945.

12. *O Estado de S. Paulo*, September 9, 1945. *Diário de Notícias*, September 11, 1945.

13. "Declarações da Comissão Episcopal da Ação Católica Brasileira," *Jornal do Commercio*, September 24–25, 1945.

14. *Jornal do Commercio* and *Folha da Manhã*, November 17, 1945. *Diário Carioca*, November 21, 1945.

5. RESISTÊNCIA DEMOCRÁTICA AND THE OAB OPPOSE THE QUEREMISTAS (SEPTEMBER–OCTOBER 1945)

1. Hugo Borghi entry in CPDOC, *Dicionário Histórico-Biográfico Brasileiro, 1930–1983* (Rio de Janeiro: Editora Forense-Universitária, 1984).

2. Getúlio Vargas entry in ibid.

3. Cleantho Paiva Leite, conversation with JWFD, Rio de Janeiro.

4. Speech of Getúlio Vargas, given in Hélio Silva, *1945: Porque depu-*

seram Vargas (Rio de Janeiro: Editora Civilização Brasileira, 1976), pp. 137–138.

5. Resistência Democrática, "Advertência à Nação," *Diário de Notícias* and *Diário Carioca*, September 16, 1945.

6. "Reuniram-se os Membros da Resistência Democrática," *Diário de Notícias*, October 26, 1945.

7. Resistência Democrática, "Advertência à Nação." "Reuniram-se os Membros da Resistência Democrática."

8. Resistência Democrática in *Diário de Notícias* and *Diário Carioca*, September 23, 1945.

9. Ibid.

10. *Diário de Notícias* and *Jornal do Commercio*, September 19, 1945.

11. *Diário de Notícias*, October 17, 1945.

12. *Diário de Notícias* and *Jornal do Commercio*, September 19, 1945.

13. *Diário de Notícias* and *Jornal do Commercio*, September 19, October 4, 1945.

14. HSP, letter to Roberto Marinho, September 22, 1945. See also *Jornal do Commercio*, September 27, 1945.

15. *Jornal do Commercio*, September 26, 27, 1945.

16. *Diário de Notícias*, October 3, 1945.

17. Ibid., October 4, 1945.

18. HSP, letters to Heitor Rocha Faria, October 6, 10, 1945.

19. Getúlio Vargas entry in *Dicionário Histórico-Biográfico Brasileiro, 1930–1983*.

20. *Diário de Notícias*, October 21, 1945. *O Estado de S. Paulo*, October 6, 26, 1945.

21. *Jornal do Commercio*, November 11, 1945.

22. Ibid., October 17, 1945. *Diário Carioca*, October 24, 1945.

23. "A LEC é anti-democrática?" *Diário Carioca*, October 19, 1945.

XI. Declining to Run for Congress and Explaining Vargas' Fall (October 1945)

1. CONDEMNING THE ALTERATION OF STATE ELECTION PROCEDURES (MID-OCTOBER 1945)

1. Virgílio A. de Mello Franco, *A Campanha da U.D.N. (1944–1945)* (Rio de Janeiro: Livraria Editora Zelio Valverde, 1946), pp. 356–357, 359.

2. Ibid., pp. 357–358.

3. *Diário de Notícias*, October 12, 1945.

4. *Diário Carioca* and *Diário de Notícias*, October 14, 1945.

5. Mello Franco, *A Campanha da U.D.N. (1944–1945)*, pp. 343–345, 349–356.

6. *Jornal do Commercio* and *Diário de Notícias*, October 17, 1945.

7. Ibid.

8. Ibid.

9. *O Globo*, October 17, 1945 (reprinted on October 17, 1995).

10. *Gazeta de Notícias*, October 19, 1945, quoted in *O Estado de S. Paulo*,

October 20, 1945. *Gazeta de Notícias* entry in CPDOC, *Dicionário Histó-rico-Biográfico Brasileiro, 1930–1983* (Rio de Janeiro: Editora Forense-Universitária, 1984). *Diário de Notícias,* October 19, 1945.

2. THE LAWYERS' PRO-GOMES RALLY (OCTOBER 19, 1945)

1. *Diário de Notícias,* October 20, 1945. HSP, letters to Henrique Dodsworth, October 8, 10, 29, 1945.

2. *Jornal do Commercio* and *Diário de Notícias,* October 20, 1945.

3. Raphael Corrêa de Oliveira, in *Diário de Notícias,* October 19, 1945.

4. *Jornal do Commercio* and *Diário de Notícias,* October 20, 1945.

5. Ibid. Carlos Lacerda, *Depoimento* (Rio de Janeiro: Editora Nova Fronteira, 1977), p. 34.

6. *Jornal do Commercio* and *Diário de Notícias,* October 20, 1945.

7. *Diário de Notícias,* October 21, 1945.

3. MACIEL FILHO RECALLS SOBRAL'S 1928 SCANDAL (OCTOBER 1945)

1. Getúlio Vargas and *A Noite* entries in CPDOC, *Dicionário Histórico-Biográfico Brasileiro, 1930–1983* (Rio de Janeiro: Editora Forense-Universitária, 1984). Adauto Lúcio Cardoso, letter in *Diário de Notícias,* October 24, 1945. André Carrazzoni, telegram to Vargas, in *A Noite,* October 17, 1945.

2. J. S. Maciel Filho, "De alma à paisana," *A Noite,* October 17, 1945.

3. Ibid.

4. Ibid. See also J. S. Maciel Filho, "A vingança dos bacharéis," *A Noite,* October 22, 1945.

5. HSP, *Destruição da Mentira pela Confissão da Verdade* (Rio de Janeiro: Jornal do Commercio, Rodrigues & Cia., 1955), pp. 5–6.

6. Ibid., pp. 6–8.

7. Ibid., pp. 8–11.

8. Ibid., p. 11. HSP, letter to F. de Barros Barreto, October 27, 1945.

9. Adauto Lúcio Cardoso, letter in *Diário de Notícias,* October 24, 1945.

10. Ibid.

11. J. S. Maciel Filho, "Um Caso de Freud," *A Noite,* October 23, 1945.

12. Hélio Lobo and *A Manhã* entries in *Dicionário Histórico-Biográfico Brasileiro, 1930–1983.*

13. "O Presidente Getúlio Vargas e a Academia Brasileira de Letras," *O Estado de S. Paulo,* October 28, 1945.

14. Ibid.

4. SOBRAL REJECTS APPEALS THAT HE RUN FOR CONGRESS (OCTOBER 27–29, 1945)

1. Alceu Amoroso Lima entry in CPDOC, *Dicionário Histórico-Biográfico Brasileiro, 1930–1983* (Rio de Janeiro: Editora Forense-Universitária, 1984). *Diário de Notícias,* October 18, 1945.

2. *Diário de Notícias,* October 17, 18, 1945.

3. *Diário de Notícias,* October 27, 1945.

4. HSP, in *Diário de Notícias*, October 28, 1945. HSP, letter to (Orlando Ribeiro) Dantas, October 27, 1945.

5. HSP, in *Diário de Notícias*, October 28, 1945.

6. HSP, letter to Horácio de Carvalho Júnior, October 29, 1945.

5. LEGALITY FOR THE PCB AND A FAMILY LIFE FOR ITS LEADER (OCTOBER 1945)

1. F. Rocha Lagoa, "Voto vencedor," on pp. 16–33 of (Tribunal Superior Eleitoral), *O Partido Comunista: Sua Condenação pela Justiça Brasileira* (Rio de Janeiro: Imprensa Nacional, 1947). See pp. 16–19, 25.

2. HSP, "O Problema Comunista no Seio da Democracia," in "Pelos Domínios do Direito," *Jornal do Commercio*, October 27, 1945.

3. Ibid.

4. F. Rocha Lagoa, "Voto vencedor," pp. 19–20.

5. "O caso da sra. Olga Prestes," *Diário Carioca*, September 12, 1945.

6. "No Rio a Filha do sr. Luiz Carlos Prestes," *Diário Carioca*, October 30, 1945.

7. HSP, letter to Lygia Prestes, October 29, 1945.

8. HSP, letter to Anita Leocádia (Prestes), October 29, 1945.

9. HSP, letter to Luiz Carlos Prestes, October 29, 1945.

10. Interview with Anita Leocádia Prestes, in *Marie Claire* (São Paulo magazine), no. 63, June 1996.

6. THE OVERTHROW OF VARGAS (OCTOBER 29, 1945)

1. Góis Monteiro entry in CPDOC, *Dicionário Histórico-Biográfico Brasileiro, 1930–1983* (Rio de Janeiro: Editora Forense-Universitária, 1984).

2. HSP, letter to Góes Monteiro, October 24, 1945, on pp. 12–14 of HSP, letter to José Linhares, November 1, 1945.

3. Ibid.

4. Lourival Coutinho, *O General Góes Depõe* (Rio de Janeiro: Livraria Editôra Coelho Branco, 1956), pp. 439, 442.

5. Ibid., pp. 439–440.

6. Ibid., pp. 442–443.

7. Ibid., pp. 444–446.

8. Ibid., pp. 446–454. Mauro Renault Leite and Luiz Gonzaga Novelli Júnior, *Marechal Eurico Gaspar Dutra: O dever da verdade* (Rio de Janeiro: Editora Nova Fronteira, 1983), p. 718. In the same volume see various *depoimentos*, such as those of Benjamim Vargas (p. 744) and Oswaldo Cordeiro de Farias (pp. 727–732). José Caó, *Dutra* (São Paulo: Instituto Progresso Editorial, 1949), p. 241.

9. Coutinho, *O General Góes Depõe*, p. 454. Alzira Vargas do Amaral Peixoto, "A Vida de Getúlio Vargas Contada por Sua Filha, Alzira Vargas, ao Journalista Raul Giudicelli," Chapter 8, *Fatos & Fotos*, August 3, 1963.

10. Coutinho, *O General Góes Depõe*, pp. 447, 456. Armando Trompowsky entry in *Dicionário Histórico-Biográfico Brasileiro, 1930–1983*.

11. Coutinho, *O General Góes Depõe*, pp. 455–456. "Proclamação do General Góis Monteiro ao Exército," *O Estado de S. Paulo*, October 30, 1945.
12. Oswaldo Cordeiro de Farias, interview, Rio de Janeiro, July 30, 1963. Alzira Vargas do Amaral Peixoto, "A Vida de Getúlio Vargas," *Fatos & Fotos*, August 3, 1963.
13. Luiz Carlos Prestes, interview, Rio de Janeiro, September 5, 1963. Oswaldo Cordeiro de Farias, interview, July 30, 1963.
14. *O Estado de S. Paulo*, October 30, 1945. Interview with Anita Leocádia Prestes, in *Marie Claire*, no. 63, June 1996.
15. José Linhares entry in *Dicionário Histórico-Biográfico Brasileiro, 1930–1983. Jornal do Commercio*, October 31, 1945. HSP, quoted in Note 15 on p. 73 of Alberto Venancio Filho, *Notícia Histórica da Ordem dos Advogados do Brasil (1930–1980)* (Rio de Janeiro: n.p., 1982).

7. SOBRAL EXPLAINS THE FALL OF VARGAS (NOVEMBER 1945)

1. Alberto Venancio Filho, *Notícia Histórica da Ordem dos Advogados do Brasil (1930–1980)* (Rio de Janeiro: n.p., 1982), pp. 72–73. *Jornal do Commercio*, October 31, 1945.
2. *Jornal do Commercio*, October 31, 1945.
3. HSP, "Modo Urgente da Legitimação da Autoridade no Brasil," in "Pelos Domínios do Direito," *Jornal do Commercio*, November 10, 1945.
4. Ibid.
5. HSP, letter to (Richard) Pattee, November 24, 1945.
6. HSP, letters to Jair Etienne Dessaune and Mário C. Vilela, November 10, 1945.
7. HSP, telegram to Góes Monteiro, November 22, 1945.

XII. Shocked by the Electorate's Message (December 1945)

1. FINDING FAULT WITH PRESIDENT LINHARES (NOVEMBER 1945)

1. HSP, letter to José Linhares, November 1, 1945, p. 6.
2. Ibid., pp. 5–11.
3. HSP, "A contaminação do presente pelos erros da ditadura," *Jornal do Commercio*, November 3–4, 1945.
4. Ibid.
5. Ibid.
6. HSP, "Modo urgente da legitimação da autoridade no Brasil," in "Pelos Domínios do Direito," *Jornal do Commercio*, November 10, 1945.
7. Ibid.
8. HSP, letter to (Antônio de) Sampaio Dória, n.d.
9. Ibid.
10. José Linhares entry in CPDOC, *Dicionário Histórico-Biográfico Brasileiro, 1930–1983* (Rio de Janeiro: Editora Forense-Universitária, 1984).
11. HSP, "A imparcialidade do poder em face das eleições políticas," in "Pelos Domínios do Direito," *Jornal do Commercio*, November 17, 1945.

12. Benedicto Valladares, *Tempos Idos e Vividos: Memórias* (Rio de Janeiro: Editôra Civilização Brasileira, 1966), p. 282.

2. LEADERS OF THE LEC DEFEND GOMES (NOVEMBER 1945)

1. "Discurso do Sr. Sobral Pinto," *Jornal do Commercio*, November 21, 1945.

2. (Laura Fagundes, Alberto Venancio Filho, José Motta Maia), *Instituto dos Advogados Brasileiros: 150 Anos de História, 1843-1993* (Rio de Janeiro: Editora Destaque, 1995), pp. 203-204.

3. Ibid. "Instituto dos Advogados," *Jornal do Commercio*, November 25, 30, 1945.

4. *Jornal do Commercio*, November 19-20, 22, 1945.

5. Ibid. *O Estado de S. Paulo*, November 28, December 2, 1945.

6. Osvaldo Peralva, interview, Rio de Janeiro, September 14, 1963.

7. *Diário Carioca*, November 18, 22, 23, 25, 27, 28, 29, 30, December 1, 1945.

8. Roberto Sabóia de Medeiros, "Perscrutando os corações," *O Estado de S. Paulo*, December 1, 1945.

9. *O Estado de S. Paulo*, November 29, December 1, 1945.

10. *Diário Carioca*, November 21, 1945.

11. Ibid., November 21, 22, 1945.

12. Eduardo Gomes entry in CPDOC, *Dicionário Histórico-Biográfico Brasileiro, 1930-1983* (Rio de Janeiro: Editora Forense-Universitária, 1984). *Diário Carioca*, November 21, 22, 1945.

13. *Diário Carioca*, November 29, 1945. *O Estado de S. Paulo*, December 1, 1945.

14. *O Estado de S. Paulo*, November 29, 1945.

15. *Diário Carioca*, December 2, 1945.

16. "Telegrama da LEC contra o gen. Dutra" and "O Arcebispo D. Jaime Câmara desmente a campanha de Dutra," *Diário Carioca*, December 2, 1945.

3. SOBRAL, RECOMMENDING CANDIDATES, DISTRESSES THE PDC (NOVEMBER 29, 1945)

1. HSP, "A sinceridade como elemento integrante do Direito Público," in "Pelos Domínios do Direito," *Jornal do Commercio*, November 24, 1945.

2. HSP, letter to Paulo Seabra, December 20, 1945.

3. HSP, "Como cumprir o dever eleitoral," *Jornal do Commercio*, November 29, 30, December 1, 1945, *Diário Carioca*, November 30, 1945.

4. Ibid.

5. Ibid.

6. Osório Lopes, in *Jornal do Commercio*, November 30, 1945.

7. HSP, letter to Osório (Lopes), November 30, 1945.

8. Osório Lopes, in *Jornal do Commercio*, December 2, 1945.

9. HSP, letter to Paulo Seabra, December 20, 1945.

4. THE ELECTION RESULTS SURPRISE AND DISAPPOINT SOBRAL (DECEMBER 1945)

1. Armando Trompowsky entry in CPDOC, *Dicionário Histórico-Biográfico Brasileiro, 1930–1983* (Rio de Janeiro: Editora Forense-Universitária, 1984).

2. *The New York Times*, dateline Rio de Janeiro, November 5, 1945. Eurico Gaspar Dutra entry in *Dicionário Histórico-Biográfico Brasileiro, 1930–1983*.

3. Stanley Hilton, *Oswaldo Aranha: Um Biográfia* (Rio de Janeiro: Editora Objetiva, 1994), p. 429. Aranha, Dutra, and Vargas entries in *Dicionário Histórico-Biográfico Brasileiro, 1930–1983*.

4. Eurico Gaspar Dutra interview, Rio de Janeiro, July 28, 1963.

5. Carlos E. Cortés, *Gaúcho Politics in Brazil* (Albuquerque: University of New Mexico Press, 1974), p. 117.

6. Ibid. *O Estado de S. Paulo*, January 8, 17, 1946.

7. *Jornal do Commercio*, December 28, 1945.

8. Partido Republicano and Getúlio Vargas entries in *Dicionário Histórico-Biográfico Brasileiro, 1930–1983*.

9. Liga Eleitoral Católica entry in ibid. *A Noite*, December 7, 31, 1945.

10. HSP, "O espírito de cooperação no regimen democrático," in "Pelos Domínios do Direito," *Jornal do Commercio*, December 22, 1945.

11. HSP, "As verdadeiras bases da boa democracia," in "Pelos Domínios do Direito," *Jornal do Commercio*, December 15, 1945.

12. Ibid.

13. HSP, "O espírito de cooperação no regimen democrático."

5. SOBRAL PINTO, THE CONSCIENCE OF BRAZIL

1. HSP, "Modo Urgente da Legitimação da Autoridade no Brasil," in "Pelos Domínios do Direito," *Jornal do Commercio*, November 10, 1945.

2. HSP, letter to Adroaldo (Mesquita da Costa), January 8, 1946.

3. HSP, letter to Jaime de Barros Câmara, April 27, 1944.

4. Notes about the life of HSP furnished to JWFD by Roberto Sobral Pinto Ribeiro by e-mail from Rio de Janeiro, March 27, 2000, and by Tito Lívio Cavalcanti de Medeiros in Rio de Janeiro, January 14, 1996. See also *Jornal do Brasil*, December 4, 1976, *O Estado de S. Paulo*, February 15, 1986, February 18, 1981, and *Folha de S. Paulo*, November 21, 1987.

5. Evandro Lins e Silva, "Sobral Pinto, o Monstro," *Jornal do Brasil*, December 8, 1991.

6. Ibid.

7. Joaquim de Sales, "Movimento Operário Social Cristão," in "Boletim do Dia," *Diário Carioca*, August 17, 1945.

8. Roberto Sisson entry in CPDOC, *Dicionário Histórico-Biográfico Brasileiro, 1930–1983* (Rio de Janeiro: Editora Forense-Universitária, 1984).

9. HSP, letter to (Roberto) Sisson, January 17, 1946.

10. Ibid.

INDEX

ABI (Brazilian Press Association), 44, 165, 190, 215, 222–223
Abyssinia, 145
Academy of Letters. *See* Brazilian Academy of Letters
Ação Católica, 86, 245
Ação Católica Brasileira: Sobral Pinto's role in, xii, 37, 43, 48, 88, 136, 145, 226, 250; and Alceu Amoroso Lima, 37, 45, 71–72, 87, 111, 145; Yamamoto's speech for, 87; leadership of, 88; Bishop Costa on political nature of, 112; reports on district activities of, 137; and Círculos Operários, 139; and American Catholic Seminar, 141; new orientation of, in 1943, 142–143; and Vargas, 145; and World War II, 145; and Dom Jayme de Barros Câmara, 189–190, 251; and prohibition of officers from holding government posts, 189–190, 267, 294; and Communist Party in Brazil, 221; and working class, 245; and Movimento Operário Social Cristão, 247–248. *See also* Liga Eleitoral Católica
Ação Integralista Brasileira (Green Shirts), xi, 35–36, 39, 44, 45, 74, 78–79, 81–84, 89, 94, 144, 187, 238
Ação rescisória, 129
Ação Universitária Católica, 42

Acioly, Hildebrando, 245, 256, 283–284
Adultery, xii, 19–22, 96, 141, 143, 263–266
AGIR, 191–192
AIB. *See* Ação Integralista Brasileira
Alagoas, 49, 66, 68
Albuquerque, Epitácio Pessoa Cavalcanti de, 182–184
Albuquerque, Olímpio de Sá e, 8–9, 11–13
Albuquerque, Severino Sombra de, 28
Aleixo, Pedro, 70, 135, 155, 157–160, 204–205, 245, 275
Aliança Liberal, 23, 24, 25, 26
Aliança Nacional Libertadora (ANL), 45–50, 60, 68, 74, 75, 87, 94–96, 153–154, 199, 238, 247
Almeida, Antônio de, 116
Almeida, José Américo de, 55, 275–276
Almeida, Miguel Osório de, 192
Amado, Gilberto, 17
Amado, Jorge, 100, 143, 145–148, 228
Amazonas, 23
Amazônia, 175–181
América Football Club, 5
Amnesty for political prisoners, 199, 220, 221–223, 228, 229–230, 235, 237, 238
Anchieta School, 3–4, 16
Andrada, Antônio Carlos de, 30, 50, 135, 230